POLITICAL ORDER IN CHANGING SOCIETIES

Written under the auspices of the
Center for International Affairs
Harvard University

Delivered in part as the
Henry L. Stimson Lectures
Yale University

Political Order in Changing Societies

Samuel P. Huntington

Foreword by Francis Fukuyama

New Haven and London, Yale University Press

Printed in the United States of America.

Library of Congress Control Number: 2005932004

ISBN-13: 978-0-300-11620-5 (cloth : alk. paper)
ISBN-10: 0-300-11620-9 (cloth : alk. paper)

A catalogue record for this book is available from the British Library.

The paper in this book meets the guidelines for permanence and
durability of the Committee on Production Guidelines for Book Longevity
of the Council on Library Resources.

10 9 8 7 6 5 4 3

*For Nancy,
Timothy, and Nicholas*

Contents

Tables

Foreword by Francis Fukuyama

It is an immense honor for me to write the Foreword to the new paperback edition of Samuel P. Huntington's *Political Order in Changing Societies*. This book, which first appeared in 1968, was one of the classics of late twentieth-century social science, a work that had enormous influence on the way people thought about development, both in academia and in the policy world. The breadth of knowledge about developing countries, as well as the analytical insight that *Political Order* brought to bear, was astonishing, and cemented Samuel Huntington's reputation as one of the foremost political scientists of his generation.

In order to understand the book's intellectual significance, it is necessary to place it in the context of the ideas that were dominant in the 1950s and early 1960s. This was the heyday of "modernization theory," probably the most ambitious American attempt to create an integrated, empirical theory of human social change. Modernization theory had its origins in the works of late nineteenth-century European social theorists like Henry Maine, Émile Durkheim, Karl Marx, Ferdinand Tönnies, and Max Weber. These authors established a series of concepts (e.g., status/contract; mechanical/organic solidarity; *Gemeinschaft/Gesellschaft;* charismatic/bureaucratic-rational authority) to describe the changes in social norms and relationships that took place as human societies made the transition from agricultural to industrial production. While basing their works primarily on the experiences of early modernizers like Britain or the United States, they sought to draw from them general laws of social development.

European social theory was killed by the two world wars; the ideas it generated migrated to the United States and were taken up by a generation of American academics after the Second World War at places like Harvard's Department of Comparative Politics, the MIT Center for International Studies, and the Social Science Research Council's Committee on Comparative Politics. The Harvard department, led by Weber's protégé Talcott Parsons, hoped to create an integrated, interdisciplinary social science that would combine economics, sociology, political science, and anthropology.

The period from the late 1940s to the early 1960s also corresponded to the dissolution of European colonial empires and the emergence of what became known as the third or developing world, newly independent countries with great aspirations to modernize and catch up with their former colonial masters. Scholars like Edward Shils, Daniel Lerner, Lucian Pye, Gabriel Almond, David Apter, and Walt Whitman Rostow saw these momentous developments as a laboratory for social theory, as well as a great opportunity to help developing countries raise living standards and democratize their political systems.

Modernization theorists placed a strong normative value on being modern, and in their view, the good things of modernity tended to go together. Economic development, changing social relationships like urbanization and the breakdown of primary kinship groups, higher and more inclusive levels of education, normative shifts towards values like "achievement" and rationality, secularization, and the development of democratic political institutions were all seen as an interdependent whole. Economic development would fuel better education, which would lead to value change, which would promote modern politics, and so on in a virtuous circle.

Political Order in Changing Societies appeared against this backdrop and directly challenged these assumptions. First, Huntington argued that political decay was at least as likely as political development, and that the actual experience of newly independent countries was one of increasing social and political disorder. Second, he suggested that the good things of modernity often operated at cross-purposes. In particular, if social mobilization outpaced the development of political institutions, there would be frustration as new social actors found themselves unable to participate in the political system. The result was a condition he labeled praetorianism, and was the leading cause of insurgencies, military coups, and weak or disorganized governments. Economic development and political development were not part of the same, seamless process of modernization; the latter had its own separate logic as institutions like political parties and legal systems were created or evolved into more complex forms.

Huntington drew a practical implication from these observations, namely, that political order was a good thing in itself and would not automatically arise out of the modernization process. Rather the contrary: without political order, neither economic nor social development could proceed successfully. The different components of modernization needed to be sequenced. Premature increases in political participation — including events like early elections — could destabilize fragile political systems. Huntington thus laid the groundwork for a development strategy that came to be called the "authoritarian transition," whereby a modernizing dictatorship provided political order, a rule of law, and the conditions for successful economic and social development. Once these building blocks were in place, other aspects of modernity, like democracy and civic participation, could be added. (Huntington's student Fareed Zakaria would write a book in 2003, *The Future of Freedom,* making a somewhat updated variant of this argument.)

The significance of Huntington's book must be seen against the backdrop of U.S. foreign policy at the time it was published. The year 1968 was a high-water mark in the Vietnam War, when troop strength swelled to half a million and the Tet offensive undermined the U.S. public's confidence. Many modernization theorists hoped their academic work would have useful implications for American policy; Walt Rostow's book *The Stages of Economic Growth* was a guide for the new U.S. Agency for International Development as it sought to buffer countries like South Vietnam and Indonesia against the appeals of communism. But by the late 1960s, there were not a lot of success stories to which Americans could point. The competing communist and Western nation-building strategies in North and South Vietnam ended with the latter's eventual defeat.

Huntington suggested that there was another way forward, through modernizing authoritarianism, a point of view that brought considerable opprobrium on him in the highly polarized context of the United States in the late 1960s. But it was exactly this kind of leader — Park Chung-Hee in Korea, Chiang Ching-Kuo in Taiwan, Lee Kwan Yew in Singapore, and Suharto in Indonesia — who brought about the so-called Asian Miracle, even as Vietnam was going communist.

It is safe to say that *Political Order* finally killed off modernization theory. It was part of a pincer attack, the other prong of which was the critique from the Left that said that modernization theorists enshrined an ethnocentric European or North American model of social development as a universal one for humanity to follow. American social science found itself suddenly without an overarching theory, and began its subsequent slide into its current methodological Balkanization.

What are we to make of Huntington's arguments, nearly four decades after they were originally laid out? Many developing countries are now more than two generations removed from independence. Enormous changes, including the East Asian Miracle, the collapse of communism, and what Huntington himself would label the Third Wave of democratizations, have occurred in the years since *Political Order* was written. In what ways do these events confirm, bolster, or weaken his observations?

There are many ways in which Huntington's observations have been vindicated. He argued that both traditional and modernized societies tended to be stable; problems occurred in the early stages of modernization, when traditional social structures were upended by new expectations. Economic growth could be stabilizing, but growth followed by sudden setback created potentially revolutionary situations. It remains largely true that the worst cases of instability have occurred in countries at relatively early stages of modernization, or in countries facing setbacks.

The problem of social mobilization outpacing political institutionalization clearly continues to occur. The most notable example was the Iranian revolution of 1978, when excessively rapid state-driven modernization ran afoul of traditional social actors; merchants in the bazaar combined with radical students to produce an Islamic revolution. Today in Andean countries like Venezuela, Bolivia, and Ecuador, new social actors (particularly indigenous groups left out of the formal political system) are undermining weak institutions and leaving chaos in their wake. The Suharto regime in Indonesia was destabilized by the 1997–98 financial crisis, which came against a backdrop of steadily rising expectations, and one could argue that radical Islamist terrorism is driven at least in part by the massive drop in Saudi per-capita income that occurred in the two decades prior to September 2001.

Huntington is further correct that political development follows its own logic independent of economic development. While there is evidence that long-term economic growth breeds stronger democratic institutions (or, more exactly, makes them less vulnerable to setbacks), this is true only at a relatively high level of per-capita GDP. For poor countries, political order and competent institutions are a precondition for economic growth. Sub-Saharan Africa's internal conflicts and weak governments are powerful inhibitors of the other dimensions of development.

Finally, *Political Order* was clearly prescient in focusing on political decay as a special object of study. The post–Cold War world has been subject to substantial political decay, from the collapse of the former Soviet Union to series of weak and failing states like Haiti, Liberia, Sierra Leone, Somalia, Sudan, and Afghanistan.

If one compares the periods before and after the book was written, the years 1945–68 saw a far higher level of political disorder than 1968–2006. In the first period, coups, insurgencies, and peasant revolts occurred in virtually every part of the developing world, while in the second period, large areas of stability have emerged. Part of the reason for this change is that successful political development has occurred in many places, especially in East Asia. These developments suggest that Huntington was pointing to a transitional problem to some extent. But the degree of overall stability is surprising. The Arab Middle East, for example, has seen relatively little political violence since the end of the Lebanese civil war, with the exception of Iraq and the on-going Israeli-Palestinian conflict. In the post-1968 period, long-serving leaders in Morocco, Libya, Jordan, Syria, and Egypt either have turned over or are preparing to turn over leadership to their sons. Indeed, many observers argue that the region is *too* stable; the political stasis that has overtaken most regimes there has blocked political participation and bred resentment. Since the return of democracy in the 1980s, Latin America has weathered debt and currency crises without military coups or return to authoritarianism, despite recent trouble in the Andes and Haiti. While agrarian revolts drag on in Nepal, Colombia, and the Philippines, they are far less common now than in the 1950s and 1960s.

One development that doesn't fit neatly into *Political Order*'s framework is the collapse of the former Soviet Union. The book's first page contains the remarkable assertion that the United States, Great Britain, and the Soviet Union were equally developed in political terms, although the first two countries were liberal democracies and the last a communist dictatorship. The notion that a country could have a high degree of political institutionalization without being democratic shocked many people at the time but underscored Huntington's point that political order and democracy were not necessarily interdependent and could work at cross-purposes.

In retrospect, it would appear that the former Soviet Union's apparent degree of political development was something of a Potemkin village. Through sheer political willpower and violence, the Bolsheviks created a remarkably artificial system that looked very powerful, virtually until the moment it collapsed. The problem was a moral one: people living under the system, including many who eventually climbed to the top ranks of the Communist Party, ultimately did not believe in its legitimacy. Thus, while democracy can be destabilizing in the short run, it can also confer resilience in the long run.

It is in the area of political decay that Huntington's thesis needs to be not so much amended as extended. As noted above, we see a number of contemporary cases of classic Huntingtonian political decay, where participation has outrun institutionalization. But if one looks at the universe of weak and failed states that has emerged in the past two decades, there are clearly other forces at work. One factor in particular is the peculiar nature of the contemporary international system, one that despite good intentions arguably promotes political decay.

If one examines historical cases of state formation and state building in the regions of the world that have strong states (primarily Europe and East Asia), the uncomfortable truth emerges that violence has always been a key ingredient. Charles Tilly has argued that the modern European state emerged out of the military competition that took place among the decentralized political actors there. The Chinese, Japanese, and Korean states were all forcibly unified at the beginning of their histories, and required continuing violence to keep them together. Even the United States, which prides itself on being a constitutional democracy, owes its national unity to a bloody civil war that took the lives of more than half a million of its citizens.

Today's international system does not look kindly on interstate violence and the kind of wars of conquest and consolidation that as recently as the 1870s produced the present-day countries of Italy and Germany. Africa, for example, was saddled with an irrational political map upon decolonization, one that corresponded to neither geography, ethnicity, nor economic functionality. The international system supported that region's leaders' decision to retain those boundaries, even as decreasing transportation and communications costs made those boundaries more porous, and the political units more susceptible to mutual destabilization.

Today, we have a situation in which things that weaken states and promote political decay—like weapons, drugs, laundered money, security advisors, refugees, and diamonds—can cross international borders with relative ease, while the world's normative structure and the institutions built around it (e.g., the United Nations, the African Union, and the various nongovernmental organizations devoted to human rights) inhibit the kind of muscular state-building that was necessary to political development in other parts of the world. (Try to imagine what the outcome of the American Civil War might have been had it taken place in today's globalized world.) Even the well-intentioned activities of international donors and nongovernmental organizations devoted to promoting economic development have had the unanticipated effect of weakening state capacity by creating aid dependency and bypassing indigenous governments. In an ironic twist, there is enough violence and conflict in places like the Democratic Republic of the Congo and Liberia to promote untold human suffering, but not enough (or not enough of the right type) to produce strong political institutions.

Samuel Huntington's *Political Order in Changing Societies* was perhaps the last serious effort to produce a grand theory of political change. Since then, there has been a good deal of relatively useful middle-range theory related to issues like democratic transitions, institutional design, and specific regions, as well as somewhat less-useful mathematical models coming out of rational-choice political science. Perhaps all grand theories are ultimately doomed to failure owing to the underlying complexity of the subject matter or to changing circumstances over time. Or perhaps the problem is that there are simply not many thinkers of Huntington's ability, insight, and ambition, who could hope to produce a book of this scope. In the meantime, we will have to be satisfied that this classic work will remain available for future generations of students interested in the problem of political development.

Preface

The "political order" referred to in the title of this book is a goal, not a reality. The pages following are, consequently, filled with descriptions of violence, instability, and disorder. In this respect this book resembles those volumes which purport to deal with "economic development" but whose actual subjects are economic backwardness and stagnation. Economists who write about economic development presumably favor it, and this book originates in a parallel concern which I have for political stability. My effort here is to probe the conditions under which societies undergoing rapid and disruptive social and economic change may in some measure realize this goal. The indices of economic development, such as per capita gross national product, are reasonably familiar and accepted. The indices of political order or its absence in terms of violence, coups, insurrections, and other forms of instabilty are also reasonably clear and even quantifiable. Just as it is possible for economists to analyze and to debate, as economists, the conditions and policies which promote economic development, it should also be possible for political scientists to analyze and to debate in scholarly fashion the ways and means of promoting political order, whatever their differences concerning the legitimacy and desirability of that goal. Just as economic development depends, in some measure, on the relation between investment and consumption, political order depends in part on the relation between the development of political institutions and the mobilization of new social forces into politics. At least that is the framework in which I have approached the problem in this book.

My research and writing were done at the Center for International Affairs at Harvard University. This work was supported in part by the Center from its own resources, in part by a Ford Foundation grant to the University for work in international affairs, and in part by a grant from the Carnegie Corporation to the Center for a research program in Political Institutionalization and Social Change. The impetus for the overall elaboration of the

argument of the book came from the invitation of Professor
Robert Dahl and the Council on International Relations of Yale
University to deliver the Henry L. Stimson Lectures in 1966.
Portions of chapters 1, 2, and 3 appeared in *World Politics* and
Daedalus and are incorporated into this manuscript with the
permission of the publishers of these two journals. Christopher
Mitchell, Joan Nelson, Eric Nordlinger, and Steven R. Rivkin read
the manuscript in whole or in part and made valuable comments
on it. Over the past four years my thinking on the problems of
political order and social change has benefited greatly from the
insight and wisdom of my colleagues in the Harvard-MIT Faculty
Seminar on Political Development. During this period also many
students have helped me in collecting and analyzing data on
modernizing countries. Those who made substantial contributions directly relevant to this book are Richard Alpert, Margaret
Bates, Richard Betts, Robert Bruce, Allan E. Goodman, Robert
Hart, Christopher Mitchell, and William Schneider. Finally,
throughout my work on this book, Shirley Johannesen Levine
functioned as an invaluable research assistant, editor, typist, proof-
reader, and, most importantly, chief-of-staff tying together the
activities of others also performing these roles. I am profoundly
grateful to all these institutions and individuals for their support,
advice, and assistance. With all this help, the remaining errors and
deficiencies must clearly be mine alone.

S.P.H.

Cambridge, Massachusetts
April 1968

POLITICAL ORDER IN CHANGING SOCIETIES

1. Political Order and Political Decay

THE POLITICAL GAP

The most important political distinction among countries concerns not their form of government but their degree of government. The differences between democracy and dictatorship are less than the differences between those countries whose politics embodies consensus, community, legitimacy, organization, effectiveness, stability, and those countries whose politics is deficient in these qualities. Communist totalitarian states and Western liberal states both belong generally in the category of effective rather than debile political systems. The United States, Great Britain, and the Soviet Union have different forms of government, but in all three systems the government governs. Each country is a political community with an overwhelming consensus among the people on the legitimacy of the political system. In each country the citizens and their leaders share a vision of the public interest of the society and of the traditions and principles upon which the political community is based. All three countries have strong, adaptable, coherent political institutions: effective bureaucracies, well-organized political parties, a high degree of popular participation in public affairs, working systems of civilian control over the military, extensive activity by the government in the economy, and reasonably effective procedures for regulating succession and controlling political conflict. These governments command the loyalties of their citizens and thus have the capacity to tax resources, to conscript manpower, and to innovate and to execute policy. If the Politburo, the Cabinet, or the President makes a decision, the probability is high that it will be implemented through the government machinery.

In all these characteristics the political systems of the United States, Great Britain, and the Soviet Union differ significantly from the governments which exist in many, if not most, of the modernizing countries of Asia, Africa, and Latin America. These countries lack many things. They suffer real shortages of food, literacy, education, wealth, income, health, and productivity, but most of them have been recognized and efforts made to do something about them. Beyond and behind these shortages, however, there is a greater shortage: a shortage of political community and of effective, authoritative, legitimate government. "I do know," Walter Lippmann has observed, "that there is no greater necessity for men who live in communities than that they be governed, self-governed if possible, well-governed if they are fortunate, but in any event, governed." [1] Mr. Lippmann wrote these words in a moment of despair about the United States. But they apply in far greater measure to the modernizing countries of Asia, Africa, and Latin America, where the political community is fragmented against itself and where political institutions have little power, less majesty, and no resiliency—where, in many cases, governments simply do not govern.

In the mid-1950s, Gunnar Myrdal called the world's attention to the apparent fact that the rich nations of the world were getting richer, absolutely and relatively, at a faster rate than the poorer nations. "On the whole," he argued, "in recent decades the economic inequalities between developed and underdeveloped countries have been increasing." In 1966 the president of the World Bank similarly pointed out that at current rates of growth the gap in per capita national income between the United States and forty underdeveloped countries would increase fifty per cent by the year 2000. [2] Clearly, a central issue, perhaps the central issue, in international and developmental economics is the apparently remorseless tendency for this economic gap to broaden. A similar and equally urgent problem exists in politics. In politics as in economics the gap between developed political systems and underdeveloped political systems, between civic polities and corrupt polities, has broadened. This political gap resembles and is related to the economic gap, but it is not identical with it. Countries with underdeveloped economies may have highly developed political systems, and countries which have achieved high levels of economic welfare may still have disorganized and chaotic politics. Yet in the

1. Walter Lippmann, *New York Herald Tribune*, Dec. 10, 1963, p. 24.
2. Gunnar Myrdal, *Rich Lands and Poor* (New York and Evanston, Harper and Row, 1957) , p. 6; George D. Woods, "The Development Decade in the Balance," *Foreign Affairs, 44* (Jan. 1966) , 207.

twentieth century the principal locus of political underdevelopment, like that of economic underdevelopment, tends to be the modernizing countries of Asia, Africa, and Latin America.

With a few notable exceptions, the political evolution of these countries after World War II was characterized by increasing ethnic and class conflict, recurring rioting and mob violence, frequent military coups d'etat, the dominance of unstable personalistic leaders who often pursued disastrous economic and social policies, widespread and blatant corruption among cabinet ministers and civil servants, arbitrary infringement of the rights and liberties of citizens, declining standards of bureaucratic efficiency and performance, the pervasive alienation of urban political groups, the loss of authority by legislatures and courts, and the fragmentation and at times complete disintegration of broadly based political parties. In the two decades after World War II, successful coups d'etat occurred in 17 of 20 Latin American countries (only Mexico, Chile, and Uruguay maintaining constitutional processes), in a half-dozen North African and Middle Eastern states (Algeria, Egypt, Syria, the Sudan, Iraq, Turkey), in a like number of west African and central African countries (Ghana, Nigeria, Dahomey, Upper Volta, Central African Republic, Congo), and in a variety of Asian societies (Pakistan, Thailand, Laos, South Vietnam, Burma, Indonesia, South Korea). Revolutionary violence, insurrection, and guerrilla warfare wracked Cuba, Bolivia, Peru, Venezuela, Colombia, Guatemala, and the Dominican Republic in Latin America, Algeria and Yemen in the Middle East, and Indonesia, Thailand, Vietnam, China, the Philippines, Malaya, and Laos in Asia. Racial, tribal, or communal violence or tension disrupted Guyana, Morocco, Iraq, Nigeria, Uganda, the Congo, Burundi, the Sudan, Ruanda, Cyprus, India, Ceylon, Burma, Laos, and South Vietnam. In Latin America, old-style, oligarchic dictatorships in countries like Haiti, Paraguay, and Nicaragua maintained a fragile police-based rule. In the eastern hemisphere, traditional regimes in Iran, Libya, Arabia, Ethiopia, and Thailand struggled to reform themselves even as they teetered on the brink of revolutionary overthrow.

During the 1950s and 1960s the numerical incidence of political violence and disorder increased dramatically in most countries of the world. The year 1958, according to one calculation, witnessed some 28 prolonged guerrilla insurgencies, four military uprisings, and two conventional wars. Seven years later, in 1965, 42 prolonged insurgencies were underway; ten military revolts occurred; and five conventional conflicts were being fought. Political instability also increased significantly during the 1950s and 1960s. Violence and other destabilizing events were five times more frequent between 1955 and 1962 than they were between 1948 and 1954. Sixty-four of 84 countries were less stable in the latter period than in the earlier one.[3] Throughout Asia, Africa, and Latin America there was a decline in political order, an undermining of the authority, effectiveness, and legitimacy of government. There was a lack of civic morale and public spirit and of political institutions capable of giving meaning and direction to the public interest. Not political development but political decay dominated the scene.

TABLE 1.1. Military Conflicts, 1958–1965

	1958	1959	1960	1961	1962	1963	1964	1965
Prolonged, irregular or guerrilla insurgency	28	31	30	31	34	41	43	42
Brief revolts, coups, uprisings	4	4	11	6	9	15	9	10
Overt, militarily conventional wars	2	1	1	6	4	3	4	5
Total	34	36	42	43	47	59	56	57

Source: U.S. Department of Defense.

What was responsible for this violence and instability? The primary thesis of this book is that it was in large part the product of rapid social change and the rapid mobilization of new groups into politics coupled with the slow development of political institutions. "Among the laws that rule human societies," de Tocqueville observed, "there is one which seems to be more precise and clear than all others. If men are to remain civilized or to become so, the art of associating together must grow and improve in the same ratio in which the equality of conditions is increased."[4] The

3. Wallace W. Conroe, "A Cross-National Analysis of the Impact of Modernization Upon Political Stability" (unpublished M.A. thesis, San Diego State College, 1965), pp. 52–54, 60–62; Ivo K. and Rosalind L. Feierabend, "Aggressive Behaviors Within Polities, 1948–1962: A Cross-National Study," *Journal of Conflict Resolution, 10* (Sept. 1966), 253–54.

4. Alexis de Tocqueville, *Democracy in America* (ed. Phillips Bradley, New York, Knopf, 1955), 2, 118.

political instability in Asia, Africa, and Latin America derives precisely from the failure to meet this condition: equality of political participation is growing much more rapidly than "the art of associating together." Social and economic change—urbanization, increases in literacy and education, industrialization, mass media expansion—extend political consciousness, multiply political demands, broaden political participation. These changes undermine traditional sources of political authority and traditional political institutions; they enormously complicate the problems of creating new bases of political association and new political institutions combining legitimacy and effectiveness. The rates of social mobilization and the expansion of political participation are high; the rates of political organization and institutionalization are low. The result is political instability and disorder. The primary problem of politics is the lag in the development of political institutions behind social and economic change.

For two decades after World War II American foreign policy failed to come to grips with this problem. The economic gap, in contrast to the political gap, was the target of sustained attention, analysis, and action. Aid programs and loan programs, the World Bank and regional banks, the UN and the OECD, consortia and combines, planners and politicians, all shared in a massive effort to do something about the problem of economic development. Who, however, was concerned with the political gap? American officials recognized that the United States had a primary interest in the creation of viable political regimes in modernizing countries. But few, if any, of all the activities of the American government affecting those countries were directly concerned with the promotion of political stability and the reduction of the political gap. How can this astonishing lacuna be explained?

It would appear to be rooted in two distinct aspects of the American historical experience. In confronting the modernizing countries the United States was handicapped by its happy history. In its development the United States was blessed with more than its fair share of economic plenty, social well-being, and political stability. This pleasant conjuncture of blessings led Americans to believe in the unity of goodness: to assume that all good things go together and that the achievement of one desirable social goal aids in the achievement of others. In American policy toward modernizing countries this experience was reflected in the belief that political stability would be the natural and inevitable result of the achievement of, first, economic development and then of social reform. Throughout the 1950s the prevailing assumption of American policy was that economic development—the elimination of poverty, disease, illiteracy—was necessary for political development and political stability. In American thinking the causal chain was: economic assistance promotes economic development, economic development promotes political stability. This dogma was enshrined in legislation and, perhaps more important, it was ingrained in the thinking of officials in AID and other agencies concerned with the foreign assistance programs.

If political decay and political instability were more rampant in Asia, Africa, and Latin America in 1965 than they were fifteen years earlier, it was in part because American policy reflected this erroneous dogma. For in fact, economic development and political stability are two independent goals and progress toward one has no necessary connection with progress toward the other. In some instances programs of economic development may promote political stability; in other instances they may seriously undermine such stability. So also, some forms of political stability may encourage economic growth; other forms may discourage it. India was one of the poorest countries in the world in the 1950s and had only a modest rate of economic growth. Yet through the Congress Party it achieved a high degree of political stability. Per capita incomes in Argentina and Venezuela were perhaps ten times that in India, and Venezuela had a phenomenal rate of economic growth. Yet for both countries stability remained an elusive goal.

With the Alliance for Progress in 1961, social reform—that is, the more equitable distribution of material and symbolic resources—joined economic development as a conscious and explicit goal of American policy toward modernizing countries. This development was, in part, a reaction to the Cuban Revolution, and it reflected the assumption among policymakers that land and tax reforms, housing projects, and welfare programs would reduce social tensions and deactivate the fuse to Fidelismo. Once again political stability was to be the by-product of the achievement of another socially desirable goal. In fact, of course, the relationship between social reform and political stability resembles that between economic development and political stability. In some circumstances reforms may reduce tensions and encourage peaceful rather than violent change. In other circumstances, however, reform may well exacerbate tensions, precipitate violence, and be a catalyst of rather than a substitute for revolution.

A second reason for American indifference to political development was the absence in the American historical experience of the need to found a political order. Americans, de Tocqueville said, were born equal and hence never had to worry about creating equality; they enjoyed the fruits of a democratic revolution without having suffered one. So also, America was born with a government, with political institutions and practices imported from seventeenth-century England. Hence Americans never had to worry about creating a government. This gap in historical experience made them peculiarly blind to the problems of creating effective authority in modernizing countries. When an American thinks about the problem of government-building, he directs himself not to the creation of authority and the accumulation of power but rather to the limitation of authority and the division of power. Asked to design a government, he comes up with a written constitution, bill of rights, separation of powers, checks and balances, federalism, regular elections, competitive parties—all excellent devices for limiting government. The Lockean American is so fundamentally anti-government that he identifies government with restrictions on government. Confronted with the need to design a political system which will maximize power and authority, he has no ready answer. His general formula is that governments should be based on free and fair elections.

In many modernizing societies this formula is irrelevant. Elections to be meaningful presuppose a certain level of political organization. The problem is not to hold elections but to create organizations. In many, if not most, modernizing countries elections serve only to enhance the power of disruptive and often reactionary social forces and to tear down the structure of public authority. "In framing a government which is to be administered by men over men," Madison warned in *The Federalist*, No. 51, "the great difficulty lies in this: you must first enable the government to control the governed; and in the next place oblige it to control itself." In many modernizing countries governments are still unable to perform the first function, much less the second. The primary problem is not liberty but the creation of a legitimate public order. Men may, of course, have order without liberty, but they cannot have liberty without order. Authority has to exist before it can be limited, and it is authority that is in scarce supply in those modernizing countries where government is at the mercy of alienated intellectuals, rambunctious colonels, and rioting students.

It is precisely this scarcity that communist and communist-type movements are often able to overcome. History shows conclusively that communist governments are no better than free governments in alleviating famine, improving health, expanding national product, creating industry, and maximizing welfare. But the one thing communist governments can do is to govern; they do provide effective authority. Their ideology furnishes a basis of legitimacy, and their party organization provides the institutional mechanism for mobilizing support and executing policy. To overthrow the government in many modernizing countries is a simple task: one battalion, two tanks, and a half-dozen colonels may suffice. But no communist government in a modernizing country has been overthrown by a military coup d'etat. The real challenge which the communists pose to modernizing countries is not that they are so good at overthrowing governments (which is easy), but that they are so good at making governments (which is a far more difficult task). They may not provide liberty, but they do provide authority; they do create governments that can govern. While Americans laboriously strive to narrow the economic gap, communists offer modernizing countries a tested and proven method of bridging the political gap. Amidst the social conflict and violence that plague modernizing countries, they provide some assurance of political order.

POLITICAL INSTITUTIONS: COMMUNITY AND POLITICAL ORDER

Social Forces and Political Institutions

The level of political community a society achieves reflects the relationship between its political institutions and the social forces which comprise it. A social force is an ethnic, religious, territorial, economic, or status group. Modernization involves, in large part, the multiplication and diversification of the social forces in society. Kinship, racial, and religious groupings are supplemented by occupational, class, and skill groupings. A political organization or procedure, on the other hand, is an arrangement for maintaining order, resolving disputes, selecting authoritative leaders, and thus promoting community among two or more social forces. A simple political community may have a purely ethnic, religious, or occupational base and will have little need for highly developed political institutions. It has the unity of Durkheim's mechanical solidarity. The more complex and heterogeneous the society, however, the more the achievement and maintenance of political community become dependent upon the workings of political institutions.

In practice, the distinction between a political institution and a social force is not a clear-cut one. Many groups may combine significant characteristics of both. The theoretical distinction between the two, however, is clear. All men who engage in political activity may be assumed to be members of a variety of social groupings. The level of political development of a society in large part depends upon the extent to which these political activists also belong to and identify with a variety of political institutions. Clearly, the power and influence of social forces varies considerably. In a society in which all belong to the same social force, conflicts are limited and are resolved through the structure of the social force. No clearly distinct political institutions are necessary. In a society with only a few social forces, one group—warriors, priests, a particular family, a racial or ethnic group—may dominate the others and effectively induce them to acquiesce in its rule. The society may exist with little or no community. But in a society of any greater heterogeneity and complexity, no single social force can rule, much less create a community, without creating political institutions which have some existence independent of the social forces that gave them birth. "The strongest," in Rousseau's oft-quoted phrase, "is never strong enough to be always the master, unless he transforms strength into right and obedience into duty." In a society of any complexity, the relative power of the groups changes, but if the society is to be a community, the power of each group is exercised through political institutions which temper, moderate, and redirect that power so as to render the dominance of one social force compatible with the community of many.

In the total absence of social conflict, political institutions are unnecessary; in the total absence of social harmony, they are impossible. Two groups which see each other only as archenemies cannot form the basis of a community until those mutual perceptions change. There must be some compatibility of interests among the groups that compose the society. In addition, a complex society also requires some definition in terms of general principle or ethical obligation of the bond which holds the groups together and which distinguishes its community from other communities. In a simple society community is found in the immediate relation of one person to another: husband to wife, brother to brother, neighbor to neighbor. The obligation and the community are direct; nothing intrudes from the outside. In a more complex society, however, community involves the relation of individual men or groups to something apart from themselves. The obligation is to some principle, tradition, myth, purpose, or code of behavior that the persons and groups have in common. Combined, these elements constitute Cicero's definition of the commonwealth, or "the coming together of a considerable number of men who are united by a common agreement upon law and rights and by the desire to participate in mutual advantages." *Consensus juris* and *utilitatis communio* are two sides of political community. Yet there is also a third side. For attitudes must be reflected in behavior, and community involves not just any "coming together" but rather a regularized, stable, and sustained coming together. The coming together must, in short, be institutionalized. And the creation of political institutions involving and reflecting the moral consensus and mutual interest is, consequently, the third element necessary for the maintenance of community in a complex society. Such institutions in turn give new meaning to the common purpose and create new linkages between the particular interests of individuals and groups.

The degree of community in a complex society thus, in a rough sense, depends on the strength and scope of its political institutions. The institutions are the behavioral manifestation of the moral consensus and mutual interest. The isolated family, clan, tribe, or village may achieve community with relatively little conscious effort. They are, in a sense, natural communities. As societies become larger in membership, more complicated in structure, and more diverse in activities, the achievement or maintenance of a high level of community becomes increasingly dependent upon political institutions. Men are, however, reluctant to give up the image of social harmony without political action. This was Rousseau's dream. It remains the dream of statesmen and soldiers who imagine that they can induce community in their societies without engaging in the labor of politics. It is the eschatological goal of the Marxists who aim to re-create at the end of history a perfect community where politics is superfluous. In fact, this atavistic notion could only succeed if history were reversed, civilization undone, and the levels of human organization reduced to family and hamlet. In simple societies community can exist without politics or at least without highly differentiated political institutions. In a complex society community is produced by political action and maintained by political institutions.

Historically, political institutions have emerged out of the interaction among and disagreement among social forces, and the gradual development of procedures and organizational devices for resolving those disagreements. The breakup of a small homogeneous ruling class, the diversification of social forces, and increased interaction among such forces are preconditions for the emergence of political organizations and procedures and the eventual creation of political institutions. "Conscious constitution-making appears to have entered the Mediterranean world when the clan organization weakened and the contest of rich and poor became a significant factor in politics." [5] The Athenians called upon Solon for a constitution when their polity was threatened by dissolution because there were "as many different parties as there were diversities in the country" and "the disparity of fortune between the rich and the poor, at that time, also reached its height." [6] More highly developed political institutions were required to maintain Athenian political community as Athenian society became more complex. The reforms of Solon and of Cleisthenes were responses to the social-economic change that threatened to undermine the earlier basis of community. As social forces became more variegated, political institutions had to become more complex and authoritative. It is precisely this development, however, which failed to occur in many modernizing societies in the twentieth century. Social forces were strong, political institutions weak. Legislatures and executives, public authorities and political parties remained fragile and disorganized. The development of the state lagged behind the evolution of society.

5. Francis D. Wormuth, *The Origins of Modern Constitutionalism* (New York, Harper, 1949) , p. 4.
6. Plutarch, *The Lives of the Noble Grecians and Romans* (trans. John Dryden, New York, Modern Library, n.d.) , p. 104.

Criteria of Political Institutionalization

Political community in a complex society thus depends upon the strength of the political organizations and procedures in the society. That strength, in turn, depends upon the *scope of support* for the organizations and procedures and their *level of institutionalization*. Scope refers simply to the extent to which the political organizations and procedures encompass activity in the society. If only a small upper-class group belongs to political organizations and behaves in terms of a set of procedures, the scope is limited. If, on the other hand, a large segment of the population is politically organized and follows the political procedures, the scope is broad. Institutions are stable, valued, recurring patterns of behavior. Organizations and procedures vary in their degree of institutionalization. Harvard University and the newly opened suburban high school are both organizations, but Harvard is much more of an institution than the high school. The seniority system in Congress and President Johnson's select press conferences are both procedures, but seniority was much more institutionalized than were Mr. Johnson's methods of dealing with the press.

Institutionalization is the process by which organizations and procedures acquire value and stability.[7] The level of institutionalization of any political system can be defined by the adaptability, complexity, autonomy, and coherence of its organizations and procedures. So also, the level of institutionalization of any particular organization or procedure can be measured by its adaptability, complexity, autonomy, and coherence. If these criteria can be identified and measured, political systems can be compared in terms of their levels of institutionalization. And it will also be possible to measure increases and decreases in the institutionalization of the particular organizations and procedures within a political system.

7. For relevant definitions and discussions of institutions and institutionalization, see Talcott Parsons, *Essays in Sociological Theory* (rev. ed. Glencoe, Ill., Free Press, 1954), pp. 143, 239; Charles P. Loomis, "Social Change and Social Systems," in Edward A. Tiryakian, ed., *Sociological Theory, Values, and Sociocultural Change* (New York, Free Press, 1963), pp. 185 ff. For a parallel but different use of the concept of institutionalization in relation to modernization, see the work of S. N. Eisenstadt, in particular his "Initial Institutional Patterns of Political Modernisation," *Civilisations, 12* (1962), 461–72, and *13* (1963), 15–26; "Institutionalization and Change," *American Sociological Review, 24* (April 1964), 235–47; "Social Change, Differentiation and Evolution," ibid., *24* (June 1964), 375–86.

Adaptability-Rigidity. The more adaptable an organization or procedure is, the more highly institutionalized it is; the less adaptable and more rigid it is, the lower its level of institutionalization. Adaptability is an acquired organizational characteristic. It is, in a rough sense, a function of environmental challenge and age. The more challenges that have arisen in its environment and the greater its age, the more adaptable it is. Rigidity is more characteristic of young organizations than of old ones. Old organizations and procedures, however, are not necessarily adaptable if they have existed in a static environment. In addition, if over a period of time an organization has developed a set of responses for effectively dealing with one type of problem, and if it is then confronted with an entirely different type of problem requiring a different response, the organization may well be a victim of its past successes and be unable to adjust to the new challenge. In general, however, the first hurdle is the biggest one. Success in adapting to one environmental challenge paves the way for successful adaptation to subsequent environmental challenges. If, for instance, the probability of successful adjustment to the first challenge is 50 per cent, the probability of successful adjustment to the second challenge might be 75 per cent, to the third challenge 87.5 per cent, to the fourth 93.75 per cent, and so on. Some changes in environment, moreover, such as changes in personnel, are inevitable for all organizations. Other changes in environment may be produced by the organization itself—for instance, if it successfully completes the task it was originally created to accomplish. So long as it is recognized that environments can differ in the challenges they pose to organizations, the adaptability of an organization can in a rough sense be measured by its age.[8] Its age, in turn, can be measured in three ways.

One is simply chronological: the longer an organization or procedure has been in existence, the higher the level of institutionalization. The older an organization is, the more likely it is to continue to exist through any specified future time period. The probability that an organization which is one hundred years old will survive one additional year, it might be hypothesized, is perhaps

8. Cf. William H. Starbuck, "Organizational Growth and Development," in James G. March, ed., *Handbook of Organizations* (Chicago, Rand McNally, 1965) , p. 453: "the basic nature of adaptation is such that the longer an organization survives, the better prepared it is to continue surviving."

one hundred times greater than the probability that an organization one year old will survive one additional year. Political institutions are thus not created overnight. Political development, in this sense, is slow, particularly when compared to the seemingly much more rapid pace of economic development. In some instances particular types of experience may substitute for time: fierce conflict or other serious challenges may transform organizations into institutions much more rapidly than normal circumstances. But such intensive experiences are rare, and even with such experiences time is still required. "A major party," Ashoka Mehta observed, in commenting on why communism was helpless in India, "cannot be created in a day. In China a great party was forged by the revolution. Other major parties can be or are born of revolutions in other countries. But it is simply impossible, through normal channels, to forge a great party, to reach and galvanize millions of men in half a million villages." [9]

A second measure of adaptability is generational age. So long as an organization still has its first set of leaders, so long as a procedure is still performed by those who first performed it, its adaptability is still in doubt. The more often the organization has surmounted the problem of peaceful succession and replaced one set of leaders by another, the more highly institutionalized it is. In considerable measure, of course, generational age is a function of chronological age. But political parties and governments may continue for decades under the leadership of one generation. The founders of organizations—whether parties, governments, or business corporations—are often young. Hence the gap between chronological age and generational age is apt to be greater in the early history of an organization than later in its career. This gap produces tensions between the first leaders of the organization and the next generation immediately behind them, which can look forward to a lifetime in the shadow of the first generation. In the middle of the 1960s the Chinese Communist Party was 45 years old, but in large part it was still led by its first generation of leaders. An organization may of course change leadership without changing generations of leadership. One generation differs from

9. Ashoka Mehta, in Raymond Aron, ed., *World Technology and Human Destiny* (Ann Arbor, University of Michigan Press, 1963), p. 133.

another in terms of its formative experiences. Simple replacement of one set of leaders by another, e.g. in surmounting a succession crisis, counts for something in terms of institutional adaptability, but it is not as significant as a shift in leadership generations, that is, the replacement of one set of leaders by another set with significantly different organizational experiences. The shift from Lenin to Stalin was an intra-generation succession; the shift from Stalin to Khrushchev was an inter-generation succession.

Thirdly, organizational adaptability can be measured in functional terms. An organization's functions, of course, can be defined in an almost infinite number of ways. (This is a major appeal and a major limitation of the functional approach to organizations.) Usually an organization is created to perform one particular function. When that function is no longer needed, the organization faces a major crisis: it either finds a new function or reconciles itself to a lingering death. An organization that has adapted itself to changes in its environment and has survived one or more changes in its principal functions is more highly institutionalized than one that has not. Functional adaptability, not functional specificity, is the true measure of a highly developed organization. Institutionalization makes the organization more than simply an instrument to achieve certain purposes.[10] Instead its leaders and members come to value it for its own sake, and it develops a life of its own quite apart from the specific functions it may perform at any given time. The organization triumphs over its function.

Organizations and individuals thus differ significantly in their cumulative capacity to adapt to changes. Individuals usually grow up through childhood and adolescence without deep commitments to highly specific functions. The process of commitment begins in late adolescence. As the individual becomes more and more committed to the performance of certain functions, he finds it increasingly difficult to change those functions and to unlearn the responses he has acquired to meet environmental changes. His personality has been formed; he has become "set in his ways." Organizations, on the other hand, are usually created to perform very specific functions. When the organization confronts a changing environment, it must, if it is to survive, weaken its commitment to

10. See the very useful discussion in Philip Selznick's small classic, *Leadership in Administration* (New York, Harper and Row, 1957), pp. 5 ff.

its original functions. As the organization matures, it becomes "unset" in its ways.[11]

In practice, organizations vary greatly in their functional adaptability. The YMCA, for instance, was founded in the mid-nineteenth century as an evangelical organization to convert the single young men who, during the early years of industrialization, were migrating in great numbers to the cities. With the decline in need for this function, the "Y" successfully adjusted to the performance of many other "general service" functions broadly related to the legitimizing goal of "character development." Concurrently, it broadened its membership base to include, first, non-evangelical Protestants, then Catholics, then Jews, then old men as well as young, and then women as well as men! [12] As a result the organization has prospered, although its original functions disappeared with the dark, satanic mills. Other organizations, such as the Woman's Christian Temperance Union and the Townsend Movement, have had greater difficulty in adjusting to a changing environment. The WCTU "is an organization in retreat. Contrary to the expectations of theories of institutionalization, the movement has not acted to preserve organizational values at the expense of past doctrine."[13] The Townsend Movement has been torn between those who wish to remain loyal to the original function and those who put organizational imperatives first. If the latter are successful, "the dominating orientation of leaders and members shifts *from the implementation of the values the organization is taken to represent* (by leaders, members, and public alike) , *to maintaining the organizational structure as such,* even at the loss of the organization's central mission."[14] The conquest of polio posed a similar acute crisis for the National Foundation for Infantile Paralysis.

11. Cf. Starbuck, pp. 473–75, who suggests that older organizations are less likely than younger ones to resist changes in goals but more likely to resist changes in social structure and task structure.

12. See Mayer N. Zald and Patricia Denton, "From Evangelism to General Service: The Transformation of the YMCA," *Administrative Science Quarterly, 8* (Sept. 1963) , 214 ff.

13. Joseph R. Gusfield, "Social Structure and Moral Reform: A Study of the Woman's Christian Temperance Union," *American Journal of Sociology, 61* (Nov. 1955) , 232; and Gusfield, "The Problem of Generations in an Organizational Structure," *Social Forces, 35* (May, 1957) , 323 ff.

14. Sheldon L. Messinger, "Organizational Transformation: A Case Study of a Declining Social Movement," *American Sociological Review, 20* (Feb. 1955) , 10; italics in original.

The original goals of the organization were highly specific. Should the organization dissolve when these goals were achieved? The dominant opinion of the volunteers was that the organization should continue. "We can fight polio," said one town chairman, "if we can organize people. If we can organize people like this we can fight anything." Another asked: "Wouldn't it be a wonderful story to get polio licked, and then go on to something else and get that licked and then go on to something else? It would be a challenge, a career." [15]

The problems of functional adaptability are not very different for political organizations. A political party gains in functional age when it shifts its function from the representation of one constituency to the representation of another; it also gains in functional age when it shifts from opposition to government. A party that is unable to change constituencies or to acquire power is less of an institution than one that is able to make these changes. A nationalist party whose function has been the promotion of independence from colonial rule faces a major crisis when it achieves its goal and has to adapt itself to the somewhat different function of governing a country. It may find this functional transition so difficult that it will, even after independence, continue to devote a large portion of its efforts to fighting colonialism. A party which acts this way is less of an institution than one, like the Congress Party, which drops its anticolonialism after achieving independence and quite rapidly adapts itself to the tasks of governing. Industrialization has been a major function of the Communist Party of the Soviet Union. A major test of the institutionalization of the Communist Party will be its success in developing new functions now that the major industrializing effort is behind it. A governmental organ that can successfully adapt itself to changed functions, such as the British Crown in the eighteenth and nineteenth centuries, is more of an institution than one which cannot, such as the French monarchy in the eighteenth and nineteenth centuries.

Complexity-Simplicity. The more complicated an organization is, the more highly institutionalized it is. Complexity may involve

15. David L. Sills, *The Volunteers* (Glencoe, Ill., Free Press, 1957), p. 266. Chapter 9 of this book is an excellent discussion of organizational goal replacement with reference to the YMCA, WCTU, Townsend Movement, Red Cross, and other case studies.

both multiplication of organizational subunits, hierarchically and functionally, and differentiation of separate types of organizational subunits. The greater the number and variety of subunits the greater the ability of the organization to secure and maintain the loyalties of its members. In addition, an organization which has many purposes is better able to adjust itself to the loss of any one purpose than an organization which has only one purpose. The diversified corporation is obviously less vulnerable than that which produces one product for one market. The differentiation of subunits within an organization may or may not be along functional lines. If it is functional in character, the subunits themselves are less highly institutionalized than the whole of which they are a part. Changes in the functions of the whole, however, are fairly easily reflected by changes in the power and roles of its subunits. If the subunits are multifunctional, they have greater institutional strength, but they may also, for that very reason, contribute less flexibility to the organization as a whole. Hence, a political system with parties of "social integration," in Sigmund Neumann's terms, has less institutional flexibility than one with parties of "individual representation." [16]

Relatively primitive and simple traditional political systems are usually overwhelmed and destroyed in the modernization process. More complex traditional systems are more likely to adapt to these new demands. Japan, for instance, was able to adjust its traditional political institutions to the modern world because of their relative complexity. For two and a half centuries before 1868 the emperor had reigned and the Tokugawa shogun had ruled. The stability of the political order, however, did not depend solely on the stability of the shogunate. When the authority of the shogunate decayed, another traditional institution, the emperor, was available to become the instrument of the modernizing samurai. The overthrow of the shogun involved not the collapse of the political order but the "restoration" of the emperor.

The simplest political system is that which depends on one individual. It is also the least stable. Tyrannies, Aristotle pointed out, are virtually all "quite short-lived." [17] A political system with sev-

16. Sigmund Neumann, "Toward a Comparative Study of Political Parties," in Neumann, ed., *Modern Political Parties* (Chicago, University of Chicago Press, 1956), pp. 403–05.

17. Aristotle, *Politics* (trans. Ernest Barker, Oxford, Clarendon Press, 1946), p. 254.

eral different political institutions, on the other hand, is much more likely to adapt. The needs of one age may be met by one set of institutions; the needs of the next by a different set. The system possesses within itself the means of its own renewal and adaptation. In the American system, for instance, President, Senate, House of Representatives, Supreme Court, and state governments have played different roles at different times in history. As new problems arise, the initiative in dealing with them may be taken first by one institution, then by another. In contrast, the French system of the Third and Fourth Republics centered authority in the National Assembly and the national bureaucracy. If, as was frequently the case, the Assembly was too divided to act and the bureaucracy lacked the authority to act, the system was unable to adapt to environmental changes and to deal with new policy problems. When in the 1950s the Assembly was unable to handle the dissolution of the French empire, there was no other institution, such as an independent executive, to step into the breach. As a result, an extraconstitutional force, the military, intervened in politics, and in due course a new institution, the de Gaulle Presidency, was created which was able to handle the problem. "A state without the means of some change," Burke observed of an earlier French crisis, "is without the means of its conservation." [18]

The classical political theorists, preoccupied as they were with the problem of stability, arrived at similar conclusions. The simple forms of government were most likely to degenerate; the "mixed state" was more likely to be stable. Both Plato and Aristotle suggested that the most practical state was the "polity" combining the institutions of democracy and oligarchy. A "constitutional system based absolutely, and at all points," Aristotle argued, "on either the oligarchical or the democratic conception of equality is a poor sort of thing. The facts are evidence enough: constitutions of this sort never endure." A "constitution is better when it is composed of more numerous elements." [19] Such a constitution is more likely to head off sedition and revolution. Polybius and Cicero elaborated this idea more explicitly. Each of the "good" simple forms of government—kingship, aristocracy, and democracy—is likely to degenerate into its perverted counterpart—tyranny, oligarchy, and

18. Edmund Burke, *Reflections on the Revolution in France* (Chicago, Regnery, 1955), p. 37.

19. *Politics*, pp. 60, 206.

mobocracy. Instability and degeneration can only be avoided by combining elements from all the good forms into a mixed state. Complexity produces stability. "The simple governments," Burke echoed two thousand years later, "are fundamentally defective, to say no worse of them." [20]

Autonomy-Subordination. A third measure of institutionalization is the extent to which political organizations and procedures exist independently of other social groupings and methods of behavior. How well is the political sphere differentiated from other spheres? In a highly developed political system, political organizations have an integrity which they lack in less developed systems. In some measure, they are insulated from the impact of nonpolitical groups and procedures. In less developed political systems, they are highly vulnerable to outside influences.

At its most concrete level, autonomy involves the relations between social forces, on the one hand, and political organizations, on the other. Political institutionalization, in the sense of autonomy, means the development of political organizations and procedures that are not simply expressions of the interests of particular social groups. A political organization that is the instrument of a social group—family, clan, class—lacks autonomy and institutionalization. If the state, in the traditional Marxist claim, is really the "executive committee of the bourgeoisie," then it is not much of an institution. A judiciary is independent to the extent that it adheres to distinctly judicial norms and to the extent that its perspectives and behavior are independent of those of other political institutions and social groupings. As with the judiciary, the autonomy of political institutions is measured by the extent to which they have their own interests and values distinguishable from those of other institutions and social forces. As also with the judiciary, the autonomy of political institutions is likely to be the result of competition among social forces. A political party, for instance, that expresses the interests of only one group in society—whether labor, business, or farmers—is less autonomous than one that articulates and aggregates the interests of several social groups. The latter type of party has a clearly defined existence apart from particular social forces. So also with legislatures, executives, and bureaucracies.

Political procedures, like political organizations, also have vary-

20. Burke, *Reflections on the Revolution in France*, p. 92.

ing degrees of autonomy. A highly developed political system has procedures to minimize, if not to eliminate, the role of violence in the system and to restrict to explicitly defined channels the influence of wealth in the system. To the extent that political officials can be toppled by a few soldiers or influenced by a few dollars, the organizations and procedures lack autonomy. Political organizations and procedures which lack autonomy are, in common parlance, said to be corrupt.

Political organizations and procedures that are vulnerable to nonpolitical influences from within the society are also usually vulnerable to influences from outside the society. They are easily penetrated by agents, groups, and ideas from other political systems. Thus a coup d'etat in one political system may easily "trigger" coup d'etats by similar groups in other less developed political systems.[21] In some instances, apparently, a regime can be overthrown by smuggling into the country a few agents and a handful of weapons. In other instances, a regime may be overthrown by the exchange of a few words and a few thousand dollars between a foreign ambassador and some disaffected colonels. The Soviet and American governments presumably spend substantial sums attempting to bribe high officials of less well-insulated political systems, sums they would not think of wasting in attempting to influence high officials in each other's political system.

In every society affected by social change, new groups arise to participate in politics. Where the political system lacks autonomy, these groups gain entry into politics without becoming identified with the established political organizations or acquiescing in the established political procedures. The political organizations and procedures are unable to stand up against the impact of a new social force. Conversely, in a developed political system the autonomy of the system is protected by mechanisms that restrict and moderate the impact of new groups. These mechanisms either slow down the entry of new groups into politics or, through a process of political socialization, impel changes in the attitudes and behavior of the most politically active members of the new group. In a highly institutionalized political system, the most important positions of leadership can normally only be achieved by

21. See Samuel P. Huntington, "Patterns of Violence in World Politics," in Huntington, ed., *Changing Patterns of Military Politics* (New York, Free Press, 1962), pp. 44-47.

those who have served an apprenticeship in less important positions. The complexity of a political system contributes to its autonomy by providing a variety of organizations and positions in which individuals are prepared for the highest offices. In a sense, the top positions of leadership are the inner core of the political system; the less powerful positions, the peripheral organizations, and the semipolitical organizations are the filters through which individuals desiring access to the core must pass. Thus the political system assimilates new social forces and new personnel without sacrificing its institutional integrity. In a political system that lacks such defenses, new men, new viewpoints, new social groups may replace each other at the core of the system with bewildering rapidity.

Coherence-Disunity. The more unified and coherent an organization is, the more highly institutionalized it is; the greater the disunity of the organization, the less it is institutionalized. Some measure of consensus, of course, is a prerequisite for any social group. An effective organization requires, at a minimum, substantial consensus on the functional boundaries of the group and on the procedures for resolving disputes which come up within those boundaries. The consensus must extend to those active in the system. Nonparticipants, or those only sporadically and marginally participant in the system, do not have to share the consensus and usually, in fact, do not share it to the same extent as the participants.[22]

In theory, an organization can be autonomous without being coherent and coherent without being autonomous. In actuality, however, the two are often closely linked together. Autonomy becomes a means to coherence, enabling the organization to develop an esprit and style that become distinctive marks of its behavior. Autonomy also prevents the intrusion of disruptive external forces, although, of course, autonomy does not protect against disruption from internal sources. Rapid or substantial expansions in the membership of an organization or in the participants in a system tend to weaken coherence. The Ottoman Ruling Institution, for instance, retained its vitality and coherence as long as admission was restricted and recruits were "put through an elaborate

22. See, e.g., Herbert McCloskey, "Consensus and Ideology in American Politics," *American Political Science Review, 18* (June 1964) , 361 ff.; Samuel Stouffer, *Communism, Conformity, and Civil Liberties* (Garden City, N.Y., Doubleday, 1955) , passim.

education, with selection and specialization at every stage." The Institution perished when "everybody pressed in to share its privileges. . . . Numbers were increased; discipline and efficiency declined." [23]

Unity, esprit, morale, and discipline are needed in governments as well as in regiments. Numbers, weapons, and strategy all count in war, but major deficiencies in any one of those may still be counterbalanced by superior coherence and discipline. So also in politics. The problems of creating coherent political organizations are more difficult but not fundamentally different from those involved in the creation of coherent military organizations. "The sustaining sentiment of a military force," David Rapoport has argued,

> has much in common with that which cements any group of men engaged in politics—the willingness of most individuals to bridle private or personal impulses for the sake of general social objectives. Comrades must trust each other's ability to resist the innumerable temptations that threaten the group's solidarity; otherwise, in trying social situations, the desire to fend for oneself becomes overwhelming. [24]

The capacities for coordination and discipline are crucial to both war and politics, and historically societies which have been skilled at organizing the one have also been adept at organizing the other. "The relationship of efficient social organization in the arts of peace and in the arts of group conflict," one anthropologist has observed, "is almost absolute, whether one is speaking of civilization or subcivilization. Successful war depends upon team work and consensus, both of which require command and discipline. Command and discipline, furthermore, can eventually be no more than symbols of something deeper and more real than they themselves." [25] Societies, such as Sparta, Rome, and Britain, which have been admired by their contemporaries for the authority and justice of their laws, have also been admired for the coherence and

23. Arnold J. Toynbee, *A Study of History* (abridgement of Vols. I–VI by D. C. Somervell, New York, Oxford University Press, 1947) , pp. 176–77.

24. David C. Rapoport, "A Comparative Theory of Military and Political Types," in Huntington, ed., *Changing Patterns of Military Politics,* p. 79.

25. Harry Holbert Turney-High, *Primitive War* (Columbia, S.C., University of South Carolina Press, 1949) , pp. 235–36.

discipline of their armies. Discipline and development go hand in hand.

Political Institutions and Public Interests

Political institutions have moral as well as structural dimensions. A society with weak political institutions lacks the ability to curb the excesses of personal and parochial desires. Politics is a Hobbesian world of unrelenting competition among social forces —between man and man, family and family, clan and clan, region and region, class and class—a competition unmediated by more comprehensive political organizations. The "amoral familism" of Banfield's backward society has its counterparts in amoral clanism, amoral groupism, amoral classism. Morality requires trust; trust involves predictability; and predictability requires regularized and institutionalized patterns of behavior. Without strong political institutions, society lacks the means to define and to realize its common interests. The capacity to create political institutions is the capacity to create public interests.

Traditionally the public interest has been approached in three ways.[26] It has been identified with either abstract, substantive, ideal values and norms such as natural law, justice, or right reason; or with the specific interest of a particular individual ("L'état, c'est moi"), group, class (Marxism), or majority; or with the result of a competitive process among individuals (classic liberalism) or groups (Bentleyism). The problem in all these approaches is to arrive at a definition that is concrete rather than nebulous and general rather than particular. Unfortunately, in most cases, what is concrete lacks generality and what is general lacks concreteness. One partial way out of the problem is to define the public interest in terms of the concrete interests of the governing institutions. A society with highly institutionalized governing organizations and procedures is more able to articulate and achieve its public interests. "Organized (institutionalized) political communities," as Friedrich argues, "are better adapted to reaching decisions and developing policies than unorganized com-

26. See, in general, Glendon Schubert, The Public Interest (Glencoe, Ill., Free Press, 1960); Carl J. Friedrich, ed., Nomos V: The Public Interest (New York, American Society of Political and Legal Philosophy, 1962); Douglas Price, "Theories of the Public Interest," in Lynton K. Caldwell, ed., Politics and Public Affairs (Bloomington, Indiana University Press, 1962), pp. 141–60; Richard E. Flathman, The Public Interest (New York, Wiley, 1966).

munities." [27] The public interest, in this sense, is not something which exists a priori in natural law or the will of the people. Nor is it simply whatever results from the political process. Rather it is whatever strengthens governmental institutions. The public interest is the interest of public institutions. It is something created and brought into existence by the institutionalization of government organizations. In a complex political system, many governmental organizations and procedures represent many different aspects of the public interest. The public interest of a complex society is a complex matter.

Democrats are accustomed to thinking of governmental institutions as having representative functions, that is, as expressing the interests of some other set of groups (their constituency). Hence they tend to forget that governmental institutions have interests of their own. These interests not only exist, they are also reasonably concrete. The questions "What is the interest of the Presidency? What is the interest of the Senate? What is the interest of the House of Representatives? What is the interest of the Supreme Court?" are difficult but not completely impossible to answer. The answers would furnish a fairly close approximation of the "public interest" of the United States. Similarly, the public interest of Great Britain might be approximated by the specific institutional interests of the Crown, Cabinet, and Parliament. In the Soviet Union, the answer would involve the specific institutional interests of the Presidium, Secretariat, and Central Committee of the Communist Party.

Institutional interests differ from the interests of individuals who are in the institutions. Keynes' percipient remark that "In the long run we are all dead" applies to individuals, not institutions. Individual interests are necessarily short-run interests. Institutional interests, however, exist through time; the proponent of the institution has to look to its welfare through an indefinite future. This consideration often means a limiting of immediate goals. The "true policy," Aristotle remarked, "for democracy and oligarchy alike, is not one which ensures the greatest possible amount of either, but one which will ensure the longest possible life for both." [28] The official who attempts to maximize power or

27. Carl J. Friedrich, *Man and His Government* (New York, McGraw-Hill, 1963), p. 150; italics in original.
28. *Politics*, p. 267.

other values in the short run often weakens his institution in the
long run. Supreme Court justices may, in terms of their immediate individual desires, wish to declare an act of Congress unconsti-
tutional. In deciding whether it is in the public interest to do so,
however, presumably one question they should ask themselves is
whether it is in the long-term institutional interest of the Supreme
Court for them to do so. Judicial statesmen are those who, like
John Marshall in *Marbury vs. Madison*, maximize the institutional power of the Court, in such a way that it is impossible for
either the President or Congress to challenge it. In contrast, the
Supreme Court justices of the 1930s came very close to expanding
their immediate influence at the expense of the long-term interests
of the Court as an institution.

"What's good for General Motors is good for the country" contains at least a partial truth. "What's good for the Presidency is good
for the country," however, contains more truth. Ask any reasonably informed group of Americans to identify the five best presidents and the five worst presidents. Then ask them to identify the
five strongest presidents and the five weakest presidents. If the
identification of strength with goodness and weakness with bad-
ness is not 100 per cent, it will almost certainly not be less than 80
per cent. Those presidents—Jefferson, Lincoln, the Roosevelts,
Wilson—who expanded the powers of their office are hailed as the
beneficent promoters of the public welfare and national interest.
Those presidents, such as Buchanan, Grant, Harding, who failed
to defend the power of their institution against other groups are
also thought to have done less good for the country. Institutional
interest coincides with public interest. The power of the presidency is identified with the good of the polity.

The public interest of the Soviet Union is approximated by the
institutional interests of the top organs of the Communist Party:
"What's good for the Presidium is good for the Soviet Union."
Viewed in these terms, Stalinism can be defined as a situation in
which the personal interests of the ruler take precedence over the
institutionalized interests of the party. Beginning in the late
1930s, Stalin consistently weakened the party. No party congress
was held between 1939 and 1952. During and after World War II
the Central Committee seldom met. The party secretariat and
party hierarchy were weakened by the creation of competing
organs. Conceivably this process could have resulted in the dis-

placement of one set of governing institutions by another, and some American experts and some Soviet leaders did think that governmental organizations rather than party organizations would become the ruling institutions in Soviet society. Such, however, was neither the intent nor the effect of Stalin's action. He increased his personal power, not the governmental power. When he died, his personal power died with him. The struggle to fill the resulting vacuum was won by Khrushchev who identified his interests with the interests of the party organization, rather than by Malenkov who identified himself with the governmental bureaucracy. Khrushchev's consolidation of power marked the reemergence and revitalization of the principal organs of the party. While they acted in very different ways and from different motives, Stalin weakened the party just as Grant weakened the Presidency. Just as a strong Presidency is in the American public interest, so also a strong party is in the Soviet public interest.

In terms of the theory of natural law, governmental actions are legitimate to the extent that they are in accord with the "public philosophy." [29] According to democratic theory, they derive their legitimacy from the extent to which they embody the will of the people. According to the procedural concept, they are legitimate if they represent the outcome of a process of conflict and compromise in which all interested groups have participated. In another sense, however, the legitimacy of governmental actions can be sought in the extent to which they reflect the interests of governmental institutions. In contrast to the theory of representative government, under this concept governmental institutions derive their legitimacy and authority not from the extent to which they represent the interests of the people or of any other group, but to the extent to which they have distinct interests of their own apart from all other groups. Politicians frequently remark that things "look different" after they are in office than they did when they were competing for office. This difference is a measure of the institutional demands of office. It is precisely this difference in perspective that legitimizes the demands of the officeholder on his fellow citizens. The interests of the president, for instance, may coincide partially and temporarily first with those of one group and then

29. See Walter Lippmann, *The Public Philosophy* (Boston, Little Brown, 1955), esp. p. 42, for his definition of the public interest as "what men would choose if they saw clearly, thought rationally, acted disinterestedly and benevolently."

with those of another. But the interest of the Presidency, as Neustadt has emphasized,[30] coincides with that of no one else. The president's power derives not from his representation of class, group, regional, or popular interests, but rather from the fact that he represents none of these. The presidential perspective is unique to the Presidency. Precisely for this reason it is both a lonely office and a powerful one. Its authority is rooted in its loneliness.

The existence of political institutions (such as the Presidency or Central Committee) capable of giving substance to public interests distinguishes politically developed societies from undeveloped ones. It also distinguishes moral communities from amoral societies. A government with a low level of institutionalization is not just a weak government; it is also a bad government. The function of government is to govern. A weak government, a government which lacks authority, fails to perform its function and is immoral in the same sense in which a corrupt judge, a cowardly soldier, or an ignorant teacher is immoral. The moral basis of political institutions is rooted in the needs of men in complex societies.

The relation between the culture of society and the institutions of politics is a dialectical one. Community, de Jouvenel observes, means "the institutionalization of trust," and the "essential function of public authorities" is to "increase the mutual trust prevailing at the heart of the social whole." [31] Conversely, the absence of trust in the culture of the society provides formidable obstacles to the creation of public institutions. Those societies deficient in stable and effective government are also deficient in mutual trust among their citizens, in national and public loyalties, and in organization skills and capacity. Their political cultures are often said to be marked by suspicion, jealousy, and latent or actual hostility toward everyone who is not a member of the family, the village, or, perhaps, the tribe. These characteristics are found in many cultures, their most extensive manifestations perhaps being in the Arab world and in Latin America. "Mistrust among the Arabs," one acute observer has commented,

> is internalized early within the value system of the child. . . . Organization, solidarity, and cohesion are lacking. . . . Their public-mindedness is not developed and their

30. See Richard E. Neustadt, *Presidential Power* (New York, John Wiley, 1960), passim, but esp. pp. 33–37, 150–51.

31. Bertrand de Jouvenel, *Sovereignty* (Chicago, University of Chicago Press, 1963), p. 123.

social consciousness is weak. The allegiance towards the state is shaky and identification with leaders is not strong. Furthermore, there prevails a general mistrust of those that govern and lack of faith in them.[32]

In Latin America similar traditions of self-centered individualism and of distrust and hatred for other groups in society have prevailed. "There is no good faith in America, either among men or among nations," Bolívar once lamented. "Treaties are paper, constitutions books, elections battles, liberty anarchy, and life a torment. The only thing one can do in America is emigrate." Over a century later the same complaint was heard: "With a politics of ambush and permanent mistrust, one for the other," argued an Ecuadorean newspaper, "we cannot do otherwise than create ruin and destruction in the national soul; this kind of politics has wasted our energies and made us weak." [33]

Other countries outside the Arab and Iberian cultures have manifested similar characteristics. In Ethiopia the "mutual distrust and lack of cooperation which inform the political climate of the country are directly related in a very low regard for man's capacity for solidarity and consensus. . . . The idea that it is possible to transcend the prevailing atmosphere of anxiety and suspicion by trusting one another . . . has been slow to appear and extremely rare." Iranian politics have been labeled the "politics of distrust." Iranians, it is argued, find "it exceptionally difficult to trust one another or to work together over time in any significant numbers." In Burma the child is taught to feel "safe only among his family while all outsiders and especially strangers are sources of danger to be treated with caution and suspicion." As a result, the Burmese find "it difficult to conceive of themselves in any way associated with objective and regulated systems of human relationships." Even a country as "Western" and as economically developed as Italy may have a political culture of "relatively unrelieved political alienation and of social isolation and distrust." [34]

32. Sania Hamady, *Temperament and Character of the Arabs* (New York, Twayne, 1960), pp. 101, 126, 230.

33. Simón Bolívar, quoted in Kalman H. Silvert, ed., *Expectant Peoples* (New York, Random House, 1963), p. 347; *El Dia*, Quito, Nov. 27, 1943, quoted in Bryce Wood, *The Making of the Good Neighbor Policy* (New York, Columbia University Press, 1961), p. 318.

34. Donald N. Levine, "Ethiopia: Identity, Authority, and Realism," in Lucian W. Pye and Sidney Verba, eds., *Political Culture and Political Development* (Prince-

The prevalence of distrust in these societies limits individual loyalties to groups that are intimate and familiar. People are and can be loyal to their clans, perhaps to their tribes, but not to broader political institutions. In politically advanced societies, loyalty to these more immediate social groupings is subordinated to and subsumed into loyalty to the state. "The love to the whole," as Burke said, "is not extinguished by this subordinate partiality. . . . To be attached to the subdivision, to love the little platoon we belong to in society, is the first principle (the germ, as it were) of public affections." In a society lacking political community, however, loyalties to the more primordial social and economic groupings—family, clan, village, tribe, religion, social class—compete with and often supersede loyalty to the broader institutions of public authority. In Africa today tribal loyalties are strong; national and state loyalties weak. In Latin America in the words of Kalman Silvert, "An innate distrust of the state coupled with the direct representation of economic and occupational interest in the government are destructive of party strength, erode pluralism, and deny the sweeping grandeur possible to enlightened political action in its broadest senses." [35] "The state in the Arab environment," one scholar has noted, "was always a weak institution, weaker than other social establishments such as the family, the religious community, and the ruling class. Private interest was always paramount over public interest." In a similar vein, H. A. R. Gibb has commented that "it is precisely the great weakness of Arab countries that, since the breakdown of the old corporations, no social institutions have been evolved through which the public will can be canalized, interpreted, defined, and mobilized. . . . There is, in short, no functioning organ of social democracy at all." [36] So also, Italians practiced within the family "virtues other men usually dedicate to the welfare of their country at large; the Italians' family loyalty is their true patriotism. . . . All official

ton, Princeton University Press, 1965) , pp. 277–78; Andrew F. Westwood, "Politics of Distrust in Iran," *Annals*, *358* (March 1965) , 123–36; Lucian W. Pye, *Politics, Personality and Nation-Building* (New Haven, Yale University Press, 1962) , pp. 205, 292–93; Gabriel Almond and Sidney Verba, *The Civic Culture* (Boston, Little Brown, 1965) , p. 308.

35. Silvert, pp. 358–59.

36. P. J. Vatikiotis, *The Egyptian Army in Politics* (Bloomington, Indiana University Press, 1961) , pp. 213–14; H. A. R. Gibb, "Social Reform: Factor X," in Walter Z. Laqueur, ed., *The Middle East in Transition* (New York, Praeger, 1958) , p. 8.

and legal authority is considered hostile by them until proved friendly or harmless." [37] Thus in a politically backward society lacking a sense of political community, each leader, each individual, each group pursues and is assumed to be pursuing its own immediate short-run material goals without consideration for any broader public interest.

Mutual distrust and truncated loyalties mean little organization. In terms of observable behavior, the crucial distinction between a politically developed society and an underdeveloped one is the number, size, and effectiveness of its organizations. If social and economic change undermine or destroy traditional bases of association, the achievement of a high level of political development depends upon the capacity of the people to develop new forms of association. In modern countries, in de Tocqueville's words, "the science of association is the mother of science; the progress of all the rest depends upon the progress it has made." The most obvious and most striking contrast between Banfield's village and an American town of similar size is the latter's "buzz of [associational] activity having as its purpose, at least in part, the advancement of community welfare." [38] The Italian village, in contrast, had only one association, and it did not engage in any public spirited activity. The absence of associations, this low level of organizational development, is characteristic of societies whose politics are confused and chaotic. The great problem in Latin America, as George Lodge has pointed out, is that "there is relatively little social organization in the sense that we know it in the United States." The result is a "motivation-organization vacuum" that makes democracy difficult and economic development slow. The ease with which traditional societies have adapted their political systems to the demands of modernity depends almost directly on the organizational skills and capacities of their people. Only those rare peoples possessed in large measure of such skills, such as the Japanese, have been able to make a relatively easy transition to a developed economy and a modern polity. The "problems of development and modernization," in Lucian Pye's words, are "rooted in the need to create more effective, more adaptive, more complex, and more rationalized organizations. . . . The ultimate test of

37. Luigi Barzini, *The Italians* (New York, Atheneum, 1964) , p. 194.
38. De Tocqueville, 2, 118; Edward C. Banfield, *The Moral Basis of a Backward Society* (Glencoe, Ill., Free Press, 1958) , p. 15.

development is the capacity of a people to establish and maintain large, complex, but flexible organizational forms." [39] The capacity to create such institutions, however, is in short supply in the world today. It is precisely the ability to meet this moral need and to create a legitimate public order which, above all else, communists offer modernizing countries.

POLITICAL PARTICIPATION: MODERNIZATION AND POLITICAL DECAY

Modernization and Political Consciousness

Modernization is a multifaceted process involving changes in all areas of human thought and activity. It is, as Daniel Lerner has said, "a process with some distinctive *quality* of its own, which would explain why modernity is felt as a *consistent whole* among people who live by its rules." The principal aspects of modernization, "urbanization, industrialization, secularization, democratization, education, media participation do not occur in haphazard and unrelated fashion." Historically they have been "so highly associated as to raise the question whether they are genuinely independent factors at all—suggesting that perhaps they went together so regularly because, in some historical sense, they *had* to go together." [40]

At the psychological level, modernization involves a fundamental shift in values, attitudes, and expectations. Traditional man expected continuity in nature and society and did not believe in the capacity of man to change or control either. Modern man, in contrast, accepts the possibility of change and believes in its desirability. He has, in Lerner's phrase, a "mobile personality" that adjusts to changes in his environment. These changes typically require the broadening of loyalties and identifications from concrete and immediate groups (such as the family, clan, and village) to larger and more impersonal groupings (such as class and nation). With this goes an increasing reliance on universalistic rather than particularistic values and on standards of achievement rather than of ascription in judging individuals.

At the intellectual level, modernization involves the tremen-

39. George C. Lodge, "Revolution in Latin America," *Foreign Affairs, 44* (Jan. 1966), 177; Pye, pp. 38, 51.

40. Daniel Lerner, *The Passing of Traditional Society* (Glencoe, Ill., Free Press, 1958), p. 438; italics in original.

dous expansion of man's knowledge about his environment and the diffusion of this knowledge throughout society through increased literacy, mass communications, and education. Demographically, modernization means changes in the patterns of life, a marked increase in health and life expectancy, increased occupational, vertical, and geographical mobility, and, in particular, the rapid growth of urban population as contrasted with rural. Socially, modernization tends to supplement the family and other primary groups having diffuse roles with consciously organized secondary associations having much more specific functions. The traditional distribution of status along a single bifurcated structure characterized by "cumulative inequalities" gives way to pluralistic status structures characterized by "dispersed inequalities." [41] Economically, there is a diversification of activity as a few simple occupations give way to many complex ones; the level of occupational skill rises significantly; the ratio of capital to labor increases; subsistence agriculture gives way to market agriculture; and agriculture itself declines in significance compared to commercial, industrial, and other nonagricultural activities. There tends to be an expansion of the geographical scope of economic activity and a centralization of such activity at the national level with the emergence of a national market, national sources of capital, and other national economic institutions. In due course the level of economic well-being increases and inequalities in economic well-being decrease.

Those aspects of modernization most relevant to politics can be broadly grouped into two categories. First, social mobilization, in Deutsch's formulation, is the process by which "major clusters of old social, economic and psychological commitments are eroded or broken and people become available for new patterns of socialization and behavior." [42] It means a change in the attitudes, values, and expectations of people from those associated with the traditional world to those common to the modern world. It is a consequence of literacy, education, increased communications, mass media exposure, and urbanization. Secondly, economic development refers to the growth in the total economic activity

41. Robert A. Dahl, *Who Governs?* (New Haven, Yale University Press, 1961), pp. 85–86.

42. Karl W. Deutsch, "Social Mobilization and Political Development," *American Political Science Review*, 55 (Sept. 1961), 494.

and output of a society. It may be measured by per capita gross national product, level of industrialization, and level of individual welfare gauged by such indices as life expectancy, caloric intake, supply of hospitals and doctors. Social mobilization involves changes in the aspirations of individuals, groups, and societies; economic development involves changes in their capabilities. Modernization requires both.

The impact of modernization on politics is varied. Numerous authors have defined political modernization in even more numerous ways. Most of these definitions focus on the differences between what are assumed to be the distinctive characteristics of a modern polity and of a traditional polity. Political modernization is naturally then held to be movement from the one to the other. Approached in this manner, the most crucial aspects of political modernization can be roughly subsumed under three broad headings. First, political modernization involves the rationalization of authority, the replacement of a large number of traditional, religious, familial, and ethnic political authorities by a single secular, national political authority. This change implies that government is the product of man, not of nature or of God, and that a well-ordered society must have a determinate human source of final authority, obedience to whose positive law takes precedence over other obligations. Political modernization involves assertion of the external sovereignty of the nation-state against transnational influences and of the internal sovereignty of the national government against local and regional powers. It means national integration and the centralization or accumulation of power in recognized national lawmaking institutions.

Secondly, political modernization involves the differentiation of new political functions and the development of specialized structures to perform those functions. Areas of particular competence—legal, military, administrative, scientific—become separated from the political realm, and autonomous, specialized, but subordinate organs arise to discharge those tasks. Administrative hierarchies become more elaborate, more complex, more disciplined. Office and power are distributed more by achievement and less by ascription. Thirdly, political modernization involves increased participation in politics by social groups throughout society. Broadened participation in politics may enhance control of the people by the government, as in totalitarian states, or it may enhance control of the government by the people, as in some democratic ones. But in all modern states the citizens become directly involved in and affected by governmental affairs. Rationalized authority, differentiated structure, and mass participation thus distinguish modern polities from antecedent polities.

It is, however, a mistake to conclude that in practice modernization means the rationalization of authority, differentiation of structure, and expansion of political participation. A basic and frequently overlooked distinction exists between political modernization defined as movement from a traditional to a modern polity and political modernization defined as the political aspects and political effects of social, economic, and cultural modernization. The former posits the direction in which political change theoretically should move. The latter describes the political changes which actually occur in modernizing countries. The gap between the two is often vast. Modernization in practice always involves change in and usually the disintegration of a traditional political system, but it does not necessarily involve significant movement toward a modern political system. Yet the tendency has been to assume that what is true for the broader social processes of modernization is also true for political changes. Social modernization, in some degree, is a fact in Asia, Africa, Latin America: urbanization is rapid, literacy is slowly increasing; industrialization is being pushed; per capita gross national product is inching upward; mass media circulation is expanding. All these are facts. In contrast progress toward many of the other goals which writers have identified with political modernization—democracy, stability, structural differentiation, achievement patterns, national integration—often is dubious at best. Yet the tendency is to think that because social modernization is taking place, political modernization also must be taking place. As a result, many sympathetic Western writings about the underdeveloped areas in the 1950s had the same air of hopeful unreality which characterized much of the sympathetic Western writing about the Soviet Union in the 1920s and 1930s. They were suffused with what can only be described as "Webbism": that is, the tendency to ascribe to a political system qualities which are assumed to be its ultimate goals rather than qualities which actually characterize its processes and functions.

In actuality, only some of the tendencies frequently encompassed in the concept "political modernization" characterized the "modernizing" areas. Instead of a trend toward competitiveness and democracy, there was an "erosion of democracy" and a tendency to autocratic military regimes and one-party regimes.[43] Instead of stability, there were repeated coups and revolts. Instead of a unifying nationalism and nation-building, there were repeated ethnic conflicts and civil wars. Instead of institutional rationalization and differentiation, there was frequently a decay of the administrative organizations inherited from the colonial era and a weakening and disruption of the political organizations developed during the struggle for independence. Only the concept of political modernization as mobilization and participation appeared to be generally applicable to the "developing" world. Rationalization, integration, and differentiation, in contrast, seemed to have only a dim relation to reality.

More than by anything else, the modern state is distinguished from the traditional state by the broadened extent to which people participate in politics and are affected by politics in large-scale political units. In traditional societies political participation may be widespread at the village level, but at any levels above the village it is limited to a very small group. Large-scale traditional societies may also achieve relatively high levels of rationalized authority and of structural differentiation, but again political participation will be limited to the relatively small aristocratic and bureaucratic elites. The most fundamental aspect of political modernization, consequently, is the participation in politics beyond the village or town level by social groups throughout the society and the development of new political institutions, such as political parties, to organize that participation.

The disruptive effects of social and economic modernization on politics and political institutions take many forms. Social and economic changes necessarily disrupt traditional social and political groupings and undermine loyalty to traditional authorities. The leaders, secular and religious, of the village are challenged by a new elite of civil servants and schoolteachers who represent the authority of the distant central government and who possess skills, resources, and aspirations with which the traditional village or

43. On the "erosion of democracy" and political instability, see Rupert Emerson, *From Empire to Nation* (Cambridge, Harvard University Press, 1960), Chap. 5; and Michael Brecher, *The New States of Asia* (London, Oxford University Press, 1963), Chap. 2.

tribal leaders cannot compete. In many traditional societies the most important social unit was the extended family, which itself often constituted a small civil society performing political, economic, welfare, security, religious, and other social functions. Under the impact of modernization, however, the extended family begins to disintegrate and is replaced by the nuclear family which is too small, too isolated, and too weak to perform these functions. A broader form of social organization is replaced by a narrower one, and the tendencies toward distrust and hostility—the war of one against all—are intensified. The amoral familism which Banfield found in southern Italy is typical not of a traditional society, but of a backward society in which the traditional institution of the extended family has disintegrated under the impact of the first phases of modernization.[44] Modernization thus tends to produce alienation and anomie, normlessness generated by the conflict of old values and new. The new values undermine the old bases of association and of authority before new skills, motivations, and resources can be brought into existence to create new groupings.

The breakup of traditional institutions may lead to psychological disintegration and anomie, but these very conditions also create the need for new identifications and loyalties. The latter may take the form of reidentification with a group which existed in latent or actual form in traditional society or they may lead to identification with a new set of symbols or a new group which has itself evolved in the process of modernization. Industrialization, Marx argued, produces class consciousness first in the bourgeoisie and then in the proletariat. Marx focused on only one minor aspect of a much more general phenomenon. Industrialization is only one aspect of modernization and modernization induces not just class consciousness but new group consciousness of all kinds: in tribe, region, clan, religion, and caste, as well as in class, occupation, and association. Modernization means that all groups, old as well as new, traditional as well as modern, become increasingly aware of themselves as groups and of their interests and claims in relation to other groups. One of the most striking phenomena of modernization, indeed, is the increased consciousness, coherence, organization, and action which it produces in many social forces which existed on a much lower level of conscious identity and or-

44. See Banfield, pp. 85 ff.

ganization in traditional society. The early phases of modernization are often marked by the emergence of fundamentalist religious movements, such as the Moslem Brotherhood in Egypt and the Buddhist movements in Ceylon, Burma, and Vietnam, which combine modern organizational methods, traditional religious values, and highly populist appeals.

So also in much of Africa tribal consciousness was almost unknown in traditional rural life. Tribalism was a product of modernization and the western impact on a traditional society. In southern Nigeria, for instance, Yoruba consciousness only developed in the nineteenth century and the term, Yoruba, was first used by Anglican missionaries. "Everyone recognizes," Hodgkin has observed, "that the notion of 'being a Nigerian' is a new kind of conception. But it would seem that the notion of 'being a Yoruba' is not very much older." Similarly, even in the 1950s, an Ibo leader, B. O. N. Eluwa, could travel through Iboland attempting to convince the tribesmen that they were Ibos. But the villagers, he said, simply "couldn't even imagine all Ibos." The efforts of Eluwa and other Ibo leaders, however, successfully created a sense of Iboness. Loyalty to tribe "is in many respects a *response* to modernization, a product of the very forces of change which colonial rule brought to Africa." [45]

A traditional society may possess many potential sources of identity and association. Some of these may be undermined and destroyed by the process of modernization. Others, however, may achieve a new consciousness and become the basis for new organization because they are capable—as for instance are tribal associations in African cities or caste associations in India—of meeting many of the needs for personal identity, social welfare, and economic advancement which are created by the process of modernization. The growth of group consciousness thus has both integrating and disintegrating effects on the social system. If villagers learn to shift their primary identity from a village to a tribe of many villages; if plantation workers cease to identify simply with their fellow workers on the plantation and instead identify with planta-

45. Thomas Hodgkin, "Letter to Dr. Biobaku," *Odü*, No. 4 (1957), p. 42, quoted in Immanuel Wallerstein, "Ethnicity and National Integration in West Africa," *Cahiers d'Etudes Africaines*, No. 3 (Oct. 1960); David Abernethy, "Education and Politics in a Developing Society: The Southern Nigerian Experience" (unpublished Ph.D. dissertation, Harvard University, 1965), p. 307; italics in original.

tion workers in general and with an organization of plantation workers in general; if Buddhist monks broaden their allegiances from their local temple and monastery to a national Buddhist movement—each of these developments is a broadening of loyalty and in that sense presumably a contribution to political modernization.

The same group consciousness, however, can also be a major obstacle to the creation of effective political institutions encompassing a broader spectrum of social forces. Along with group consciousness, group prejudice also "develops when there is intensive contact between different groups, such as has accompanied the movement toward more centralized political and social organizations." [46] And along with group prejudice comes group conflict. Ethnic or religious groups which had lived peacefully side by side in traditional society become aroused to violent conflict as a result of the interaction, the tensions, the inequalities generated by social and economic modernization. Modernization thus increases conflict among traditional groups, between traditional groups and modern ones, and among modern groups. The new elites based on Western or modern education come into conflict with the traditional elites whose authority rests on ascribed and inherited status. Within the modernized elites, antagonisms arise between politicians and bureaucrats, intellectuals and soldiers, labor leaders and businessmen. Many, if not most, of these conflicts at one time or another erupt into violence.

Modernization and Violence

The Poverty and Modernization Theses. The relation between modernization and violence is complex. More modern societies are generally more stable and suffer less domestic violence than less modern societies. One study produced a correlation of .625 (n = 62) between political stability and a composite index of modernity defined in terms of eight social and economic variables. Both the level of social mobilization and the level of economic development are directly associated with political stability. The relation between literacy and stability is particularly high. The frequency of revolutions also varies inversely with the educational

46. "Report on Preliminary Results of Cross-Cultural Study of Ethnocentrism," by Robert A. LeVine and Donald T. Campbell, *Carnegie Corporation of New York Quarterly* (Jan. 1966) , p. 7.

level of the society, and deaths from domestic group violence vary inversely with the proportion of children attending primary school. Economic well-being is similarly associated with political order: in 74 countries, the correlation between per capita gross national product and deaths from domestic group violence was

TABLE 1.2. Per Capita GNP and Violent Conflicts, 1958–1965

Economic group	Number of countries	Number with conflicts	Per cent of total countries affected	Number of conflicts in group	Rate of conflicts for all nations in group
Very poor (under $100)	38	32	87%	72	1.9
Poor ($100–$249)	32	22	69	41	1.3
Middle income ($250–$749)	37	18	48	40	1.1
Rich (above $750)	27	10	37	11	.4
Total	134	82	61%	164	1.2

Source: U.S. Department of Defense and Escott Reid, *The Future of the World Bank* (Washington, D.C., International Bank for Reconstruction and Development, 1965), pp. 64–70.

—.43. A different study of 70 countries for the years 1955–60 found a correlation of —.56 between per capita gross national product and the number of revolutions. During the eight years between 1958 and 1965, violent conflicts were more than four times as prevalent in very poor nations as they were in rich nations; 87 per cent of the very poor countries suffered significant outbreaks of violence as compared to only 37 per cent of the rich countries.[47]

Clearly countries which have high levels of both social mobilization and economic development are more stable and peaceful politically. Modernity goes with stability. From this fact it is an easy step to the "poverty thesis" and the conclusions that economic and social backwardness is responsible for instability and hence

47. Feierabend, "Aggressive Behaviors," pp. 258–62; Bruce M. Russett et al., *World Handbook of Political and Social Indicators* (New Haven, Yale University Press, 1964), p. 273; Raymond Tanter and Manus Midlarsky, "A Theory of Revolution," *Journal of Conflict Resolution, 11* (Sept. 1967), 271–72; Raymond Tanter, "Dimensions of Conflict Behavior Within Nations, 1955–1960: Turmoil and Internal War," *Papers, Peace Research Society, 3* (1965), 175.

that modernization is the road to stability. "There can, then, be no question," as Secretary McNamara said, "but that there is an irrefutable relationship between violence and economic backwardness." Or in the words of one academic analyst, "all-pervasive poverty undermines government—of any kind. It is a persistent cause of instability and makes democracy well-nigh impossible to practice." [48] If these relationships are accepted, then obviously the promotion of education, literacy, mass communications, industrialization, economic growth, urbanization, should produce greater political stability. These seemingly clear deductions from the correlation between modernity and stability are, however, invalid. In fact, modernity breeds stability, but modernization breeds instability.

The apparent relationship between poverty and backwardness, on the one hand, and instability and violence, on the other, is a spurious one. It is not the absence of modernity but the efforts to achieve it which produce political disorder. If poor countries appear to be unstable, it is not because they are poor, but because they are trying to become rich. A purely traditional society would be ignorant, poor, and stable. By the mid-twentieth century, however, all traditional societies were also transitional or modernizing societies. It is precisely the devolution of modernization throughout the world which increased the prevalence of violence about the world. For two decades after World War II American foreign policy toward the modernizing countries was in large part devoted to promoting economic and social development because these would lead to political stability. The success of this policy is, however, written in both the rising levels of material well-being and the rising levels of domestic violence. The more man wages war against "his ancient enemies: poverty, disease, ignorance" the more he wages war against himself.

By the 1960s every backward nation was a modernizing nation. Evidence, nonetheless, did exist to suggest that causes of violence in such nations lay with the modernization rather than with the backwardness. Wealthier nations tend to be more stable than those less wealthy, but the poorest nations, those at the bottom of the international economic ladder, tend to be less prone to violence and instability than those countries just above them. Even Secre-

48. Speech by Robert S. McNamara, Montreal, Quebec, May 18, 1966, *New York Times*, May 19, 1966, p. 11; Brecher, pp. 62-63.

tary McNamara's own statistics offered only partial support for his proposition. The World Bank, for instance, classified six of the twenty Latin American republics as "poor," that is, they had per capita gross national products of less than $250. Six of the twenty countries were also suffering from prolonged insurgencies in February 1966. Only one country, Bolivia, however, fell into both categories. The probability of insurgency in those Latin American countries which were not poor was twice as high as it was in those countries which were poor. Similarly, 48 out of 50 African countries and territories were classified as poor, and eleven of these were suffering from insurgency. Certainly, however, the probabilities of insurgency in the two African countries which were not poor—Libya and South Africa—were just as high as in the remaining 37 poor countries and territories. Moreover, the insurgency which did exist in 11 countries seemed to be related in four cases to continued colonial rule (e.g., Angola, Mozambique) and in the other seven to marked tribal and racial differences among the population (e.g. Nigeria, Sudan). Colonialism and ethnic heterogeneity would seem to be much better predictors of violence than poverty. In the Middle East and Asia (excluding Australia and New Zealand) 10 out of 22 countries classified as poor were suffering from insurgencies in February 1966. On the other hand, three out of the four countries which were not poor (Iraq, Malaysia, Cyprus, Japan) were also experiencing insurgencies. Here again, the likelihood of insurgency in the richer countries was about twice that in the poorer countries. Here also, ethnic heterogeneity appeared to be a better predictor of insurgency than poverty.

The weakness of the direct correlation between poverty and instability is also suggested by other evidence. While a correlation of —.43 (n = 74) existed between per capita GNP and deaths from domestic group violence, the largest amount of violence was found not in the poorest countries with per capita GNPs of less than $100, but in those slightly more wealthy with per capita GNPs between $100 and $200. Above $200 the amount of violence tended to decline significantly. These figures led to the conclusion that "underdeveloped nations must expect a fairly high level of civil unrest for some time, and that the very poor states should probably expect an increase, not a decrease, in domestic violence over the next few decades." [49] So also, Eckstein found that the 27 countries in

49. Hayward R. Alker, Jr. and Bruce M. Russett, "The Analysis of Trends and Patterns," in Russett et al., pp. 306–07. See also Ted Gurr with Charles Ruttenberg.

which internal wars were rare between 1946 and 1959 were divided into two groups. Nine were highly modern (e.g. Australia, Denmark, Sweden), while 18 were "relatively underdeveloped countries whose elites have remained tied closely to the traditional types and structures of life." Among these were a number of still backward European colonies plus such countries as Ethiopia, Eritrea, Liberia, and Saudi Arabia.[50] Somewhat similarly, a division of countries according to their levels of literacy also suggested a bell-shaped pattern of instability. Ninety-five per cent of those countries in the middle range with 25 to 60 per cent literacy were unstable as compared to 50 per cent of those countries with less than 10 per cent literacy and 22 per cent of those countries with more than 90 per cent literacy. In another analysis mean instability scores were calculated for 24 modern countries (268), 37 transitional countries (472), and 23 traditional countries (420).[51]

TABLE 1.3. Literacy and Stability

Level of literacy	Number of countries	Number of unstable countries	Per cent unstable
Below 10%	6	3	50.0
10%–25%	12	10	83.3
25%–60%	23	22	95.6
60%–90%	15	12	80.0
Over 90%	23	5	21.7

Source: Ivo K. and Rosalind L. Feierabend and Betty A. Nesvold, "Correlates of Political Stability" (paper presented at Annual Meeting, American Political Science Association, Sept. 1963), pp. 19–21.

The sharp difference between the transitional and modern countries demonstrates graphically the thesis that modernity means stability and modernization instability. The small difference between the traditional societies and the transitional societies reflects the fact that the line drawn between the two was a purely arbitrary one intended to produce a group of "traditional" countries

The Conditions of Civil Violence: First Tests of a Causal Model (Princeton, Princeton University, Center of International Studies, Research Monograph No. 28, 1967), pp. 66–67.

50. Harry Eckstein, "Internal War: The Problem of Anticipation," in Ithiel de Sola Pool et al., Social Science Research and National Security (Washington, D.C., Smithsonian Institution, 1963), pp. 120–21.

51. Feierabend, p. 263.

equal in size to the modern group. Hence virtually all the societies classified as traditional were actually in the early phases of transition. Again, however, the data suggest that if a purely traditional society existed, it would be more stable politically than those in the transitional phase.

The modernization thesis thus explains why the poverty thesis could acquire a certain seeming validity in the late twentieth century. It also explains seeming reversals in the relation between modernity and stability for particular sets of countries. In Latin America, for instance, the wealthiest countries are at the middle levels of modernization. Consequently, it is not surprising that they should be more unstable than the more backward Latin American countries. As we have seen, in 1966 only one of the six poorest Latin American countries, but five of the 14 wealthier Latin American countries, suffered from insurgency. Communist and other radical movements have been strong in Cuba, Argentina, Chile, and Venezuela: four of the five wealthiest of the 20 Latin American republics and three of the five most literate republics. The frequency of revolution in Latin America is directly related to the level of economic development. For the continent as a whole the correlation of per capita income and number of revolutions is .50 (n = 18); for nondemocratic states it is much higher (r = .85; n = 14).[52] Thus, the data on Latin America which suggest a positive relationship between modernity and instability actually bolster the argument that relates modernization to instability.

This relationship also holds for variations within countries. In modernizing countries, violence, unrest, and extremism are more often found in the wealthier parts of the country than in the poorer sections. In analysing the situation in India, Hoselitz and Weiner found that "the correlation between political stability and economic development is poor or even negative." Under British rule political violence was most prevalent in the "economically most highly developed provinces"; after independence violence remained more likely in the industrialized and urban centers than

52. Manus Midlarsky and Raymond Tanter, "Toward a Theory of Political Instability in Latin America," *Journal of Peace Research, 4* (1967), 215. See also Robert D. Putnam's discovery of a positive association between economic development (but not social mobilization) and military intervention in Latin America: "Toward Explaining Military Intervention in Latin American Politics," *World Politics, 20* (Oct. 1967), 94–97.

"in the more backward and underdeveloped areas of India." [53] In numerous underdeveloped countries the standard of living in the major cities is three or four times that prevalent in the country-side, yet the cities are often the centers of instability and violence while the rural areas remain quiet and stable. Political extremism is also typically stronger in the wealthier than in the poorer areas. In fifteen Western countries, the communist vote was largest in the most urbanized areas of the least urbanized countries.[54] In Italy the center of communist strength was the prosperous north rather than the poverty-stricken south. In India the communists were strongest in Kerala (with the highest literacy rate among Indian states) and in industrialized Calcutta, not in the economically more backward areas. In Ceylon, "In a fundamental sense, the areas of Marxist strength are the most Westernized" and those with the highest per capita income and education.[55] Thus, within countries, it is the areas which are modernizing rather than those which remain traditional that are the centers of violence and extremism.

Not only does social and economic modernization produce political instability, but the degree of instability is related to the rate of modernization. The historical evidence with respect to the West is overwhelming on this point. "The *rapid* influx of large numbers of people into *newly* developing urban areas," Kornhauser observes, "invites mass movements." So also, the European and particularly the Scandinavian experience demonstrates that wherever "industrialization occurred *rapidly,* introducing sharp *discontinuities* between the pre-industrial and industrial situation, more rather than less extremist working-class movements emerged." [56] Similarly, the combined rate of change on six of eight indicators of modernization (primary and postprimary education; caloric consumption; cost of living; radios; infant mortality; urbanization; literacy; and national income) for 67 countries between 1935 and 1962 correlated .647 with political instability in those coun-

53. Bert F. Hoselitz and Myron Weiner, "Economic Development and Political Stability in India," *Dissent, 8* (Spring 1961), 173.

54. William Kornhauser, *The Politics of Mass Society* (Glencoe, Ill., Free Press, 1959), pp. 143–44.

55. William Howard Wriggins, *Ceylon: Dilemmas of a New Nation* (Princeton, Princeton University Press, 1960), pp. 134–35, 138–40.

56. Kornhauser, p. 145 (italics in original); Seymour Martin Lipset, *Political Man* (Garden City, N.Y., Doubleday, 1960), p. 68 (italics in original).

tries between 1955 and 1961. "The higher the rate of change toward modernity, the greater the political instability, measured statically or dynamically." The overall picture which emerges of an unstable country is:

> one exposed to modernity; disrupted socially from the traditional patterns of life; confronted with pressures to change their ways, economically, socially and politically; bombarded with new and "better" ways of producing economic goods and services; and frustrated by the modernization process of change, generally, and the failure of their government to satisfy their ever-rising expectations, particularly.[57]

Political instability was rife in twentieth-century Asia, Africa, and Latin America in large part because the rate of modernization was so much faster there than it had been in the earlier modernizing countries. The modernization of Europe and of North America was spread over several centuries; in general, one issue or one crisis was dealt with at a time. In the modernization of the non-Western parts of the world, however, the problems of the centralization of authority, national integration, social mobilization, economic development, political participation, social welfare have arisen not sequentially but simultaneously. The "demonstration effect" which the early modernizers have on the later modernizers first intensifies aspirations and then exacerbates frustrations. The differences in the rate of change can be dramatically seen in the lengths of time which countries, in Cyril Black's formulation, required for the consolidation of modernizing leadership. For the first modernizer, England, this phase stretched over 183 years, from 1649 to 1832. For the second modernizer, the United States, it lasted 89 years, from 1776 to 1865. For 13 countries which entered it during the Napoleonic period (1789–1815), the average period was 73 years. But for 21 of the 26 countries which began it during the first quarter of the twentieth century and had emerged by the 1960s, the average was only 29 years.[58] In a similar vein, Karl Deutsch estimates that during the nineteenth century the principal indicators of social mobilization in modernizing countries changed at about the rate of 0.1 per cent per year, while in

57. Conroe, "A Cross-National Analysis," pp. 65–73, 86–87; Feierabend, pp. 263–67.
58. Cyril E. Black, *The Dynamics of Modernization* (New York, Harper and Row, 1966), pp. 90–94.

twentieth-century modernizing countries they change at about the rate of 1 per cent per year. Clearly the tempo of modernization has increased rapidly. Clearly, also, the heightened drive for social and economic change and development was directly related to the increasing political instability and violence that characterized Asia, Africa, and Latin America in the years after World War II.

Social Mobilization and Instability. The relationship between social mobilization and political instability seems reasonably direct. Urbanization, increases in literacy, education, and media exposure all give rise to enhanced aspirations and expectations which, if unsatisfied, galvanize individuals and groups into politics. In the absence of strong and adaptable political institutions, such increases in participation mean instability and violence. Here in dramatic form can be clearly seen the paradox that modernity produces stability and modernization instability. For 66 nations, for example, the correlation between the proportion of children in primary schools and the frequency of revolution was —.84. In contrast, for 70 nations the correlation between the rate of change in primary enrollment and political instability was .61.[59] The faster the enlightenment of the population, the more frequent the overthrow of the government.

The rapid expansion of education has had a visible impact on political stability in a number of countries. In Ceylon, for instance, the school system expanded rapidly between 1948 and 1956. This "increase in the number of students graduating in the indigenous languages satisfied some ambitions but contributed new social pressures among the articulate educated middle classes." It was, apparently, directly related to the electoral overturn of the government in the elections of 1956 and to the increased instability affecting Ceylon during the following six years.[60] Similarly, in Korea during the 1950s Seoul became "one of the largest education centers of the world." Its law schools, it is estimated, produced about eighteen times as many graduates in 1960 as the field could absorb. At the lower levels of education, the expansion was even more striking, with the literacy rate increasing

59. Tanter and Midlarsky, p. 272, citing forthcoming *Dimensions of Nations* by Rummel, Sawyer, Tanter, and Guetzkow; Conroe, p. 66.

60. Wriggins, pp. 119, 245. On the Feierabend-Nesvold-Conroe index, instability in Ceylon increased from 3:012 during 1948–54 to 4:089 for 1955–62; see Conroe, Table I.

from less than 20 per cent in 1945 to over 60 per cent in the early 1960s.[61] This expansion of awareness presumably shared some responsibility for the political instability of Korea during the early 1960s, the principal source of which was students. Students and unemployed university graduates were, indeed, a common concern in the 1960s to the nationalist military regime in Korea, the socialist military regime in Burma, and the traditional military regime in Thailand. The extent to which higher education in many modernizing countries is not calculated to produce graduates with the skills relevant to the country's needs creates the paradoxical but common situation "of a country in which skilled labor is a scarce resource, and yet in which highly educated persons are in superabundant supply." [62]

In general, the higher the level of education of the unemployed, alienated, or otherwise dissatisfied person, the more extreme the destabilizing behavior which results. Alienated university graduates prepare revolutions; alienated technical or secondary school graduates plan coups; alienated primary school leavers engage in more frequent but less significant forms of political unrest. In West Africa, for instance, "disgruntled and restless though they are, these school-leavers stand not at the center but on the perimeter of significant political events. The characteristic forms of political disturbance for which they are responsible are not revolutions but acts of arson, assault, and intimidation directed against political opponents." [63]

The problems posed by the rapid expansion of primary education have caused some governments to reassess their policies. In a debate on education in the Eastern Region of Nigeria in 1958, for instance, Azikiwe suggested that primary education could become an "unproductive social service," and one cabinet member warned that the United Kingdom followed "the pattern of industry and increased productivity first, free education second. Never free education first, as there must be jobs for the newly educated to take up, and only industry, trade and commerce can

61. Gregory Henderson, *Korea: The Politics of the Vortex* (Cambridge, Harvard University Press, forthcoming, 1968) , p. 170.

62. Hoselitz and Weiner, p. 177.

63. David Abernethy and Trevor Coombe, "Education and Politics in Developing Countries," *Harvard Educational Review*, 35 (Summer 1965) , 292.

provide such jobs in bulk. . . . We must hesitate to create political problems of unemployment in the future." [64] Literates and semiliterates may furnish recruits for extremist movements generating instability. Burma and Ethiopia had equally low per capita incomes in the 1950s: the relative stability of the latter in comparison to the former perhaps reflected the fact that fewer than 5 per cent of the Ethiopians were literate but 45 per cent of the Burmese were.[65] Similarly, Cuba had the fourth highest literacy rate in Latin America when it went communist, and the only Indian state to elect a communist government, Kerala, also has the highest literacy rate in India. Clearly, the appeals of communism are usually to literates rather than illiterates. Much has been made of the problems caused by the extension of suffrage to large numbers of illiterates; democracy, it has been argued, cannot function satisfactorily if the vast bulk of the voting population cannot read. Political participation by illiterates, however, may well, as in India, be less dangerous to democratic political institutions than participation by literates. The latter typically have higher aspirations and make more demands on government. Political participation by illiterates, moreover, is likely to remain limited, while participation by literates is more likely to snowball with potentially disastrous effects on political stability.

Economic Development and Instability. Social mobilization increases aspirations. Economic development, presumably, increases the capacity of a society to satisfy those aspirations and therefore should tend to reduce social frustrations and the consequent political instability. Presumably, also, rapid economic growth creates new opportunities for entrepreneurship and employment and thereby diverts into money-making ambitions and talents which might otherwise go into coup-making. It can, however, also be argued to the contrary that economic development itself is a highly destabilizing process and that the very changes which are needed to satisfy aspirations in fact tend to exacerbate those aspirations. Rapid economic growth, it has been said:

1. disrupts traditional social groupings (family, class, caste) , and thus increases "the number of individuals who are

64. Quoted in Abernethy, p. 501.
65. Deutsch, "Social Mobilization and Political Development," p. 496.

déclassé . . . and who are thus in circumstances conducive to revolutionary protest"; [66]

2. produces *nouveaux riches* who are imperfectly adjusted to and assimilated by the existing order and who want political power and social status commensurate with their new economic position;

3. increases geographical mobility which again undermines social ties, and, in particular, encourages rapid migration from rural areas to cities, which produces alienation and political extremism;

4. increases the number of people whose standard of living is falling, and thus may widen the gap between rich and poor;

5. increases the incomes of some people absolutely but not relatively and hence increases their dissatisfaction with the existing order;

6. requires a general restriction of consumption in order to promote investment and thus produces popular discontent;

7. increases literacy, education, and exposure to mass media, which increase aspirations beyond levels where they can be satisfied;

8. aggravates regional and ethnic conflicts over the distribution of investment and consumption;

9. increases capacities for group organization and consequently the strength of group demands on government, which the government is unable to satisfy.

To the extent that these relationships hold, economic growth increases material well-being at one rate but social frustration at a faster rate.

The association of economic development, particularly rapid economic development, with political instability received its classic statement in de Tocqueville's interpretation of the French Revolution. The revolution, he said, was preceded by "an advance as rapid as it was unprecedented in the prosperity of the nation." This "steadily increasing prosperity, far from tranquilizing the

66. Mancur Olson, Jr., "Rapid Growth as a Destabilizing Force," *Journal of Economic History*, *23* (Dec. 1963) , 532. This list of the destabilizing effects of economic growth is drawn primarily from Olson's article.

population, everywhere promoted a spirit of unrest" and "it was precisely in those parts of France where there had been most improvement that popular discontent ran highest." Similar conditions of economic improvement, it has been argued, preceded the Reformation, the English, American, and Russian revolutions, and the agitation and discontent in England in the late eighteenth and early nineteenth centuries. The Mexican revolution similarly followed twenty years of spectacular economic growth. The rate of change in per capita gross national product for seven years before a successful revolt correlated very highly with the extent of violence in such revolts in Asian and Middle Eastern countries between 1955 and 1960, although not in Latin America. The experience of India, it has been argued, from the 1930s through the 1950s also shows "that economic development, far from enhancing political stability, has tended to be politically unstabilizing." [67] All this data is, of course, also consistent with the finding that during World War II discontent about promotions was more widespread in the Air Force than in other services despite or because of the fact that promotions were more frequent and rapid in the Air Force than in the other services.[68]

Much specific evidence thus exists of an apparent association between rapid economic growth and political instability. On a more general level, however, the link between the two is not so clear. During the 1950s the correlation between rate of economic growth and domestic group violence for 53 countries was a mildly negative one of —.43. West Germany, Japan, Roumania, Yugoslavia, Austria, the U.S.S.R., Italy, and Czechoslovakia had very high rates of economic growth and little or no domestic violence. Bolivia, Argentina, Honduras, and Indonesia, on the other hand, had many deaths from domestic violence but very low, and in some cases even negative, growth rates. Similarly, the correlation for seventy countries of the rate of change in national income between 1935 and 1962 and level of political instability between 1948 and 1962 was —.34; the correlation between the change in national income

67. Alexis de Tocqueville, *The Old Regime and the French Revolution* (Garden City, N.Y., Doubleday, 1955) , pp. 173, 175–76; Crane Brinton, *The Anatomy of Revolution* (New York, Vintage, 1958) , p. 264; Olson, pp. 544–47; Tanter and Midlarsky, pp. 272–74; Hoselitz and Weiner, p. 173, for the quotation on India.

68. See Samuel A. Stouffer et al., *The American Soldier* (Princeton, Princeton University Press, 1949) , *1*, 251–58, 275–76.

and the variations in stability for the same countries in the same years was —.45. In a similar vein, Needler found that in Latin America economic growth was a precondition for institutional stability in countries with high rates of political participation.[69]

TABLE 1.4. Rapid Economic Growth and Political Instability

Annual growth of GNP per capita	Deaths from Domestic Group Violence in 53 Countries, 1950–62 (per 1,000,000 population)				
	NONE	LOW .1–9.9	MODERATE 10–99	HIGH 100–1,335	TOTAL
Very high, 6% and over	4	3	0	0	7
High, 4%–5.9%	0	6	1	2	9
Moderate, 2%–3.9%	8	5	1	3	17
Low, 1%–1.9%	3	4	6	1	14
Very low, below 1%	0	1	2	3	6
Total	15	19	10	9	53

Source: Bruce Russett et al., *World Handbook of Political and Social Indicators* (New Haven, Yale University Press, 1964) , Tables 29 and 45. Periods for the growth figures vary but are generally for 7 to 12 years centering on the 1950s.

This conflicting evidence suggests that the relationship, if any, between economic growth and political instability must be a complicated one. Perhaps the relationship varies with the level of economic development. At one extreme, some measure of economic growth is necessary to make instability possible. The simple poverty thesis falls down because people who are really poor are too poor for politics and too poor for protest. They are indifferent, apathetic, and lack exposure to the media and other stimuli which would arouse their aspirations in such manner as to galvanize them into political activity. "The abjectly poor, too," Eric Hoffer observed, "stand in awe of the world around them and are not hospitable to change. . . . There is thus a conservatism of the destitute as profound as the conservatism of the privileged, and the former is as much a factor in the perpetuation of a social order as

69. Conroe, pp. 65–69; Martin C. Needler, *Political Development in Latin America: Instability, Violence, and Evolutionary Change* (New York, Random House, forthcoming) , Chap. 5.

the latter." [70] Poverty itself is a barrier to instability. Those who are concerned about the immediate goal of the next meal are not apt to worry about the grand transformation of society. They become marginalists and incrementalists concerned simply with making minor but absolutely essential improvements in the existing situation. Just as social mobilization is necessary to provide the motive for instability, so also some measure of economic development is necessary to provide the means for instability.

At the other extreme, among countries which have reached a relatively high level of economic development, a high rate of economic growth is compatible with political stability. The negative correlations between economic growth and instability reported above are, in large part, the result of combining both highly developed and underdeveloped countries into the same analysis. Economically developed countries are more stable and have higher rates of growth than economically less developed countries. Unlike other social indicators, the rate of economic growth tends to vary directly with the level of development rather than inversely with it. In countries which are not wealthy, the rate of economic growth is not related significantly to political instability one way or another: for 34 countries with per capita GNP below $500 the correlation between rate of economic growth and deaths from domestic group violence was —.07. Thus, the relation between the rate of economic growth and political instability varies with the level of economic development. At low levels, a positive relation exists, at medium levels no significant relation, and at high levels a negative relationship.

The Gap Hypothesis. Social mobilization is much more destabilizing than economic development. The gap between these two forms of change furnishes some measure of the impact of modernization on political stability. Urbanization, literacy, education, mass media, all expose the traditional man to new forms of life, new standards of enjoyment, new possibilities of satisfaction. These experiences break the cognitive and attitudinal barriers of the traditional culture and promote new levels of aspirations and wants. The ability of a transitional society to satisfy these new as-

70. Eric Hoffer, *The True Believer* (New York, New American Library, 1951), p. 17; Daniel Goldrich, "Toward an Estimate of the Probability of Social Revolutions in Latin America: Some Orienting Concepts and a Case Study," *Centennial Review*, 6 (Summer 1962), 394 ff. See also below, pp. 278 ff.

pirations, however, increases much more slowly than the aspirations themselves. Consequently, a gap develops between aspiration and expectation, want formation and want satisfaction, or the aspirations function and the level-of-living function.[71] This gap generates social frustration and dissatisfaction. In practice, the extent of the gap provides a reasonable index to political instability.

The reasons for this relationship between social frustration and political instability are somewhat more complicated than they may appear on the surface. The relationship is, in large part, due to the absence of two potential intervening variables: opportunities for social and economic mobility and adaptable political institutions. Since Puritanism, the go-getting economic innovator and the dedicated revolutionary have had qualitatively different goals but strikingly similar high aspirations, both the product of a high level of social mobilization.[72] Consequently, the extent to which social frustration produces political participation depends in large part on the nature of the economic and social structure of the traditional society. Conceivably this frustration could be removed through social and economic mobility if the traditional society is sufficiently "open" to offer opportunities for such mobility. In part, this is precisely what occurs in rural areas, where outside opportunities for horizontal mobility (urbanization) contribute to the relative stability of the countryside in most modernizing countries. The few opportunities for vertical (occupational and income) mobility within the cities, in turn, contribute to their greater instability. Apart from urbanization, however, most modernizing countries have low levels of social-economic mobility. In relatively few societies are the traditional structures likely to encourage economic rather than political activity. Land and any other types of economic wealth in the traditional society are tightly held by a relatively small oligarchy or are controlled by foreign corporations and investors. The values of the traditional society often are hostile to entrepreneurial roles, and such roles consequently may be largely monopolized by an ethnic minority

71. These are terms employed by Deutsch, pp. 493 ff.; James C. Davies, "Toward a Theory of Revolution," *American Sociological Review*, 27 (Feb. 1962) , 5 ff.; Feierabend, pp. 256–62; Charles Wolf, *Foreign Aid: Theory and Practice in Southern Asia* (Princeton, Princeton University Press, 1960) , pp. 296 ff.; and Tanter and Midlarsky, pp. 271 ff.

72. For the relation between n-Achievement and communism, see David C. McClelland, *The Achieving Society* (Princeton, Van Nostrand, 1961) , pp. 412–13.

(Greeks and Armenians in the Ottoman Empire; Chinese in southeast Asia; Lebanese in Africa). In addition, the modern values and ideas which are introduced into the system often stress the primacy of government (socialism, the planned economy), and consequently may also lead mobilized individuals to shy away from entrepreneurial roles.

In these conditions, political participation becomes the road for advancement of the socially mobilized individual. Social frustration leads to demands on the government and the expansion of political participation to enforce those demands. The political backwardness of the country in terms of political institutionalization, moreover, makes it difficult if not impossible for the demands upon the government to be expressed through legitimate channels and to be moderated and aggregated within the political system. Hence the sharp increase in political participation gives rise to political instability. The impact of modernization thus involves the following relationships:

$$(1) \quad \frac{\text{Social mobilization}}{\text{Economic development}} = \text{Social frustration}$$

$$(2) \quad \frac{\text{Social frustration}}{\text{Mobility opportunities}} = \text{Political participation}$$

$$(3) \quad \frac{\text{Political participation}}{\text{Political institutionalization}} = \text{Political instability}$$

The absence of mobility opportunities and the low level of political institutionalization in most modernizing countries produce a correlation between social frustration and political instability. One analysis identified 26 countries with a low ratio of want formation to want satisfaction and hence low "systemic frustration" and 36 countries with a high ratio and hence high "systemic frustration." Of the 26 satisfied societies, only six (Argentina, Belgium, France, Lebanon, Morocco, and the Union of South Africa) had high degrees of political instability. Of the 36 dissatisfied countries, only two (Philippines, Tunisia) had high levels of political stability. The overall correlation between frustration and instability was .50. The differences in Communist voting strength in Indian states can also in part be explained by the ratios between social mobilization and economic well-being in these states. Similarly, in Latin America, constitutional stability has been shown to be a function of economic development and politi-

cal participation. Sharp increases in participation produce instability unless they are accompanied by corresponding shifts in the
level of economic well-being.[73]

Political instability in modernizing countries is thus in large
part a function of the gap between aspirations and expectations
produced by the escalation of aspirations which particularly occurs
in the early phases of modernization. In some instances, a similar
gap with similar results may be produced by the decline in expectations. Revolutions often occur when a period of sustained economic growth is followed by a sharp economic downturn. Such
downturns apparently occurred in France in 1788–89, in England
in 1687–88, in America in 1774–75, before Dorr's rebellion in
1842, in Russia (as a result of the war) in 1915–17, in Egypt in
1952, and in Cuba in 1952–53 (when Castro launched his first attack on Batista). In addition, in Latin America coups d'etat occur
more frequently during years when economic conditions worsen
than in those years marked by increases in real per capita incomes.[74]

Inequality and Instability. "In all these cases," Aristotle observed of political change in Greece, "the cause of sedition is always to be found in inequality." [75] Political inequality is, by definition, almost an inherent aspect of political instability. What
about economic inequality? The paucity of data on the distribution of income and wealth makes it difficult to test the proposition
that economic inequality is associated with political instability.
For eighteen countries a correlation of .34 was found between the
Gini index of inequality in income before taxes and deaths from
political violence; for twelve countries the correlation of income
inequality after taxes and political violence was .36.[76] More substantial evidence exists, however, to link inequalities in land ownership to political instability. In a study of 47 countries, Russett
found a correlation of .46 between a Gini index of inequality in
land ownership and deaths from domestic group violence. Lower
correlations existed between unequal land ownership and frequency of violent incidents. The relationship of the concentration

73. Feierabend, p. 259; Wolf, Chap. 9; Needler, Chap. 5.
74. See Davies, pp. 5 ff.; Tanter and Midlarsky, passim; Martin C. Needler, "Political Development and Military Intervention in Latin America," *American Political
Science Review, 60* (Sept. 1966), 617–18.
75. Aristotle, *Politics*, p. 205.
76. Russett et al., p. 272.

of land ownership to violence was, however, greatly strengthened when the percentage of the population engaged in agriculture was also taken into account. In highly agricultural countries, presumably the social-economic mobility opportunities for those in agriculture are less and hence inequality in land ownership should be more directly related to violence. This is, indeed, the case, and the correlation of inequality in land ownership with violent deaths was found to be about .70 in agricultural countries.[77]

Modernization affects economic inequality and thus political instability in two ways. First, wealth and income are normally more unevenly distributed in poor countries than in economically developed countries.[78] In a traditional society this inequality is accepted as part of the natural pattern of life. Social mobilization, however, increases awareness of the inequality and presumably resentment of it. The influx of new ideas calls into question the legitimacy of the old distribution and suggests the feasibility and the desirability of a more equitable distribution of income. The obvious way of achieving a rapid change in income distribution is through government. Those who command the income, however, usually also command the government. Hence social mobilization turns the traditional economic inequality into a stimulus to rebellion.

Secondly, in the long run, economic development produces a more equitable distribution of income than existed in the traditional society. In the short run, however, the immediate impact of economic growth is often to exacerbate income inequalities. The gains of rapid economic growth are often concentrated in a few groups while the losses are diffused among many; as a result, the number of people getting poorer in the society may actually increase. Rapid growth often involves inflation; in inflation prices typically rise faster than wages with consequent tendencies toward a more unequal distribution of wealth. The impact of Western legal systems in non-Western societies often encourages the replacement of communal forms of land ownership with private ownership

77. Bruce M. Russett, "Inequality and Instability: The Relation of Land Tenure to Politics," World Politics, 16 (April 1964), 442–54.

78. See Simon Kuznets, "Qualitative Aspects of the Economic Growth of Nations: VIII. Distribution of Income by Size," Economic Development and Cultural Change, 11 (Jan. 1963), 68; UN Social Commission, Preliminary Report on the World Social Situation (New York, United Nations, 1952), pp. 132–33; Gunnar Myrdal, An International Economy (New York, Harper, 1956), p. 133.

and thus tends to produce greater inequalities in land ownership than existed in the traditional society. In addition, in less developed societies the distribution of income in the more modern, nonagricultural sector is typically more unequal than it is in the agricultural. In rural India in 1950, for instance, five per cent of the families received 28.9 per cent of the income; but in urban India five per cent of the families received 61.5 per cent of the income.[79] Since the overall distribution of income is more equal in the less agricultural, developed nations, the distribution of income within the nonagricultural sector of an underdeveloped country is much more unequal than it is in the same sector in a developed country.

In particular modernizing countries the impact of economic growth on economic inequality may become quite noticeable. The twenty years before the revolution in Mexico witnessed a tremendous growth in economic inequalities, particularly in land ownership. In the 1950s the gap between wealth and poverty in Mexico and in Latin America generally was again tending to increase. The gap between high and low incomes in the Philippines was also reported to have increased significantly during the 1950s. Similarly, Pakistan's rapid economic growth in the late 1950s and early 1960s gave rise to "tremendous disparities in income" and tended to produce "relative stagnation at the bottom of the social pyramid." [80] In African countries independence brought to the few who assumed power frequent opportunities to amass immense wealth at a time when the standard of living for the bulk of their populations remained stationary or even declined. The earlier independence came in the evolution of a colonial society, the greater the economic—and political—inequality which independence fastened on that society.

Economic development increases economic inequality at the same time that social mobilization decreases the legitimacy of that

79. Kuznets, pp. 46–58.

80. Gustav F. Papanek, *Pakistan's Development: Social Goals and Private Incentives* (Cambridge, Harvard University Press, 1967), pp. 207, 67–72, 176–78, and Barbara Ward (Lady Jackson), Notes for Seminar, Harvard University, Center for International Affairs, March 11, 1965. See also David Wurfel, "The Philippine Elections: Support for Democracy," *Asian Survey*, 2 (May 1962), 25; John J. Johnson, *The Military and Society in Latin America* (Stanford, Stanford University Press, 1964), pp. 94–95.

inequality. Both aspects of modernization combine to produce political instability.

Modernization and Corruption

Corruption is behavior of public officials which deviates from accepted norms in order to serve private ends. Corruption obviously exists in all societies, but it is also obviously more common in some societies than in others and more common at some times in the evolution of a society than at other times. Impressionistic evidence suggests that its extent correlates reasonably well with rapid social and economic modernization. Political life in eighteenth-century America and in twentieth-century America, it would appear, was less corrupt than in nineteenth-century America. So also political life in seventeenth-century Britain and in late nineteenth-century Britain was, it would appear, less corrupt than it was in eighteenth-century Britain. Is it merely coincidence that this high point of corruption in English and American public life coincided with the impact of the industrial revolution, the development of new sources of wealth and power, and the appearance of new classes making new demands on government? In both periods political institutions suffered strain and some measure of decay. Corruption is, of course, one measure of the absence of effective political institutionalization. Public officials lack autonomy and coherence, and subordinate their institutional roles to exogenous demands. Corruption may be more prevalent in some cultures than in others but in most cultures it seems to be most prevalent during the most intense phases of modernization. The differences in the level of corruption which may exist between the modernized and politically developed societies of the Atlantic world and those of Latin America, Africa, and Asia in large part reflect their differences in political modernization and political development. When the leaders of military juntas and revolutionary movements condemn the "corruption" in their societies, they are, in effect, condemning the backwardness of their societies.

Why does modernization breed corruption? Three connections stand out. First, modernization involves a change in the basic values of the society. In particular it means the gradual acceptance by groups within the society of universalistic and achievement-based norms, the emergence of loyalties and identifications of individuals and groups with the nation-state, and the spread of the assumption that citizens have equal rights against the state and equal obligations to the state. These norms usually, of course, are first accepted by students, military officers, and others who have been exposed to them abroad. Such groups then begin to judge their own society by these new and alien norms. Behavior which was acceptable and legitimate according to traditional norms becomes unacceptable and corrupt when viewed through modern eyes. Corruption in a modernizing society is thus in part not so much the result of the deviance of behavior from accepted norms as it is the deviance of norms from the established patterns of behavior. New standards and criteria of what is right and wrong lead to a condemnation of at least some traditional behavior patterns as corrupt. "What Britons saw as corrupt and Hausa as oppressive," one scholar has noted of northern Nigeria, "Fulani might regard as both necessary and traditional." [81] The calling into question of old standards, moreover, tends to undermine the legitimacy of all standards. The conflict between modern and traditional norms opens opportunities for individuals to act in ways justified by neither.

Corruption requires some recognition of the difference between public role and private interest. If the culture of the society does not distinguish between the king's role as a private person and the king's role as king, it is impossible to accuse the king of corruption in the use of public monies. The distinction between the private purse and public expenditures only gradually evolved in Western Europe at the beginning of the modern period. Some notion of this distinction, however, is necessary to reach any conclusion as to whether the actions of the king are proper or corrupt. Similarly, according to traditional codes in many societies, an official had the responsibility and obligation to provide rewards and employment to members of his family. No distinction existed between obligation to the state and obligation to the family. Only when such a distinction becomes accepted by dominant groups within the society does it become possible to define such behavior as nepotism and hence corruption. Indeed, the introduction of achievement standards may stimulate greater family identification and more felt need to protect family interests against the threat posed by

81. M. G. Smith, "Historical and Cultural Conditions of Political Corruption Among the Hausa," *Comparative Studies in Society and History*, 6 (Jan. 1964), 194.

alien ways. Corruption is thus a product of the distinction between public welfare and private interest which comes with modernization.

Modernization also contributes to corruption by creating new sources of wealth and power, the relation of which to politics is undefined by the dominant traditional norms of the society and on which the modern norms are not yet accepted by the dominant groups within the society. Corruption in this sense is a direct product of the rise of new groups with new resources and the efforts of these groups to make themselves effective within the political sphere. Corruption may be the means of assimilating new groups into the political system by irregular means because the system has been unable to adapt sufficiently fast to provide legitimate and acceptable means for this purpose. In Africa, corruption threw "a bridge between those who hold political power and those who control wealth, enabling the two classes, markedly apart during the initial stages of African nationalist governments, to assimilate each other." [82] The new millionaires buy themselves seats in the Senate or the House of Lords and thereby become participants in the political system rather than alienated opponents of it, which might have been the case if this opportunity to corrupt the system were denied them. So also recently enfranchised masses or recently arrived immigrants use their new power of the ballot to buy themselves jobs and favors from the local political machine. There is thus the corruption of the poor and the corruption of the rich. The one trades political power for money, the other money for political power. But in both cases something public (a vote or an office or decision) is sold for private gain.

Modernization, thirdly, encourages corruption by the changes it produces on the output side of the political system. Modernization, particularly among the later modernizing countries, involves the expansion of governmental authority and the multiplication of the activities subjected to governmental regulation. In Northern Nigeria, "oppression and corruption tended to increase among the Hausa with political centralization and the increase of governmental tasks." All laws, as McMullan has pointed out, put some group at a disadvantage, and this group consequently becomes a

82. M. McMullan, "A Theory of Corruption," *The Sociological Review, 9* (July 1961), 196.

potential source of corruption.[83] The multiplication of laws thus multiplies the possibilities of corruption. The extent to which this possibility is realized in practice depends in large part upon the extent to which the laws have the general support of the population, the ease with which the law can be broken without detection, and the profit to be made by breaking it. Laws affecting trade, customs, taxes plus those regulating popular and profitable activities such as gambling, prostitution, and liquor, consequently become major incentives to corruption. Hence in a society where corruption is widespread the passage of strict laws against corruption serves only to multiply the opportunities for corruption.

The initial adherence to modern values by a group in a transitional country often takes an extreme form. The ideals of honesty, probity, universalism, and merit often become so overriding that individuals and groups come to condemn as corrupt in their own society practices which are accepted as normal and even legitimate in more modern societies. The initial exposure to modernism tends to give rise to unreasonable puritanical standards even as it did among the Puritans themselves. This escalation in values leads to a denial and rejection of the bargaining and compromise essential to politics and promotes the identification of politics with corruption. To the modernizing zealot a politician's promise to build irrigation ditches for farmers in a village if he is elected seems to be just as corrupt as an offer to pay each villager for his vote before the election. Modernizing elites are nationalistic and stress the overriding preeminence of the general welfare of society as a whole. Hence in a country like Brazil, "efforts by private interests to influence public policy are considered, as in Rousseau, *inherently* 'corrupt.' By the same token government action which is fashioned in deference to particular claims and pressures from society is considered 'demagogy.' "[84] In a society like Brazil the modernizing elements condemn as corrupt ambassadorial appointments to reward friends or to appease critics and the establishment of government projects in return for interest group support. In the extreme case the antagonism to corruption may take the form of the intense fanatical puritanism characteristic of most revolutionary and some military regimes in at least their early phases.

83. Smith, p. 194; McMullan, pp. 190–91.
84. Nathaniel Leff, "Economic Development Through Bureaucratic Corruption," *American Behavioral Scientist, 8* (Nov. 1964) , 132; italics in original.

Paradoxically, this fanatical anticorruption mentality has ultimate effects similar to those of corruption itself. Both challenge the autonomy of politics: one substituting private goals for public ones and the other replacing political values with technical ones. The escalation of standards in a modernizing society and the concomitant devaluation and rejection of politics represent the victory of the values of modernity over the needs of society.

Reducing corruption in a society thus often involves both a scaling down of the norms thought appropriate for the behavior of public officials and at the same time changes in the general behavior of such officials in the direction of those norms. The result is a greater congruence between prevalent norms and prevalent behavior at the price of some inconsistency in both. Some behavior comes to be accepted as a normal part of the process of politics, as "honest" rather than "dishonest graft," while other, similar behavior comes to be generally condemned and generally avoided. Both England and the United States went through this process: at one point the former accepted the sale of peerages but not of ambassadorships, while the latter accepted the sale of ambassadorships but not of judgeships. "The result in the U.S.A.," as one observer has noted, "is a patchwork: the scope of political patronage has been greatly reduced and the cash bribery of higher public servants largely eliminated. At the same time, large areas of public life have so far remained more or less immune to reform, and practices that in one sphere would be regarded as corrupt are almost taken for granted in another." [85] The development within a society of the ability to make this discrimination is a sign of its movement from modernization to modernity.

The functions, as well as the causes, of corruption are similar to those of violence. Both are encouraged by modernization; both are symptomatic of the weakness of political institutions; both are characteristic of what we shall subsequently call praetorian societies; both are means by which individuals and groups relate themselves to the political system and, indeed, participate in the system in ways which violate the mores of the system. Hence the society which has a high capacity for corruption also has a high capacity for violence. In some measure, one form of deviant behavior may substitute for the other, but, more often, different social

85. Colin Leys, "What Is the Problem About Corruption?" *Journal of Modern African Studies, 3* (1965), 230.

forces simultaneously exploit their differing capacities for each. The prevalence of violence, however, does pose a greater threat to the functioning of the system than the prevalence of corruption. In the absence of agreement on public purposes, corruption substitutes agreement on private goals, while violence substitutes conflict over public or private ends. Both corruption and violence are illegitimate means of making demands upon the system, but corruption is also an illegitimate means of satisfying those demands. Violence is more often a symbolic gesture of protest which goes unrequited and is not designed to be requited. It is a symptom of more extreme alienation. He who corrupts a system's police officers is more likely to identify with the system than he who storms the system's police stations.

Like machine politics or clientalistic politics in general, corruption provides immediate, specific, and concrete benefits to groups which might otherwise be thoroughly alienated from society. Corruption may thus be functional to the maintenance of a political system in the same way that reform is. Corruption itself may be a substitute for reform and both corruption and reform may be substitutes for revolution. Corruption serves to reduce group pressures for policy changes, just as reform serves to reduce class pressures for structural changes. In Brazil, for instance, governmental loans to trade association leaders have caused them to give up "their associations' broader claims. Such betrayals have been an important factor in reducing class and trade association pressure upon the government." [86]

The degree of corruption which modernization produces in a society is, of course, a function of the nature of the traditional society as well as of the nature of the modernizing process. The presence of several competing value systems or cultures in a traditional society will, in itself, encourage corruption in that society. Given a relatively homogeneous culture, however, the amount of corruption likely to develop during modernization would appear to be inversely related to the degree of social stratification in the traditional society. A highly articulated class or caste structure means a highly developed system of norms regulating behavior between individuals of different status. These norms are enforced both by the individual's socialization into his own group and by the expectations and potential sanctions of other groups. In such a society fail-

86. Leff, p. 137.

ure to follow the relevant norms in intergroup relations may lead to intense personal disorganization and unhappiness.

Corruption, consequently, should be less extensive in the modernization of feudal societies than it is in the modernization of centralized bureaucratic societies. It should have been less in Japan than in China and it should have been less in Hindu cultures than in Islamic ones. Impressionistic evidence suggests that these may well be the case. For Western societies, one comparative analysis shows that Australia and Great Britain have "fairly high levels of class voting" compared to the United States and Canada. Political corruption, however, appears to have been more extensive in the latter two countries than in the former, with Quebec perhaps being the most corrupt area in any of the four countries. Consequently, "the more class-polarized countries also seem to have less political corruption." [87] Similarly, in the "mulatto" countries (Panama, Cuba, Venezuela, Brazil, Dominican Republic, and Haiti) of Latin America, "there appears to be greater social equality and much less rigidity in the social structure" than in the Indian (Mexico, Ecuador, Guatemala, Peru, Bolivia) or *mestizo* (Chile, Colombia, El Salvador, Honduras, Nicaragua, Paraguay) countries. Correspondingly, however, the relative "absence of an entrenched upper class means also the relative absence of a governing class ethic, with its sense of noblesse oblige" and hence "there seems little doubt that it is countries in this socioracial category in which political graft reaches its most flagrant heights." Pérez Jiménez in Venezuela, Batista in Cuba, and Trujillo in the Dominican Republic all came from non-upper-class backgrounds and all became multimillionaires in office. So also, "Brazil and Panama are notorious for more 'democratic,' more widely-distributed, graft-taking." [88] The prevalence of corruption in the African states may well be related to the general absence of rigid class divisions. "The rapid mobility from poverty to wealth and from one occupation to another," one observer has noted of Africa, "has prevented the development of class phenomena, that is, of hereditary status or class consciousness." [89] The same mobility, however, multiplies the opportunities for and the

---

87. Robert R. Alford, *Party and Society* (Chicago, Rand McNally, 1963) , p. 298.
88. Needler, *Political Development in Latin America*, Chap. 6, pp. 15–16.
89. Peter C. Lloyd, "The Development of Political Parties in Western Nigeria," *American Political Science Review, 49* (Sept. 1955) , 695.

attractions of corruption. Similarly, the Philippines and Thailand, both of which have had reasonably fluid and open societies with relatively high degrees of social mobility, have been characterized by frequent reports of widespread political corruption.

In most forms corruption involves an exchange of political action for economic wealth. The particular forms that will be prevalent in a society depend upon the ease of access to one as against the other. In a society with multiple opportunities for the accumulation of wealth and few positions of political power, the dominant pattern will be the use of the former to achieve the latter. In the United States, wealth has more commonly been a road to political influence than political office has been a road to wealth. The rules against using public office to obtain private profit are much stricter and more generally obeyed than those against using private wealth to obtain public office. That striking and yet common phenomenon of American politics, the cabinet minister or presidential assistant who feels forced to quit office *in order* to provide for his family, would be viewed with amazement and incredulity in most parts of the world. In modernizing countries, the reverse situation is usually the case. The opportunities for the accumulation of wealth through private activity are limited by traditional norms, the monopoly of economic roles by ethnic minorities, or the domination of the economy by foreign companies and investors. In such a society, politics becomes the road to wealth, and those enterprising ambitions and talents which cannot find what they want in business may yet do so in politics. It is, in many modernizing countries, easier for an able and ambitious young man to become a cabinet minister by way of politics than to become a millionaire by way of business. Consequently, contrary to American practice, modernizing countries may accept as normal widespread use of public office to obtain private wealth while at the same time taking a stricter view of the use of private wealth to obtain public office. Corruption, like violence, results when the absence of mobility opportunities outside politics, combined with weak and inflexible political institutions, channels energies into politically deviant behavior.

The prevalence of foreign business in a country in particular tends to promote corruption both because the foreigners have less scruples in violating the norms of the society and because their control of important avenues to economic well-being forces potential native entrepreneurs to attempt to make their fortunes through politics. Taylor's description of the Philippines undoubtedly has widespread application among modernizing countries: "Politics is a major industry for the Filipinos; it is a way of life. Politics is the main route to power, which, in turn, is the main route to wealth. . . . More money can be made in a shorter time with the aid of political influence than by any other means." [90] The use of political office as a way to wealth implies a subordination of political values and institutions to economic ones. The principal purpose of politics becomes not the achievement of public goals but the promotion of individual interests.

In all societies the *scale* of corruption (i.e. the average value of the private goods and public services involved in a corrupt exchange) increases as one goes up the bureaucratic hierarchy or political ladder. The *incidence* of corruption (i.e. the frequency with which a given population group engages in corrupt acts) on a given level in the political or bureaucratic structure, however, may vary significantly from one society to another. In most political systems, the incidence of corruption is high at the lower levels of bureaucratic and political authority. In some societies, the incidence of corruption seems to remain constant or to increase as one goes up the political hierarchy. In terms of frequency as well as scale, national legislators are more corrupt than local officials; high level bureaucrats are more corrupt than low level ones; cabinet ministers are the most corrupt of all; and the president or top leader the most corrupt among them. In such societies the top leader—the Nkrumah, Sarit, San Martín, Pérez Jiménez, Trujillo—may make off with tens if not hundreds of millions of dollars. In such a system corruption tends to accentuate already existing inequalities. Those who gain access to the most political power also have the more frequent opportunities to gain access to the most wealth. Such a pattern of top-heavy corruption means a very low level of political institutionalization, since the top political institutions in the society which should be most independent of outside influences are in fact most susceptible to such influences. This pattern of corruption is not necessarily incompatible with political stability so long as the avenues of upward mobility through the political machine or the bureaucracy remain open. If, however,

90. George E. Taylor, *The Philippines and the United States: Problems of Partnership* (New York, Praeger, 1964), p. 157.

the younger generation of politicians sees itself indefinitely excluded from sharing in the gains of the older leaders, or if the
colonels in the army see little hope of promotion and the chance
to share in the opportunities open only to generals, the system becomes liable to violent overthrow. In such a society both political
corruption and political stability depend upon vertical mobility.

The expectation of more corruption at the top is reversed in
other societies. In these societies the incidence of corrupt behavior
increases as one goes down the political or bureaucratic hierarchy.
Low-level bureaucratic officials are more likely to be corrupt than
high-level ones; state and local officials are more likely to be corrupt than national ones; the top national leadership and the national cabinet are comparatively free from corruption, while the
town council and local offices are deeply involved in it. Scale and
incidence of corruption are inversely related. This pattern would
seem to be generally true for highly modern societies, such as the
United States, and also for at least some modernizing societies,
such as India. It is also probably the dominant pattern in communist states. The crucial factor in this type of society is the existence of fairly strong national political institutions which socialize
rising political leaders into a code of values stressing the public responsibilities of the political leadership. National political institutions are reasonably autonomous and differentiated, while lower-
level and local political individuals and organizations are more
closely involved with other social forces and groups. This pattern
of corruption may directly enhance the stability of the political
system. The top leaders of the society remain true to the stated
norms of the political culture and accept political power and
moral virtue as substitutes for economic gain. Low-level officials,
in turn, are compensated for their lack of political standing by
their greater opportunity to engage in corruption. Their envy of
the power of their leaders is tempered by the solace of their own
petty graft.

Just as the corruption produced by the expansion of political
participation helps to integrate new groups into the political system, so also the corruption produced by the expansion of governmental regulation may help stimulate economic development.
Corruption may be one way of surmounting traditional laws or
bureaucratic regulations which hamper economic expansion. In
the United States during the 1870s and 1880s corruption of state

legislatures and city councils by railroad, utility, and industrial corporations undoubtedly speeded the growth of the American economy. "Many economic activities would be paralyzed," Weiner observes of India, "were it not for the flexibility which *bakshish* contributes to the complex, rigid, administrative system." [91] In somewhat similar fashion, during the Kubitschek era in Brazil a high rate of economic development apparently corresponded with a high rate of parliamentary corruption, as industrializing entrepreneurs bought protection and assistance from conservative rural legislators. It has even been suggested that one result of governmental efforts to reduce corruption in societies such as Egypt is to produce additional obstacles to economic development. In terms of economic growth, the only thing worse than a society with a rigid, overcentralized, dishonest bureaucracy is one with a rigid, overcentralized, honest bureaucracy. A society which is relatively uncorrupt—a traditional society for instance where traditional norms are still powerful—may find a certain amount of corruption a welcome lubricant easing the path to modernization. A developed traditional society may be improved—or at least modernized—by a little corruption; a society in which corruption is already pervasive, however, is unlikely to be improved by more corruption.

Corruption naturally tends to weaken or to perpetuate the weakness of the government bureaucracy. In this respect, it is incompatible with political development. At times, however, some forms of corruption can contribute to political development by helping to strengthen political parties. "The corruption of one government," Harrington said, ". . . is the generation of another." [92] Similarly, the corruption of one governmental organ may help the institutionalization of another. In most modernizing countries, the bureaucracy is overdeveloped in comparison with the institutions responsible for aggregating interests and handling the input side of the political system. Insofar as the governmental bureaucracy is corrupted in the interests of the political parties, political development may be helped rather than hindered. Party

91. Myron Weiner, *The Politics of Scarcity* (Chicago, University of Chicago Press, 1962), p. 253. See in general Joseph S. Nye, "Corruption and Political Development: A Cost-Benefit Analysis," *American Political Science Review*, 61 (June 1967), 417–27.

92. James Harrington, quoted in Sabine, *A History of Political Thought* (rev. ed. New York, Henry Holt, 1950), p. 501.

patronage is only a mild form of corruption, if indeed it deserves to be called that at all. For an official to award a public office in return for a payment to the official is clearly to place private interest over public interest. For an official to award a public office in return for a contribution of work or money to a party organization is to subordinate one public interest to another, more needy, public interest.

Historically strong party organizations have been built either by revolution from below or by patronage from above. The nineteenth-century experience of England and the United States is one long lesson in the use of public funds and public office to build party organization. The repetition of this pattern in the modernizing countries of today has contributed directly to the building of some of the most effective political parties and most stable political systems. In the later modernizing countries the sources of private wealth are too few and too small to make a major contribution to party building. Just as government in these countries has to play a more important role in economic development than it did in England and the United States, so also it must play a more important role in political development. In the 1920s and the 1930s, Ataturk used the resources of the Turkish government to foster the development of the Republican Peoples Party. After its creation in 1929 the Mexican Revolutionary Party similarly benefited from governmental corruption and patronage. The formation of the Democratic Republican Party in Korea in the early 1960s was directly helped by the use of governmental monies and governmental personnel. In Israel and India, governmental patronage has been a major source of strength for Mapai and Congress. The corruption in West Africa derived in part from the needs of the political parties. And, of course, in the most obvious and blatant case of all, communist parties, once they acquire power, directly subordinate governmental bureaucracies and governmental resources to their own purposes.

The rationale for corrupting the bureaucracy on behalf of the parties does not derive simply from a preference for one organization as against another. Corruption is, as we have seen, a product of modernization and particularly of the expansion of political consciousness and political participation. The reduction of corruption in the long run requires the organization and structuring of that participation. Political parties are the principal institution of modern politics which can perform this function. Corruption thrives on disorganization, the absence of stable relationships among groups and of recognized patterns of authority. The development of political organizations which exercise effective authority and which give rise to organized group interests—the "machine," the "organization," the "party"—transcending those of individual and social groups reduces the opportunity for corruption. Corruption varies inversely with political organization, and to the extent that corruption builds parties, it undermines the conditions of its own existence.

Corruption is most prevalent in states which lack effective political parties, in societies where the interests of the individual, the family, the clique, or the clan predominate. In a modernizing polity the weaker and less accepted the political parties, the greater the likelihood of corruption. In countries like Thailand and Iran where parties have had a semilegality at best, corruption on behalf of individual and family interests has been widespread. In the Philippines where political parties are notoriously weak, corruption has again been widely prevalent. In Brazil, also, the weakness of political parties has been reflected in a "clientelistic" pattern of politics in which corruption has been a major factor.[93] In contrast, it would seem that the incidence of corruption in those countries where governmental resources have been diverted or "corrupted" for party-building is on the whole less than it is where parties have remained weak. The historical experience of the West also reflects this pattern. The parties which at first are the leeches on the bureaucracy in the end become the bark protecting it from more destructive locusts of clique and family. Partisanship and corruption, as Henry Jones Ford argued, "are really antagonistic principles. Partisanship tends to establish a connection based upon an avowed public obligation, while corruption consults private and individual interests which secrete themselves from view and avoid accountability of any kind. The weakness of party organization is the opportunity of corruption."[94]

93. See Leff, pp. 10–12.
94. Henry Jones Ford, *The Rise and Growth of American Politics* (New York, Macmillan, 1858), pp. 322–23.

The City-Country Gap: Urban Breakthrough and
Green Uprising

One crucial political result of modernization is the gap it produces between countryside and city. This gap is, indeed, a preeminent political characteristic of societies undergoing rapid social and economic change. It is the primary source of political instability in such societies and a principal, if not the principal, obstacle to national integration. Modernization is, in large part, measured by the growth of the city. The city becomes the locus of new economic activities, new social classes, new culture and education, which make it fundamentally different from the more tradition-bound countryside. At the same time modernization may also impose new demands on the countryside which intensify its hostility toward the city. The city dweller's feelings of intellectual superiority to and contempt for the backward peasant are matched by the country dweller's feelings of moral superiority to and yet envy of the city slicker. The city and the countryside become different nations, different ways of life.

Historically, the emigration of the peasant from village cottage to city slum was a decisive and irreversible change. In the later modernizing countries, however, the very process of modernization itself has made the move less decisive and has reduced the gap between city and countryside. The radio brings the language and the hopes of the city to the village; the bus brings the language and the beliefs of the village to the city. City cousins and country cousins are more often in contact with each other. The modern infrastructure of modernization has thus narrowed the rural-urban gap, but it has not eliminated it. The differences are still fundamental. The standard of living in the city is often four or five times that of the countryside. Most of those in the city are literate; a substantial majority of those in the countryside are illiterate. The economic activities and opportunities in the city are almost infinitely more varied than those in the countryside. The culture of the city is open, modern, secular; that of the countryside remains closed, traditional, and religious. The difference between the city and the countryside is the difference between the most modern and the most traditional parts of society. A fundamental problem of politics in a modernizing society is the development of the means for bridging this gap and re-creating through political means the social unity which modernization has destroyed.

The expansion of political participation is reflected in the changing relationship between city and countryside and their changing patterns of political instability and stability. In a typical traditional phase, the countryside dominates the city both politically and socially, and in the countryside a small aristocratic group of landowners dominates a large passive peasant mass. Outside the village the level of political participation is low. It is limited to aristocrats, landowners, high bureaucratic officials, ecclesiastics, and high-ranking military officers. All these are drawn from the same small ruling elite, and the distinctions among the various roles and functions are still relatively primitive. Except in centralized bureaucratic empires, the city plays a minor or secondary role in most traditional societies. It may well be the seat of government, but the government itself requires few professional officials and is dominated by the rural elite whose wealth and power is based upon their control of land. In such a society, the countryside is preeminent and both city and countryside are stable.

Modernization changes the nature of the city and the balance between city and countryside. Economic activities multiply in the city and lead to the emergence of new social groups and to the development of a new social consciousness by old social groups. New ideas and new techniques imported from outside the society make their appearance in the city. In many cases, particularly where the traditional bureaucracy is fairly well developed, the first groups within the traditional society to be exposed to modernity are the military and civilian bureaucrats. In due course, students, intellectuals, merchants, doctors, bankers, artisans, entrepreneurs, teachers, lawyers, and engineers emerge on the scene. These groups develop feelings of political efficacy and demand some form of participation in the political system. The urban middle class, in short, makes its appearance in politics and makes the city the source of unrest and opposition to the political and social system which is still dominated by the country.

Eventually the urban elements assert themselves and overthrow the ruling rural elite, thereby marking the end of the traditional political system. This urban breakthrough is usually accompanied by violence, and at this point the politics of the society becomes highly unstable.[95] The city is still but a small growth in society as a whole, but the groups within the city are able to employ their superior skills, location, and concentration to dominate the politics of the society at the national level. In the absence of effective political institutions, politics becomes a city game fought out among the elements of the emerging urban middle class. The community is divided by a fundamental gap; the society is still rural but its politics have become urban. The city is becoming the dominant source of political power, but the middle-class groups in the city are committed to opposition first to the rural elite which they have dislodged but then also to each other. The sources of instability in a modernizing society are seldom in its poorest or most backward areas; they are almost always in the most advanced sectors of the society. As politics becomes more and more urban, it becomes less and less stable.

At this point the re-creation of political stability requires an alliance between some urban groups and the masses of the population in the countryside. A crucial turning point in the expansion of political participation in a modernizing society is the inauguration of the rural masses into national politics. This rural mobilization or "Green Uprising" is far more important politically for the later modernizing countries than it was for most early modernizers. In the latter, urbanization and industrialization usually reached high levels before the bulk of the rural population became available for political mobilization. The rural population was less important numerically when it became more involved politically. The one major exception was the United States. In eighteenth-century America, the war of independence, the norms of equality and democracy, the relatively high levels of literacy and education, and the relatively widespread distribution of land ownership (outside the south) combined to produce extensive agrarian political participation before the rise of the city. Somewhat similarly, in later modernizing countries the telescoping of modernization tends to spread political consciousness and the possibility of political action through the countryside at a time when urban development and industrialization are still at relatively low levels. In these countries, consequently, the key to political stability is the extent to

95. See Chap. 4 for a more detailed analysis of breakthrough coups and the politics of radical praetorianism.

which the rural masses are mobilized into politics within the existing political system rather than against the system.

The timing, the method, and the auspices of the Green Uprising thus decisively influence the subsequent political evolution of the society. The uprising may occur rapidly or it may occur slowly and proceed through several stages. It usually takes one of four forms. In a colonial society, the Green Uprising may occur under the auspices of the nationalist intellectuals who, as in India and Tunisia, mobilize peasant groups into politics within the framework of the nationalist movement to support them in their struggles with the imperial power. Once independence is achieved, however, the problem for the nationalist leaders is to organize and sustain this rural participation and support. If the nationalist party fails to do this, some other group of urban leaders opposed to it or opposed to the political system of which it is a part may move to win the support of the peasants. In a competitive party system, the Green Uprising often takes the form of one segment of the urban elite developing an appeal to or making an alliance with the crucial rural voters and mobilizing them into politics so as to overwhelm at the polls the more narrowly urban-based parties. The victories of Jefferson and Jackson over the Adamses had their twentieth-century counterparts in Turkey, Ceylon, Burma, Senegal, the Sudan, and other modernizing countries. Thirdly, the Green Uprising may take place, in part at least, under military leadership, if as in South Korea and perhaps Egypt a rural-oriented military junta comes to power and then attempts to develop a broad power base in the countryside to overwhelm and contain its urban opponents. Finally, if no group within the political system takes the lead in mobilizing the peasants into politics, some group of urban intellectuals may mobilize and organize them into politics against the political system. This results in revolution.

Each form of the Green Uprising involves the mobilization of the peasants for political combat. If there is no combat, there is no mobilization. The crucial differences involve the target of the uprising and the framework in which it occurs. In the nationalist case, the target is the imperial power and the mobilization takes place within the framework of a nationalist movement which replaces the imperial power as the source of legitimacy in the political system. In the competitive case, the target is the ruling party

TABLE 1.5. Political Modernization: Changes in Urban-Rural Power and Stability

Phase	City	Countryside	Comments
1. Traditional Stability	Stable Subordinate	Stable Dominant	Rural elite rules; middle class absent; peasants dormant
2. Modernization Take-off	Unstable Subordinate	Stable Dominant	Urban middle class appears and begins struggle against rural elite
3. Urban Breakthrough	Unstable Dominant	Stable Subordinate	Urban middle class displaces rural elite; peasants still dormant
A4. Green Uprising: Containment	Unstable Subordinate	Stable Dominant	Peasant mobilization within system reestablishes stability and rural dominance
A5. Fundamentalist Reaction	Stable Dominant	Unstable Subordinate	Middle class grows and becomes more conservative; working class appears; shift of dominance to city produces rural fundamentalist reaction
B4. Green Uprising: Revolution	Unstable Subordinate	Unstable Dominant	Peasant mobilization against system overthrows old structures
B5. Modernizing Consolidation	Stable Dominant	Unstable Subordinate	Revolutionaries in power impose modernizing reforms on peasantry
6. Modern Stability	Stable Dominant	Stable Subordinate	Countryside accepts modern values and city rule

and the mobilization takes place within the framework of the political system but not within the framework of the ruling party. In the military case, the target is usually the former ruling oligarchy and the mobilization is part of the effort by the military leaders to construct a new political framework. In the revolutionary case, the target is the existing political system and its leadership and the mobilization takes place through an opposition political party whose leadership is dedicated to replacing the existing political system.

The instability of the city—the instability of coups, riots, and demonstrations—is, in some measure, an inescapable characteristic of modernization. The extent to which this instability manifests itself depends upon the effectiveness and the legitimacy of the political institutions of the society. Urban instability is thus minor but universal. Rural instability, on the other hand, is major but avoidable. If urban elites identified with the political system fail to lead the Green Uprising, the way is opened for an opposition group to come to power through revolution with the support of the peasants and to create a new institutional framework in the form of a single party to bridge the gap between country and city. If urban elites identified with the political system are, however, able to bring the peasants into politics on their side, they are able to surround and to contain the instability of the city. The rural strength of the regime enables it to survive the hostility of the city in the early phases of modernization. The price of rural support, however, is the modification or abandonment by the regime of many of its Western or modern values and practices. Thus, paradoxically, the Green Uprising has either a highly traditionalizing impact on the political system or a profoundly revolutionary one.

If revolution is avoided, in due course the urban middle class changes significantly; it becomes more conservative as it becomes larger. The urban working class also begins to participate in politics, but it is usually either too weak to challenge the middle class or too conservative to want to do so. Thus, as urbanization proceeds, the city comes to play a more effective role in the politics of the country, and the city itself becomes more conservative. The political system and the government come to depend more upon the support of the city than upon that of the countryside. Indeed, it now becomes the turn of the countryside to react against the prospect of domination by the city. This reaction often takes the form of rural protest movements of a fundamentalist character, which vainly attempt to undermine the power of the city and to stop the spread of urban culture. When these opposition movements are stalemated or defeated, modernization, in its political sense, has reached modernity. Both city and countryside again become stable, but the dominant power now rests with the former rather than with the latter. The society which was once unified by a rural traditional culture is now unified by a modern urban one.

Whether a society evolves through a more or a less revolutionary path thus depends upon the choices made by its leaders and their urban opponents after the city asserts its role in the political system. At this point either the leaders of the system mobilize the peasantry into politics as a stabilizing force to contain urban disorder or the opposition mobilizes them into politics as a revolutionary force to join in the violent destruction of the existing political and social order. A society is, in these terms, vulnerable to revolution only when the opposition of the middle class to the political system coincides with the opposition of the peasants. Once the middle class becomes conservative, rural rebellion is still possible, but revolution is not.

POLITICAL STABILITY: CIVIC AND PRAETORIAN POLITIES

Political systems can thus be distinguished by their levels of political institutionalization and their levels of political participation. In both cases the differences are obviously differences in degree: no clear-cut line separates the highly institutionalized polity from the disorganized polity; so also no clear-cut line exists between one level of political participation and another. To analyze the changes in both dimensions, however, it is necessary to identify different categories of systems, recognizing full well that rarely will any actual political system in fact fit into any specific theoretically defined pigeonhole. In terms of institutionalization, it is perhaps enough to distinguish those systems which have achieved a high degree of political institutionalization from those which have achieved only a low degree. In terms of participation, it seems desirable to identify three levels: at the lowest level, participation is restricted to a small traditional aristocratic or bureaucratic elite; at the medium level, the middle classes have entered into politics; and in a highly participant polity, elite, middle class, and the populace at large all share in political activity.

It would be convenient to leave the matter there, but things are not quite so simple. The stability of any given polity depends upon the relationship between the level of political participation and the level of political institutionalization. The level of political institutionalization in a society with a low level of political participation may be much lower than it is in a society with a much higher level of participation, and yet the society with lower levels

Figure 1.

**POLITICAL INSTITUTIONALIZATION
AND POLITICAL PARTICIPATION**

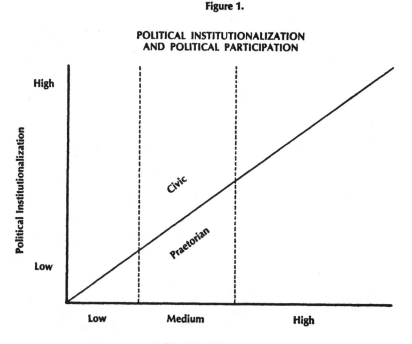

Political Participation

of both may be more stable than the society having a higher level of institutionalization and a still higher level of participation. Political stability, as we have argued, depends upon the ratio of institutionalization to participation. As political participation increases, the complexity, autonomy, adaptability, and coherence of the society's political institutions must also increase if political stability is to be maintained.

Modern polities are, in some measure, distinguished from traditional polities by their level of political participation. Developed polities are, in some measure, distinguished from underdeveloped ones by their level of political institutionalization. To these distinctions must now be added a third: the distinction between those polities where political participation is high relative to political institutionalization and those where institutionalization is high relative to participation. Political systems with low levels of institutionalization and high levels of participation are systems where social forces using their own methods act directly in the political sphere. For reasons elaborated below, such political systems are appropriately called praetorian polities. Conversely, political systems with a high ratio of institutionalization to participation may be termed civic polities. One society may thus have more highly developed political institutions than another and yet may also be more praetorian in character because of its still higher level of political participation.

Civic or praetorian societies may thus exist at various levels of political participation. The combination of the classification of societies according to their level of political participation, on the one hand, and their ratio of institutionalization to participation, on the other, produces, of course, a typology of six kinds of political systems, which are identified in Table 1.6.

TABLE 1.6. Types of Political Systems

Political Participation	Ratio of Institutionalization to Participation	
	HIGH: CIVIC	LOW: PRAETORIAN
Low: traditional	Organic (Ethiopia)	Oligarchical (Paraguay)
Medium: transitional	Whig (Chile)	Radical (Egypt)
High: modern	Participant (Soviet Union)	Mass (Argentina)

This typology may strike a familiar note to the historian of political ideas. Starting with a different set of categories but with similar concern for the conditions of political stability, our analysis has led to a typology of political systems strikingly similar to that of the classics. The ancient theorists divided political systems in two ways: according to the number of rulers and according to the nature of the rule. Their division of systems into those ruled by the one, the few, and the many corresponds in a rough sense to the distinctions made here, and by other modern political analysts, according to levels of political participation. The distinction between civic and praetorian polities corresponds roughly to the difference postulated by Plato, Aristotle, and other classical writers between legitimate or law-abiding states, where the rulers acted in the public interest, and perverted or law-neglecting systems, where the rulers acted in their own interests rather than those of the polity. "Those constitutions which consider the common interest are *right* constitutions," says Aristotle, and those "constitutions which consider only the personal interest of the rulers are all *wrong* constitutions, or *perversions* of the right forms." [96]

As the Greeks recognized, the "right" constitutions might take a variety of forms, even as today the political systems of the United States, Great Britain, and the Soviet Union differ significantly from each other. The societies with perverted constitutions, in contrast, were societies which lacked law, authority, cohesion, discipline, and consensus, where private interests dominated public ones, where there was an absence of civic obligation and civic duty, where, again, political institutions were weak and social forces strong. Plato's degenerate states were ruled by various forms of appetite: by force, wealth, numbers, and charisma. They were manifestations of what Machiavelli called the corrupt state, dominated, in the words of one commentator, by "all sorts of license and violence, great inequalities of wealth and power, the destruction of peace and justice, the growth of disorderly ambition, disunion, lawlessness, dishonesty, and contempt for religion." [97] Modern equivalents of the classical corrupt society are Kornhauser's theory of the mass society, where, in the absence of institutions, elites are accessible to masses and masses are available for mobilization by the elites, and Rapoport's concept of the praetorian state, where "private ambitions are rarely restrained by a sense of public authority; [and] the role of power (i.e. wealth and force) is maximized." [98]

It is virtually impossible to classify such states in terms of their form of government. We can have little doubt that the United States is a constitutional democracy and the Soviet Union a communist dictatorship. But what is the political system of Indonesia, of the Dominican Republic, South Vietnam, Burma, Nigeria, Ecuador, Argentina, Syria? These countries have held elections,

96. Aristotle, *Politics*, p. 112; italics in original.
97. Sabine, p. 343.
98. Kornhauser, passim; David C. Rapoport, "Praetorianism: Government Without Consensus" (unpublished Ph.D. dissertation, University of California, Berkeley, 1960); and Rapoport, in Huntington, ed., *Changing Patterns*, p. 72, where the quotation occurs.

but they are clearly not democracies in the sense in which Denmark or New Zealand is a democracy. They have had authoritarian rulers, but they are not effective dictatorships like the communist states. At other times they have been dominated by highly personalistic, charismatic rulers or by military juntas. They are unclassifiable in terms of any particular governmental form because their distinguishing characteristic is the fragility and fleetingness of all forms of authority. Charismatic leader, military junta, parliamentary regime, populistic dictator follow each other in seemingly unpredictable and bewildering array. The patterns of political participation are neither stable nor institutionalized; they may oscillate violently between one form and another. As Plato and Aristotle pointed out long ago, corrupt or praetorian societies often swing back and forth between despotism and mobrule. "Where the pre-established political authority is highly autocratic," says Kornhauser, "rapid and violent displacement of that authority by a democratic regime is highly favorable to the emergence of extremist mass movements that tend to transform the new democracy in antidemocratic directions." Rapoport finds in Gibbon an apt summary of the constitutional rhythms of the praetorian state which "floats between the extremes of absolute monarchy and wild democracy." Such instability is the hallmark of a society lacking political community and where participation in politics has outrun the institutionalization of politics.[99]

Civic polities, in contrast, have recognizable and stable patterns of institutional authority appropriate for their level of political participation. In traditional polities, these structures normally take the form of either a centralized bureaucratic empire or of a complex feudal monarchy, or some combination of these two. At the Whig level of middle-class participation, the dominant political institutions are normally parliamentary assemblies with members chosen through some limited form of elections. In the fully participant, modern polity, political parties supplement or replace the traditional political structures as the key institutions for organizing mass involvement in politics. At all levels of participation, however, political institutions are sufficiently strong to pro-

99. Edward Gibbon, *The Decline and Fall of the Roman Empire* (New York, Macmillan, 1899), *1*, 235, quoted by Rapoport in Huntington, ed., *Changing Patterns*, p. 98.

vide the basis of a legitimate political order and a working political community. The institutions impose political socialization as the price of political participation. In a praetorian society groups become mobilized into politics without becoming socialized by politics. The distinguishing characteristic of a highly institutionalized polity, in contrast, is the price it places on power. In a civic polity, the price of authority involves limitations on the resources that may be employed in politics, the procedures through which power may be acquired, and the attitudes that power wielders may hold. If the society is modern and complex, with a large number of social forces, individuals from any one of the social forces may have to make extensive changes in their behavior, values, and attitudes in the process of acquiring power through the political institutions of the society. They may well have to unlearn much which they have learned from family, ethnic group, and social class, and adapt to an entirely new code of behavior.

The development of a civic polity may have some relation to the stage of modernization and of political participation, but it is not directly dependent upon it. By the mid-twentieth century many of the more advanced Latin American nations had achieved comparatively high indices of literacy, per capita national income, and urbanization. In the mid-1950s, for instance, Argentina was economically and socially a highly developed country. Almost half the population lived in cities of over 20,000 people; 86 per cent of the people were literate; 75 per cent were engaged in nonagricultural employment; the per capita gross national product was over $500. Argentine politics, however, remained notably underdeveloped. "The public good," Sarmiento had said in the 1850s, "is a meaningless word—there is no 'public.' " A hundred years later the failure to develop effective political institutions meant the continued absence of public community. As one observer noted,

> The hard surface of military rule or the mottled aspect of Machiavellian balancing and intriguing have been the two masks of Argentine politics since 1930. The masks, most unhappily, do not disguise reality—they *are* the reality of Argentina's situation of weak government, a debility stemming from several fundamental causes. . . . The state is not firmly established as the ultimate arbiter of Argentine public life.

The other institutions competing for men's loyalties permit a high degree of protection from the dictates of the state.[100]

So long as a country like Argentina retained a politics of coup and counter-coup and a feeble state surrounded by massive social forces, it remained politically underdeveloped no matter how urbane, prosperous, and educated its citizenry.

In reverse fashion, a country may be politically highly developed with modern political institutions while still very backward in terms of modernization. India, for instance, was typically held to be the epitome of the underdeveloped society. Judged by the usual criteria of modernization, it was at the bottom of the ladder during the 1950s: per capita GNP of $72, 80 per cent illiterate, over 80 per cent of the population in rural areas, 70 per cent of the work force in agriculture, fourteen major languages, deep caste and religious differences. Yet in terms of political institutionalization, India was far from backward. Indeed, it ranked high not only in comparison with other modernizing countries in Asia, Africa, and Latin America, but also in comparison with many much more modern European countries. A well developed political system has strong and distinct institutions to perform both the "input" and the "output" functions of politics. India entered independence with not only two organizations, but two highly developed—adaptable, complex, autonomous, and coherent—institutions ready to assume primary responsibility for these functions. The Congress Party, founded in 1885, was one of the oldest and best organized political parties in the world; the Indian Civil Service, dating from the early nineteenth century, was appropriately hailed as "one of the greatest administrative systems of all time." [101] The stable, effective, and democratic government of India during its first twenty years of independence rested far more on this institutional inheritance than it did on the charisma of Nehru. In addition, the relatively slow pace of modernization and social mobilization in India did not create demands and strains which the party and the bureaucracy were unable to handle. So long as these two organizations maintained their institutional strength, it was ridiculous to think of India as politically underdeveloped no matter how low its per capita income or how high its illiteracy rate.

Almost no other country attaining independence after World War II was institutionally as well prepared as India for self-government. In countries like Pakistan and the Sudan, institutional evolution was unbalanced: the civil and military bureaucracies were more highly developed than the political parties, and the military had strong incentives to move into the institutional vacuum on the input side of the political system and to attempt to perform interest aggregation functions. This pattern, of course, has also been common in Latin America. In countries like Guate-

TABLE 1.7. Institutional Development
at Time of Independence

Input Institutions	Output Institutions	
	High	Low
High	India	N. Vietnam
Low	Sudan	Congo

mala, El Salvador, Peru, and Argentina, John J. Johnson pointed out, the military was "the country's best organized institution and is thus in a better position to give objective expression to the national will" than were parties or interest groups. In a very different category was a country like North Vietnam, which fought its way into independence with a highly disciplined political organization but which was distinctly weak on the administrative side. The Latin American parallel here would be Mexico, where, as Johnson put it, "not the armed forces but the PRI [Partido Revolucionario Institucional] is the best organized institution, and the party rather than the armed forces has been the unifying force at the national level." [102] In yet a fourth category were those unfortunate states, such as the Congo, which were born with neither political nor administrative institutions. Many of these new states deficient at independence in one or both types of institutions were also confronted by high rates of social mobilization and rapidly increasing demands on the political system.

If a society is to maintain a high level of community, the expansion of political participation must be accompanied by the development of stronger, more complex, and more autonomous political institutions. The effect of the expansion of political participa-

102. Johnson, *Military and Society*, p. 143.

tion, however, is usually to undermine the traditional political institutions and to obstruct the development of modern political ones. Modernization and social mobilization, in particular, thus tend to produce political decay unless steps are taken to moderate or to restrict its impact on political consciousness and political involvement. Most societies, even those with fairly complex and adaptable traditional political institutions, suffer a loss of political community and decay of political institutions during the most intense phases of modernization.

This decay in political institutions has been neglected or overlooked in much of the literature on modernization. As a result, the models and concepts which are hopefully entitled "developing" or "modernizing" are only partially relevant to many of the countries to which they are applied. Equally relevant would be models of corrupt or degenerating societies highlighting the decay of political organization and the increasing dominance of disruptive social forces. Who, however, has advanced such a theory of political decay or a model of a corrupt political order which might be useful in analyzing the political processes of the countries usually called "developing"? Perhaps the most relevant ideas are again the most ancient ones. The evolution of many contemporary new states, once the colonial guardians have departed, has not deviated extensively from the Platonic model.[103] Independence is followed by military coups, as the "auxiliaries" take over. Corruption by the oligarchy inflames the envy of rising groups. Conflict between oligarchy and masses erupts into civil strife. Demagogues and street mobs pave the way for the despot. Plato's description of the means by which the despot appeals to the people, isolates and eliminates his enemies, and builds up his personal strength is a far less misleading guide to what has taken place in Africa and elsewhere than many things written yesterday.[104]

103. See, in general, *The Republic*, Book VIII, and especially the description of the despotic regime (Cornford trans., New York, Oxford University Press, 1946), pp. 291–93.

104. Perhaps the closest contemporary model comes not from a social scientist but from a novelist: William Golding. The schoolboys (newly independent elites) of *The Lord of the Flies* initially attempt to imitate the behavior patterns of adults (former Western rulers). Discipline and consensus, however, disintegrate. A demagogic military leader and his followers gain or coerce the support of a majority. The symbol of authority (the conch) is broken. The voices of responsibility (Ralph) and reason (Piggy) are deserted and harassed, and reason is destroyed. In the end,

The extent to which a society undergoes complete political decomposition during the modernization process depends in large part on the nature of its traditional political institutions. If these are weak or nonexistent, or if they are destroyed by colonialism or other means, the society usually evolves directly from traditional praetorianism to an even more praetorian transitional phase with extensive urban middle-class participation in politics. If a society has a reasonably highly developed and autonomous bureaucratic structure in its traditional phase, it will face acute problems in adapting to broader political participation because of the nature of the structure. Paradoxically, those traditional systems which seem most "modern" in their structural differentiation and rationalization of authority often also have more difficulties in adapting to broader political participation than traditional political systems which are less rationalized and differentiated but institutionally more complex and pluralistic. Highly centralized bureaucratic monarchies like those of China and France seem more modern than more pluralistic feudal systems such as those of England and Japan. Yet the latter prove to be more adaptable than the former.[105] In these instances, the struggle between oligarchy and middle class tends to become muted, and the political institutions of the society prove to be sufficiently adaptable to absorb into the political system the new middle-class groups.

Societies which have high levels of middle-class political participation have strong tendencies toward instability because of the nature of the middle class and the dominance of politics by the city at the expense of the country. It is in this middle-class phase of expansion that politics is most likely to assume a praetorian cast and to become, in Macaulay's phrase, "all sail and no anchor." [106] In such a society the political system has lost its rural anchor and is tossed about in rough seas under a full head of urban sail. The strain on political institutions, even highly developed institutions,

---

the naval officer (British Marine Commandos) arrives just in time to save Ralph (Nyerere) from the "hunters" (mutinous troops).

105. See Robert T. Holt and John E. Turner, *The Political Basis of Economic Development* (Princeton, Van Nostrand, 1966).

106. Thomas B. Macaulay, letter to Henry S. Randall, Courtlandt Village, New York, May 23, 1857, printed in "What Did Macaulay Say About America?," *Bulletin of the New York Public Library*, 24 (July 1925), 477–79.

is great, and in most societies the traditional institutions inherited from the past disintegrate or collapse.

If the traditional political institutions do adapt to middle-class political participation or if, in a previously praetorian society, new political institutions are created to stabilize politics at the middle-class level, in due course these institutions face the problem of adapting to the expansion of participation to the urban working class and the rural peasantry. If the existing political institutions of the middle-class polity are capable of adjustment, the transition is made to a fully participant, highly institutionalized modern polity. If these institutions are incapable of adapting themselves to mass participation or if in the society a situation of radical praetorianism prevails, the society then moves in the direction of mass praetorianism in which the dominant social forces become the large-scale movements characteristic of a highly modern and mobilized society.

Both the mass society and the participant society have high levels of political participation. They differ in the institutionalization of their political organizations and procedures. In the mass society political participation is unstructured, inconstant, anomic, and variegated. Each social force attempts to secure its objectives through the resources and tactics in which it is strongest. Apathy and indignation succeed each other: the twin children of the absence of authoritative political symbols and institutions. The distinctive form of political participation is the mass movement combining violent and nonviolent, legal and illegal, coercive and persuasive actions. Mass society lacks organized structures which can relate the political desires and activities of the populace to the goals and decisions of their leaders. As a result, a direct relationship exists between leaders and masses; in Kornhauser's terms, the masses are available for mobilization by the leaders and the leaders are accessible to influence by the masses. In the participant polity, on the other hand, a high level of popular involvement is organized and structured through political institutions. Each social force must transform its sources of power and forms of action—be they numbers, wealth, knowledge, or potential for violence—into those which are legitimate in and institutionalized in the political system. The structure of a participant polity may assume a variety of forms, and power may be dispersed or concentrated. In all cases, however, participation is broad and is organized and structured into legitimate channels. Popular participation in politics does not necessarily mean popular control of government. Constitutional democracies and communist dictatorships are both participant polities.

The modern polity thus differs from the traditional polity in the scope of the political consciousness and political involvement of its population. The modern, developed polity differs from the traditional, developed polity in the nature of its political institutions. The institutions of the traditional polity need only structure the participation of a small segment of society. The institutions of a modern polity must organize the participation of the mass of the population. The crucial institutional distinction between the two is thus in the organizations for structuring mass participation in politics. The distinctive institution of the modern polity, consequently, is the political party. The other institutions which exist in modern political systems are adaptations of or carry-overs from traditional political systems. Bureaucracies are not distinctly modern. The bureaucracies which existed in the Chinese, Roman, Byzantine, Ottoman, and other historic empires often had high degrees of structural differentiation, elaborate systems for recruitment and promotion according to merit and achievement, and carefully worked out procedures and regulations governing their actions. Nor are assemblies and parliaments unique to the modern polity: assemblies existed in the ancient city-states, and parliaments and other meetings of the estates were common phenomena in medieval Europe, most of which were destroyed during the process of modernization. Elections are also found in nonmodern polities: elective chiefs are common in tribal societies; the *strategoi* and other magistrates were elected in Athens, the tribunes and consuls in ancient Rome. The idea and practice of constitutionalism are similarly ancient. Constitutions, laws, and courts all existed in highly developed forms long before the appearance of the modern state. So also did cabinets and executive councils. The only potential rival to the party as the distinctive institution of the modern polity is federalism.[107] The more widespread existence of federal institutions among modern states than among traditional ones reflects the same factor which accounts for the development of parties: the extension of the scope of the polity in terms of popula-

107. See William H. Riker, *Federalism: Origin, Operation, Significance* (Boston, Little Brown, 1964), pp. 1–10.

tion as well as territory. Yet federalism is neither unique to the modern world nor prevalent within it. Such, however, is precisely the case with the political party. The party is the distinctive institution of modern politics.

Cliques and factions exist in all political systems. So also do parties in the sense of informal groups competing with each other for power and influence. But parties in the sense of organizations are a product of modern politics. Political parties exist in the modern polity because only modern political systems require institutions to organize mass participation in politics. The political party as an organization had its forerunners in the revolutions of the sixteenth and seventeenth centuries. The first appearance of organized political parties, however, comes in the eighteenth century in those countries where political participation was first expanded, in America and then in France. The shift, in Rudolph's terms, from the politics of status to the politics of opinion, led to the creation of the political party as a political institution.[108] In 1800 political parties existed only in the United States; by 1900 they existed throughout the Western world. The development of political parties parallels the development of modern government. The more traditional political institutions have been able to adapt to the needs of modern politics, the less significant has been the role of the political party. Conversely, the importance of the political party in providing legitimacy and stability in a modernizing political system varies inversely with the institutional inheritance of the system from traditional society. Where traditional political institutions (such as monarchies and feudal parliaments) are carried over into the modern era, parties play secondary, supplementary roles in the political system. The other institutions are the primary source of continuity and legitimacy. Parties typically originate within the legislatures and then gradually extend themselves into society. They adapt themselves to the existing framework of the political system and typically reflect in their own operations the organizational and procedural principles embodied in that system. They broaden participation in the traditional institutions, thus adapting those institutions to the requirements of the modern polity. They help make the traditional

108. Lloyd I. Rudolph, "From the Politics of Status to the Politics of Opinion" (unpublished Ph.D. dissertation, Harvard University, 1956).

institutions legitimate in terms of popular sovereignty, but they are not themselves a source of legitimacy. Their own legitimacy derives from the contributions they make to the political system.

Where traditional political institutions collapse or are weak or nonexistent, the role of the party is entirely different from what it is in those polities with institutional continuity. In such situations, strong party organization is the only long-run alternative to the instability of a corrupt or praetorian or mass society. The party is not just a supplementary organization; it is instead the source of legitimacy and authority. In the absence of traditional sources of legitimacy, legitimacy is sought in ideology, charisma, popular sovereignty. To be lasting, each of these principles of legitimacy must be embodied in a party. Instead of the party reflecting the state, the state becomes the creation of the party and the instrument of the party. The actions of government are legitimate to the extent that they reflect the will of the party. The party is the source of legitimacy because it is the institutional embodiment of national sovereignty, the popular will, or the dictatorship of the proletariat.

Where traditional political institutions are weak or nonexistent, the prerequisite of stability is at least one highly institutionalized political party. States with one such party are markedly more stable than states which lack such a party. States with no parties or many weak parties are the least stable. Where traditional political institutions are smashed by revolution, post-revolutionary order depends on the emergence of one strong party: witness the otherwise very different histories of the Chinese, Mexican, Russian, and Turkish revolutions. Where new states emerge from colonialism with little or no inheritance of political institutions, the stability of the polity depends directly on the strength of the party.

The political party is the distinctive organization of modern politics, but in another sense it is not an entirely modern institution. The function of the party is to organize participation, to aggregate interests, to serve as the link between social forces and the government. In performing these functions, the party necessarily reflects the logic of politics, not the logic of efficiency. A bureaucracy with its differentiated structure and merit system is, by the latter logic, a more modern institution than a political party which operates on patronage, influence, and compromise. Consequently, the promoters of modernization, like the defenders of tradition, often reject and denigrate political parties. They attempt to modernize their society politically without establishing the institution that will make their society politically stable. They pursue modernity at the expense of politics and in the process fail to achieve the one because of their neglect of the other.

2. Political Modernization: America vs. Europe

THREE PATTERNS OF MODERNIZATION

Political modernization involves the rationalization of authority, the differentiation of structures, and the expansion of political participation. In the West, political modernization was spread over many centuries. The sequence and extent of its three components varied significantly in different areas of Europe and North America. Most obviously, the expansion of political participation occurred earlier and far more extensively in America than in Europe. In the eighteenth century political participation in the English colonies, in terms of the suffrage, was already widespread by English standards, not to mention Continental ones. The American Revolution removed the English Crown from the American scene and with it the only possible alternative source of legitimacy to popular sovereignty. The Revolution, as Robert Palmer stresses, made history by establishing the people as the constituent power.[1] All governments derive their just powers from the consent of the governed. Given this principle, little ground existed on which to limit the suffrage. If the people could directly establish a system of government, they certainly could participate in the system so established.

As a result the franchise and other forms of popular participation in government were rapidly expanded with independence. The property qualifications for voting, which in many states did not disenfranchise large numbers of people in any event, were changed first to taxpaying requirements and then abolished altogether. The new states admitted to the union generally came in with no economic restrictions on suffrage. By the 1830s universal white male suffrage was the norm in America. In Europe, in con-

---

1. Robert R. Palmer, *The Age of the Democratic Revolution* (2 vols. Princeton, Princeton University Press, 1959–64), *1*, 213 ff.

trast, property qualifications remained high. The Reform Act of 1832 expanded the total eligible English electorate from two to four per cent of the total population; in America 16 per cent of the total population actually voted in the presidential election in 1840. In France high property qualifications existed until 1848 when universal male suffrage was introduced only to be made somewhat less than meaningful with the coming of the Second Empire. Universal male suffrage was introduced in Germany in 1871 but in Prussia the three class system of voting remained in effect until the end of World War I. In the Low Countries and Scandinavia universal male suffrage came at the end of the nineteenth century and in the first decades of the twentieth.

The United States, moreover, pioneered in popular participation in government not only in terms of the number of people who could vote for public officials but also, and perhaps more importantly, in the number of public officials who could be voted on by the people. In Europe suffrage was normally limited to the lower house of the national parliament and to local councils; in America, in contrast, as de Tocqueville observed, "the principle of election extends to everything," and scores of officials at the national, state, and local level were subject to popular approval. De Tocqueville's dramatic contrast between the equality and democracy he saw here and the conditions he knew in Europe was, of course, only one indication of the American lead in expanding participation.

The early widespread political participation in America as contrasted with Europe often leads people to conclude that political modernization in general occurred earlier and more rapidly in the United States than in Europe. Such, however, is far from the case. In fact, the rationalization of authority and the differentiation of structures occurred much earlier and more completely in Europe than in America. The experience of the West, indeed, suggests that an inverse correlation may exist between the modernization of governmental institutions and the expansion of political participation. The former took place much more rapidly in Europe, the latter much more rapidly in America.

In terms of the modernization of governmental institutions, three distinct patterns can be identified: Continental, British, and American.[2] On the Continent the rationalization of authority and the

2. For the sake of clarity, let me make clear the geographical scope I give these terms. With appropriate apologies to Latin Americans and Canadians, I feel com-

differentiation of structures were dominant trends of the seventeenth century. "It is misleading to summarize in a single phrase any long historical process," Sir George Clark observes,

> but the work of monarchy in the seventeenth century may be described as the substitution of a simpler and more unified government for the complexities of feudalism. On one side it was centralization, the bringing of local business under the supervision or control of the government of the capital. This necessarily had as its converse a tendency toward uniformity.[3]

It was the age of the great simplifiers, centralizers, and modernizers: Richelieu, Mazarin, Louis XIV, Colbert, and Louvois in France; the Great Elector in Prussia; Gustavus Adolphus and Charles XI in Sweden; Philip IV and Olivares in Spain; and their countless imitators among the lesser realms of the Continent. The modern state replaced the feudal principality; loyalty to the state superseded loyalty to church and to dynasty. "I am more obligated to the state," Louis XIII declared on the famous "Day of Dupes," November 11, 1630, when he rejected the Queen Mother and her claims for family in favor of the Cardinal and his claims for the state. "More than any other single day," Friedrich argues, "it may be called the birthday of the modern state." [4] With the birth of the modern state came the subordination of the church, the suppression of the medieval estates, and the weakening of the aristocracy by the rise of new groups. In addition, the century witnessed the rapid growth and rationalization of state bureaucracies and public services, the origin and expansion of standing armies, and the extension and improvement of taxation. In 1600 the medieval political world was still a reality on the Continent; by 1700 it had been replaced by the modern world of nation-states.

The British pattern of institutional modernization was similar in nature to that on the Continent but rather different in results. In Britain, too, church was subordinated to state, authority was centralized, sovereignty asserted internally as well as externally,

---

pelled by the demands of brevity to use the term "America" to refer to the thirteen colonies which subsequently became the United States of America. By "Europe" I mean Great Britain and the Continent. By "the Continent" I refer to France, the Low Countries, Spain, Portugal, Sweden, and the Holy Roman Empire.

3. Sir George Clark, *The Seventeenth Century* (New York, Oxford-Galaxy, 1961), p. 91.

4. Carl J. Friedrich, *The Age of the Baroque: 1610–1660* (New York, Harper, 1952), pp. 215–16.

legal and political institutions differentiated, bureaucracies expanded, and a standing army created. The efforts of the Stuarts, however, to rationalize authority along the lines of Continental absolutism provoked a constitutional struggle, from which Parliament eventually emerged the victor. In Britain, as on the Continent, authority was centralized but it was centralized in Parliament rather than in the Crown. This, however, was no less of a revolution than occurred on the Continent and perhaps even more of one.

In America, in contrast, political institutions did not undergo revolutionary changes. Instead, the principal elements of the English sixteenth-century constitution were exported to the new world, took root there, and were given new life precisely at the time that they were being abandoned in the home country. They were essentially Tudor and hence significantly medieval in character. The Tudor century saw some steps toward modernization in English politics, particularly the establishment of the supremacy of the state over the church, the heightened sense of national identity and consciousness, and a significant increase in the power of the Crown and the executive establishment. Nonetheless, even in Elizabethan government, the first point of importance is, "the fundamental factor of continuity with the Middle Ages." [5] The sixteenth century, as Chrimes says, saw "The Zenith of the Medieval Constitution." The changes introduced by the Tudor monarchs did not have "the effect of breaking down the essential principles of the medieval Constitution, nor even its structure." [6] Among these principles and institutions were the idea of the organic union of society and government, the harmony of authorities within government, the subordination of government to fundamental law, the intermingling of the legal and political realms, the balance of powers between Crown and Parliament, the complementary representative roles of these two bodies, the vitality of local governmental authorities, and reliance on the militia for the defense of the realm.

The English colonists took these late medieval and Tudor political ideas, practices, and institutions across the Atlantic with them

---

5. A. L. Rowse, *The England of Elizabeth* (New York, Macmillan, 1951), p. 262.
6. S. B. Chrimes, *English Constitutional History* (2d ed. London, Oxford University Press, 1953), pp. 121–23. See also W. S. Holdsworth, *A History of English Law* (3d ed. London, Methuen, 1945), *4*, 209 ff.

during the great migrations in the first half of the seventeenth century. The patterns of thought and behavior which were established in the New World developed and grew but were not substantially changed during the century and a half of colonyhood. The English generation of 1603–30, Notestein remarks, was "one in which medieval ideas and practices were by no means forgotten and in which new conceptions and new ways of doing things were coming in. The American tradition, or that part derived from England, was at least in some degree established by the early colonists. The English who came over later must have found the English Americans somewhat settled in their ways." [7] The conflict with the British government in the middle of the eighteenth century served only to reinforce the colonists' adherence to their traditional institutions. In the words of our greatest constitutional historian:

> The colonists retained to a marked and unusual degree the traditions of Tudor England. In all our study of American institutions, colonial and contemporary, institutions of both public law and private law, this fact must be reckoned with. The breach between colonies and mother country was largely a mutual misunderstanding based, in great part, on the fact of this retention of older ideas in the colonies after parliamentary sovereignty had driven them out in the mother country. [8]

In the constitutional debates before the American Revolution, the colonists in effect argued the case of the old English constitution against the merits of the new British constitution which had come into existence during the century after they had left the mother country. "Their theory," as Pollard says, "was essentially medieval." [9]

7. Wallace Notestein, *The English People on the Eve of Colonization, 1603–1630* (New York, Harper, 1954) , p. xiv. See also Edward S. Corwin, *The "Higher Law" Backround of American Constitutional Law* (Ithaca, Cornell University Press, 1955) , p. 74.

8. Charles Howard McIlwain, *The High Court of Parliament and its Supremacy* (New Haven, Yale University Press, 1910) , p. 386.

9. A. F. Pollard, *Factors in American History* (New York, Macmillan, 1925) , p. 39. See also Charles Howard McIlwain, *The American Revolution: A Constitutional Interpretation* (Ithaca, Cornell University Press, 1958) , and Randolph G. Adams, *Political Ideas of the American Revolution* (3d ed. New York, Barnes and Noble, 1958) .

These ancient institutions and ideas were embodied in the state constitutions drafted after independence and in the Federal Constitution of 1787. Not only is the American Constitution the oldest written constitution in the world, but it is also a constitution that in large part simply codified and formalized on the national level practices and institutions long in existence on the colonial level. The institutional framework established in 1787 has, in turn, changed remarkably little in 175 years. Hence, the American system "can be properly understood, in its origin, development, workings, and spirit, only in the light of precedents and traditions which run back to the England of the civil wars and the period before the civil wars." [10] The American political system of the twentieth century still bears a closer approximation to the Tudor polity of the sixteenth century than does the British political system of the twentieth century. "Americanisms in politics, like Americanisms in speech," as Henry Jones Ford put it, "are apt to be Anglicisms which died out in England but survived in the new world." [11] The British broke their traditional patterns in the seventeenth century. The Americans did not do so then and have only partially done so since then. Political modernization in America has thus been strangely attenuated and incomplete. In institutional terms, the American polity has never been underdeveloped, but it has also never been wholly modern. In an age of rationalized authority, centralized bureaucracy, and totalitarian dictatorship, the American political system remains a curious anachronism. In today's world, American political institutions are unique, if only because they are so antique.

RATIONALIZATION OF AUTHORITY

In seventeenth-century Europe the state replaced fundamental law as the source of political authority and within each state a single authority replaced the many which had previously existed. America, on the other hand, continued to adhere to fundamental law as both a source of authority for human actions and as an authoritative restraint on human behavior. In addition, in America, human authority or sovereignty was never concentrated in a

10. McIlwain, *High Court*, p. 388.

11. Henry Jones Ford, *The Rise and Growth of American Politics* (New York, Macmillan, 1900), p. 5. See also James Bryce, *The American Commonwealth* (London, Macmillan, 1891), 2, 658.

single institution or individual but instead remained dispersed throughout society as a whole and among many organs of the body politic. Traditional patterns of authority were thus decisively broken and replaced in Europe; in America they were reshaped and supplemented but not fundamentally altered. The continued supremacy of law was mated to the decisive rejection of sovereignty.

Undoubtedly the most significant difference between modern man and traditional man is their outlook on man in relation to his environment. In traditional society man accepts his natural and social environment as given. What is ever will be: it is or must be divinely sanctioned; to attempt to change the permanent and unchanging order of the universe and of society is not only blasphemous but also impossible. Change is absent or imperceptible in traditional society because men cannot conceive of its existence. Modernity begins when men develop a sense of their own competence, when they begin to think first that they can understand nature and society, and then that they can control nature and society for their own purposes. Above all, modernization involves belief in the capacity of man by reasoned action to change his physical and social environments. It means the rejection of external restraints on men, the Promethean liberation of man from control by gods, fate, and destiny.

This fundamental shift from acceptance to activism manifests itself in many fields. Among the more important is law. For traditional man, law is an external prescription or restraint over which he has little control. Man discovers law but he does not make law. At most he may make supplementary emendations of an unchanging basic law to apply it to specific circumstances. Such concepts can exist only in a society where government does not make fundamental changes in society. If political bodies are to produce social change, political authority must reside in those bodies and not in external restraints which, more often than not, are identified in practice with the very social order which modernization will change.

In late medieval Europe, law was variously defined in terms of divine law, natural law, the law of reason, common law, and custom. In all these manifestations it was viewed as a relatively unchanging external authority for and restraint on human action. Particularly in England, the dominant concept was "the characteristic medieval idea of all authority as deriving from the law." As Bracton put it, "Law makes the King." [12] These ideas remained dominant through the Tudor years and were in one form or another at the basis of the writings of Fortescue, St. Germain, Sir Thomas Smith, Hooker, and Coke. Even after the Act of Supremacy, Parliament was still viewed as a law-declaring body, not a law-making body. Even during the first phases of the constitutional struggles of the seventeenth century, Prynne argued that "the Principal Liberties, Customs, Laws" of the kingdom, particularly those in the *"great Charters,"* are "FUNDAMENTAL, PERPETUAL, AND UNALTERABLE." [13]

The obverse of fundamental law is, of course, the rejection of determinate human sovereignty. For the men of 1600, as Figgis observes, "law is the true sovereign, and they are not under the necessity of considering whether King or Lords or Commons or all three together are the ultimate authority in the state." [14] The sovereignty of law permitted a multiplicity of human authorities, since no single human authority was the sole source of law. Man owed obedience to authority, but authority existed in many institutions: king, Parliament, courts, common law, custom, church, people. Sovereignty, indeed, was an alien concept to the Tudor constitution. No "lawyer or statesman of the Tudor period," as Holdsworth says, "could have given an answer to the question as to the whereabouts of the sovereign power in the English state." [15] Society and government, Crown and people, existed together in harmony in a "single body politic." The Tudor regime, says Chrimes, "was essentially the culmination of the medieval ideals of monarchical government, in alliance with the assent of parliament for certain purposes, and acknowledging the supremacy of the common law where appropriate. No one was concerned about the location of sovereignty within the State." [16] Unlike Bodin and other Continental theorists, sixteenth-century English writers simply denied the existence of sovereignty. The "whole standpoint"

12. Corwin, p. 27.
13. McIlwain, *High Court*, pp. 51 ff., 65.
14. John Neville Figgis, *The Divine Right of Kings* (Cambridge, England, Cambridge University Press, 1922) , p. 230. See also Christopher Morris, *Political Thought in England: Tyndale to Hooker* (London, Oxford University Press, 1953) , p. 1.
15. Holdsworth, *4*, 208.
16. Chrimes, pp. 122–23. See also J. B. Black, *The Reign of Elizabeth, 1558–1603* (2d ed. Oxford, Clarendon Press, 1959) , p. 206.

of the most notable expounder of the Elizabethan constitution, Sir Thomas Smith, was "nearer that of Bracton than that of Bodin." [17]

Fundamental law and the diffusion of authority were incompatible with political modernization. Modernization requires authority for change. Fundamental changes in society and politics come from the purposeful actions of men. Hence authority must reside in men, not in unchanging law. In addition, men must have the power to effect change and hence authority must be concentrated in some determinate individual or group of men. Fundamental and unchanging law may serve to diffuse authority throughout society and thus to preserve the existing social order. But it cannot serve as authority for change except for lesser changes which can be passed off as restoration. The modernization which began in the sixteenth century on the Continent and in the seventeenth century in England required new concepts of authority, the most significant of which was the simple idea of sovereignty itself, the idea that there is, in the words of Bodin, a "supreme power over citizens and subjects, unrestrained by law." One formulation of this idea was the new theory, which developed in Europe in the late sixteenth century, of the divine right of kings. Here, in effect, religious and in that sense traditional forms were used for modern purposes. "The Divine Right of Kings on its political side was little more than the popular form of expression for the theory of sovereignty." [18] The doctrine developed in France after 1594 and was introduced into England by James I. It admirably served the purposes of the modernizing monarchs of the seventeenth century: giving the sanction of the Almighty to the purposes of the mighty. It was a necessary "transition stage between medieval and modern politics." [19]

In addition, of course, other political theorists responded to the needs of the time by furnishing different and more "rational" justifications of absolute sovereignty based on the nature of man and the nature of society. On the Continent, Bodin and the Politiques looked to the creation of a supreme royal power which would

17. John Neville Figgis, "Political Thought in the Sixteenth Century," *The Cambridge Modern History* (Cambridge, 1904), *3*, 748; J. W. Allen, *A History of Political Thought in the Sixteenth Century* (New York, Barnes and Noble, 1960), p. 262.
18. Figgis, *Divine Right*, p. 237.
19. Ibid., p. 258. See Allen, p. 386; Charles Howard McIlwain, ed., *The Political Works of James I* (Cambridge, Harvard University Press, 1918).

maintain order and constitute a centralized public authority above parties, sects, and groups, all of which were to exist only on its sufferance. Bodin's *Republic* was published in 1576; Hobbes' *Leviathan* with its more extreme doctrine of sovereignty appeared in 1651. Closely linked with the idea of absolute sovereignty was the concept of the state as an entity apart from individual, family, and dynasty. Twentieth-century modernizing Marxists justify their efforts by the needs of the party; seventeenth-century modernizing monarchs justified their actions by "reason of state." The phrase was first popularized by Botero in *Della Ragion di Stato* in 1589. Its essence was briefly defined by another Italian writer in 1614 when he declared, "The reason of state is a necessary violation [*eccesso*] of the common law for the end of public utility." [20] One by one the European monarchs took to legitimizing themselves and their actions by reference to the state.

In both its religious and its secular versions, in Filmer as well as in Hobbes, the import of the new doctrine of sovereignty was the subject's absolute duty of obedience to his king. Both doctrines helped political modernization by legitimizing the concentration of authority and the breakdown of the medieval pluralistic political order. They were the seventeenth-century counterparts of the theories of party supremacy and national sovereignty which are today employed to break down the authority of traditional local, tribal, and religious bodies. In the seventeenth century mass participation in politics still lay in the future; hence rationalization of authority meant concentration of power in the absolute monarch. In the twentieth century, the broadening of participation and the rationalization of authority occur simultaneously, and hence authority must be concentrated in either a political party or in a popular charismatic leader, both of which are capable of arousing the masses as well as challenging traditional sources of authority. But in the seventeenth century the absolute monarch was the functional equivalent of the twentieth century's monolithic party.

On the Continent in the seventeenth century the medieval diffusion of authority among the estates rapidly gave way to the centralization of authority in the monarch. At the beginning of the seventeenth century, "Every country of western Christendom, from Portugal to Finland, and from Ireland to Hungary, had its

20. Quoted in Friedrich, pp. 15–16.

assemblies of estates." [21] By the end of the century most of these had been eliminated or greatly reduced in power. In France the last Estates General until the Revolution met in 1615, and the provincial estates, except in Brittany and Languedoc, did not meet after 1650.[22] By the seventeenth century only six of the original 22 Spanish kingdoms retained their *cortes*. The *cortes* in Castile was already suppressed; those in Aragon were put down by Philip II; Olivares subordinated Catalonia after a long bloody war. In Portugal the *cortes* met for the last time in 1697. In the kingdom of Naples parliamentary proceedings ended in 1642. The Great Elector put down the estates in Brandenburg and Prussia. The estates of Carniola, Styria, and Carinthia had already lost their powers to the Hapsburgs, and during the early part of the century the latter were able to curtail the powers of those in Bohemia, Moravia, and Silesia. The Danish crown became hereditary in 1665, that of Hungary in 1687. Toward the end of the century Charles XI reestablished absolute rule in Sweden.[23] By 1700 the traditional diffusion of powers had been virtually eliminated from continental Europe. The modernizers and state-builders had triumphed.

The tendencies toward the substitution of sovereignty for law and the centralization of authority also occurred in England. James I sundered the Crown from Parliament, challenged the traditional authority of the law and of the judges, advocated the divine right of kings. Kings, he said, "were the authors and makers of the laws and not the laws of the kings." [24] James was simply attempting to modernize English government and to move it along the paths which were already well-developed on the Continent. His efforts at political modernization were opposed by Coke and other conservatives who argued in terms of fundamental law and the traditional diffusion of authority. Their claims, however, were out of date in the face of the social and political changes taking place. "Coke, like most opponents of the King, had not really

21. Clark, p. 83.

22. Palmer, *I*, 461: "In 1787 demands were heard for revival of Provincial Estates in various parts of the country. It was a long-delayed reaction against Richelieu and Louis XIV, a demand to make France a constitutional monarchy, not on the English model, but on the model of a France that had long since passed away."

23. See Clark's summary of constitutional trends, pp. 86–87, and also F. L. Carsten, *Princes and Parliaments in Germany* (Oxford, Clarendon Press, 1959), pp. 436–37 and Holdsworth, *4*, 168–72.

24. James I, "The Trew Law of Free Monarchies," in McIlwain, ed., *Political Works*, p. 62.

grasped the conception of sovereignty; he maintained a position, reasonable enough in the Middle Ages, but impossible in a developed unitary state." [25] Centralization was necessary and at times it seemed that England would follow the continental pattern. But in due course the claims for royal absolutism generated counter claims for parliamentary supremacy. When James I, Filmer, and Hobbes put the king above law, they inevitably provoked Milton's argument that "the parliament is above all positive law, whether civil or common, makes or unmakes them both." The Long Parliament began the age of parliamentary supremacy. It was then that England saw "practically for the first time a legislative assembly of the modern type,—no longer a mere law-declaring, but a law-*making* machine." [26] Fundamental law suffered the same fate in England that it had on the Continent, but it was replaced by an omnipotent legislature rather than by an absolute monarchy.

American development was strikingly different from that in Europe. At the same time that the modernizing monarchs were squelching the traditional estates, that men were asserting their power to make law, that Richelieu was building an absolute state in France and Hobbes was proclaiming one in England, the old patterns of fundamental law and diffused authority were transported to a new life in the New World. The traditional view of law continued in America in two forms. First, the idea that man could only declare law and not make law remained strong in America long after it had been supplanted by positive conceptions of law in Europe. In some respects, it persisted right into the twentieth century. Secondly, the old idea of a fundamental law beyond human control was given new authority by identifying it with a written constitution. A written constitution can, of course, be viewed as a contract and as deriving its authority from conscious, positive human action. But it may also and even concurrenly be viewed as a codification of limitations already imposed upon government by custom and reason. It was in this latter sense that men accepted the idea of fundamental law in sixteenth- and seventeenth-century England and embodied it in their colonial charters and declarations of rights. The combination of both theories created a situation in which "higher law as with renewed youth, entered upon one of the great periods of its history." [27]

25. Figgis, *Divine Right*, p. 232.
26. McIlwain, *High Court*, pp. 93–96; italics in original.
27. Corwin, p. 89.

The persistence of fundamental-law doctrines went hand in hand with the rejection of sovereignty. The older ideas of the interplay of society and government and the harmonious balance of the elements of constitution continued to dominate political thought. In England, the ideas of the great Tudor political writers, Smith, Hooker, Coke, "were on the way to becoming anachronisms even as they were set down." [28] In America, on the other hand, their doctrines prospered, and Hobbes remained irrelevant. Neither the divine right of kings, nor absolute sovereignty, nor parliamentary supremacy, had a place on the western shores of the Atlantic. "Americans may be defined," as Pollard has said, "as that part of the English-speaking world which instinctively revolted against the doctrine of the sovereignty of the State and has, not quite successfully, striven to maintain that attitude from the time of the Pilgrim Fathers to the present day." The eighteenth-century argument of the colonists with the home country was essentially an argument against the legislative sovereignty of Parliament.

> It is this denial of all sovereignty which gives its profound and permanent interest to the American Revolution. . . . These are American ideas, but they were English before they were American. They were part of that medieval panoply of thought with which, including the natural equality of man, the view of taxes as grants, the laws of nature and of God, the colonists combatted the sovereignty of Parliament. They had taken these ideas with them when they shook the dust of England off their feet; indeed they left their country in order that they might cleave to these convictions. And now they come back, bringing with them these and other sheaves, to reconvert us to the views which we have held long since but lost awhile.[29]

To the extent that sovereignty was accepted in America it was held to be lodged in "the people." But apart from rare moments, such as the election of a constituent assembly or the ratification of

28. George H. Sabine, *A History of Political Theory* (rev. ed. New York, Holt, 1950), p. 455.

29. Pollard, pp. 31–33. For a perceptive discussion of the implications of this rejection of sovereignty for the way in which the political system has adapted to the most modern of problems, see Don K. Price, *The Scientific Estate* (Cambridge, Harvard University Press, 1965), passim but esp. pp. 45 ff., 58, 75–78, 165–67.

a constitution, sovereignty could never be exercised by the people. Authority existed in a multiplicity of organs each of which could justify its authority by reference to its source in the people but no one of which could conclusively demonstrate that it was more popular than the others. Popular sovereignty is as nebulous a concept as divine sovereignty. The voice of the people can be about as readily identified as the voice of God. It is thus a latent, passive, and ultimate authority, not a positive and active one.

The difference between American and European development is also manifest in the theories and practices of representation. In Europe, the elimination of the medieval representative bodies, the estates, was paralleled by a decline in the legitimacy accorded to local interests. On the Continent the absolute monarch represented or embodied the state. Beginning with the French Revolution, he was supplanted by the national assembly which represented or embodied the nation. In both instances, the collective whole had authority and legitimacy; local interests, parochial interests, group interests, as Rousseau argued, lacked legitimacy and hence had no claim for representation in the central organs of the political system.

The rationalization of authority in Britain also produced changes in representation which stand in marked contrast to the continuing American adherence to the older traditional concepts. In sixteenth-century England both King and Parliament had representative functions. The king was "the representative head of the corporate community of the realm." [30] The members of Parliament still had their traditional medieval functions of representing local communities and special interests. In the late medieval parliament, "the burgess is his town's attorney. His presence at parliament enables him to present petitions for confirmation of charters, the increase of local liberties, and redress of grievances, and to undertake private business in or near London for constituents." [31] Thus, the king represented the community as a whole, while the members of Parliament represented its component parts. The M.P. was responsible to his constituency. Indeed, an act passed during the reign of Henry V required members of Parliament to reside in their constituency. In the late sixteenth century this legal requirement began to be avoided in practice, but local residence and local ties still remained qualifications for most M.P.s. "The overwhelming localism of representation in Parliament is its dominant feature," writes Rowse of Elizabethan England, "and gives it vigor and reality. Everywhere the majority of members are local men, either gentry of the country or townsmen. The number of official members, privy councillors and such, is very small, and even they have their roots. . . . An analysis of the representation shows a very small proportion of outsiders, and still smaller of officials." [32] The members not only resided in their constituencies and represented the interests of those constituencies, but they were also paid by their constituencies for their services. Each constituency, moreover, was normally represented by two or three members of Parliament.

The constitutional revolution of the seventeenth century dealt the death blow to this "Old Tory" system of representation. It was replaced by what Beer terms the "Old Whig" system, under which the King lost his active representative functions and the M.P. became "the representative of the whole community, as well as of its component interests." [33] Parliament, as Burke phrased it in the classic statement of the Old Whig theory, is "a *deliberative* assembly of *one* nation, with *one* interest, that of the whole—where not local purposes, not local prejudices, ought to guide, but the general good, resulting from the general reason of the whole." Hence the M.P. should not be bound by authoritative instructions from his constituents and should rather subordinate their interests to the general interest of the entire society. With this new concept came a radical break with the old tradition of local residence and local payment. The last recorded instance of a constituency paying its representatives was in 1678. Increasingly during the seventeenth century members no longer resided in their constituencies. The statute was "evaded by the admission of strangers to free burghership," and it was finally repealed in 1774.[34] At the same

32. Rowse, *England of Elizabeth*, p. 306. Cf. A. F. Pollard, *The Evolution of Parliament* (2d ed. rev. London, Longmans, Green, 1926), p. 159, who argues that the nationalizing changes began in the late Tudor years.

33. Beer, pp. 614–15.

34. Herbert W. Horwill, *The Usages of the American Constitution* (London, Oxford University Press, 1925), p. 169.

time, the number of multiple-member districts declined, culminating in their complete elimination in 1885. All these developments made Parliament the collective representative of the nation
rather than a collection of representatives of individual constituencies. Thus the theory and practice of British representation
adjusted to the new fact of parliamentary supremacy.

In America, of course, the Old Tory system took on new life.
The colonial representative systems reproduced Tudor practices,
and subsequently these were established on a national scale in the
Constitution of 1787. America, like Tudor England, had a dual
system of representation: the President, like the Tudor king, represented the interests of the community as a whole; the individual
members of the legislature owed their primary loyalties to their
constituencies. The multimember constituencies which the British
had in the sixteenth century were exported to the colonial legislatures in America, adapted to the upper house of the national legislature, and extended to the state legislatures where they remained
in substantial number to the twentieth century.[35] Local residence, which had been a legal requirement and a political fact in
Tudor England, became a political requirement and a political
fact in America. It reflected "the intense localism . . . which persisted in America after it had been abandoned in the mother country." Thus in Britain many commanding political figures in the
nineteenth and twentieth centuries were able to stay in Parliament because they were able to change their constituencies.
"What a difference it would have made to the course of English
politics," as one commentator observed, "if Great Britain had not
thrown off, centuries ago, the medieval practice which America
still retains!" Contrariwise, Americans may view with astonish-
ment and disdain the gap which political modernization has created between the British M.P. and his constituents.[36]

35. Maurice Klain, "A New Look at the Constituencies: The Need for a Re-
count and a Reappraisal," *American Political Science Review*, *49* (Dec. 1955), passim, but esp. 1111–13. In 1619 the London Company aped English practice when it
summoned to the first Virginia House of Burgesses, "two Burgesses from each Plantation freely . . . elected by the inhabitants thereof."

36. Horwill, pp. 169–70, and see, *contra*, the comments of an American newspaperman covering the 1964 general election: "British members of Parliament aren't
oriented toward their constituencies. They don't even have to live in them. . . .
Constituencies tend to be regarded as political factories to provide fodder for the
national consensus in London. An American Congressman may get 1,500 to 2,000
letters a week from people who elect him. A British MP usually gets no more than
10." Roderick MacLeish, *New York Herald Tribune*, Oct. 11, 1964.

DIFFERENTIATION OF STRUCTURE

In comparing European and American developments, a distinction must be made between "functions" and "power." In this chapter, "power" (in the singular) means influence or control over the actions of others; "function" refers to particular types of activity, which may be defined in various ways. "Powers" (in the plural) will not be used, since most authors use it to mean "functions." It is thus possible to speak with the Founding Fathers of legislative, executive, and judicial functions, with Bagehot of dignified and efficient functions, and also of legal and political functions, military and civil functions, domestic and foreign functions. The exercise of any function involves some power. But functions and power are distinct dimensions. Two courts may have similar or identical judicial functions, but one may have much more power than another. Two agencies may have similar power, but their functions may differ both in substance and in number. Governmental institutions thus may be equal or unequal in power and specialized or overlapping in function.

In Europe the rationalization of authority and the centralization of power were accompanied by functional differentiation and the emergence of more specialized governmental institutions and bodies. These developments were, of course, a response to the growing complexity of society and the increasing demands upon government. Administrative, legal, judicial, military institutions developed as semi-autonomous but subordinate bodies in one way or another responsible to the political bodies (monarch or parliament) which exercised sovereignty. The dispersion of functions among relatively specialized institutions, in turn, also encouraged inequalities in power among the institutions. The legislative or law-making function carried with it more power than the administrative or law-enforcement function.

In medieval government and in Tudor government the differentiation of functions was not very far advanced. A single institution often exercised many functions, and a single function was often dispersed among several institutions. This tended to equalize power among institutions. The government of Tudor England was a "government of *fused* powers" (i.e. functions), that is, Parliament, Crown, and other institutions each performed many functions.[37] In the seventeenth and eighteenth centuries British

37. McIlwain, *High Court*, p. xi; italics in original.

government evolved toward a concentration of power and a differentiation of function. In Great Britain, as Pollard argues, "Executive, legislature, and judicature have been evolved from a common origin, and have adapted themselves to specific purposes, because without that specialization of functions English government would have remained rudimentary and inefficient. But there has been no division of sovereignty and no separation of powers." [38]

In America, in contrast, sovereignty was divided, power was separated, and functions were combined in many different institutions. This result was achieved despite rather than because of the theory of the separation of powers (i.e. functions) which was prevalent in the eighteenth century. In its pure form, the assignment of legislative, executive, and judicial functions to separate institutions would give one institution a monopoly of the dominant law-making function and thus would centralize power. This was in part what Locke wanted and even more what Jefferson wanted. It was also, of course, found in Montesquieu, but Montesquieu recognized the inequality of power which would result from the strict separation of functions. The "judiciary," he said, "is in some measure next to nothing." Consequently, to obtain a real division of power, Montesquieu divided the legislative function among three different institutions representing the three traditional estates of the realm. In practice in America, as in Tudor England, not only was power divided by dividing the legislative function but other functions were also shared among several institutions, thus creating a system of "checks and balances" which equalized power. "The constitutional convention of 1787," as Neustadt has said, "is supposed to have created a government of 'separated powers' [i.e. functions]. It did nothing of the sort. Rather, it created a government of separated institutions *sharing* powers [functions]." [39] Thus America perpetuated a fusion of functions and a division of power, while Europe developed a differentiation of functions and a centralization of power.

The passion of the Founding Fathers for the division of power, for setting ambition against ambition, for creating a constitution with a complicated system of balances exceeding that of any other, is, of course, well known. Everything is bought at a price, however,

38. Pollard, *Parliament*, p. 257.
39. Richard E. Neustadt, *Presidential Power: The Politics of Leadership* (New York, John Wiley, 1960), p. 33; italics in original.

and, as many Englishmen have pointed out, one apparent price of the division of power is governmental inefficiency. "The English constitution, in a word," Bagehot argued, "is framed on the principle of choosing a single sovereign authority, and making it good: the American, upon the principle of having many sovereign authorities, and hoping that their multitude may atone for their inferiority." [40] Fifty years later Pollard could similarly point to the separation of powers as "the reason why American efficiency, so marked in private concerns, has been so fettered in government" and why "American politics are unattractive to so many American minds." In due course, however, he hoped that the "American nation will trust a national government with the full powers of sovereignty" and that "The separation of powers will then be reduced to its true proportions as a specialization of functions." [41] Perversely, however, American institutions continued to divide power and to combine functions. This pattern can be clearly seen in the mixing in the same institution of legislative and judicial functions and of dignified and efficient functions, in the division of the legislative function among many institutions, and in the incomplete differentiation of distinct military institutions.

In medieval government no distinction existed between legislation and adjudication. On the Continent such institutions as the *Justiza* of Aragon and the French *Parlements* exercised important political functions into the sixteenth century. In England, of course, Parliament itself was viewed primarily as a court and not as a legislature down to the beginning of the seventeenth century. The courts of law, as Holdsworth observes,

> were, in the days before the functions of government had become specialized, very much more than merely judicial tribunals. In England and elsewhere they were regarded as possessing functions which we may call political, to distinguish them from those purely judicial functions which nowadays are their exclusive functions on the continent, and their principal functions everywhere. That the courts continued to exercise these larger functions, even after departments of government had begun to be differentiated, was due to the con-

40. Walter Bagehot, *The English Constitution* (London, Oxford-World's Classics, 1949) , p. 202.
41. Pollard, *Parliament*, pp. 255–57.

tinuance of that belief in the supremacy of the law which was the dominant characteristic of the political theory of the Middle Ages.[42]

In England, the supremacy of the law disappeared in the civil wars of the seventeenth century and with it disappeared the mixture of judicial and political functions. English judges followed the course of Bacon rather than Coke and became "lions under the throne" who could not "check or oppose any points of sovereignty." By the eighteenth century, Blackstone could flatly state that no court could declare invalid an act of Parliament, however unreasonable it might be. To admit such a power, he said, "were to set the judicial power above that of the legislature, which would be subversive of all government." [43] Parliament had evolved from high court to supreme legislature.

In America, on the other hand, the mixture of judicial and political functions remained. The judicial power to declare what the law is became the mixed judicial-legislative power to tell the legislature what the law cannot be. The American doctrine and practice of judicial review were undoubtedly known only in very attenuated form in late sixteenth-century and early seventeenth-century England. Indeed, the whole concept of judicial review implies a distinction between legislative and judicial functions which was not explicitly recognized at that time. It is, nonetheless, clear that Tudor and early Stuart courts did use the common law to "controul" acts of Parliament at least to the point of redefining rather sweepingly the purposes of Parliament. These actions did not represent a conscious doctrine of judicial review so much as they represented the still "undifferentiated fusion of judicial and legislative functions." [44] This fusion of legislative and judicial functions was retained by American courts and was eventually formulated into the doctrine and practice of judicial review. The legislative functions of courts in America, as McIlwain argued, are far greater than those in England, "because the like tendency was there checked by the growth in the seventeenth century of a new doctrine of parliamentary supremacy." Unlike English courts,

42. Holdsworth, 4, 169.
43. Sir William Blackstone, *Commentaries on the Laws of England*, Thomas M. Cooley, ed. (Chicago, Callaghan, 1876) , 1, 90.
44. See J. W. Gough, *Fundamental Law in English Constitutional History* (Oxford, Clarendon Press, 1955) , p. 27.

"American courts still retain much of their Tudor indefiniteness, notwithstanding our separation of departments. They are guided to an extent unknown now in England by questions of policy and expediency. The Supreme Court has acted again and again on the principle that it may reverse its decisions, a principle which the House of Lords has definitely accepted as inadmissible." [45] Foreign observers since de Tocqueville have identified the "immense political influence" of the courts as one of the most astonishing and unique characteristics of American government.

The mixing of legal and political functions in American government can also be seen in the consistently prominent role of lawyers in American politics. In fourteenth- and fifteenth-century England lawyers played an important role in the development of parliamentary proceedings, and the alliance between Parliament and the law, in contrast to the separation between the Estates General and the French *parlement,* helped to sustain parliamentary authority.[46] In Elizabethan England lawyers played an increasingly important role in Parliament. In 1593, for instance, 43 per cent of the members of the House of Commons possessed a legal education. The Speaker and the other leading figures in the House were usually lawyers. Subsequently the role of lawyers in the British Parliament declined in significance, reaching a low in the nineteenth century. In the twentieth century only about 20 per cent of the M.P.s have been lawyers. In America, on the other hand, in the colonial governments, in the state governments, and in the national government, the Tudor heritage of lawyer-legislators has continued, with lawyers often being a majority or more of the members of American legislative bodies.[47]

Every political system, as Bagehot pointed out, must gain authority and then use authority. In the modern British system these functions are performed by the dignified and efficient parts of the constitution. The assignment of each function to separate institu-

---

45. McIlwain, *High Court,* pp. ix, 385–86.

46. Holdsworth, *4,* 174, 184–85, 188–89.

47. See J. E. Neale, *The Elizabethan House of Commons* (London, Penguin, 1949), pp. 290–95; Rose, p. 307; Thompson, pp. 169–73; Donald R. Matthews, *The Social Background of Political Decision-Makers* (New York, Random House, 1954), pp. 28–31; J. F. S. Ross, *Elections and Electors* (London, Eyre and Spottiswoode, 1955), p. 444; W. L. Guttsman, *The British Political Elite* (New York, Basic Books, 1963), pp. 82, 90, 105; D. E. Butler and Richard Rose, *The British General Election of 1959* (London, Macmillan, 1960), p. 127.

tions is one aspect of the functional differentiation which is part of modernization. It can be seen most clearly, of course, in the case of the so-called constitutional monarchies, but in some degree it can be seen in almost all modern governments.[48] The American political system, however, like the older European political systems, does not assign dignified and efficient functions to different institutions. All major institutions of the American government—President, Supreme Court, House, Senate, and their state counterparts—combine in varying degrees both types of functions. This combination is, of course, most notable in the Presidency. Almost every other modern political system from the so-called constitutional monarchies of Great Britain and Scandinavia to the parliamentary republics of Italy, Germany, and France before De Gaulle, to the communist dictatorships in the Soviet Union and eastern Europe separates the chief of state from the head of government. In the Soviet system, the differentiation is carried still further to distinguish chief of state from head of government from party chief. In the United States, however, the President unites all three functions, this combination being a major source of his power but also a major limitation on his power, since the requirements of one role often conflict with the demands of another. This combination of roles perpetuates ancient practice. For the Presidency was created, as Jefferson declared in 1787, as an "elective monarchy"; the office was designed to embody much of the power of the British king; and the politics that surround it are court politics.[49]

48. Bagehot, pp. 304. See also Francis X. Sutton, "Representation and the Nature of Political Systems," *Comparative Studies in Society and History*, 2 (Oct. 1959) , 7: "the kind of distinction Bagehot made when he talked of the 'dignified' and 'efficient' parts of the English constitution is observed clearly in many states. . . . The discrimination of functions here rests, of course, on an analytical distinction relevant in any political system. It is that between symbolic representation and executive control."

49. Thomas Jefferson, Letter to James Madison, Dec. 20, 1787, *Writings* (Washington, D.C., Thomas Jefferson Memorial Association, 1903–05) , 6, 389–90; Ford, p. 293. For an elegant—and eloquent—essay on the President as King, see D. W. Brogan, "The Presidency," *Encounter*, 25 (Jan. 1964) , 3–7. I am in debt to Richard E. Neustadt for insights into the nature of the American monarchy and into the similarities between White House politics and palace politics. See also Pollard, *Factors in American History*, pp. 72–73: "down to this day the Executive in the United States is far more monarchical and monarchy far more personal than in the United Kingdom. 'He' is a single person there, but 'It' is a composite entity in Great Britain."

The Presidency is, indeed, the only survival in the contemporary world of the constitutional monarchy once prevalent throughout medieval Europe. In the sixteenth century a constitutional monarch was one who reigned and ruled, but who ruled under law (*non sub homine sed sub Deo et lege*) with due regard to the rights and liberties of his subjects, the type of monarch Fortescue had in mind when he distinguished *dominium politicum et regale* from *dominium regale*. In the seventeenth century this old-style constitutional monarch was supplanted by the new-style absolute monarch who placed himself above the law. Subsequently, the eighteenth and nineteenth centuries saw the emergence of a new so-called "constitutional monarchy" in which a "dignified" monarch reigned but did not rule. Like the absolute monarch he is a modern invention created in response to the need to fix supreme power in a single organ. The American Presidency, on the other hand, continues the older, original type of constitutional monarchy. In functions and power American Presidents are Tudor kings. In institutional role, as well as in personality and talents, Lyndon Johnson far more closely resembled Elizabeth I than did Elizabeth II. Britain preserved the form of the old monarchy, but America preserved the substance. Today America still has a king, Britain only a Crown.

In most modern states the legislative function is in theory in the hands of a large representative assembly, parliament, or supreme soviet. In practice, however, it is performed by a relatively small body of men—a cabinet or presidium—which exercises its power in all fields of government activity. In America, however, the legislative function remains divided among three distinct institutions and their subdivisions, much as it was once divided among the different estates and other constituted bodies in late medieval Europe. On the national level this arrangement derives not from the ideas of any European theorist but rather from the "institutional history of the colonies between 1606 and 1776." [50] The relations among burgesses, councils, and governors in the colonies, in turn, reflected the relations among Crown, Lords, and Commons in the late sixteenth century.

In modern politics, the division of power between two bodies in

---

50. Benjamin F. Wright, "The Origins of the Separation of Powers in America," *Economics, 13* (May 1933), 169 ff.

a legislative assembly generally varies inversely with the effective power of the assembly as a whole. The Supreme Soviet has little power but is truly bicameral; the British Parliament has more power but is effectively unicameral. America, however, is unique in preserving a working bicameralism directly inherited from the sixteenth century. Only in Tudor times did the two houses of Parliament become formally and effectively distinguished, one from the other, on an institutional basis. "The century started with Parliament a unitary institution, truly bi-cameral only in prospect." When it ended, the growth in "the power, position, and prestige of the House of Commons" had made Parliament "a political force with which the Crown and government had to reckon." [51] The sixteenth century represented a peak of bicameralism in English parliamentary history. Each house often quashed bills which had passed the other house, and to resolve their differences the houses resorted to conference committees. Originally used as an "occasional procedure," in 1571 the conference committee was transformed into "a normal habit." In Elizabethan Parliaments, conferences were requested by one or the other house on most bills, the conference delegations were at times instructed not to yield on particular items, and when there were substantial differences between the versions approved by the two houses, the conference committee might substantially rewrite the entire bill, at times at the urging and with the advice of the Queen and her councillors. Although all this sounds very contemporary, it is, in fact, very Tudor, and the conference committee procedure was carried over into the colonial legislatures and then extended to the national level. In Great Britain, however, the practice died out with the rise of cabinet responsibility to the Commons. The last real use of "Free Conferences," where discussion and hence politics were permitted, occurred about 1740.[52]

The participation of two assemblies and the chief executive in the legislative process caused the continuation in America of many other legislative methods familiar to Tudor government. An assembly which legislates must delegate some of its work to subordi-

51. J. E. Neale, *Elizabeth I and Her Parliaments* (New York, St. Martin's, 1958), *I*, 16–17.

52. Ibid., pp. 235, 287, 387–88, 412–13; G. F. M. Campion, *An Introduction to the Procedure of the House of Commons* (London, Philip Allan, 1929), p. 199; Ada C. McCown, *The Congressional Conference Committee* (New York, Columbia University Press, 1927), pp. 23–37.

nate bodies or committees. Committees made their appearance in the Tudor Parliament in the 1560s and 1570s. The practice of referring bills to committees soon became almost universal, and, as the committees assumed more and more of the functions of the House, they became larger and more permanent. The committees were also frequently dominated by those with special interests in the legislation that they considered. Bills concerned with local and regional problems went to committees composed of members from those regions and localities.[53] By the turn of the century the larger committees had evolved into standing committees which considered all matters coming up within a general sphere of business. The active role of the Commons in the legislative process compelled it to resort to this committee procedure. The procedure, in turn, was exported to the colonies in the early seventeenth century—particularly to the Virginia House of Burgesses —where it also met a real need, and 150 years later was duplicated in the early sessions of the national Congress. At the same time in England, however, the rise of the cabinet undermined the committee system which had earlier existed in Parliament; the old standing committees of the House of Commons became empty formalities, indistinguishable from Committees of the Whole House, long before they were officially discontinued in 1832.

The division of the legislative function imposed similar duties upon the Speaker in the Tudor House of Commons and in subsequent American legislatures. The Tudor Speaker was a political leader, with a dual allegiance to the Crown and to the House. His success in large measure depended upon how well he could balance and integrate these often conflicting responsibilities. He was the "manager of the King's business" in the House, but he was also the spokesman for the House to the Crown and the defender of its rights and privileges. He could exercise much influence in the House by his control, subject to veto by the House, over the order in which bills were called up for debate and by his influence on the "timing and framing of questions." The struggle between Crown and Parliament in the seventeenth century, however, made it impossible for the Speaker to continue his loyalties to both. His overriding duty was now to the House, and, in due course, the impartiality of Onslow in the eighteenth century (1727–61) became the norm for Speakers in the nineteenth and twentieth centuries.

53. Rowse, p. 307.

Thus in Britain an office which had once been weighted with politics, efficient as well as dignified, radically changed its character and became that of a depoliticized, impartial presiding officer. In America, on the other hand, the political character of the Tudor Speakership was perpetuated in the colonial assemblies and eventually in the national House of Representatives.[54]

The sharing of the legislative function among two assemblies and the chief executive gives a strikingly Tudor character to the contemporary American lawmaking process. In Elizabethan England, as Rowse observes, the "relations between Crown and Parliament were more like those between President and Congress than those that subsist in England today." [55] The Tudor monarchs had to badger, wheedle, cajole, and persuade the Commons to give them the legislation they wanted. At times they were confronted by unruly Parliaments which pushed measures the monarch did not want or debated issues the monarch wished to silence. Generally, of course, the monarch's "legislative program," consisting primarily of requests for funds, was approved. At other times, however, the Commons would rear up and the monarch would have to withdraw or reshape his demands. Burghley, who was in charge of Parliamentary relations for Elizabeth, "kept a close eye on proceedings and received from the Clerks during the session lists showing the stages of all bills in both Houses." [56] Elizabeth regularly attempted to win support in the Commons for her proposals by sending messages and "rumors" to the House, by exhorting and instructing the Speaker on how to handle the business of the House, by "receiving or summoning deputations from the Houses to Whitehall and there rating them in person," and by "descending magnificently upon Parliament in her coach or open chariot and addressing them" personally or through the Lord Keeper.[57]

Although the sovereign did not "lack means of blocking obnoxious bills during their progress through the two Houses," almost every session of Parliament passed some bills which the Crown did not want, and the royal veto was exercised. Although used more

54. Neale, *House of Commons*, p. 381 and passim; Holdsworth, *4*, 177; Campion, *2*, 52–54.
55. Rowse, p. 294.
56. Neale, *House of Commons*, p. 411.
57. Rowse, pp. 294–95.

frequently against private bills than against public ones, important public measures might also be stopped by the Crown. During her reign Elizabeth I apparently approved 429 bills and vetoed approximately 71. The veto, however, was not a weapon which the Crown could use without weighing costs and gains: "politics—the art of the possible—were not entirely divorced even from Tudor monarchy. Too drastic or ill-considered a use of the royal veto might have stirred up trouble." [58] The tactics of a Henry VIII or Elizabeth I in relation to their Parliaments thus differed little from those of a Kennedy or Johnson in relation to their Congresses. A similar distribution of power imposed similar patterns of executive-legislative behavior.

The Tudor monarchs did perhaps have some advantage over American Presidents in that some, although not all, of their Privy Councillors sat in Parliament. These councillors were the principal managers of the Crown's business in Parliament, performing the functions of the majority leaders in Congress. At times, like the majority leaders, they would feel compelled to put their loyalty to the House above their loyalty to the Crown. The practice of Privy Councillors sitting in Parliament, however, was never wholly accepted as desirable, and in the seventeenth century continuing efforts were made to keep "place men" out of Parliament. These culminated in the Act of Settlement of 1701, the relevant provisions of which were subsequently written into the American Constitution, although they almost immediately became ineffective in England. Thus, American practice developed one aspect of the earlier English thought and behavior, while later British practice developed another.[59] The relationships between chief executive and legislature, however, made American cabinet and executive officers resemble the English and British cabinets and councils of the sixteenth, seventeenth, and eighteenth centuries. Reflecting this similarity and the drastic change which took place in the role of the British cabinet is the fact that in the United States the executive leadership is still called "the Administration," as it was in eighteenth-century Britain, while in Britain itself, it is now termed "the Government."

58. Neale, *House of Commons*, pp. 410–12, and Neale, *Elizabeth I and Her Parliaments*, passim.

59. See Campion, pp. 37–38; Pollard, *Parliament*, pp. 237–38; Richard F. Fenno, *The President's Cabinet* (Cambridge, Harvard University Press, 1959), pp. 10–13.

The differentiation of specialized administrative structures also took place much more rapidly in Europe than it did in America. The contrast can be strikingly seen in the case of military institutions. A modern military establishment includes a standing army recruited voluntarily or through conscription and commanded by a professional officer corps. In Europe a professional officer corps emerged during the first half of the nineteenth century. By 1870 the major continental states had developed most of the principal institutions of professional officership. England, however, lagged behind the Continent in developing military professionalism, and the United States lagged behind Great Britain. Not until the turn of the century did the United States have many of the institutions of professional officership which the European states had acquired many decades earlier. The division of power among governmental institutions perpetuated the mixing of politics and military affairs and enormously complicated the emergence of a modern system of objective civilian control. In most areas of civil life Americans have been willing to accept functional differentiation and specialized competence as inherent and even desirable aspects of modernization. Even after World War II, however, many Americans still adhered to a "fusionist" approach to civil-military relations and believed that military leadership and military institutions should mirror the attitudes and characteristics of civil society.[60]

American reluctance to accept a standing army also contrasts with the much more rapid modernization in Europe. In the sixteenth century European military forces consisted of feudal levies, mercenaries, and local militia. In England the militia was an ancient institution, and the Tudors formally organized it on a county basis under the Lord Lieutenants to take the place of the private retinues of the feudal lords. This development was a step toward "domestic tranquility and military incompetence," and in 1600, "Not a single western country had a standing army: the only one in Europe was that of the Turks."[61] By the end of the cen-

---

60. See Huntington, *The Soldier and the State* (Cambridge, Harvard-Belknap, 1957) , passim.

61. J. H. Hexter, *Reappraisals in History* (Evanston, Ill., Northwestern University Press, 1962) , p. 147, and Clark, p. 84. On the fundamental changes in European military practice, see Michael Roberts, *The Military Revolution: 1560–1660* (Belfast, Queen's University, n.d.) .

tury, however, all the major European powers had standing armies. Discipline was greatly improved, uniforms introduced, regulations formalized, weapons standardized, and effective state control extended over the military forces. The French standing army dates from Richelieu; the Prussian from the actions of the Great Elector in 1655; the English from the Restoration of 1660. In England the county militia continued in existence after 1660, but steadily declined in importance.

In America, on the other hand, the militia became the crucial military force at the same time that it was decaying in Europe. The militia was the natural military system for societies whose needs were defensive rather than offensive and intermittent rather than constant. The seventeenth-century colonists continued, adapted, and improved upon the militia system which had existed in Tudor England. In the next century, they identified militia with popular government, and standing armies became the symbol of monarchical tyranny. "On the military side," as Vagts says, "the war of the American Revolution was in part a revolt against the British standing army." [62] But in terms of military institutions, it was a reactionary revolt. The standing armies of George III represented modernity, the colonial militias embodied traditionalism. The American commitment to this military traditionalism, however, became all the more complete as a result of the War of Independence. Hostility to standing armies and reliance on the militia as the first line of defense of a free people became popular dogma and constitutional doctrine, however much it might be departed from in practice. Fortunately the threats to security in the nineteenth century were few, and hence the American people were able to go through that century with a happy confidence in an ineffective force which was protecting them from a nonexistent danger. The militia legacy, however, remained a continuing element in American military affairs far into the much more tumultuous twentieth century. It was concretely manifest in the political influence and military strength of the National Guard. Even after World War II, the idea that an expert military force is better than a citizen-soldier force had still to win wholehearted acceptance on the western side of the Atlantic.

62. Alfred Vagts, *A History of Militarism* (rev. ed. New York, Meridian Books, 1959), p. 92. See generally Louis Morton, "The Origins of American Military Policy," *Military Affairs*, 22 (Summer 1958), 75–82.

Tudor Institutions and Mass Participation

Among the peoples of western civilization, the Americans were the first to achieve widespread political participation but the last to modernize their traditional political structures. In America, Tudor institutions and popular participation united in a political system which remains as baffling to understand as it is impossible to duplicate. In Europe, on the other hand, the rationalization of authority and the differentiation of structure clearly preceded the expansion of political participation. How can these differences in political modernizat.on be explained?

In large part, they are directly related to the prevalence of foreign war and social conflict in Europe as contrasted with America. On the Continent the late sixteenth and the seventeenth centuries were periods of intense struggle and conflict. For only three years during the entire seventeenth century was there a complete absence of fighting on the European continent. Several of the larger states were more often at war during the century than they were at peace. The wars were usually complex affairs involving many states tied together in dynastic and political alliances. War reached an intensity in the seventeenth century which it never had previously and which was exceeded later only in the twentieth century.[63] The prevalence of war directly promoted political modernization. Competition forced the monarchs to build their military strength. The creation of military strength required national unity, the suppression of regional and religious dissidents, the expansion of armies and bureaucracies, and a major increase in state revenues. "The most striking fact" in the history of seventeenth-century conflict, Clark observes,

> is the great increase in the size of armies, in the scale of warfare. . . . Just as the modern state was needed to create the standing army, so the army created the modern state, for the influence of the two causes was reciprocal. . . . The growth of the administrative machine and of the arts of government was directed and conditioned by the desire to turn the natural and human resources of the country into military

63. Clark, p. 98; Quincy Wright, *A Study of War* (Chicago, University of Chicago Press, 1942), *1, 235-40.* See also Sir George Clark, *War and Society in the Seventeenth Century* (Cambridge, Cambridge University Press, 1958), passim.

power. The general development of European institutions was governed by the fact that the continent was becoming more military, or, we may say, more militaristic.[64]

War was the great stimulus to state building.

In recent years much has been written about "defensive modernization" by the ruling groups in nonwestern societies such as Egypt under Mohammad Ali, the eighteenth- and nineteenth-century Ottoman Empire, and Meiji Japan. In all these cases, intense early efforts at modernization occurred in the military field, and the attempts to adopt European weapons, tactics, and organization led to the modernization of other institutions in society. What was true of these societies was also true of seventeenth-century Europe. The need for security and the desire for expansion prompted the monarchs to develop their military establishments, and the achievement of this goal required them to centralize and to rationalize their political machinery.

Largely because of its insular position, Great Britain was a partial exception to this pattern of war and insecurity. Even so, one major impetus to the centralization of authority in English government came from the efforts of the Stuart kings to get more taxes to build and man more ships to compete with the French and other continental powers. If it were not for the English Channel, the Stuart centralization probably would have succeeded. In America, in the seventeenth century, however, continuing threats came only from the Indians. The nature of this threat plus the dispersed character of the settlements meant that the principal defense force had to be the settlers themselves organized into militia units. There was little incentive to develop European-type military forces and a European-type state to support and control them.

Civil harmony also contributed significantly to the preservation of Tudor political institutions in America. Those institutions reflected the relative unity and harmony of English society during

64. Clark, *Seventeenth Century*, pp. 98, 101–02. See also Wright, *Study of War, 1*, 256: "it would appear that the political order of Europe changed most radically and rapidly in the seventeenth and twentieth centuries when war reached greatest intensity. The seventeenth century witnessed the supercession of feudalism and the Holy Roman Empire by the secular sovereign states of Europe. The twentieth century appears to be witnessing the supercession of the secular sovereign states by something else. Exactly what cannot yet be said."

the sixteenth century. English society, which had been racked by the Wars of the Roses in the fifteenth century, welcomed the opportunity for civil peace that the Tudors afforded. Social conflict was minimal during the sixteenth century. The aristocracy had been almost eliminated during the civil wars of the previous century. England was not perhaps a middle-class society but the differences between social classes were less then than they had been earlier and much less than they were to become later. Individual mobility rather than class struggle was the keynote of the Tudor years. "The England of the Tudors was an 'organic state' to a degree unknown before Tudor times, and forgotten almost immediately afterward." [65] Harmony and unity made it unnecessary to fix sovereignty in any particular institution; it could remain dispersed so long as social conflict was minimal.

The only major issue which disrupted the Tudor consensus, of course, was religion. Significantly, in sixteenth-century English history the Act of Supremacy means the supremacy of the state over the church, not the supremacy of one governmental institution over another or one class over another. After the brief interlude of the Marian struggles, however, the shrewd politicking and popular appeal of Elizabeth restored a peace among religious groups which was virtually unique in Europe at that time. The balance between Crown and Parliament and the combination of an active monarchy and common law depended upon this social harmony. Meanwhile on the Continent, civil strife had already reached a new intensity before the end of the sixteenth century. France alone had eight civil wars during the 36 years between 1562 and 1598, a period roughly comprising the peaceful reign of Elizabeth in England. The following 50 years saw Richelieu's struggles with the Huguenots and the wars of the Fronde. Spain was racked by civil strife, particularly between 1640 and 1652 when Philip IV and Olivares attempted to subdue Catalonia. In Germany, princes and parliaments fought each other. Where, as frequently happened, estates and princes espoused different religions, the controversy over religion inevitably broke the medieval balance of powers between princes and parliaments.[66]

English harmony ended with the sixteenth century. Whether the gentry were rising, falling or doing both in seventeenth-

65. McIlwain, *High Court*, p. 336; Rowse, pp. 223 ff.
66. Friedrich, pp. 20–21; Sabine, pp. 372–73.

century England, forces were at work in society disrupting Tudor social peace. The efforts to reestablish something like the Tudor balance broke down before the intensity of social and religious conflict. The brief period of Crown power between 1630 and 1640, for instance, gave way "to a short-lived restoration of something like the Tudor balance of powers during the first year of the Long Parliament (1641). This balance might perhaps have been sustained indefinitely, but for the rise of acute religious differences between the Crown and the militant Puritan party in the Commons." [67] In England, as in France, civil strife led to the demand for strong centralized power to reestablish public order. The breakdown of unity in society gave rise to irresistible forces to reestablish that unity through government.

Both Puritan and Cavalier emigrants to America escaped from English civil strife. The process of fragmentation, in turn, encouraged homogeneity, and homogeneity encouraged "a kind of immobility." [68] In America environment reinforced heredity, as the common challenges of the frontier combined with the abundance of land to help perpetuate the egalitarian characteristics of Tudor society and the complexity of Tudor political institutions. And, paradoxically, as Hartz has pointed out, the Framers of the Constitution of 1787 reproduced these institutions on the federal level in the expectation that the social divisions and conflict within American society made necessary a complex system of checks and balances. In reality, however, their Constitution was successful only because their view of American society was erroneous. So also, only the absence of significant social divisions permitted the continued transformation of political issues into legal ones through the peculiar institution of judicial review.[69] Divided societies cannot exist without centralized power; consensual societies cannot exist with it.

In continental Europe, as in most contemporary modernizing countries, rationalized authority and centralized power were ne-

67. Chrimes, p. 138.

68. Louis Hartz, *The Founding of New Societies* (New York, Harcourt, Brace and World, 1964), pp. 3, 4, 6, 23. Hartz's theory of fragmentation furnishes an excellent general framework for the analysis of the atrophy of settlement colonies, while his concept of the American liberal consensus in large part explains the preservation of Tudor political institutions.

69. Louis Hartz, *The Liberal Tradition in America* (New York, Harcourt, Brace, 1955), pp. 9-10, 45-46, 85-86, 133-34, 281-82.

cessary not only for unity but also for progress. The opposition to modernization came from traditional interests: religious, aristocratic, regional, and local. The centralization of power was necessary to smash the old order, break down the privileges and restraints of feudalism, and free the way for the rise of new social groups and the development of new economic activities. In some degree a coincidence of interest did exist between the absolute monarchs and the rising middle classes. Hence European liberals often viewed favorably the concentration of authority in an absolute monarch, just as modernizers today frequently view favorably the concentration of authority in a single "mass" party.

In America, on the other hand, the absence of feudal social institutions made the centralization of power unnecessary. Since there was no aristocracy to dislodge, there was no need to call into existence a governmental power capable of dislodging it.[70] This great European impetus to political modernization was missing. Society could develop and change without having to overcome the opposition of social classes with a vested interest in the social and economic status quo. The combination of an egalitarian social inheritance plus the plenitude of land and other resources enabled social and economic development to take place more or less spontaneously. Government often helped to promote economic development, but (apart from the abolition of slavery) it played only a minor role in changing social customs and social structure. In modernizing societies, the centralization of power varies directly with the resistance to social change. In the United States, where the resistance was minimal, so also was the centralization.

The differences in social consensus between Europe and America also account for the differences in the manner in which political participation expanded. In Europe this expansion was marked by discontinuities on two levels. On the institutional level, democratization meant the shift of power from monarchical ruler to popular assembly. This shift began in England in the seventeenth century, in France in the eighteenth century, and in Germany in the nineteenth century. Where medieval assemblies survived the age of absolutism, they usually became the vehicle through which popular sovereignty was asserted against royal supremacy. The royal powers and prerogative were gradually limited or termi-

70. Ibid., p. 43.

nated; parliament emerged as the dominant institution; and in due course extensions of the suffrage made it representative of the nation.

In countries where assemblies or estates did not survive absolutism, the transition to participant government was more difficult. In these systems, the rationalization of authority and the differentiation of structure had often been carried so far as to close off opportunities for popular participation through traditional institutions. Consequently, the monarchy was often overthrown by revolutionary action and a popularly elected assembly installed in its place: Rousseau was the natural legatee of Richelieu. Countries such as France and Prussia which took the lead in modernizing their political institutions in the seventeenth century thus had the most difficulty in maintaining stable democracy in the twentieth century. Countries where the seventeenth-century tendencies toward absolute monarchy were either defeated (England), stalemated (Sweden), or absent (America), later tended to develop more viable democratic institutions. The continued vitality of medieval estates and pluralistic assemblies is associated with subsequent democratic tendencies. "It is no accident, surely," Carsten observes, "that the liberal movement of the nineteenth century was strongest in those areas of Germany where the Estates survived the period of absolute government." [71] Similarly, in seventeenth-century Spain, Catalonia was the principal locus of feudal opposition to the centralizing and rationalizing efforts of Olivares, but in the twentieth century it has been the principal locus of Spanish liberalism and constitutionalism. In eighteenth-century Europe also, the conservative and even reactionary efforts of the "constituted bodies" to maintain and to restore their privileges laid the basis for later popular participation and popular resistance against despotism.[72]

On the electoral level, the expansion of participation in Europe meant the gradual extension of the suffrage for the assembly from aristocracy to upper bourgeoisie, lower bourgeoisie, peasants, and urban workers. This process is clearly seen in the English reform acts of 1832, 1867, 1884, and 1918. Where no assembly existed, the creation of a popular assembly was also at times accompanied by the introduction of universal male suffrage which, in turn, directly

71. Carsten, p. 434; Friedrich, pp. 20–25.
72. Palmer, *1*, passim, but esp. pp. 323–407.

encouraged political instability. In both cases, control of the assembly determined control of the government, and hence struggles over who should vote for the assembly were often intense and sometimes violent. In America, on the other hand, no class differences existed as in Europe, and hence the social basis for conflict over suffrage extensions was less than in Europe. In addition, the continuation of the pluralistic institutions of medieval constitutionalism reduced the apparent significance of suffrage extensions. In a system of checks and balances with many institutions competing for power, it seemed natural enough that at least one of these institutions (usually the lower house of the assembly) should be elected by popular suffrage. Once this was granted, however, the competition between social forces and between governmental institutions produced the gradual democratization of the other institutions.

In America, thus, the unity of society and the division of government made the latter the principal focus of democratization. The American equivalent of the Reform Act of 1832 was the change in the nature of the Electoral College produced by the rise of political parties, and the resulting transformation of the Presidency from an indirectly elected, semi-oligarchical office to a popular one. The other major steps in the expansion of popular participation in the United States involved the extension of the electoral principle to all the state governors, to both houses of the state legislature, to many state administrative offices and boards, to the judiciary in many states, and to the United States Senate. In Europe the broadening of participation meant the extension of the suffrage for one institution to all classes of society while in America it meant the extension of the suffrage by the one class in society to all (or almost all) institutions of government.

Why did the early and rapid expansion of political participation fail to breed violence and instability in the United States? At least in part, the answer lies in the relative complexity, adaptability, autonomy, and coherence of the traditional political institutions which existed in America in the seventeenth and eighteenth centuries. These institutions were, in particular, sufficiently variegated at the local, state, and eventually national levels so as to provide many avenues for political participation. The multiplicity of institutions furnished multiple means of access to political power. Those groups unable to influence the national government might be able to dominate state or local governments. Those who could not elect chief executives might still control legislatures or at least legislative committees. Those who were forever weak numerically might find support in judicial bodies anxious to assert their power and to locate a constituency. With rare exceptions most of the significant social and economic groups in American society in the eighteenth and nineteenth centuries could find some way of participating in government and of compounding their influence with governmental authority.

In Europe the expansion of participation was linked to the centralization of power: "the democratic movement had to be unitary and centralizing, because it had to destroy before it could construct." [73] In America, on the other hand, the expansion of participation was linked with the dispersion of power and the maintenance of the established units of government. Only a modernizing autocrat like Hamilton could advance in America the type of centralization favored by the democrats of Europe. The democratization of many institutions of government, however, equalized their power and thus moderated its own effects. At the same time it also legitimated and reinforced the pluralistic inheritance from the past. As Madison recognized, the most popular branch of government would also be the most powerful one. Time and again the establishment of links between governmental institutions and rising social forces reinvigorated political institutions which, without that connection, would have lost their powers like the monarchs and second chambers of Europe. Thus, the institutional pluralism preserved from the past first encouraged the expansion of political participation and then was strengthened by it.

In Europe the opposition to modernization within society forced the modernization of the political system. In America, the ease of modernization within society precluded the modernization of political institutions. The United States thus combines the world's most modern society with one of the world's more antique polities. The American political experience is distinguished by frequent acts of creation but few, if any, of innovation. Since the Revolution constitutions have been drafted for 38 new political systems, but the same pattern of government has been duplicated over and over again. The new constitutions of Alaska and Hawaii

73. Ibid., 2, 350–51.

in the 1950s differed only in detail from the constitution of Massachusetts, originally drafted by John Adams in 1780. When else in history has such a unique series of opportunities for political experiment and innovation been so almost totally wasted?

This static quality of the political system contrasts with the prevalence of change elsewhere in American society. A distinguishing feature of American culture, Robin Williams has argued, is its positive orientation toward change. In a similar vein, two observers have noted, "In the United States change itself is valued. The new is good; the old is unsatisfactory. Americans gain prestige by being among the first to own next year's automobile; in England, much effort is devoted to keeping twenty-five-year-old cars in operating condition." [74] In three centuries, a few pitifully small and poor rural settlements strung along the Atlantic seaboard and populated in large part by religious exiles were transformed into a huge, urbanized, continental republic, the world's leading economic and military power. America has given the world its most modern and efficient economic organizations. It has pioneered social benefits for the masses: mass production, mass education, mass culture. Economically and socially, everything has been movement and change. In governmental structure, however, the only significant institutional innovation has been federalism, and this, in itself, of course, was made possible only because of the traditional hostility to the centralization of authority. Fundamental social and economic change has thus been combined with political stability and continuity. In a society dedicated to what is shiny new, the polity remains quaintly old.

The distinctive American contributions to politics are in the organization of popular participation.[75] The one major political institution invented in America is, of course, the political party. Americans created the caucus before the Revolution and commit-

74. Robin Williams, *American Society* (2d ed. rev. New York, Knopf, 1961), p. 571; Eli Ginzberg and Ewing W. Reilley, *Effecting Change in Large Organizations* (New York, Columbia University Press, 1957), pp. 18–19.

75. So also are the distinctive American contributions to the language of politics. As was pointed out above, pp. 98, 119, many of the terms Americans use to describe their governmental institutions were once used in England but have in the course of political modernization dropped from usage there. The opposite is true with respect to the language of political participation and the institutions to organize that participation. Here many of the terms (like the institutions) were either invented in the United States (caucus, gerrymander) or were given a new and specifically political meaning (citizen, primary, machine, boss, spoils, ticket, lobby).

tees of correspondence during the revolutionary crisis. Upon these beginnings at the end of the eighteenth century they organized the first political parties. American parties, in turn, directly reflect the nature of political modernization in America. They were created in the United States before they appeared elsewhere as a response to the earlier expansion of political participation there. Ambitious politicians had to mobilize and to organize the electorate if they were to succeed in the competition for power. In New York City, in 1800, for instance, the Jeffersonian Republican leaders determined that to win the election they would have to carry New York State and to carry the state they would have to carry New York City. To achieve this end, Aaron Burr in effect innovated the party machine. Burr, as one scholar has said,

> faced severe odds, for the Federalists were ably led by his old adversary, Alexander Hamilton, who had won the previous election decisively, and the Republicans were divided. Burr quietly persuaded the older party leaders to unite on one ticket of eminent local Republicans; shrewdly waited to announce his ticket until after Hamilton had pieced together an inferior one . . . ; organized his lieutenants solidly on a ward-by-ward basis; card-indexed the voters, their political history, attitudes and how to get them to the polls; set up committees to canvass for funds from house to house; put the heat on wealthy Republicans for bigger donations; organized rallies; enlisted in his cause the members of the Tammany Society, then ? struggling fraternal group; debated publicly with Hamilton; and spent ten hours straight at the polls on the last day of the three-day election.[76]

The result was a decisive victory for Burr and for the institutional innovations which he brought to American politics.

The early expansion of political participation in America thus explains why mass political organizations originated there. In similar but reverse fashion, the absence of rationalization and differentiation and the continuation of traditional political institutions also explains why American political parties never became as strongly organized as British or Continental parties. The existence of a complex structure of government left fewer functions for

76. James MacGregor Burns, *The Deadlock of Democracy* (Englewood Cliffs, N.J., Prentice-Hall, 1963), p. 34.

parties to perform, and made their general role in the political system less important than it was in Europe. American parties tended to be looser, less cohesive, and less disciplined than European parties and they generally avoided involvement in the diversity of ancillary social and economic activities which characterized European parties, particularly of the left. American parties, in some sense, bear the same relation to European parties that American governmental institutions bear to European governmental institutions. In comparison, "American parties have a very archaic general structure." [77] Paradoxically, the form of political organization which originated in America was developed into a much stronger and complex structure in western Europe and was carried to its fullest and most complete development in the Soviet Union.

Modernity is thus not all of a piece. The American experience demonstrates conclusively that some institutions and some aspects of a society may become highly modern while other institutions and other aspects retain much of their traditional form and substance. Indeed, this may be a natural state of affairs. In any system some sort of equilibrium or balance must be maintained between change and continuity. Change in some spheres renders unnecessary or impossible change in others. In America the continuity and stability of governmental institutions has permitted the rapid change of society, and the rapid change in society has encouraged continuity and stability in government. The relation between polity and society may well be dialectical rather than complementary. In other societies, such as Latin America, a rigid social structure and the absence of social and economic change have been combined with political instability and the weakness of political institutions. A good case can be made, moreover, that the latter is the result of the former. [78]

This combination of modern society and Tudor political institutions explains much that is otherwise perplexing about political ideas in America. In Europe the conservative is the defender of traditional institutions and values, particularly those in society rather than in government. Conservatism is associated with the church, the aristocracy, social customs, the established social order. The attitude of conservatives toward government is ambivalent; it

77. Maurice Duverger, *Political Parties* (New York, John Wiley, 1954), p. 22.
78. Merle Kling, "Toward a Theory of Power and Political Instability in Latin America," *Western Political Quarterly, 9* (March 1956), 21–35.

is viewed as guarantor of social order; but it also is viewed as the generator of social change. Society rather than government has been the principal conservative concern. European liberals, on the other hand, have had a much more positive attitude toward government. Like Turgot, Price, and Godwin, they have viewed the centralization of power as the precondition of social reform. They have supported the gathering of power into a single place—first the absolute monarch, then the sovereign people—where it can then be used to change society.

In America, on the other hand, these liberal and conservative attitudes have been thoroughly confused and partly reversed. Conservatism has seldom flourished because it has lacked social institutions to conserve. Society is changing and modern, while government, which the conservative views with suspicion, has been relatively unchanging and antique. With a few exceptions, such as a handful of colleges and churches, the oldest institutions in American society are governmental institutions. The absence of established social institutions, in turn, has made it unnecessary for American liberals to espouse the centralization of power as did European liberals. John Adams could combine Montesquieu's polity with Turgot's society much to the bafflement of Turgot. Nineteenth-century Europeans had every reason to be fascinated by America; it united a liberal society which they were yet to experience with a conservative politics which they had in large part forgotten.

These conservative institutions could well change more rapidly in the future than they did in the past. External security and internal consensus have been the principal factors militating against the modernization of American political institutions. The former disappeared in the early twentieth century; the latter appears at times to be on the verge of disruption. The political institutions suited to a society which did not have to worry about external dangers may be inappropriate for one continually involved in a balance of terror, cold war, and military interventions in distant portions of the globe. So also, the problems of race relations and poverty strengthen demands for action by the national government. The needs of national defense and social reform could undermine the traditional pluralism inherited from the past and hasten the centralization of authority and structural differentiation in American political institutions.

TUDOR POLITY AND MODERNIZING SOCIETIES

Much has been made of the relevance to the currently modernizing countries of Asia, Africa, and Latin America of the earlier phases of modernization in the United States. It has been argued that the United States was and still should be a revolutionary power. The American Revolution, it has been said, "started a chain reaction" beginning with the French Revolution and leading on to the Russian Revolution, which was "the American Revolution's child, though an unwanted and unacknowledged one." [79] But the effort to see connections and/or parallels between what happened in America in the eighteenth century and what is happening in Asia, Africa, and elsewhere in the twentieth century can only contribute to monstrous misunderstandings of both historical experiences. The American Revolution was not a social revolution like the French, Russian, Chinese, Mexican, or Cuban revolutions; it was a war of independence. Moreover, it was not a war of independence of natives against alien conquerors, like the struggles of the Indonesians against the Dutch or the Vietnamese or the Algerians against the French, but instead a war of settlers against the home country. Any recent parallels are in the relations of the Algerian *colons* to the French Republic or the Southern Rhodesians to the United Kingdom. It is here, in the last of the European "fragments" to break their European ties, that the eighteenth-century experience of America may be duplicated. These, however, are not parallels of which American liberal intellectuals and statesmen like to be reminded.

The case for the relevance of the American experience to the contemporary modernizing countries has also been couched in terms of the United States as "The First New Nation." The United States, it has been argued, was the first nation "of any consequence to emerge from the colonial dominance of Western Europe as a sovereign state in its own right, and to that extent it shares something in common with the 'emerging nations' of today, no matter how different they may be in other respects." [80] The

79. Arnold J. Toynbee, "If We Are to Be the Wave of the Future," *New York Times Magazine*, Nov. 13, 1960, p. 123.

80. See Seymour Martin Lipset, *The First New Nation* (New York, Basic Books, 1963) , Part I; J. Leiper Freeman, "The Colonial Stage of Development: The American Case" (unpublished paper, Comparative Administration Group, 1963) , p. 4.

phrase "new nation," however, fails to distinguish between state and society and hence misses crucial differences between the American experience and those of the contemporary modernizing countries. The latter are, for the most part, more accurately described by the title of another book: "Old Societies and New States." [81] America, on the other hand, was historically a new society but an old state. Hence the problems of government and political modernization which the contemporary modernizing states face differ fundamentally from those which ever confronted the United States.

In most countries of Asia, Africa, and Latin America, modernization confronts tremendous social obstacles. The gaps between rich and poor, between modern elite and traditional mass, between the powerful and the weak, which are the common lot of "old societies" trying to modernize today, contrast markedly with the "pleasing uniformity" of the "one-estate" which existed in eighteenth-century America. As in seventeenth-century Europe these gaps can only be overcome by the creation of powerful, centralized authority in government. The United States never had to construct such authority in order to modernize its society, and hence its experience has little to offer modernizing countries today. America, de Tocqueville said, "arrived at a state of democracy without having to endure a democratic revolution" and "was born equal without having to become so." So also American society was born modern, and it hence was never necessary to construct a government powerful enough to make it so. An antique polity is compatible with a modern society but it is not compatible with the modernization of a traditional society.

The Latin American experience, for instance, is almost exactly the reverse of that of the United States. After independence the United States continued essentially the same political institutions which it had had before independence and which were perfectly suited to its society. At independence the Latin American countries inherited and maintained an essentially feudal social structure. They attempted to superimpose on this social structure republican political institutions copied from the United States and revolutionary France. Such institutions had no meaning in a feudal society. These early efforts at republicanism left Latin

81. See Clifford Geertz, ed., *Old Societies and New States: The Quest for Modernity in Asia and Africa* (New York, Free Press, 1963).

America with weak governments which until the twentieth century lacked the authority and power to modernize the society.
Liberal, pluralistic, democratic governments serve to perpetuate
antiquated social structure. Thus in Latin America an inherent
conflict exists between the political goals of the United States—elections, democracy, representative government, pluralism, constitutionalism—and its social goals—modernization, reform, social welfare, more equitable distribution of wealth, development of a middle class. In the North American experience these goals did not
conflict. In Latin America, they often clash head on. The variations of the North American political system which North Americans would like to reproduce in Latin America are simply too
weak, too diffuse, too dispersed to mobilize the political power
necessary to bring about fundamental change. Such power can be
mobilized by revolution, as it was in Mexico and Cuba, and an historical function of revolutions is to replace weak governments by
strong governments capable of achieving social change. The question for Latin America and similarly situated countries is whether
other ways exist short of violent revolution for generating the political power necessary to modernize traditional societies.

If a parallel exists between seventeenth-century modernization
and twentieth-century modernization, the implications of the
former for the latter are clear. Despite arguments to the contrary,
the countries where modernization requires the concentration of
power in a single, monolithic, hierarchical, but "mass" party are
not likely to be breeding grounds for democracy.[82] Mass participation goes hand-in-hand with authoritarian control. As in Guinea
and Ghana, it is the twentieth-century weapon of modernizing
centralizers against traditional pluralism. Democracy, on the other
hand, is more likely in those countries which preserve elements of
traditional social and political pluralism. Its prospects are bright-
est where traditional pluralism is adapted to modern politics, as appears to be the case with the caste associations of India and as may

82. See Immanuel Wallerstein, *Africa: The Politics of Independence* (New York,
Vintage, 1961), pp. 159–63, and Ruth Schachter (Morgenthau), "Single-Party Sys-
tems in West Africa," *American Political Science Review*, 55 (June 1961), 294–307,
for the case for the liberal and democratic potential of single-party states. For
more realistic evaluations, see Martin Kilson, "Authoritarian and Single-Party
Tendencies in African Politics," *World Politics*, 15 (Jan. 1963), 262–94, and Aristide
Zolberg, "The African Mass-Party State in Perspective," (paper prepared for APSA
Annual Meeting, September 1964).

be the case with tribal associations in some parts of Africa. So also, the most democratic Arab country—indeed, perhaps the only democratic Arab country—has a highly traditional politics of confessional pluralism.[83] Like the states of seventeenth-century Europe the non-Western countries of today can have political modernization or they can have democratic pluralism, but they cannot normally have both.

In each historical period one type of political system usually seems to its contemporaries to be particularly relevant to the needs and demands of the age. In the era of European state-building in the seventeenth century, the "pattern-state," to use Sir George Clark's phrase, was the Bourbon monarchy of France. Indeed, the new state which emerged in that century, as Clark argues, "may be called the French type of monarchy not only because it reached its strongest and most logical expression in France, but also because it was consciously and deliberately copied elsewhere from the Bourbon model."[84] This type of centralized, absolute monarchy met the paramount needs of the time. In the late eighteenth and nineteenth centuries, the pattern-state was the British parliamentary system. The countries of Europe then faced the problems of democratization and the incorporation into the polity of the lower social orders. The British system furnished the model for this phase of modernization. Today, in much of Asia, Africa, and Latin America, political systems face simultaneously the needs to centralize authority, to differentiate structure, and to broaden participation. It is not surprising that the system which seems most relevant to the simultaneous achievement of these goals is a one-party system. If Versailles set the standard for one century and Westminster for another, the Kremlin may well be the most relevant model for many modernizing countries in this century. Just as the heads of minor German principalities aped Louis XIV, so also the heads of equally small and fragile African states will ape Lenin and Mao. The primary need their countries face is the accumulation and concentration of power, not its dispersion, and it is in

83. See Lloyd I. and Susanne Hoeber Rudolph, "The Political Role of India's Caste Associations," *Pacific Affairs, 33* (March 1960) , 5–22; Lloyd I. Rudolph, "The Modernity of Tradition: The Democratic Incarnation of Caste in India," *American Political Science Review, 59,* (Dec. 1965) , 975–89; and Michael C. Hudson, "Pluralism, Power, and Democracy in Lebanon" (paper prepared for APSA Annual Meeting, September 1964) .

84. Clark, *Seventeenth Century,* pp. 83, 90–91.

Moscow and Peking and not in Washington that this lesson is to be learned.

Nor should this irrelevance of the American polity come as a great surprise. Historically foreigners have always found American society more attractive than the American polity. Even in the seventeenth and eighteenth centuries, as Beloff observes, "The political appeal of the new country was less potent than the social one." [85] De Tocqueville was far more impressed by the democracy of American society and customs than he was by its democratic institutions of government. In the last century Europeans have found much to emulate in American business organization and in American culture, but they have found little reason to copy American political institutions. Parliamentary democracies and one-party dictatorships abound throughout the world. But surely one of the striking features of world politics is the rarity of other political systems which reflect in practice the American model.

The irrelevance of the American polity to the rest of the world, however, must not be overdone. It is of little use to societies which must modernize a traditional order. But as the American experience itself demonstrates, a Tudor polity is quite compatible with a modern society. Consequently it is possible, although far from necessary, that as other societies become more fully modern, as the need to disestablish old, traditional, feudal, and local elements declines, the need to maintain a political system capable of modernization may also disappear. Such a system will, of course, have the advantage of tradition and of being associated with successful social change. So the probabilities are that it will not change greatly. But at least the possibility exists that there may be some evolution toward an American-type system. The "end of ideology" in western Europe, the mitigation of class conflict, the tendencies toward an "organic society," all suggest that the European countries could now tolerate more dispersed and relaxed political institutions. Some elements of the American system seem to be creeping back into Europe from which they were exported three centuries ago.[86]

85. Max Beloff, *The Age of Absolutism: 1660–1815* (London, Hutchinson, 1954), pp. 168–69.

86. See, e.g., Stephen Graubard, ed., *A New Europe?* (Boston, Houghton Mifflin, 1964); Stanley Hoffmann, "Europe's Identity Crisis: Between the Past and America," *Daedalus, 93* (Fall 1964), 1249, 1252–53. On the role of the courts see: Taylor Cole, "Three Constitutional Courts: A Comparison," *American Political Science Review, 53* (Dec. 1959), 963–84, and Gottfried Dietze, "America and Europe—Decline and Emergence of Judicial Review," *Virginia Law Review, 44* (Dec. 1958), 1233–72.

Judicial review has made a partial and timorous reappearance on the Continent. After de Gaulle, the constitution of the Fifth Republic might well shake down to something not too far removed from the constitution of the American Republic. In Britain Mr. Wilson was accused, before and after coming to power, of acting like Mr. President. These are small straws in the wind. They may not mean anything. But if they do mean something, they mean that the New Europe may eventually come to share some of the old institutions which the New World has preserved from an older Europe.

3. Political Change in Traditional Polities

POWER, INSTITUTIONS, AND POLITICAL MODERNIZATION

To cope successfully with modernization, a political system must be able, first, to innovate policy, that is, to promote social and economic reform by state action. Reform in this context usually means the changing of traditional values and behavior patterns, the expansion of communications and education, the broadening of loyalties from family, village, and tribe to nation, the secularization of public life, the rationalization of authority structures, the promotion of functionally specific organizations, the substitution of achievement criteria for ascriptive ones, and the furthering of a more equitable distribution of material and symbolic resources. A second requirement for a political system is the ability to assimilate successfully into the system the social forces produced by modernization and achieving a new social consciousness as a result of modernization. In due course, these social groups demand participation in the political system, and the system either provides for this participation in ways harmonious with the continued existence of the system, or it alienates the groups from the system and produces overt or covert civil strife and secession.

What political conditions, more specifically, what power conditions, are conducive to policy innovation in modernizing societies? In more complex systems, the evidence in general suggests that policy innovations are encouraged by a power distribution which is neither highly concentrated nor widely dispersed. In attempting to synthesize the literature on innovation in organizations, for instance, James Q. Wilson has concluded that the rate of proposal of innovations is directly proportional to the diversity of an organization while the rate of adoption of innovations is inversely proportional to the diversity of the organization.[1] By organizational di-

---

1. James Q. Wilson, "Innovation in Organization: Notes Toward a Theory," in James D. Thompson, ed., *Approaches to Organizational Design* (Pittsburgh, University of Pittsburgh Press, 1966), pp. 193–218.

versity he means the complexity of the organization's task structure and the complexity of its incentive system. In terms of large-
scale political systems "diversity" can be roughly equated with dispersion of power. So modified and extended, the Wilson proposition would then hold that a political system where power was dispersed would have many proposals and few adoptions and one
where power was concentrated would have few proposals but
many adoptions. Policy innovation in the United States and the
Soviet Union may indeed approximate these models.[2] As Wilson
points out, however, this double-barreled proposition in itself says
nothing about what level of diversity or what distribution of
power will produce the highest rate of innovation except to suggest that the rate will be lower at the extremes—that is where
power is totally concentrated or completely dispersed—than it will
be in the middle of the continuum.

Starting from this theory, however, it may be possible to identify some qualifications enabling us to relate the probability of innovation to the distribution of power. In the process of political
modernization today the agenda of innovation is fairly well
known. It is perhaps significant that power was more widely dispersed in the earlier countries to modernize—Great Britain, northwestern Europe, the United States—than it has been in those
which modernized later. The initial proposal of the various innovations which together constitute modernization could only take
place in societies where many groups could take the initiative. Societies which modernized later do not need the same degree of diversity or dispersion to develop proposals for modernizing innovations. Indeed, the only minimum requirement is the exposure of
at least some groups in the society to the earlier modernization of
the West. In the later modernizing societies the proposal of innovations (in the sense of their promotion within the society by
some significant social group) requires less organizational diversity and dispersion of power than it did in the earlier modernizing
societies.

The process of adoption rather than the process of proposal thus
becomes the critical phase of innovation in the later modernizing

2. Zbigniew Brzezinski and Samuel P. Huntington, *Political Power: USA/USSR*
(New York, Viking, 1964), Chap. 4. See also Mayer N. Zald and Patricia Denten,
"From Evangelism to General Service: The Transformation of the YMCA," *Admin-
istrative Science Quarterly, 8* (Sept. 1963), 214–34.

societies. These societies differ from the United States in the number and strength of the sources of opposition to modernizing reform. Traditional social forces, interests, customs, and institutions are strongly entrenched. The change or destruction of these traditional forces requires the concentration of power in the agents of modernization. Modernization is associated with a marked redistribution of power within the political system: the breakdown of local, religious, ethnic, and other power centers and the centralization of power in the national political institutions. Tribes and villages with more highly concentrated power structures innovate more easily and more rapidly than those with more dispersed power structures.[3] In towns and cities rapid economic and population growth is associated with the concentration of power in a small entrepreneurial elite. A decline in civic growth is similarly associated with a dispersion of power among a large number of groups, and the much disputed differences between Atlanta and New Haven thus become functions of age rather than method. In the United States social changes, such as desegregation, seem to take place earlier and easier in situations and organizations where power is concentrated than where it is dispersed.[4] It thus seems reasonable to conclude that in a modernizing society policy innovation will vary more or less directly with the concentration of power in its political system.

The overthrow of entrenched traditional interests often requires the mobilization of new social forces into politics, and the second key requirement of a modernizing system is the capacity to assimilate into the system the social forces which result from modernization. In many instances these will be new social groupings, e.g. entrepreneurs or urban workers, which did not exist in traditional society. At least equally important, however, is the capacity of the system to incorporate traditional social groupings which

3. See, for example, Norman E. Whitten, Jr., "Power Structure and Socio-cultural Change in Latin American Communities," *Social Forces, 43* (March 1965), 320–29, and also David E. Apter, *The Politics of Modernization* (Chicago, University of Chicago Press, 1965), Chap. 3; Ethel M. Albert, "Socio-political Organization and Receptivity to Change: Some Differences Between Ruanda and Urundi," *Southwestern Journal of Anthropology, 16* (Spring 1960), 46–74.

4. See, e.g., Kenneth Clark, "Desegregation: An Appraisal of the Evidence," *Journal of Social Issues, 9* (1953), 54–58, 72–76. H. Douglas Price's forthcoming manuscript demonstrates how the concentration of power in a city is related to rapid economic and population growth and the dispersion of power to tne decline in such growth.

acquire political consciousness during the process of modernization. The development of group consciousness leads the groups to make claims on the political system and to demand participation in the political system. The test of a system is, in some measure, its capacity to respond to these demands. Successful assimilation depends upon both the receptivity of the system and the adaptability of the entering group, that is, the willingness of the group to relinquish some of its values and claims in order to gain admittance to the system. Generally these two qualities are directly related: group adaptability is enhanced by system receptivity. Systems also tend to be more receptive to new social groups which did not previously exist in the society than they are to old social groups which were previously excluded from the system but which develop new political consciousness. The assimilation of industrial entrepreneurs and industrial workers, consequently, poses fewer problems to a modernizing society than the assimilation of peasants.

The assimilation of new groups into the political system means, in effect, the expansion of the power of the political system. Like the wealth of an economy, power in a polity exists in two dimensions not just one. It can be expanded and contracted as well as concentrated and dispersed. Power, as Parsons has said,

> has to be divided or allocated, but it also has to be produced and it has collective as well as distributive functions. It is the capacity to mobilize the resources of the society for the attainment of goals for which a general "public" commitment has been made, or may be made. It is mobilization, above all, of the action of persons and groups, which is *binding* on them by virtue of their position in the society.[5]

More generally, the amount of power in a society depends upon the number and intensity of the influence relationships within the society, that is, relationships in which action by one person or group produces changes in the behavior of another person or group. Political systems thus differ in their distribution of power and also in their accumulation of power. The increased production of wealth depends upon industrialization; so also, the increased production of power depends upon the assimilation of new

5. Talcott Parsons, "The Distribution of Power in American Society," *World Politics, 10* (1957), 140; italics in original.

groups into the political system. Economic systems differ in their capacities to expand their wealth through industrialization, that is, their receptivity to new forms of economic activity; so also, political systems differ in their capacity to expand their power through assimilation, that is, their receptivity to new types of political groups and political resources. Modern political systems differ from traditional ones in the amount of power in the system, not in its distribution. In both traditional political systems and in modern ones, power may be concentrated or dispersed. In the modern system, however, more of the society is involved in more power relationships than is true in a traditional system; more people participate politically in the former than in the latter. The modern polity simply has more power than the traditional polity.

TABLE 3.1. Political Systems and Power Configurations

Distribution of Power	Amount of Power	
	SMALL	LARGE
Concentrated	Bureaucratic empire; absolute monarchy	Totalitarian dictatorship
Dispersed	Feudalism; "pyramidal structures"	Constitutional democracy

Here again is an important difference between the American and communist approaches to political development. Americans typically tend to think of power in zero-sum terms: a gain in power for one person or group must be matched by a loss of power by other people or groups. The communist approach, on the other hand, emphasizes the "collective" or expansible aspect of power. Power is something which has to be mobilized, developed, and organized. It must be created. The American failure to recognize this is reflected in the oft expressed fears that the communists or some other hostile group may "seize" power in a backward or modernizing country. At times these statements seem to imply that power is something which may be lying around on the floor of the capitol or the presidential palace, and that a group of conspirators may sneak in and run off with it. There is a failure to recognize that most such countries are suffering from the absence of power in their political systems. There is little or none around to be grabbed, and that which does exist can be lost as easily as it can be gained. The problem is not to seize power but to make power, to mobilize groups into politics and to organize their participation in politics. This takes time, and it also usually requires struggle, and these are precisely the terms in which the communist elites view political change.

Modernization thus involves, as Frey has suggested, changes in both the distribution of power within a political system and in the amount of power in the system.[6] Logically, changes in one dimension have no necessary relationship to changes in the other dimension. Nonetheless, the two may well be connected historically. The expansion of wealth in a society is related to the allocation of wealth in the society. Poor countries typically have extremes of luxury and poverty. In the early stages of economic growth, wealth becomes even more concentrated. In later phases, however, economic expansion makes possible a broader sharing of material benefits. The wealthiest countries typically have the most equitable distribution of wealth. The relation between the concentration and expansion of power may be somewhat similar in the process of political modernization. In an early stage, modernization requires changes in traditional social, economic, and cultural beliefs and behavior, hence policy innovations, and hence the concentration of power. The gap between the powerful and the weak becomes greater. At the same time, the social and economic change encouraged by the policy innovation leads new groups to demand entry into the political system and requires the expansion of the system. In a third phase, much later, the expansion of the system may make possible a new dispersion of power within the system.

Depending upon one's perspective, one can thus define political modernization to mean either the concentration of power, the expansion of power, or the dispersion of power, and peculiarly enough, political scientists have indeed defined political modernization in each of these ways. At one point or another in a country's history, each does constitute "modernization," and in turn each poses challenges to the adaptability of the political system. Typi-

6. See Frederick W. Frey, *The Turkish Political Elite* (Cambridge, Mass., M.I.T. Press, 1965), Chap. 13 and esp. pp. 406–19, and "Political Development, Power and Communications in Turkey," in Lucian W. Pye, ed., *Communications and Political Development* (Princeton, N.J., Princeton University Press, 1963), pp. 298–305. On p. 309 n. Frey suggests that political development involves the concentration and expansion of power. See also his "Democracy and Reform in Developing Societies" (unpublished paper presented at Seminar on Political Development, University of Minas Gerais, Brazil, 1966).

cally, the first challenge of modernization to a dispersed, weakly articulated and organized, feudalistic traditional system is to concentrate the power necessary to produce changes in the traditional society and economy. The second problem is then to expand the power in the system to assimilate the newly mobilized and politically participant groups, thus creating a modern system. This challenge is the predominant one in the modernizing world today. At a later stage the system is confronted with the demands of the participant groups for a greater dispersion of power and for the establishment of reciprocal checks and controls among groups and institutions. Many of the communist states of eastern Europe are grappling with the problem of adaptation to the pressures for the dispersion of power.

Political systems thus differ according to the amount of power in the system and the distribution of power in the system. More significantly, in terms of policy innovation and group assimilation, political systems differ in their capacity to concentrate power and their capacity to expand power. These capacities of the system will be directly affected by the nature of its political institutions. Praetorian systems which lack any effective institutions are incapable of either the sustained concentration of power necessary for reform or the sustained expansion of power involved in the identification of new groups with the system. Power is neither concentratable nor expansible, except on a temporary basis. The distinctive characteristic is the rapid shift from extreme concentration to extreme dispersion and between the rapid expansion and the rapid contraction of power. At times, a populistic dictator, a charismatic leader, or a military junta may both expand power and concentrate it. But these developments are inevitably temporary and are replaced by the dispersion of power among many social forces and by the reappearance of apathy and alienation on the part of the populace. The shift back and forth between one weak dictator and many weak parties symbolizes the inability of the system to effect significant change in the accumulation or distribution of power.

At the opposite extreme, the great utility and the great appeal of the single-party system in modernizing countries is that it is an institution which, in large measure, promotes both concentration (and hence innovation) and also expansion (and hence group assimilation). In various ways the established one-party systems in Mexico and Tunisia, North Korea and North Vietnam have all demonstrated both these capacities. Similar capabilities are also likely to exist in dominant-party systems, where there is a single major party and a multiplicity of smaller, more parochial, ethnic and ideological parties. In countries with this type of system, such as India and Israel, the minor parties play a significant role as bell-wethers or warning devices, the rise and fall in their votes indicating to the dominant party the directions in which it must move to maintain its dominant position either by assimilating new groups or by innovating policies. Ideological dogma and electoral pressure combine to induce the dominant party to maintain its innovative and assimilative capacities.

More competitive two-party or multiparty systems may have considerable capacity for expansion and the assimilation of groups but less capability for the concentration of power and the promotion of reform. Political competition in a two-party system, for instance, may serve to mobilize new groups into politics and in this sense to expand the power of the system, but at the same time this mobilization also tends to divide power and to fracture the existing consensus on modernization. The typical manifestation of this is the "ruralizing election," such as took place in Turkey in 1950, in Ceylon in 1956, and in Burma in 1960.[7] The mere existence of a multiple party system, however, does not guarantee expansibility. The impetus to expand comes from competition, not multiplicity, and a political system may have many parties with little competition among them. Even in a two-party system, implicit or explicit (as in Colombia after 1957) arrangements may be made to limit the competition between the parties and thereby reduce the capacity of the system to expand its power and assimilate new groups. The ability of both traditional systems and modern ones to promote reforms and to assimilate groups thus varies with the nature of their political institutions. Modern systems will be discussed in the later chapters of this book. The question to be confronted here is: What are the capacities of the traditional monarchy for the expansion and concentration of power?

7. See below, Chapter 7, pp. 448 ff.

TRADITIONAL POLITICAL SYSTEMS

Traditional political systems come in varied shapes and sizes: village democracies, city-states, tribal kingdoms, patrimonial states, feudal polities, absolute monarchies, bureaucratic empires, aristocracies, oligarchies, theocracies. The bulk of the traditional polities which have faced the challenges of modernization, however, can be subsumed under two broad categories familiar in political analysis. "The kingdoms known to history," observed Machiavelli, "have been governed in two ways: either by a prince and his servants, who, as ministers by his grace and permission, assist in governing the realm; or by a prince and by barons, who hold their positions not by favour of the ruler but by antiquity of blood." Machiavelli cited the Turks as an example of the former, and the French polity of his day as an example of the latter. Mosca drew a somewhat similar distinction between bureaucratic and feudal states. The "feudal state" was "that type of political organization in which all the executive functions of society—the economic, the judicial, the administrative, the military—are exercised simultaneously by the same individuals, while at the same time the state is made up of small social aggregates, each of which possesses all the organs that are required for self-sufficiency." In the bureaucratic state, on the other hand, "the central power conscripts a considerable portion of the social wealth by taxation and uses it first to maintain a military establishment and then to support a more or less extensive number of public services." In a similar manner, Apter distinguishes between hierarchical and pyramidal authority structures.[8] The key element in all these distinctions is the extent to which power is concentrated or dispersed. The two historical traditional polities which are most representative of these two types are the bureaucratic empire, on the one hand, and the feudal system, on the other.

In the centralized, bureaucratic state, the king possesses, as Machiavelli says, "more authority" than he does in the dispersed feudal state. In the former he directly or indirectly appoints all the

8. Niccolò Machiavelli, *The Prince and The Discourses* (New York, The Modern Library, 1940), p. 15; Gaetano Mosca, *The Ruling Class* (New York, McGraw-Hill, 1939), pp. 80 ff.; David E. Apter, *The Politics of Modernization* (Chicago, University of Chicago Press, 1965), pp. 81 ff. See also S. N. Eisenstadt, "Political Struggle in Bureaucratic Societies," *World Politics, 9* (Oct. 1956), 18–19, and *The Political Systems of Empires* (New York, Free Press, 1963), pp. 22–24.

officials, while in the latter office and power are hereditary within an aristocratic class. The bureaucratic state, consequently, is characterized by considerable social and political mobility—those from the lowest orders may reach the highest offices—while the feudal state is more highly stratified and only rarely do men pass from one *Stand* to another. In the bureaucratic state, "there is always a greater specialization in the functions of government than in a feudal state." [9] The bureaucratic state thus tends toward the separation of functions and the concentration of power while the feudal state tends toward the fusion of functions and the division of power. In the bureaucratic state all land is often in theory owned by the king and in practice he exercises primary control over its disposition. In the feudal state land ownership is usually dispersed and hereditary; its control is in large part beyond the influence of the monarch. In the bureaucratic polity the king or emperor is the sole source of legitimacy and authority; in the feudal polity he shares this legitimacy with the nobility whose sources of authority over their subjects are independent of the monarch's authority over them. The essence of the bureaucratic state is the one-way flow of authority from superior to subordinate; the essence of the feudal state is the two-way system of reciprocal rights and obligations between those at different levels in the social-political-military structure. Clearly all the traditional political systems known to history cannot be squeezed into these two categories. Yet, all traditional polities are characterized by a greater or lesser centralization of power, and the mere fact that these categories have constantly reappeared in political analysis suggests that they do have a general relevance and validity.

In addition to this differentiation in terms of overall functional specialization and distribution of power, it is also possible to distinguish between traditional political systems in terms of the role of the monarch. In some polities, bureaucratic or feudal, the monarch may play a passive role. He reigns and does not rule, but neither popular sovereignty nor party sovereignty is accepted in principle and neither is institutionalized in electoral procedures, parties, and parliaments. The king remains the principal source of legitimacy in the system, but actual power is exercised by a bureaucratic or feudal oligarchy acting in his name. Thailand and

9. Mosca, p. 83.

Laos were oligarchical monarchies in the mid-twentieth century; Japan was in the nineteenth and early twentieth centuries. In other traditional polities, bureaucratic or feudal, the monarch may play an active role. He is the principal source of legitimacy and in addition he rules as well as reigns. A ruling monarchy is not necessarily an absolute monarchy. The actual powers of government may be shared with other institutions and groups, but in all cases the monarch also plays an active, efficient, political role in the governing process. Twentieth-century ruling monarchies range from those which closely approximate the absolute model, such as Ethiopia and Saudi Arabia, through those in which some institutional and constitutional restraints exist on the monarch (such as Iran and Afghanistan), to those in which there may be active competition and collaboration between the monarch, on the one hand, and armies, parliaments, and political parties, on the other (Morocco, Greece).

TABLE 3.2. Traditional Political Systems

Political Structure	Role of Monarch	
	ACTIVE (RULING)	PASSIVE (OLIGARCHICAL)
Centralized (Bureaucratic)	Roman Empire Ethiopia China	Korea Meiji Japan Thailand
Dispersed (Feudal)	Medieval Europe	Tokugawa Japan

Both the oligarchical monarchy and the ruling monarchy are, of course, traditional political systems, and hence must be distinguished from the modern, parliamentary monarchy. In the latter the monarch reigns, but the ultimate source of legitimacy lies not in him but in the people. The monarch is the chief of state, the symbol of national continuity, identity, and unity. The efficient powers of government are exercised by a cabinet produced by political parties and responsible to a popularly elected parliament. The efficient powers of the monarch are usually limited to the possibility of exercising some discretion in the selection of a prime minister if no single leader or party commands a clear majority in parliament. This is, of course, the familiar form of constitutional monarchy found in the British Commonwealth, the Low Countries, Scandinavia, and modern Japan.

The pattern of change by which these various types of traditional political systems have introduced reforms into their societies and assimilated groups into their polities can, of course, be seen in full in the evolution of the historical bureaucratic empires of Europe and Asia (e.g. Russian, Ottoman, Chinese) and in the evolution of European monarchies and principalities from medieval times down through the nineteenth century. The lessons to be learned from such study are, however, not only of historical interest. Indeed, the experience of the traditional monarchies highlights many of the dilemmas of political modernization which in

TABLE 3.3. Types of Contemporary Monarchies

| | Traditional | | Modern |
	RULING	OLIGARCHICAL	PARLIAMENTARY
Principal function of monarch	Rule and reign	Reign	Reign
Principal source of legitimacy	Monarchy	Monarchy	People
Principal efficient authorities	Monarchy, bureaucracy, army, and perhaps parties	Army and bureaucracy	Cabinet, parties and parliament
Scope of political participation	Narrow to medium	Narrow	Broad

less dramatic form confront other types of states as well. In addition, there still remain in the contemporary world a number of antique and rather curious political systems in which legitimacy and power reside largely in the highly traditional institutions of an hereditary monarchy. Most of these monarchies exist today in countries which are beginning to undergo rapid social, economic, and cultural change. One purpose of our analysis is to explore the problems which modernization poses to such traditional political systems. To what extent are kings simply the doomed relics of a fading historical era? Can monarchial systems cope with modernizing problems? To what extent are the political evolutions of such regimes likely to be in the direction of democracy, dictatorship, or revolution?

In the 1960s perhaps fifteen of the world's sovereign entities were ruling or oligarchical monarchies, and remnants of tribal monarchies still existed in Uganda, Burundi, Lesotho, and perhaps elsewhere in Africa. No traditional monarchy was a major power, but Iran, Ethiopia, and Thailand had each more than twenty million people, and a total of about 150,000,000 people throughout the world lived under this type of political system. In comparison with other less developed countries, the monarchies tended to rank fairly low on most indices of social and economic development. In 1957, to be sure, in terms of per capita income, both the richest country in the world (Kuwait, $2,900) and the poorest (Nepal, $45) were ruling monarchies. But the general pattern is quite different. Eight of 14 traditional monarchies had per capita national incomes of $100 or less; four ranked between $100 and $200, only two had per capita incomes over $200. So also, in only two of the 14 countries was more than half of the population literate, while in ten less than 20 per cent of the population was literate. In 11 of the 14 less than a quarter of the people lived in cities over 20,000 population, and in eight countries less than 10 per cent of the population lived in cities this size.[10]

While the traditional monarchies were typically at low levels of economic and social development, they also, typically, suffered somewhat less from problems of national identity and national integration than do most underdeveloped countries. Most ruling monarchies did not experience colonial rule or else had relatively indirect or brief experiences with colonial rule. They were typically located where the competing imperialisms of larger powers collided with each other and produced a stand-off which enabled the smaller, indigeneous monarchy to maintain its independence, however shakily. Thailand was between the English and the French, Nepal between China and India, Afghanistan and Iran between the English and the Russians, Ethiopia at the juncture point of English, French, and Italian imperialisms. The colonial experiences of Libya and Morocco were, in some measure, limited by the competition between Great Britain and Italy, on the one hand, and France and Spain, on the other. Most of the other contemporary traditional monarchies were in the Arabian peninsula, in large parts of which neither Ottoman nor European rule was effectively exercised. In some instances, such as Ethiopia, Thailand, and Iran, claims could be made for the continuous existence of the monarchy through several centuries. While several tradi-

10. Figures are from Russett et al., *World Handbook of Political and Social Indicators.*

tional monarchies, such as Morocco and Ethiopia, had substantial ethnic minorities, even their problems of national integration seemed relatively simple compared to those of most countries in Asia and Africa. One key problem for traditional monarchies, consequently, was how to preserve the headstart which independence and national institutions of authority gave them in the face of the needs for rapid social and economic change and for broader political participation which challenges the capabilities of those institutions.

The traditional monarchies thus posed fascinating problems for the student of political development. Their fate, however, was also of some interest to policy-makers. As a result of the historical conditions associated with their continued independence, many traditional monarchies occupied strategic geographical positions. At one time or another, Greece, Iran, Afghanistan, Thailand, and Laos, were all the focus of Cold War struggles. Morocco, Libya, Saudi Arabia, Ethiopia, and Thailand were sites of important American overseas bases. In addition, most of the traditional monarchies were on the Western side in the Cold War. The United States, consequently, had a significant interest in their future political development. The replacement of their political systems by revolution, chaos, instability, or radically nationalist regimes presumably would be less in the American national interest than the peaceful evolution of those political systems. Finally, while the traditional monarchies are, in general, no richer and no poorer in natural resources than other developing states, they have played a key role in the production of one of the crucial essentials of a modern economy. Between one fifth and one quarter of the world's oil comes from countries where the king rules as well as reigns.

POLICY INNOVATION: REFORM VS. LIBERTY

Traditional monarchies are, in today's world, rarely, if ever, traditionalizing monarchies. The monarchial oligarchies are (like the Meiji samurai, the Young Turks, or the Thai Promoters of 1932) modernizing oligarchies and the ruling monarchs are modernizing monarchs. Modernization has thinned the ranks of monarchs, but produced a higher proportion of modernizing monarchies than ever existed before in history. The impetus of these rulers toward reform and change may well be greater than among the less traditional, nationalist leaders who have come to power following the retreat of Western imperialism. The latter can claim modern legitimacy, and hence can afford to devote more attention to the spoils of power. The traditional legitimacy of the former, in contrast, is more open to question. They must prove themselves by good works. Thus they become the protagonists of the royal revolution from above. In so doing, they fall, of course, into a familiar mold, populated by the centralizing and nation-building monarchs of seventeenth- and eighteenth-century Europe and by such diverse nineteenth-century types as Mahmud II, Alexander II, Chulalongkorn, and the Taewongun.

While the patterns of monarchial innovation and centralization are strikingly similar across centuries and cultures, the primary incentives and motives behind these changes have shifted significantly over the years. For the absolute monarchies of seventeenth-century Europe external threats and conflicts furnished the principal impetus to innovation and centralization. The "defensive modernization" by non-Western states in the nineteenth century stemmed from similar fear of foreign invasion and conquest. The dispersion of power and the absence of modernizing innovations could be maintained only so long as the society remained isolated from outside threats. Japanese feudalism (like American pluralism) persisted into the late nineteenth century, because "the pressure of the international struggle, which in other cases enforced reform and the elimination of feudalism, was entirely absent from Japan for two centuries in Tokugawa times." [11] The inability to continue this isolation produced the Meiji era of centralization and reform.

Similarly the eighteenth-century dispersion of power in the Ottoman Empire between the Sultan and the Grand Vezir and among "the three great engines of state—the military, the bureaucratic, and the religious" could not be maintained once the armies of the French Revolution appeared in the Middle East. Selim III and Mahmud II became "convinced that this reciprocity of power, this mutuality of influence with regard to specific issues, was a barrier to Ottoman progress in the face of Western pressure. They believed that centralization of power in the hands of the Sultan was a prerequisite to modernization." [12] So also, the

11. Rushton Coulborn, "The End of Feudalism," in Coulborn, ed., *Feudalism in History* (Hamden, Conn., Archon Books, 1965), p. 303.

12. Frey, "Political Development, Power and Communications," pp. 310–11.

Opium War stimulated the first glimmerings of reform in China; the Japanese victory over China in 1895 led to the "One Hundred Days" of 1898; and the intervention of Western powers following the Boxer Rebellion even converted the Dowager Empress to the cause.

In Iran, the increasing incursions from the Russians and British plus the Japanese victory over Russia in 1905 led to the constitutionalist movement, and the post-World War I policies of Reza Shah were clearly motivated in large part by the desire to preserve the territorial integrity and independence of his country against British and possible Russian influence. In Russia itself the reforms of Alexander II followed hard on the catastrophes of the Crimean War and those of Stolypin were made possible by the Japanese victory in 1905. If the existing dynasty or monarchy proved incapable of inaugurating reforms itself, it might well be overthrown and replaced by a new dynasty (as in Iran) or the monarchy might be displaced entirely, as in Turkey after World War I or in Egypt after the Palestine War. Political modernization is thus often the child of military failure. Success in modernization and in the centralization of power, conversely, increases the probability of military success. In Africa, for instance, the "successful national aggrandizement" of the Baganda was associated with the centralized, hierarchical despotism of the Kabaka.[13]

For the traditional monarchies of the twentieth century, security considerations have undoubtedly also loomed large. Perhaps even more important, however, has been the recognition of the need for modernization for domestic reasons. The principal threat to the stability of a traditional society comes not from invasion by foreign armies but from invasion by foreign ideas. The printed and the spoken word can move quicker and penetrate further than can regiments and tanks. The stability of twentieth-century traditional monarchies is endangered from within rather than from without. The monarch is forced to modernize and to attempt to change his society by the fear that if he does not, someone else will. Nineteenth-century monarchs modernized to thwart imperialism; twentieth-century monarchs modernize to thwart revolution.

The priorities of innovation in traditional monarchies vary with the nature of the traditional polity. In a bureaucratic polity, authority is already centralized, and the principal problem is to con-

13. Apter, *Modernization*, p. 104.

vert the traditional bureaucracy to the implementation of modernizing reforms. In a feudal system or other traditional polity where power is widely dispersed, the indispensable prerequisite to policy innovation is the centralization of power. The crucial struggle is between the monarch and his bureaucratic servants, on the one hand, and the autonomous centers of traditional power, local, aristocratic, and religious, on the other. The effective opposition to the monarch varies inversely with the extent to which the society is bureaucratized. To implement his modernizing reforms, the monarch has to pursue centralization with unflagging zest. Seventeenth-century European monarchs struggled, in most cases successfully, to end the medieval diffusion of authority, to abolish the estates, and to establish secular authority over the church. The pattern was repeated in the non-Western monarchies as they became affected by Western influence. Mahmud II was appropriately termed the Peter the Great of the Ottoman Empire. "The first essential of this task, as Mahmud saw it, was the centralization of all power in his own hands, and the elimination of all intermediate authorities, both in the capital and in the provinces. All power deriving from inheritance, from tradition, from usage, or from popular or local assent was to be suppressed, and the sovereign power alone was to remain the sole source of authority in the Empire." So also, in twentieth-century Ethiopia, the principal goal of Haile Selassie has been "to eliminate once and for all the semi-autonomous strength of the powerful provincial nobles and to centralize power and prestige in his person to a degree never before realized in Ethiopia." [14]

Modernization frequently requires not only a shift in power from regional, aristocratic, and religious groups to central secular, national institutions, but also the concentration of authority in a single individual within those institutions. The claims of the state and of the nation have to be asserted by the monarch against the more parochial claims of family, class, and clan. The "birthday" of the modern state in France, when Louis XIII rejected the Queen Mother and her claims for family in favor of Richelieu and his claims for the state, has been replicated in most twentieth-century

14. Bernard Lewis, *The Emergence of Modern Turkey* (London, Oxford University Press, 1961), p. 88; Donald N. Levine, "Ethiopia: Identity, Authority, and Realism," in Pye and Verba, eds., *Political Culture and Political Development*, p. 272; Levine, *Wax and Gold* (Chicago, University of Chicago Press, 1965), pp. 212–13; Margery Perham, *The Government of Ethiopia* (London, Faber and Faber, 1947), p. 76. See, in general, Eisenstadt, "Political Struggle," pp. 15–33.

monarchies. The birthday of the modern state in Afghanistan might be set as March 12, 1963, when King Mohammed Zahir ousted his cousin Mohammed Daud as effective ruler of the country and banned future participation in politics by members of the royal family. For Saudi Arabia the modern state may date from March 20, 1964, when the replacement of King Saud by Prince Faisal, in effect, represented the assertion of the priority of public objectives and public needs over the claims of family and kinship; the immense personal expenditures by the king, his relatives, and his offspring were cut back from over 15 per cent to 6 per cent of the national budget and the funds saved assigned to education, communication, and social welfare. This transfer of power involved an intense political struggle between Faisal and Saud which split the royal family and came close to open violence.

The priority which modernizing monarchs accord to particular reforms varies from one country to another. No monarch starts out with an entirely traditional society, and most countries which modernize in this manner require a succession of modernizing monarchs. The prerequisite of reform, however, is the consolidation of power. Hence, first attention is given to the creation of an efficient, loyal, rationalized, and centralized army. Military power must be unified. The prerequisite to all his other reforms for Mahmud II was the suppression of the Janissaries. So also Manelik in Ethiopia and Reza Shah in Iran gave first attention to the creation of a centralized military force. The second priority is, typically, to create a more effective government bureaucracy. If the traditional polity already possesses a large bureaucracy with some specialization of function and recruitment based on achievement according to traditional criteria, the problems of reforming the bureaucracy are likely to be overwhelming. For this reason, reform in the centralized bureaucratic empires (e.g. Russian, Chinese, and Ottoman) was more difficult to implement and in general less extensive than was reform in polities which had been feudal in character and consequently where the creation of administrative services could start de novo. In these circumstances, as in the absolute monarchies of Europe, the monarch was able to bring in more new men and to employ social and political mobility to his own advantage. The transition from traditional ascription to modern achievement, in short, is easier than the transition from traditional achievement to modern achievement.

Military and administrative reform provide both the impetus

and the means for changes in the society. The increased activity of the government typically requires more drastic reorganization of the fiscal system and the imposition of new, indirect taxes on customs and commerce. Changes in the legal system, encouragement of economic development and industrialization, expansion of transportation and communications, improvements in public health, increases in the quality and quantity of education, alteration of traditional social mores (on such matters as the role of women), and steps toward secularization and the divorce of the religious bodies from public affairs usually follow. Effectuating changes such as these obviously requires patience and fortitude. In most societies, periods of intensive reform alternate with periods of quiescence or even of traditionalizing countermoves. Even more than for the modern reformer, the traditional reformer has to move slowly if he is to succeed at all. Once the old order has been overthrown, the dominant atmosphere in a society is usually sympathetic to the idea of reform.

Within a traditional society, however, the royal reformer is obviously in a minority. Consequently, to act too quickly and too sweepingly is to mobilize latent opposition into active opposition. The Hundred Days of Kuang Hsu in 1898 provide one dramatic example of how the effort to do everything at once brings everything to a speedy halt. A somewhat similar and almost equally unsuccessful case of imperial utopianism is furnished by the Revolutionary Emperor, Joseph II, who between 1780 and 1790 tried out on the Hapsburg domains almost every reform which the French Revolution was later to introduce into France. He attacked and subordinated the church, ordering the abolition of the contemplative religious orders and the confiscation of their property, the shift in responsibility for the poor from church to state, the toleration of Protestants, the supremacy of civil courts in marriage, and the incorporation of the clergy into the state bureaucracy. He established equal penalties for nobles and commoners convicted of crimes. He opened the civil service to the bourgeoisie and the Army to the Jews. He attacked serfdom, declaring that every peasant should be a citizen, an entrepreneur, a taxpayer, and a potential soldier. Peasants were to have secure tenure of their land with freedom to sell and to mortgage it. He wanted a uniform tax on land, with "no difference between the possessions of men, to whatever estate or order they might belong."

Five months before the fall of the Bastille, he issued a dramatic decree providing that peasants should own their own land, keeping 70 per cent of their income for themselves, and paying 18 per cent to their former landlords and 12 per cent to the state.[15] In effect, a revolution from above had been tried and had failed in the Austro-Hungarian empire before the revolution from below started in France.

The principal political forces in a traditional society are usually the monarch, the church, the landowning aristocracy, and the army. If the polity is heavily bureaucratized or becomes so, the civil officials also assume a crucial role. As modernization proceeds, new groupings emerge including, first, an intelligentsia, then a commercial or entrepreneurial group, and then professional and managerial types. In due course an urban working class may develop and eventually the peasantry, which has existed outside the political realm, becomes politically aware and active. The problem of the monarch attempting to reform a traditional society is to create and to maintain a favorable balance among these social forces. The religious authorities, the landowners, the military, and the bureaucracy are preeminent in the first stages of modernization. The success of the monarch depends in large part on the extent to which he can win the support of the latter two against the former two. To the extent that the monarch remains dependent upon the support of the church and the aristocracy he will be limited in his ability to undertake reform. If the church is an integral part of the traditional establishment, the success of the monarch depends upon his ability to expand his authority over it, to secure control over its appointments and its finances. In these cases, as in the Ottoman Empire and in twentieth-century Ethiopia and Morocco, conflict between church and monarch will probably be muted and delayed. The church will, in some measure, be like the army: a source of traditional loyalty to the institution of monarchy despite the undoubted opposition of its top leaders to the policies which the monarch pursues. On the other hand, if church and state are separate, if the church has an autonomous hierarchy and independent control of land and wealth, it is very likely to be an active source of opposition to the monarch. A landowning aristocracy is inherently independent of the monarch and is almost in-

15. See R. R. Palmer's discussion, *The Age of the Democratic Revolution, 1,* 373–84.

evitably opposed to his reforms. The success of the monarch, consequently, depends upon his ability to develop a bureaucracy with a corporate interest distinct from that of the aristocracy and recruited at least in part from nonaristocratic elements of the population. The growth of despotism is thus associated with increased social and political mobility.

The principal political division in a modernizing monarchy is thus between the monarch and his bureaucratic supporters, on the one hand, and the religious and aristocratic opposition, on the other. The goal of the latter is the preservation of the traditional society and their privileged position within that society. In struggling to achieve this goal, their interests, as traditional and conservative as they may be, eventually lead them to espouse and to articulate modern values of liberty, constitutionalism, representative government against the monarch's goals of reform and centralization. This poses the classic dilemma of the first phase of political modernization: traditional pluralism confronts modernizing despotism, liberty is pitted against equality. R. R. Palmer aptly summed up this dilemma in his description of the Belgian revolt of 1787 against the modernizing reforms of Joseph II:

> The issue was clear. It was between social change and constitutional liberty. Reform could come at the cost of arbitrary government overriding the articulate will and historic institutions of the country. Or liberty would be preserved at the cost of perpetuating archaic systems of privilege, property, special rights, class structure, and ecclesiastical participation in the state. . . . It was a revolution against the innovations of a modernizing government—in a sense, a revolution *against* the Enlightenment. It was not in this respect untypical of the time.[16]

What was true of the Hapsburg domains in the eighteenth century was repeated in the Romanov and Ottoman Empires in the nineteenth century. In the late 1850s as Alexander II moved to emancipate the serfs, he was met by proposals from the nobility for a national assembly. These moves to limit imperial power were supported by both "oligarchs who desired to increase the influence of the nobility and genuine believers in constitutionalism. . . ." Alexander II vigorously pushed emancipation but rejected as-

16. Ibid., *1*, 347; italics in original.

semblies on the ground that they would "establish in our country an oligarchic form of government." The interests of the serfs, as W. E. Mosse says, were far safer in the hands of the tsar and his officials in the Ministry of the Interior "than in those of any elected assembly possible in Russia at that time. It is easy to imagine what would have happened to liberation in a 'constitutional' assembly dominated by the 'planters' and their friends." [17] Here truly was a case where despotism "can be a liberating force, which, by 'breaking the chain of custom which lies so heavy on the savage,' may clear the way for more complex institutions, for a wider and more varied range of human action." [18]

In the Ottoman Empire Mahmud II was followed in 1839 by Sultan Abdulmecid who inaugurated in the so-called Tanzimat a new period of reform. These reforms eventually gave rise to a constitutional opposition, the Young Ottomans, generated, like most oppositions, in Paris. Its leader, Namik Kemal, was inspired by Montesquieu and wanted to replace Ottoman absolutism with a constitutional system. All of this sounds liberal and modern. In actual fact, however, Namik Kemal had to appeal to traditionalism to find restraints which could be applied to an Ottoman sultan. In effect, he became a defender of Islamic traditions against the Tanzimat reforms. He argued that the reforms had abolished old rights and privileges without creating new ones; that the Sultan should be subordinate to Islamic law; that at one time the Ottoman Empire had possessed representative bodies which should be reestablished; and that, indeed, the Janissaries, the bulwark of the old order, which Mahmud II had displaced in 1826, were in reality the "armed consultative assembly of the nation." [19] What a peculiar and fascinating combination of modern liberalism and traditional pluralism! The Young Ottomans successfully overthrew the sultan in 1876 and forced his successor to adopt a constitution modeled on the Belgian Constitution of 1831. The constitution, however, functioned for all of about a year. The new sultan, Abdulhamid, dissolved parliament in 1878 and reestablished the partnership of despotism and reform.

17. W. E. Mosse, *Alexander II and the Modernization of Russia* (London, English Universities Press, 1958) , pp. 69–70, 131–32.

18. C. C. Wrigley, "The Christian Revolution in Buganda," *Comparative Studies in Society and History*, 2 (Oct. 1959) , 48, quoting J. G. Frazer, *Lectures on the Early History of the Kingship* (London, Macmillan, 1905) , p. 86.

19. See Lewis, *Emergence of Modern Turkey*, pp. 137–56.

The constitutionalist movement in Iran, at the turn of the century, was a similar combination of traditionalism and liberty. In 1896 a new monarch ascended the Iranian throne who lacked the prestige of his predecessor. Many Persians had also been traveling abroad and absorbed ideas of limited government. In 1906 the country suddenly erupted into revolt and the Shah was forced to grant a constitution, again one, incidentally, modeled on the Belgian Constitution of 1831. Again the combination of forces which produced this step toward constitutionalism was a motley crew, including on its liberal side students, merchants, intellectuals, and in its traditionalist wing tribal groups, religious leaders, and the civic guilds. The Iranian Constitution was more successful than the Ottoman Constitution; it is, indeed, still in effect today. But its authority varied inversely with the speed of modernization and reform. During the 1920s and 1930s Reza Shah quietly forgot about the constitution while he modernized his country. Similarly, the most significant reform which his son, Mohammed Shah, undertook, the land reform of 1961–62, was accomplished only when the Shah also evaded the constitution and got rid of Parliament.

Against the liberal-conservative opposition, where does the modernizing monarch secure support for his reforms? His problem is a ticklish one. The policies of the monarchy are reformist; but the institution of monarchy is highly traditional. Just as his opponents combine traditional pluralists and modern constitutionalists, so also must the modernizing monarch build a coalition to support himself from both modernizing and traditional sources. In practice, modernizing monarchs may receive support from four sources, three within their society and one outside it.

The first and most crucial source of support is, of course, the state bureaucracy. The bureaucracy is the natural enemy of the aristocracy, and through his control of the bureaucracy the monarch can bring individuals from nonaristocratic social groups into positions of power. Normally, however, he cannot do this on a wholesale basis without weakening the authority of the bureaucracy and possibly provoking more stubborn and outright aristocratic resistance. He can promote individuals but not social groups. He must, instead, attempt to blend new men and old in his bureaucracy so that it retains the prestige of the latter while serving the ends of the former. The most important element in the bureaucracy is, of course, the military officer corps. In many cases, such as the Ottoman Empire, the military officers may share the goals of the monarch. In other instances, such as Iran and Ethiopia, the dominant elements in the officer corps may have essentially traditional values but for that very reason remain loyal to the monarch because he is the traditional source of authority. In any event, the power of the monarch in large part depends on his army and the recognition of an identity of interest between the army and the crown.

A determined monarch and an efficient bureaucracy can have considerable impact on a traditional society. Rarely, however, will their power be sufficient to put through significant reforms. They need the support of other groups. In western Europe, of course, the classic source of such support was the middle class: the new financial, commercial, and eventually industrial bourgeoisie. In many societies, however, the middle class is not strong enough to be helpful. The great problem with the Revolutionary Emperor, as Palmer points out, was that Joseph's position "expressed no general or public demand, no groups of interested parties with formulated ideas and habits of working together. There was no one to whom he could appeal. His important followers were his own bureaucrats and officials." [20] In the Hapsburg realms, there simply were not sufficient middle-class elements to give the monarch effective support. In many modernizing monarchies the tradition of etatism, of officialdom being the preferred career for the indigenous elite groups, prevents the emergence of an autonomous middle class. Commercial and financial functions are performed by ethnic minorities—Greeks and Armenians in the Ottoman Empire and in Ethiopia, Chinese in Thailand—who consequently cannot be a major source of political support.

In addition, even if there is an indigenous middle class, it may well be a source of opposition to the monarch. In the eighteenth century Voltaire and the new middle class could enthuse over benevolent despotism. This was before the era of popular sovereignty and political parties. The ideology and outlook of twentieth-century intellectuals and middle-class groups, however, tends to describe even the most benevolent despotism as a feudal anachronism. Monarchy is simply out of style in middle-class circles. However much they may support the social and economic policies

20. Palmer, *Democratic Revolution*, *1*, 381.

of the modernizing monarch, they oppose the monarchy as an institution. They oppose the restrictions a modernizing monarchy imposes on freedom of communication, elections, and parliaments, and they inevitably see the monarch's reforms as too little and too late, an insincere sop designed to mask a hard commitment to the preservation of the status quo. Hence, in a country like Iran the urban middle class, far from being a source of support for the modernizing monarchy, ranks with the traditional clergy as its most deadly enemy. The intensity of middle-class opposition, indeed, normally exceeds that of all other social groups.

A third potential source of support consists of the masses of the population. Kings are usually popular, or at least more popular than local aristocrats and feudal landowners. Many of the reforms proposed by the monarchs benefit the large masses of the common people, in the countryside and in the cities. In the 1860s in Korea the Taewongun mobilized support from the lower classes and other previously outcaste groups in his effort to centralize power and to push modernizing reforms. In Buganda the chiefly oligarchy regularly attempted to limit the authority of each new monarch. But, "in each case, the Kabaka has appealed over the heads of the chiefs and the administration to the public and has succeeded in mustering popular support for the traditional idea of the all-powerful king." [21] There are, however, many problems involved in obtaining and maintaining such broader support. The appeal to the masses, much more than to the bourgeoisie, is liable to provoke even more extreme opposition on the part of the traditional elite, this in accord with the general proposition that ingroups are more likely to take in new groups than old out-groups. Second, the fears of the aristocrats may well be justified, the appeal to the masses may go too far, and the peasants may take things into their own hands. Joseph II had this problem when the peasants reacted to his sweeping agrarian reform by refusing to work and to pay taxes or rent to anyone, and by plundering the houses and estates and attacking the persons of their former landlords. Third, while the masses may well be capable of spontaneous and erratic violence, they are not likely to be capable of sustained, organized, intelligent political support, and a monarch is ill-equipped to organize broad-based popular groups. A final difficulty is that fre-

21. Lloyd Fallers, "Despotism, Status Culture and Social Mobility in an African Community," *Comparative Studies in Society and History, 2* (1959) , 30.

quently the masses do not share the goals of the monarch. On fairly specific bread-and-butter economic issues, such as agrarian reforms which will benefit the peasants at the expense of the landed aristocracy, there will be a coincidence of interest. The long-run stability of the monarchy, as Stolypin and Amini recognized, may well depend upon its ability to mobilize peasant support by means of such reforms. But on other issues of legal reform, secularization, changes in customs, even education, the masses, particularly the peasant masses, may be very traditional, and they may well line up behind other traditional elites, such as the clergy or the local landlords, to oppose the modernizing policies of the monarch.

A fourth potential source of support is a foreign government or some other body outside the political system. For a modernizing monarch who is a stranger in his own country this may well be a highly undesirable but necessary source of backing. The support of the United States was for a time an indispensable element in the coalition which kept the Shah of Iran in power. Here the roles and the interplay of all the various social forces can be seen quite clearly. The opposition to the Shah came from the nationalist middle class and from the traditional clergy. His principal sources of support were the army, the bureaucracy, and the United States. Originally the landed aristocracy was also identified with the monarchy. As a result of the crisis of 1961, however, the government came to view the current opposition of the landlords as less of a risk than the future opposition of the peasantry. In effect, the government tried to reconstitute its coalition, to bring into politics new social forces, consisting of small landlords and peasantry, which would furnish it with a popular base and reduce its dependence on the security forces and the United States. In Iran support by a foreign power bought time for the modernizing monarch to try to develop broader sources of support from among his own people.

Support from external sources, however, also endangers the ability of the monarch to capitalize on what in the long-run may be the most potent sentiments among all groups in the society, the sentiments of nationalism. Those monarchs survive who identify themselves with popular nationalism; those monarchs perish who remain more committed to traditional values, class perspectives, and family interests than to national ones. The fate of rulers of multinational empires, such as the Ottoman empire or the Austro-Hungarian empire, is a foregone conclusion. So also a foreign dynasty such as the Manchus has difficulty identifying itself with the rising spirit of nationalism both because of its own foreign origins and because of its inability to defend the country against the incursions of other foreigners. In Japan, on the other hand, the throne became identified with the assertion of nationalism and the new military and industrial programs designed to insure national independence, and state Shinto was developed as the link between the new patriotism and the old imperial values.

In Iran, Reza Shah was able to make himself the institutional embodiment of Iranian nationalism against foreign influence during the 1920s and 1930s. The crisis of the monarchy in the 1940s and early 1950s stemmed largely from the fact that his son proved incapable of monopolizing Iranian nationalist sentiments. Instead these became increasingly expressed through the National Front, which directed its ire first at the Russians and then at the British and Americans. When the climax came, foreign support and intervention played some role—and perhaps a decisive role—in keeping the Shah on his throne. The price was the intensification of middle-class and reactionary nationalist opposition to the monarchy. In the decade after 1953 the Shah made major efforts to develop a contrast between his "positive nationalism" and the "negative nationalism" of Mossadeq and the National Front. But many groups still felt that the monarch was in some measure disloyal to the nation he governed. In terms of support from his own polity a monarch should aim to be dethroned by a foreign power rather than maintained by such powers. The exiling by the French and the British of the Sultan of Morocco and the Kabaka of Buganda in the last stages of colonial rule made possible the subsequent return of these kings to their thrones with the overwhelmingly enthusiastic support of their people.

GROUP ASSIMILATION: PLURALISM VS. EQUALITY

"A bureaucratic state," Mosca argues, "is just a feudal state that has advanced and developed in organization and so grown more complex"; bureaucratic states are characteristic of societies at higher "levels of civilization," feudal states, of societies at more primitive levels of civilization.[22] This relation between political

22. Mosca, p. 81.

form and level of development seems reasonable enough. In contrast to feudal polities, bureaucratic systems do manifest more differentiated political institutions, more complicated administrative structures, greater specialization and division of labor, more equality of opportunity and social mobility, and greater predominance of achievement criteria over ascriptive ones. All these features presumably reflect a higher level of political modernization than is found in dispersed or feudal polities. At the same time, the centralization of power in the bureaucratic polity enhances the capability of the state to bring about modernizing reforms in society.

Yet the equation of modernity with centralization and the ability to innovate policy is incomplete at best. In fact, the more "modern" a traditional polity becomes in this sense, the more difficulty it has in adapting to the expansion of participation which is the inevitable consequence of modernization. The power which is sufficiently concentrated in the monarchy to promote reform may become too concentrated to assimilate the social forces released by reform. Modernization creates new social groups and new social and political consciousness in old groups. A bureaucratic monarchy is quite capable of assimilating individuals; more than any other traditional political system it provides avenues of social mobility for the intelligent and the artful. Individual mobility, however, clashes with group participation. The hierarchy and centralization of power which makes it easier for the monarchy to absorb individuals also creates obstacles to the expansion of power necessary to assimilate groups.

The problem is at root one of legitimacy. The legitimacy of the reforms depends on the authority of the monarch. But the legitimacy of the political system in the long run depends upon the participation within it of a broader range of social groups. Elections, parliaments, political parties are the methods of organizing that participation in modern societies. Yet the modernizing reforms of the traditional monarch require the absence of elections, parliaments, and political parties. The success of the reforms, on the other hand, undermines the legitimacy of the monarchy. The support for the monarchy in the traditional society came originally from groups which were loyal to it as a traditional institution even though they may have disapproved of its modernizing policies. As society changes, however, new groups appear which may approve of the modernizing tendencies of the monarch but which disapprove thoroughly of the monarchy as an institution. The broadening of participation in traditional society in the early stages of evolution benefits traditional forces. It is precisely for this reason that the monarch weakens or abolishes traditional assemblies, estates, councils, and parliaments. The success of the monarch's reforms then produces groups sympathetic to modernization and anxious to participate in politics but lacking the institutional means for doing so.

This dilemma is a product of the distinctive character of the monarchy as an institution. The modernizing policies of the monarch require the destruction or weakening of the traditional institutions which could have facilitated the expansion of political participation. The traditional character of the monarchy as an institution, on the other hand, makes difficult if not impossible the creation of modern channels and institutions of political participation. Other types of elites working through other types of institutions may be able both to promote reform from above and also to mobilize support from below and provide broader channels of political participation. A single-party system usually has this capability, and this perhaps is one reason why bureaucratic monarchies, when their time is over, so often are replaced by single-party regimes. A military ruler may also centralize power for reform and then face the need to expand power for group participation. He is, however, far more free than the monarch to organize a political party, to create new structures of political participation (such as Basic Democracies) , and to adapt himself to coexistence with legislatures and elections. The modernizing monarch is the prisoner of the institution that makes his modernization possible. His policies require the expansion of political participation but his institution does not permit it. The success of modernization in the first stage depends upon strengthening the power of this traditional institution, whose legitimacy the process of modernization progressively undermines.

In addition, the inability of the monarchy to adapt to broadened political participation eventually limits the ability of the monarch to innovate social reforms. The effectiveness of the monarch depends upon his legitimacy and the decline in the latter erodes the former. The success of his reforms diminishes the monarch's impetus to innovate policy and increases his concern for the preservation of his institution. A gap opens between the increasingly modern society and the traditional polity which gave it birth; able to transform the society, but unable to transform itself, the monarchial parent is eventually devoured by its modern progeny.

Many societies offer evidence of the contrast in the ability to expand participation satisfactorily between those traditional polities in which power was highly centralized and which consequently had the capacity for policy innovation and those in which power was dispersed and which consequently possessed less of such capacity. In the western world, as we have seen, the centralization of power and modernizing reforms occurred earlier on the Continent than they did in England, and earlier in England than they did in America.[23] In the eighteenth century the French centralized despotism was viewed as the vehicle of reform and progress; only conservatives such as Montesquieu could see advantages in what was generally held to be the corrupt, disorganized, fractionated and backward English political system. Yet the centralization of power under traditional auspices also worked to obstruct the expansion of political participation, while the polities where power remained dispersed were better able to assimilate rising social classes into the political system. So also, in America the centralization of power was even less advanced than in England and the expansion of political participation proceeded even more rapidly and smoothly. Thus, the polities which were less modern politically in the seventeenth and eighteenth centuries came to be more modern politically in the nineteenth century.

A similar difference in evolution exists between China and Japan. In the mid-nineteenth century, authority and power were far more centralized in China than in Japan: one was a bureaucratic empire, the other still essentially feudal. Japanese society was highly stratified and permitted little social mobility; Chinese society was more open and permitted the movement of individuals up and down the social and bureaucratic ladder. In Japan heredity was, in Reischauer's phrase, "the basic source of authority," while in China it played a much smaller role, and advancement in the bureaucracy was based on an elaborate system of examinations.[24]

23. See above, Chap. 2.

24. Edwin O. Reischauer, *The United States and Japan* (rev. ed. Cambridge, Mass., Harvard University Press, 1957), p. 157.

As Lockwood suggests, an observer of 1850 asked to judge the potential for future development of the two countries "would have placed his bet unhesitatingly on China." Politically,

> the feudal heritage of Japan . . . tended to conserve political power in the hands of a self-conscious warrior caste, [whose] traditional skills and habits of domination over an unfree people were dubious assets for modernization, to say the least. . . . By comparison, China alone among the Asian peoples brought to the modern world a tradition of egalitarianism, of personal freedom and social mobility, of private property freely bought and sold, of worldly pragmatism and materialism, of humane political ideals sanctioned by the right of rebellion, of learning as the key to public office.[25]

The same feudal system, however, which made Tokugawa Japan seem so backward compared with Ch'ing China also furnished the social basis for the expansion of political participation and the integration of both the traditional clans and the newer commercial groups into the political system. In Japan the "potential leadership, because of feudal political institutions, was much more widespread, not only among the 265 'autonomous' han but even among the various social groups with their differing functions in society. If one geographical area or sector of Japanese society failed to respond adequately to the crisis created by Western pressures, another one would; in fact, this is what happened."[26] The gap between the symbolic end of feudalism (1868) and the organization of the first modern political party (1881) was sufficiently brief so that the latter could be built on the wreckage of the former. Thus, in Japan the broadening and institutionalizing of political participation went on simultaneously with the introduction of modernizing policy innovations. In China, on the other hand, Confucian values and attitudes delayed the conversion of the political elite to the cause of reform, and, once it was converted, the centralization

25. William W. Lockwood, "Japan's Response to the West: The Contrast with China," *World Politics, 9* (1956), 38–41.

26. Edwin O. Reischauer and John K. Fairbank, *East Asia: The Great Tradition* (Boston, Houghton Mifflin, 1960), pp. 672–73. For an analysis along somewhat similar lines attempting to explain why England and Japan developed economically more rapidly than France and China, see Robert T. Holt and John E. Turner, *The Political Basis of Economic Development* (Princeton, N.J., Van Nostrand, 1966), passim, but esp. pp. 233–91.

of authority precluded the peaceful assimilation of the social groups produced by modernization.

The patterns of evolution in Africa do not seem to differ significantly from those of Europe and Asia. Ruanda and Urundi, for instance, were two traditional societies of similar size, similar geography, similar economies, and similar ethnic make-up of about 85 per cent Bahutu tribesmen and about 15 per cent Watutsi warriors who comprised the political and economic elite. The principal differences between the two kingdoms were in the distribution of power and the flexibility of social structure. The *mwami* or king of Ruanda "was an absolute monarch who governed through a highly centralized organization and by principles that enabled him effectively to control his militarily powerful feudatories." In Urundi, on the other hand, the king shared power with the royal clan or *baganwa*, whose members "were by hereditary right the ruling class of Urundi." In Ruanda the king might make grants of land to members of the royal family, but they "had no special rights or powers." The *baganwa* of Urundi, however, could appoint their own subordinates "to lead their personal armies and to administer their lands." Not infrequently these personal armies, in typical feudal fashion, would be used against the king. Thus, while the king of Urundi was in theory absolute, in practice he was "with respect to the *baganwa* virtually *primus inter pares* in a decentralized state." The systems of royal marriage and of inheriting the throne tended to "consolidate royal power" in Ruanda but contributed to "weakening royal power" in Urundi. Similarly the foreign wars which were typical of Ruanda also "consolidated the royal power by increasing the royal treasury and thus putting at the king's disposal new lands, cows, and other goods for distribution to his successful feudatories." [27] In Urundi, in contrast, civil wars among the rival princes helped to reduce royal authority.

While Ruanda was, in some respects, more conservative and traditional than Urundi, clearly it was also more centralized and bureaucratic while Urundi was more dispersed and feudal. The receptivity of the two societies to social-economic change reflected these differences. The Ruandans demonstrated "greater intellec-

---

27. Albert, pp. 54–60. See also René Lemarchand, "Political Instability in Africa: The Case of Rwanda and Burundi" (unpublished paper), p. 34. On the traditional system in Ruanda in general, see Jacques Maquet, *The Premise of Inequality in Ruanda* (London, Oxford University Press, 1961).

tual quickness for 'book-learning' " and greater "interest in and ability to learn European ways—in the school system, in religious instruction, and in response to economic or political reforms proposed by the Europeans." The Ruandans appraised "European culture as holding out to them the opportunity to increase their prestige and power, and they tend to act to make it as much as possible their own." For the Rundi, on the other hand, "the new institutions and ways seem to be received as new impositions from above, accepted out of necessity rather than welcomed or pursued, avoided as far as possible." These differences in receptivity to change were found in large measure to be the result of the difference between "a strongly centralized and a decentralized political system." [28]

The ability to expand political power and to assimilate groups into the political system, however, would appear to vary in just the reverse way between the two systems. In the more modern and "progressive" Ruanda the process of political change involved a violent revolution in 1959, in which the previously subordinate Hutu turned on their Watutsi rulers, slaughtered several thousand of them, ousted the *mwami,* established a Hutu-dominated republic, and drove some 150,000 Tutsi into exile. As in Russia, China, and the Ottoman Empire, the centralized monarchy in Ruanda was replaced by a single-party regime. In late 1963 raids by Watutsi guerrillas across the borders into Ruanda provoked another savage tribal massacre in which the Hutu apparently killed over 10,000 more of the Tutsi remaining within their borders, floating their bodies down the Ruzizi River to Burundi and hacking and maiming thousands of others. Kigali, the capital of Ruanda, was reported to be pervaded with the stench of human flesh. "In a few weeks," one European resident observed, "Ruanda slipped back 500 years." [29] The centralized, hierarchical, more open traditional Ruandan political system was thus able to adapt to social and economic reforms but was clearly unable to provide for the peaceful absorption of the previously excluded social groups into the political system. The result was bloody revolution and conflict in which about half the Watutsi population of over 400,000 had by 1966 been either killed or forced into exile.

28. Albert, pp. 66–67, 71–73.
29. *New York Times,* January 22, 1964, p. 2, Feb. 9, 1964, p. 1; *Newsweek, 63* (Feb. 24, 1964) , 51.

The political evolution of Burundi was hardly a model of peaceful progress. In the space of four years, two premiers were assassinated and one badly wounded. Nonetheless the violence was kept limited, and tribal massacres avoided. "Whereas in Rwanda majority rule struck at the very roots of the traditional system of stratification and directly threatened the elitist nature of the political system, in Burundi, where cleavages were less consistent, the forces of tradition and modernity coalesced in relative harmony." [30] The weaker, decentralized Urundi monarchy was carried over into independence as a constitutional monarchy, political parties developed based upon aristocratic clans and cutting across tribal lines, and the leaders of the country were drawn from both tribal groups. The tensions caused by independence and the impact of the tribal conflict in Ruanda, however, led the monarch to assume a more active role in the political system. This tendency toward the centralization of power "coinciding with the extension of political participation to the peasantry, not only destroyed the old pattern of balanced tensions among the *ganwa* but, in effect, paved the way for a polarization of ethnic feeling between Hutu and Tutsi." [31] In the 1965 election the Hutu came to dominate the parliament. The king responded by challenging parliament's authority and asserting more vigorously his power to rule as well as reign. These actions stimulated some Hutu to attempt a coup in October 1965, which failed and triggered the execution by the government of a number of Bahutu leaders. As a result, the crown, in effect, became the prisoner of the Tutsi; another coup in July 1966 replaced the king with his son; a third coup in the fall of 1966 ended the monarchy entirely and established a Watutsi-dominated republic. During all this instability, however, Burundi still avoided the mass slaughter of its neighbor and, indeed, the instability which it did suffer was in some measure a result of that slaughter. The inability of Tutsi and Hutu to live together in peace under Ruanda's centralized system was definitely established. Their ability to coexist in Burundi's decentralized system remained unproven but still possible.[32]

30. Lemarchand, "Political Instability," p. 18.

31. René Lemarchand, "Social Change and Political Modernization in Burundi" (paper prepared for Annual Meeting, African Studies Association, October 24-26, 1966), pp. 43-44.

32. Of interest here are Ted Gurr's predictions of civil violence in 1961-63 for 119 polities through regression analyses using 29 variables measuring primarily

The differences in political evolution in these two African states are paralleled by similar differences in other states with comparable political systems. In Uganda, for instance, the Banyoro developed a highly centralized state system while their neighbors, the Iteso, lacked such a system, had a widely dispersed power structure, "and, judged by Western standards, existed in a state of near anarchy." In contrast to the Banyoro with their more modern traditional system, however, the Iteso adapted much more quickly to modern forms of organized political participation. They "have swiftly abandoned much of their traditional social organization and have been relatively quick to accommodate themselves to new forms of association." [33]

Similarly, David Apter found that the ability of African political systems to adjust to modernization was a function of their traditional value systems and their traditional structures of authority. Societies with consummatory value systems were unlikely to adapt successfully to the modern world. Among societies with instrumental value systems, patterns of adaptation were largely determined by the hierarchical or pyramidal character of the traditional authority structure. An hierarchical system with high social mobility, such as existed in Buganda, reacted similarly to that in Ruanda and very rapidly absorbed modern social, economic, and technical practices. But the system had very limited ability to expand political participation. The Baganda strongly opposed the organization of political parties and other types of institutional devices to structure such participation. They resisted the introduction of elections in 1958 because, as the Prime Minister of Buganda argued, "from time immemorial the Baganda have known no other ruler above their Kabaka in his Kingdom, and still they do not recognize any other person whose authority does not derive

---

national integration, social mobilization, economic development, governmental penetration of the economy, and military-internal security forces. For 99 polities his predictions were reasonably good, but not for our two central African states. Of the 119 polities, that in which violence most exceeded the prediction was Rwanda; in Burundi, in contrast, violence fell farther below the prediction than in any other state save one. Conceivably, these extreme deviations are explained by the contrasting social-political authority structures of the two societies. See Ted Gurr with Charles Ruttenberg, *The Conditions of Civil Violence: First Tests of a Causal Model* (Princeton, Princeton University, Center of International Studies, Research Monograph No. 28, 1967), pp. 100–06.

33. Fred G. Burke, *Local Government and Politics in Uganda* (Syracuse, N.Y., Syracuse University Press, 1964), p. 124.

from the Kabaka and is exercised on his behalf." [34] In short, authority cannot derive from representative sources. As a result, Buganda became a distinct and somewhat indigestible entity within independent Uganda. Its representatives within the central government formed the principal opposition party, the Kabaka Yekka ("Kabaka Only"), dedicated to the preservation of the authority of the monarch. In an effort at compromise the Kabaka was made President of Uganda, while the Prime Minister was the leader of the principal nationalist party, the United Peoples Congress, which drew its strength primarily from the non-Bugandan portions of Uganda. In due course, however, this effort to reconcile modern and traditional patterns of authority broke down. Early in 1966 Prime Minister Obote concentrated power in his own person and ousted the Kabaka from the Presidency. A few months later, the Ugandan army moved in on Buganda, suppressed resistance to the central authority, and after a brief siege seized the Kabaka's palace and drove him into exile, ending, at least temporarily, Buganda's traditional centralized monarchy. Bugandan leaders alleged 15,000 of their tribesmen were killed. Thus, the traditional Bugandan hierarchical monarchy was unable to absorb modern forms of political participation, and the modern political system of Uganda was unable to absorb the traditional Bugandan monarchy. The "instrumental-hierarchical type of system," as Apter put it, "can innovate with ease until the kingship principle is challenged, at which point the entire system joins together to resist change. In other words, such systems are highly resistant to political rather than other forms of modernization, and in particular cannot easily supplant the hierarchical principle of authority with a representative one." [35]

The fate of Buganda may be contrasted with the evolution of the Fulani-Hausa system of northern Nigeria. Like Buganda, this too had an instrumental value structure. Unlike Buganda, authority was organized primarily on a pyramidal basis. As a result, the Fulani-Hausa were much less active than the Baganda in social, economic, and cultural modernization. In many ways they remained highly traditional. Like the Baganda in Uganda, the Fulani-Hausa also remained outside the main currents of modern

34. Apter, *Modernization*, p. 114 n.

35. David E. Apter, "The Role of Traditionalism in the Political Modernization of Ghana and Uganda," *World Politics, 13* (1960), 48.

nationalist politics which developed during the decade preceding independence in both countries. Unlike the Baganda, however, the Fulani-Hausa did adapt themselves to participation in a modern polity. Indeed, they were able "to organize themselves . . . successfully for modern political life, in fact, to the point of dominating nearly all of Nigeria." Early in 1966 this preeminent role of the northerners was ended by a military coup led by Ibos from eastern Nigeria. Unlike the Ugandan government, however, the new central government in Nigeria was not willing or able to attempt to overthrow the dispersed power structures in the north, and instead a series of compromises was gradually worked out between the central government and the northern authorities. The instrumental-pyramidal system of the Fulani-Hausa, as Apter put it, "is adaptive while remaining conservative. Given to compromise and negotiation, and with a clear notion of secular interests, the Fulani-Hausa nevertheless do not become easily engaged in massive development or imbued with ideas of change and progress." [36] Obviously the process of evolution is far from finished, but it would not seem unreasonable to predict that the northern Nigerian emirs may well adapt to the expansion of political participation in ways not too dissimilar from those of the English aristocracy.

Thus, the evidence is fairly conclusive that the more pluralistic in structure and dispersed in power a traditional political system, the less violent is its political modernization and the more easily it adapts to the broadening of political participation. These conditions make possible the emergence of a modern, participant political system which is more likely to be democratic than authoritarian. Paradoxical as it may seem, dispersed or feudal traditional systems characterized by rigid social stratification and little social mobility more often give birth to modern democracy than do the more differentiated, egalitarian, open, and fluid bureaucratic traditional systems with their highly centralized power. The experience of seventeenth- and eighteenth-century Europe is reproduced in twentieth-century Asia and Africa. Those traditional systems which are most modern before the expansion of political participation have the greatest difficulty in dealing with the consequences of that expansion.

36. Apter, *Modernization*, p. 99.

THE KING'S DILEMMA: SUCCESS VS. SURVIVAL

In Morocco and Iran, Ethiopia and Libya, Afghanistan and Saudi Arabia, Cambodia and Nepal, Kuwait and Thailand, traditional monarchies grappled with modernization in the second half of the twentieth century. These political systems were involved in a fundamental dilemma. On the one hand, centralization of power in the monarchy was necessary to promote social, cultural, and economic reform. On the other hand, this centralization made difficult or impossible the expansion of the power of the traditional polity and the assimilation into it of the new groups produced by modernization. The participation of these groups in politics seemingly could come only at the price of the monarchy. This is a problem of some concern to the monarch: Must he be the victim of his own achievements? Can he escape the dilemma of success vs. survival? More broadly put, are there any means which may provide for a less rather than a more disruptive transition from the centralizing authority needed for policy innovation to the expansible power needed for group assimilation?

The problem basically involves the relation between traditional and modern authority. Three possible strategies are open to the monarch. He could attempt to reduce or to end the role of monarchical authority and to promote movement toward a modern, constitutional monarchy in which authority was vested in the people, parties, and parliaments. Or a conscious effort might be made to combine monarchical and popular authority in the same political system. Or the monarchy could be maintained as the principal source of authority in the political system and efforts made to minimize the disruptive effects upon it of the broadening of political consciousness.

Transformation

In modern constitutional monarchies, the king reigns but does not rule; authority derives from popular consent through elections, parties, and legislatures. Is there any reason why the remaining ruling monarchies cannot, if the monarch so wills, be peacefully transformed into modern reigning monarchies? In theory, this should be feasible, but the traditional monarchies which existed in the second half of the twentieth century were almost all highly centralized regimes. The only major exceptions were Afghanistan, where tribal pluralism had long supported a dispersion of power, and Morocco, where colonialism had generated an experience with parties unique among ruling monarchies. Historically no case exists of a peaceful direct shift from absolute monarchy to an electoral regime, with a government responsible to parliament, and a king who reigned but did not rule. In most countries such a change would involve a basic transfer of legitimacy from the sovereignty of the monarch to the sovereignty of the people, and such changes usually require either time or revolution. Contemporary modern constitutional monarchies almost invariably developed out of feudal rather than centralized traditional polities. "The less the area of his prerogative," Aristotle observed, "the longer will the authority of a king last unimpaired." In Japan, for instance, the emperor was the traditional source of legitimacy but he virtually never ruled. The shifts of power from the shogunate to the Meiji oligarchy to the party regimes of the 1920s to the military juntas of the 1930s could all be legitimated through the emperor. So long as the emperor did not attempt active rule himself, monarchical legitimacy did not compete with but instead reinforced the authority of people, parties, and parliament." It is hard to overestimate," Mendel has observed, "the symbolic power of the Japanese imperial institution to legitimize relatively smooth transitions of popular leadership." [37]

An alternative course of accommodation is for the traditional ruling monarch to abandon his formal claims to legitimacy in the interests of maintaining his actual power to govern. In 1955 Sihanouk abdicated as king of Cambodia, turned the throne over to his father, organized a political party, won the parliamentary elections, and returned to the government as premier. When his father died in 1960 the constitutional monarchy was formally continued and the queen ascended the throne; but the constitution was amended to provide also for a chief of state selected by parliament, and Sihanouk was elected to that position. Thus, in a manner somewhat similar to that of the English aristocracy, Sihanouk maintained the substance of traditional elite rule by accommodating it to the forms of popular legitimacy.

The more usual shift, however, is not from ruling monarchy to

37. Aristotle, *Politics*, pp. 243–44; Douglas H. Mendel, Jr., "Japan as a Model for Developing Nations" (paper prepared for Annual Meeting, American Political Science Association, September 8, 1965), pp. 8–9.

parliamentary monarchy but from ruling monarchy to oligarchic monarchy. Monarchical legitimacy is maintained but effective rule is transferred from the monarch to a bureaucratic elite. This was, in effect, what happened with the Young Turk revolt of 1908 in the Ottoman Empire, and for the next decade a military junta exercised effective power in the name of the sultan. The revolution of 1932 transformed Thailand from an absolute monarchy to a limited monarchy. A military-dominated oligarchy ruled the country in the name of the monarch, with cliques within the oligarchy replacing each other regularly through means of fairly limited and usually bloodless coups. This oligarchical regime, like that of the Young Turks, represented some broadening of participation over what existed previously. It did not, however, involve the creation of any institutionalized capacity to absorb additional social groups. Thailand still did not have an expansible political system, and the 1932 pattern of events which overthrew the absolute monarchy seemed likely to have its parallel in the future with the revolutionary overthrow of the military oligarchy.

The more vigorously a monarch exercises authority, the more difficult it is to transfer that authority to another institution. It is, one may assume, virtually impossible for a modernizing monarch who has struggled to centralize power and to force through reforms against strong traditionalist opposition to release his grasp and voluntarily to assume a dignified rather than an efficient role. It is quite natural for him to feel that he is indispensable to the order, unity, and progress of his country, that his subjects would indeed be lost without him. Once when asked why he did not become a constitutional monarch, the Shah of Iran is reported to have replied: "When the Iranians learn to behave like Swedes, I will behave like the King of Sweden." [38] Any similar monarchial modernizer is likely to have equally strong paternalistic sentiments. In addition, the polity and the society themselves come to reflect the expectation of authoritative monarchical rule. The possible weakening of that rule opens up the prospect of rival claimants for power and ambiguous principles of legitimacy. The uncertainty and fear of what may replace monarchical legitimacy and kingly rule may become a powerful sentiment among many groups militating against change. If royal authority disappears what else

38. Quoted by Claire Sterling, "Can Dr. Amini Save Iran?," *The Reporter, 30* (August 17, 1961), 36.

will bind the community together? In the extreme case, the existence of the community may become completely identified with the authority of the monarchy.

In part for this reason, the successful transition from ruling to constitutional monarchy may be facilitated by accidents of birth, health, and death which indicate that the authoritative exercise of monarchical power is not indispensable to political stability. The timely appearance of a mad monarch, a child king, or a playboy prince can play a key role in preserving institutional continuity. George III's insanity (if it was that) was a boon to constitutional evolution in Great Britain. The modernization of Japan was eased by the fact that the Meiji Emperor was fifteen when he was "restored" to power. So also, the shift from absolute to limited monarchy in Thailand was certainly aided by the circumstance that King Prajadhipok was a reasonably passive and ineffectual ruler, who gladly acquiesced in the Revolution of 1932 and then abdicated three years later, turning the throne over to a sixteen-year-old schoolboy in Switzerland. The transition from ruling monarchs to reigning monarchs in Iran and Morocco would be facilitated if Mohammad Shah and Hassan II abdicated or died before their children reach maturity. In the 1960s the Crown Prince of Ethiopia was a rather weak, easygoing fellow, purportedly sympathetic to assuming a limited, constitutional rule when he succeeded to the throne. He was, however, also reported to be anxious to pursue the conflicting objective of reinvigorating the process of reform which had slowed down in the late 1950s. Once on the throne, he would thus have to choose between the potential political virtues of passivity and the immediate social need for activism. The almost universal experience of his own and other countries suggests that the latter is likely to be overriding.

Coexistence

If modernization is unavoidable, what can be done about expanding the power of the political system to make it bearable? Is there any reason why it should be impossible to combine monarchial rule and party government, to institutionalize competitive coexistence in the polity of two independent sources of power? Such a compromise may last for a substantial length of time—as it did, indeed, in Imperial Germany for almost half a century—but the relationship will always be an uneasy one. The pressures in such a system are either for the monarch to become only a symbol or for him to attempt to limit the expansion of the political system, thus precipitating a constitutional crisis such as occurred in Greece in 1965. In actual practice, other institutions of authority were weak or nonexistent in most post-World War II traditional monarchies. With a few exceptions, all possessed legislative bodies of one sort or another; in general, however, these were obedient instruments of royal rule. If, at times, they did attempt to act independently and to assert an authority of their own, it usually took the form of attempting to block the monarch's reform proposals. In Iran parliament had maintained an institutional life since the inauguration of the constitution in 1906 and was sufficiently vigorous and sufficiently conservative that Premier Amini had to insist on its dissolution as the price of accepting the premiership in 1961. "At present," Amini commented, "the Majlis is a luxury for which the Iranian people are not yet ready." [39]

The continuing problem in any effort to institutionalize the coexistence of monarchial and popular legitimacy concerns the dual responsibility of the premier and his cabinet to king and parliament. In actual fact, in virtually all the post-World War II ruling monarchies, the premier remained primarily responsible to the king rather than to parliament. In Iran he could not be a member of parliament, and a similar provision was included in the Afghan constitution of 1964. Inevitably, friction developed if the premier attempted to act independently of the throne. The Iranian Shah was careful to limit the freedom of action for most of his premiers and to oust those who showed signs of developing other sources of support. When a premier did do this, as in the case of Mossadeq, the result was a constitutional crisis.

Political parties were weak or nonexistent in most of the traditional monarchies. In the mid-1960s no political parties existed in Ethiopia, Saudi Arabia, or Libya. In Nepal and Thailand they had been abolished. The absence of a colonial experience for most monarchies removed a major incentive to the formation of popular movements and political parties. Where monarchies were subjected to colonialism, the monarchy itself, as in Morocco and Buganda, served as a substitute for or a competitor with political parties as a focus for nationalist sentiments. Where political

39. Quoted in Donald N. Wilber, *Contemporary Iran* (New York, Praeger, 1963), p. 126.

parties do exist in monarchial regimes, they are usually little more than parliamentary cliques lacking any significant organized mass support.

The most notable effort to combine monarchial and modern sources of authority after World War II was in Morocco. Thanks in part to its colonial experience Morocco developed much stronger political parties than did most ruling monarchies. The dominant party at the time of independence in 1956 was the Istiqlal, which had been founded in 1943 and which had supplemented the monarch as the promoter of Moroccan independence. In effect, the Moroccan system, as one political leader wrote, was to be neither a "traditional, feudal, absolute monarchy" nor a modern constitutional monarchy with the crown performing a purely symbolic role. Instead the system was "a variation of the absolute monarchy, based on a reenforcement of Islam . . . engaging the personal responsibility of the King." [40] Inevitably, however, the claims of party and throne made it difficult if not impossible to maintain a cabinet responsible to both. Zartman neatly summarizes Moroccan problems in this respect:

> In the first two Councils of Ministers, Mohammed V tried to create a government of national unity under an independent leader. Both eventually fell because they ignored party claims as well as realities. Certain members in the third government, and all members of the Council which followed it, were chosen as non-party technicians, as logically consistent with the quasivizirial system in force. Yet in a young country such as Morocco, everyone and everything is political, and there are no non-partisan technicians. The government was torn between responsibility to the king and responsibility to party groups, between its vizirial and ministerial nature. Therefore, it too fell, since it was not responsible before the political groups which could make its work impossible, and since these groups were not committed by the collective responsibility of the Council.
>
> Even had there been no catalytic pressure from the prince to increase his governing role, the government would naturally have tended to seek a stable position as a purely vizirial

40. 'Adberrahim Bou'abid, quoted in I. William Zartman, *Destiny of a Dynasty: The Search for Institutions in Morocco's Developing Society* (Columbia, S.C., University of South Carolina Press, 1964), p. 17.

or a purely ministerial system, simply to be comfortable in its role. Against partisan tendencies naturally pushing towards the latter system, the king acted in the other direction; the last government under Mohammed V, its continuation, and then succeeding governments under Hassan II were vizirial governments, with their members separately designated and individually responsible to the king.[41]

A monarch can also try to organize his own political party and to attempt to institutionalize popular support for his continuingly active rule. After the death of Mohammed V in 1961, the new king, Hassan II, in an effort to move the regime in a more constitutional direction, promulgated a constitution in 1962. The principal participants in the elections which took place in May 1963 under this constitution were the Istiqlal, which by now was a conservative party, the National Union of Popular Forces, a leftist socialist party, and a party of what were essentially the King's Friends, called the Front for the Defense of Constitutional Institutions. The king had hoped that the Front would gain a working majority, but in fact it got only 69 seats out of 144. In the United States a broad consensus makes it possible for a President to work with a Congress dominated not only by men of the opposite party but by men of opposing policy viewpoints. In a modernizing country, the issues are deeper, passions more intense, and in a case like this, opposing principles of legitimacy are at stake. Government became stalemated, and in June 1965 Hassan shut up Parliament and decided to rule by himself. Parliament, he said at the time, was "paralysed by futile debate," parliamentary government would accelerate the degradation of the system, and "resolute action" was necessary. "The country cries out for a strong stable government." [42] This effort to combine monarchical rule and parliamentary government ended in failure. Subsequent events suggested that the king might be becoming more and more dependent on and perhaps the prisoner of the bureaucracy and the security forces.

Efforts to combine active political parties with a ruling monarchy were no more successful in Iran. Political parties in Iran

41. Zartman, pp. 60–61.

42. *New York Times*, June 8, 1965; Ronald Steel, "Morocco's Reluctant Autocrat," *The New Leader*, August 30, 1965.

historically were much weaker than they were in Morocco. In the late 1940s and in the 1950s, however, the Tudeh Party and the National Front did develop sufficient strength and appeal to block the Shah in the Majlis or Parliament and in 1953 to challenge the very existence of the monarchy. After recovering a surer seat on his throne, the Shah discouraged the development of political parties which might become autonomous foci of power. In the late 1950s he sponsored the formation of a "two party system," with a government party and an opposition party, the latter being led by a close personal and political associate of the Shah. In the elections of 1960 the Shah tried to promote the candidacy of men who would be sympathetic to his program. The conservative opposition to the Shah, however, encouraged the more radical nationalist opposition to the monarchy to reappear and the Shah was forced to void the elections on the grounds of corruption and the dominance of the electoral process by reactionary elements. Finally in September 1963, the Shah got a Parliament which would support him by the fairly direct method of in effect designating the candidates. Questioned about this apparent deviation from the usual democratic procedure, he is reported to have said: "So what. Was it not better that this [i.e. his] organization do it than that it be done by politicians for their own purposes? For the first time we have a Majlis and a Senate truly representing the people—not the landlords." [43] Thus in Iran the monarch subordinated the parliament and the parties while in Morocco he suspended and displaced them. In neither country has it been possible to combine an active ruling monarch and active autonomous political parties. An autonomous parliament opposes the monarch's reforms; autonomous parties challenge the monarch's rule.

In the 1950s and the 1960s the dominant trend among the remaining ruling monarchies was toward the reassertion of monarchial power. In 1954 in Iran, as we have seen, Mohammed Shah successfully reestablished the throne as the center of authority, and in 1963 Hassan II did the same in Morocco. In Nepal in 1950 King Tribhuvan overthrew the Ranas who had dominated the government as prime ministers. In 1959 his successor, King Mahendra, experimented with parliamentary democracy and permitted

43. Quoted by Jay Walz, *New York Times*, September 25, 1963. See also Andrew F. Westwood, "Elections and Politics in Iran," *Middle East Journal*, *15* (1961), 153 ff.

elections to be held in which the Nepali Congress Party won a majority in the legislature. This effort at combining monarchial and parliamentary authority lasted eighteen months. In December 1960 in a royal coup the king suspended the constitution, abolished the Nepali Congress Party, jailed the prime minister and other political leaders, and successfully reestablished direct royal rule.[44] In Afghanistan in 1963 King Zahir, like King Tribhuvan, displaced a strong prime minister and asserted his own authority to govern, making efforts, however, to inaugurate a constitutional regime. Similarly in Bhutan in 1964 the king assumed all powers of the state after a struggle with the country's first family. Even Greece in 1965 saw a struggle between the power of a prime minister with broadly based political organization and that of the monarchy, from which the latter emerged with at least a temporary victory. While these efforts reversed earlier tendencies toward a dispersion of power, the ruling monarchs in countries like Libya, Saudi Arabia, Jordan, and Ethiopia showed no signs of relinquishing their firm grasp on power or of accepting other sources of legitimacy. The political pressures of modernization seemingly made neither a feasible alternative.

Maintenance

Little prospect thus exists for significant changes in the political institutions and sources of legitimacy of modernizing monarchies. Barring such fundamental changes, what capacities, if any, do the monarchies have for adaptation and survival in a modernizing world? To what extent can the ruling monarchy become a viable institution? The problem is not a new one. Alexander II's policy, Mosse observes,

> was likely to be opposed from two different directions. Reform could not but hurt the vested interests of landowners, merchants, and officials; refusal to admit participation of the public in government could not but antagonize the liberals. Alexander's reign combined reform and repression; the combination pleased no important section of the population.[45]

44. Eugene B. Mihaly, *Foreign Aid and Politics in Nepal* (London, Oxford University Press, 1965), p. 108; Anirudha Gupta, *Politics in Nepal* (Bombay, Allied Publishers, 1964), pp. 157–60; Bhuwan Lal Joshi and Leo E. Rose, *Democratic Innovations in Nepal* (Berkeley and Los Angeles, University of California Press, 1966), pp. 384–88.

45. Mosse, pp. 176–77.

How can the monarch cope with the problem while still maintaining his authority? Conceivably he can placate the liberals by attempting to absorb them into the government; or he can placate the conservatives by backing away from reform; or he can proceed with reform and intensify repression so as to squelch the opposition of both liberals and conservatives.

One modern aspect of a centralized, bureaucratic monarchy is the extent to which it provides for individual mobility. In theory in most such monarchies and in practice in many, able men from the humblest backgrounds can rise up through the bureaucracy to the highest posts beneath the monarch. Is there any reason why this ability of the traditional monarchy cannot provide the means for assimilating the upwardly mobile individuals produced by modernization? In the initial phases of modernization, the monarch does precisely this. The appointment of modern men to the bureaucracy is, indeed, necessary for reform and is a crucial means by which the monarch reduces his dependence on the traditional elites in the bureaucracy. In the 1960s Faisal of Arabia and Zahir of Afghanistan asserted their power against oligarchic traditionalists by appointing for the first time in both countries cabinets dominated by commoners. (Afghanistan may well be the only country in history where at one time Ph.D.s made up half the cabinet.) In Iran after the 1963 elections a new wave of energetic and progressive middle-class experts was brought into the government under the leadership of Premier Hassan Ali Mansur. In Ethiopia after 1945 the emperor created what was in effect a "new nobility" composed of old-line aristocrats who were given honorific offices, ambitious opportunists, and skilled technicians.[46] Undoubtedly these appointments reconciled to the monarchy many who otherwise would have opposed it.

The ability of the traditional monarchy to reduce discontent through this process of individual absorption declines, however, as modernization progresses. The Ethiopian system, for instance, was not able to absorb significant numbers of the new intelligentsia who began to appear after 1955. In the absence of substantial employment opportunities in private business and in the presence of traditional contempt for private employment, it may well be simply beyond the financial and physical capacity of the bureaucracy to absorb the educated manpower produced by modernization.

46. Levine, *Wax and Gold*, pp. 185–93.

The natural wealth of the monarchy here becomes a key factor: the absorptive capacity of the Middle Eastern oil monarchies presumably exceeds considerably that of other realms less fluidly endowed. In addition, while some who mount the bureaucratic ladder will identify entirely with the system which has provided them the opportunity for advancement, others may still have very ambivalent loyalties to that system. A common figure in all traditional monarchies is the modern, progressive, educated bureaucrat struggling with his conscience as he attempts to balance the reforms he may be able to promote from within the system against the rewards which he has received for participating in that system. "We have been kept from acting," one Ethiopian intellectual remarked sadly, "by fear and the sweetness of office." [47]

A final limitation on the effects of individual absorption is that while this may well involve some of the most active middle-class leaders with the future of the regime, it does not provide a means for the assimilation of the middle-class and lower-class groups into the system as groups. It is a delaying action. New groups with new interests will still appear in the society; a high level of individual mobility may reduce the intensity and skill with which these interests are advanced, but it will not eliminate the interests as such. The problem of assimilating the groups into the system remains although it may well be made less urgent.

A second possible alternative is for the modernizing monarch to stop modernizing. The dilemma stems from his efforts to combine traditional authority and modern reform. He could escape from the dilemma by giving up the idea of reform, by becoming, in effect, an un-modernizing monarch or a traditionalizing monarch. This may not be as way out as it sounds. Presumably every society can arrive at its own fusion of traditional and modern elements. Party competition in democratic modernizing countries gives renewed strength to traditionalizing movements. Maybe the problem of the modernizing monarch can be solved by slowing down the processes of modernization and reform, coming to an accommodation with the traditional elements in society, and enlisting their support in the maintenance of a partially modern but not modernizing system. Certainly monarchs can shape the pace and direction of changes in the different sectors of society in ways which will be least destabilizing for their regime. Like the Ethi-

47. Ibid., p. 215.

opian government, they may, for instance, reduce the number of students studying abroad and place obstacles to the development of closely knit student bodies in the colleges in their own country. The problems in the application of this tactic are, first, that once the process of modernization starts—that is, once a core of modern-oriented intellectuals appears on the scene—it is very difficult, if not impossible, to stop or reverse the process. If the intellectuals are not brought into the bureaucracy to push the reforms of the modernizing monarch, they will certainly go underground to overthrow him. In addition, the slowdown in reform itself, while it may reduce the appearance in the future of more groups hostile to the regime also will intensify the hostility of those which already exist. "Ten years, even five years ago, the Emperor was ahead and leading us," one young Ethiopian observed in 1966. "Now it is we, the educated elite, educated by his order, who are leading, and the Emperor who lags behind." [48]

Traditionalizing policies are usually associated with more parochial and less cosmopolitan leaders. A traditionalizing monarchy requires greater isolation from the world culture than any other type of political system including totalitarian ones. Yet the traditional character of its political institutions means it will be less effective in isolating itself than a totalitarian system. For other reasons, such as foreign policy, isolation may be undesirable. The success of the Ethiopian government in securing the location of the OAU and the ECA in Addis Ababa enhances Ethiopia's international prestige at the same time that it undermines Ethiopia's political stability.

Finally, the monarch may attempt to maintain his authority by continuing to modernize but by intensifying the repression necessary to keep under control those conservatives who disapprove of the reform and those liberals who disapprove of the monarchy. The monarch's legitimacy was originally based on the acceptance throughout the society of traditional concepts of authority. As modernization proceeds, however, the new groups which are produced reject those concepts and the older groups become alienated from the monarchy as a result of his policies. Modernization erodes the support of the traditional classes and produces more enemies than friends among the modern classes. The monarch's political need to divide the bureaucracy against itself, to maintain

48. *New York Times*, March 8, 1966, p. 10.

a rapid turnover in top offices, to appoint enemies to competing positions and favorites to important ones, all reduce the effectiveness of the bureaucracy as a modernizing force. They also intensify the alienation and hostility of the middle-class intelligentsia. "I wake up screaming in the night," said one young Ethiopian official in the early 1960s, "at the thought the Emperor might die a natural death. I want him to know a judgment is being enacted on him!" [49]

The monarch becomes isolated with his army between the aristocratic and religious elites, on the one hand, and the educated middle class, on the other. As his legitimacy drains away he becomes more and more dependent upon the coercive power of the military, and thus the military come to play a more and more important role in his regime. To maintain its support the monarch must comply with its demands for symbolic and material rewards. In Ethiopia after the army had defended the emperor against the attempted coup d'etat by the Imperial Bodyguard in December 1960, the emperor had little choice but to acquiesce in its demands for higher pay. Providing pay, privileges, and equipment for the military, in turn, can absorb scarce resources which might otherwise be used for schools, roads, factories, hospitals, and other projects more directly related to reform. In Iran, the resignation of the reform prime minister, Ali Amini, in July 1962 was apparently caused in part by his desire to cut back the size of the army from 200,000 to 150,000 men in order to acquire funds for land reform and other modernizing purposes. Having just alienated substantial elements of the traditional aristocracy by introducing land reform, and it still being much too early for the peasants to be mobilized politically as a result of land reform, the Shah could hardly endanger his position with the military. He had little choice but to choose the army over Amini. The same necessity which leads the king to favor the military over other social groups also, however, leads him to attempt to weaken it against itself, to make it incapable of united action except under his leadership. Consequently monarchs often create other military forces, such as the bodyguard and the territorial militia in Ethiopia, to reduce the probability

49. Levine, *Wax and Gold*, pp. 187 ff.; Leonard Binder, *Iran* (Berkeley and Los Angeles, University of California Press, 1962) , pp. 94–95; David S. French, "Bureaucracy and Political Development in African States" (unpublished paper, Harvard University, 1966) .

that the military will act as a unit against the monarchy. Similarly, the monarch attempts to capitalize on personal rivalries among military leaders and at times on ethnic and generational differences within the officer corps. No modernizing monarchy is immune to attempts at coups d'etat, but, as in Iran and Ethiopia, the monarchs may for a while be able to defeat these attempts.

Not only does the army come to be the major organized source of support for the monarchy as modernization progresses, but the police and internal security forces also play an increasingly important role. Monarchs who pursue reform unremittingly become increasingly dependent upon sheer repression to maintain themselves in power. It is ironic but logical that, along with everything else he did, the Revolutionary Emperor, Joseph II, also created the first modern secret police system in Europe. So also, Alexander II, who began as "the tsar liberator" in due course found himself forced to become "the tsar despot." [50] The alliance of despotism and reform which characterized the nineteenth century Ottoman Empire came to a climax with the energetic and pervasive modes of repression employed by Abdulhamid II at the end of that century. The expansion of education and communications media led Abdulhamid "to erect an elaborate network of spies and informers to alert him to all slightly questionable activities of his subjects." [51]

Twentieth-century monarchies are under similar compulsions. In Morocco the reassertion of royal authority was followed by the Ben Barka affair and the increasing comments about the "repressive" nature of the regime.[52] In Saudi Arabia the first large-scale arrests of young liberals suspected of Communist or Nasserite sympathies occurred simultaneously with the new push for reform by Faisal at the time he mounted the throne. In Iran as Mohammed Shah played an increasingly important role in shaping the evolution of his country in the 1950s, the secret police organization, SAVAK, seemed to play an increasingly active role in searching out the enemies and potential enemies of the regime. Thus, in some measure the success of a monarch in modernizing his country may be gauged by the size and the efficiency of the police forces he feels it necessary to maintain. Both reform and repression are aspects of

50. Mosse, Chaps. 3, 6.
51. Frey, "Political Development, Power and Communications," pp. 311–13.
52. See, e.g., *New York Times*, November 21, 1966.

the centralization of power and the failure to expand political participation. Their logical result is revolt or revolution.

The future of the existing traditional monarchies is bleak. Their leaders have little choice but to attempt to promote social and economic reform, and to achieve this they must centralize power. This process of centralization under traditional auspices has reached the point where the peaceful adaptation of any of them, with the possible exceptions of Afghanistan and Morocco, to broader political participation seems most unlikely. The key questions concern simply the scope of the violence of their demise and who wields the violence. Three possibilities exist. In the most limited form of change, a coup d'etat changes ruling monarchies into oligarchical monarchies on the Thai model. This involves a limited broadening of participation in the system without creating an institutional capacity for any subsequent broadening of participation and probably at the cost of some capacity for policy innovation. It does, however, preserve the monarchy as a symbol of unity and legitimacy. In a country like Ethiopia such a course is probably the best that could be hoped for. A more drastic and perhaps more likely form of change in most ruling monarchies would be a Kassim-like coup which disposes of both monarch and monarchy, but which fails to produce any new principle or institutions of legitimacy. In this case, the political system degenerates into a formless, praetorian condition. The most violent solution would be a full-scale revolution in which several discontented groups join together for the demolition of the traditional political and social order, and out of which there eventually emerges a modern party dictatorship. Some existing societies with traditional monarchies, however, may be too backward even for revolution. Whichever course they take, what does seem certain is that the existing monarchies will lose some or all of whatever capability they have developed for policy innovation under traditional auspices before they gain any substantial new capability to cope with problems of political participation produced by their own reforms.

4. Praetorianism and Political Decay

Few aspects of political modernization are more striking or common than the intervention of the military in politics. Juntas and coups, military revolts and military regimes have been continuing phenomena in Latin American societies; they have been almost as prevalent in the Middle East. In the late 1950s and early 1960s many societies in southern and southeast Asia also came under military rule. In the mid 1960s the rash of military coups in Ghana, Dahomey, the Leopoldville Congo, the Central African Republic, Upper Volta, and Nigeria, added to those which had taken place earlier in Algeria, Togo, the Sudan, and the Brazzaville Congo, conclusively exposed the futility of the hopes and the arguments that Africa would somehow avoid the praetorian experience of Latin America, the Middle East, and Southeast Asia. Military interventions apparently are an inseparable part of political modernization whatever the continent and whatever the country. They pose two problems for analysis. First, what are the causes of military intervention in the politics of modernizing countries? Second, what are the consequences of intervention for modernization and for political development?

Their very prevalence suggests that many of the commonly advanced causes for their existence lack persuasiveness. It has, for instance, been argued that American military assistance is a significant factor increasing the proclivities of armies to involve themselves in politics. Such assistance, it is said, encourages the political independence of the army and gives it extra power, extra leverage, and more motivation to take action against civilian political leaders. In some circumstances this argument may have a certain partial validity. By enlarging and strengthening the military forces, military aid programs may help to aggravate the lack of balance between the input and output institutions of the political system. As the sole or principal cause of military interventions, however, military aid cannot be held guilty. Most countries which experienced military coups after receiving American military assistance experienced them equally often before they became the beneficiaries of Pentagon largesse. No convincing evidence exists of a correlation between the American military aid and military involvement in politics. And, it must be pointed out, the opposite hypothesis also is not true: the hopes of many people that the propensity of foreign military to intervene would be reduced by courses at Leavenworth, indoctrination in Anglo-American doctrines of civilian supremacy, and association with professionalized American military officers have also turned to naught. Armies which have received American, Soviet, British, and French military assistance and no military assistance have all intervened in politics. So also, armies which have received American, Soviet, British, French, and no military assistance have refrained from political intervention. Military aid and military training are by themselves politically sterile: they neither encourage nor reduce the tendencies of military officers to play a political role.[1]

It is equally fallacious to attempt to explain military interventions in politics primarily by reference to the internal structure of the military or the social background of the officers doing the intervening. Morris Janowitz, for instance, looks for the causes of military intervention in politics in the "characteristics of the military establishment" of the country and attempts to relate the propensity and ability of military officers to intervene in politics to their "ethos of public service," their skill structure, "which combines managerial ability with a heroic posture," their middle-class and lower middle-class social origins, and their internal cohesion.[2] Some evidence supports these connections, but other evidence does not. Some military men in politics have been apparently motivated by high ideals of public service; others have even more obviously been motivated by private gain. Officers with a variety of skills—managerial, charismatic, technical, and political—have all

1. On Latin America: see Charles Wolf, Jr., *United States Policy and the Third World: Problems and Analysis* (Boston, Little Brown and Company, 1967), Chap. 5; John Duncan Powell, "Military Assistance and Militarism in Latin America," *Western Political Quarterly, 18* (June 1965), 382–92; Robert D. Putnam, "Toward Explaining Military Intervention in Latin American Politics," *World Politics, 20* (Oct. 1967), 101–02, 106.

2. Morris Janowitz, *The Military in the Political Development of New Nations* (Chicago, University of Chicago Press, 1964), pp. 1, 27–29.

intervened in politics—and refrained from such intervention. So also, officers drawn from all social classes have led coups at one time or another. Nor are military forces which are internally cohesive any more likely to intervene in politics than those which are less united: to the contrary, political intervention and military factionalism are so closely related it is almost impossible to trace casual relationships between the one and the other. The effort to answer the question, "What characteristics of the military establishment of a new nation facilitate its involvement in domestic politics?" is misdirected because the most important causes of military intervention in politics are not military but political and reflect not the social and organizational characteristics of the military establishment but the political and institutional structure of the society.

Military explanations do not explain military interventions. The reason for this is simply that military interventions are only one specific manifestation of a broader phenomenon in underdeveloped societies: the general politicization of social forces and institutions. In such societies, politics lacks autonomy, complexity, coherence, and adaptability. All sorts of social forces and groups become directly engaged in general politics. Countries which have political armies also have political clergies, political universities, political bureaucracies, political labor unions, and political corporations. Society as a whole is out-of-joint, not just the military. All these specialized groups tend to become involved in politics dealing with general political issues: not just issues which affect their own particular institutional interest or groups, but issues which affect society as a whole. In every society, military men engage in politics to promote higher pay and larger military forces, even in political systems such as those of the United States and the Soviet Union, which have almost impeccable systems of civilian control. In underdeveloped societies the military are concerned not only with pay and promotion, although they are concerned with that, but also with the distribution of power and status throughout the political system. Their goals are general and diffuse as well as limited and concrete. So also with other social groups. Colonels and generals, students and professors, Moslem *ulema* and Buddhist monks, all become directly involved in politics as a whole.

Corruption in a limited sense refers to the intervention of

wealth in the political sphere. Praetorianism in a limited sense refers to the intervention of the military in politics, and clericalism to the participation of religious leaders. As yet no good word describes extensive student participation in politics. All these terms, however, refer to different aspects of the same phenomenon, the politicization of social forces. Here, for the sake of brevity, the phrase "praetorian society" is used to refer to such a politicized society with the understanding that this refers to the participation not only of the military but of other social forces as well.[3]

Scholarly analyses of social institutions in modernizing countries invariably stress the high degree of politicization of the institution with which they are concerned. Studies of the military in modernizing countries naturally focus on its active political role which distinguishes it from the military in more advanced societies. Studies of labor unions highlight "political unionism" as the distinguishing feature of labor movements in modernizing societies. Studies of universities in modernizing countries stress the active political involvement of faculty and students. Studies of religious organizations stress the extent to which the separation of church and state remains a distant goal.[4] Each group of authors looks at a particular social group in modernizing countries, more or less in isolation from other social groups, and implicitly or explicitly emphasizes its extensive involvement in politics. Clearly, such involvement is not peculiar to the military or to any other social group but rather is pervasive throughout the society. The same

3. See David Rapoport, "A Comparative Theory of Military and Political Types," in Huntington, ed., *Changing Patterns of Military Politics*, pp. 71–100, and Rapoport, "Praetorianism: Government Without Consensus," passim. See also Amos Perlmutter's independent analysis of military intervention, which in part parallels that of this chapter: "The Praetorian State and the Praetorian Army: Towards a Theory of Civil-Military Relations in Developing Politics" (unpublished paper, Institute of International Studies, University of California [Berkeley]).

4. See Bruce H. Millen, *The Political Role of Labor in Developing Countries* (Washington, D.C., The Brookings Institution, 1963); Sidney C. Sufrin, *Unions in Emerging Societies: Frustration and Politics* (Syracuse, Syracuse University Press, 1964); Edward Shils, "The Intellectuals in the Political Development of the New States," *World Politics*, *12* (April 1960), pp. 329–68; Seymour Martin Lipset, ed., "Student Politics," special issue of *Comparative Education Review*, *10* (June 1966); Donald Eugene Smith, *Religion and Politics in Burma* (Princeton, Princeton University Press, 1965); Fredrick B. Pike, *The Conflict between Church and State in Latin America* (New York, Alfred A. Knopf, 1964); Robert Bellah, ed., *Religion and Progress in Modern Asia* (New York, Free Press, 1965); Ivan Vallier, "Religious Elites in Latin America: Catholicism, Leadership and Social Change," *America Latina, 8* (1965), 93–114.

causes which produce military interventions in politics are also responsible for the political involvements of labor unions, businessmen, students, and clergy. These causes lie not in the nature of the group but in the structure of society. In particular they lie in the absence or weakness of effective political institutions in the society.

In all societies specialized social groups engage in politics. What makes such groups seem more "politicized" in a praetorian society is the absence of effective political institutions capable of mediating, refining, and moderating group political action. In a praetorian system social forces confront each other nakedly; no political institutions, no corps of professional political leaders are recognized or accepted as the legitimate intermediaries to moderate group conflict. Equally important, no agreement exists among the groups as to the legitimate and authoritative methods for resolving conflicts. In an institutionalized polity most political actors agree on the procedures to be used for the resolution of political disputes, that is, for the allocation of office and the determination of policy. Office may be assigned through election, heredity, examination, lot, or some combination of these and other means. Policy issues may be resolved by hierarchical processes, by petitions, hearings, and appeals, by majority votes, by consultation and consensus or through yet other means. But, in any event, general agreement exists as to what those means are, and the groups participating in the political game recognize their obligation to employ those means. This is true of both Western constitutional democracies and communist dictatorships. In a praetorian society, however, not only are the actors varied, but so also are the methods used to decide upon office and policy. Each group employs means which reflect its peculiar nature and capabilities. The wealthy bribe; students riot; workers strike; mobs demonstrate; and the military coup. In the absence of accepted procedures, all these forms of direct action are found on the political scene. The techniques of military intervention are simply more dramatic and effective than the others because, as Hobbes put it, "When nothing else is turned up, clubs are trumps." [5]

The absence of effective political institutions in a praetorian society means that power is fragmented: it comes in many forms and

5. Quoted by Dankwart A. Rustow, *A World of Nations* (Washington, D.C., Brookings Institution, 1967) , p. 170.

in small quantities. Authority over the system as a whole is transitory, and the weakness of political institutions means that authority and office are easily acquired and easily lost. Consequently, no incentive exists for a leader or group to make significant concessions in the search for authority. The changes which individuals make are thus imposed by the transfer of allegiance from one social group to another, rather than by a broadening of loyalty from a limited social group to a political institution embodying a multiplicity of interests. Hence the common phenomenon in praetorian politics of the "sell-out." In institutionalized systems, politicians expand their loyalties from social group to political institution and political community as they mount the ladder of authority. In the praetorian society the successful politician simply transfers his identity and loyalty from one social group to another. In the most extreme form, a popular demagogue may emerge, develop a widespread but poorly organized following, threaten the established interests of the rich and aristocrats, be voted into political office, and then be bought off by the very interests which he has attacked. In less extreme forms, the individuals who mount the ladder to wealth and power simply transfer their allegiance from the masses to the oligarchy. They are absorbed or captured by a social force with narrower interests than that to which they previously owed allegiance. The rise to the top in an institutionalized civic polity broadens a man's horizons; in a praetorian system it narrows them.

A praetorian society lacking community and effective political institutions can exist at almost any level in the evolution of political participation. At the oligarchical level, the actors in politics are relatively homogeneous even in the absence of effective political institutions. Community is still the product of social ties as well as of political action. As political participation broadens, however, the actors in politics become more numerous and their methods of political action are more diverse. As a result, conflict becomes more intense in the middle-class radical praetorian society and still more so in the mass praetorian society.

In all stages of praetorianism social forces interact directly with each other and make little or no effort to relate their private interest to a public good. In a praetorian oligarchy politics is a struggle among personal and family cliques; in a radical praetorian society the struggle among institutional and occupational groups supplements that among cliques; in mass praetorianism social classes and social movements dominate the scene. The increase in the size, strength, and diversity of social forces makes the tension and conflict among them less and less tolerable. In an institutionalized society the participation of new groups in the political system reduces tensions; through participation, new groups are assimilated into the political order: as, for instance, the classic case of the extension of the suffrage in Great Britain. In praetorian societies, however, the participation of new groups exacerbates rather than reduces tensions. It multiplies the resources and methods employed in political action and thus contributes to the disintegration of the polity. New groups are mobilized but not assimilated. The expansion of political participation in Great Britain made Disraeli's two nations into one. The expansion of participation in Argentina made the same two nations into mortal enemies.

The stability of a civic polity thus varies directly with the scope of political participation; the stability of a praetorian society varies inversely with the scope of political participation. Its durability declines as participation rises. Praetorian oligarchies may last centuries; middle-class systems, decades; mass praetorian systems usually only a few years. Either the mass praetorian system is transformed through the conquest of power by a totalitarian party, as in Weimar Germany, or the more traditional elites attempt to reduce the level of participation through authoritarian means, as in Argentina. In a society without effective political institutions and unable to develop them, the end result of social and economic modernization is political chaos.

Oligarchical to Radical Praetorianism: Breakthrough Coups and the Soldier as Reformer

Oligarchical praetorianism dominated nineteenth-century Latin America. The imperial rule of both Spain and Portugal did not encourage the development of autonomous local political institutions. The war of independence produced an institutional vacuum—in Morse's phrase it "decapitated" the state [6]—which the creoles attempted to fill by copying the constitutional arrangements of the United States and republican France. Inevitably

6. Richard M. Morse, "The Heritage of Latin America," in Louis Hartz, ed., *The Founding of New Societies* (New York, Harcourt, Brace and World, 1964), p. 161.

these could not take root in a society which remained highly oligarchical and feudal. This left Latin America with entrenched social forces and weak and ineffective political institutions incapable of modernizing society. The result was a pattern of corporate or syndicalist politics which in most countries persisted through the expansions of political participation. Even in the twentieth century oligarchical praetorianism still existed in the countries of the Caribbean, Central America, and the Andes, and in Paraguay. It was also a common phenomenon in the Middle East. There the disintegration of Ottoman authority and its only partial or indirect replacement by British or French rule created a vacuum of legitimacy and an absence of effective political institutions.

In oligarchical praetorianism the dominant social forces are the great landowners, the leading clergy, and the wielders of the sword. Social institutions are still relatively undifferentiated, and the members of the ruling class easily and frequently combine political, military, religious, social, and economic leadership roles. The most active groups in politics are still basically rural in nature. Families, cliques, and tribes struggle unremittingly with each other for power, wealth, and status. Politics assumes an individualistic Hobbesian pattern. No consensus exists on the means of resolving disputes; few, if any, political organizations or institutions exist.

Almost all praetorian oligarchies eventually evolve into radical praetorian systems. Not all radical praetorian systems, however, have been praetorian oligarchies. Some evolve from centralized traditional monarchies. Such political systems ordinarily have a high degree of legitimacy and effectiveness so long as political participation is limited. Their political institutions, however, remain rigid and fragile in the face of social change. They are unable to adapt to the emergence of middle-class groups into politics. The appearance of such groups leads to the overthrow or breakdown of the traditional monarchical system of rule and heralds the movement of the society into a praetorian phase. The society evolves from a civic traditional order to a radical praetorian one. Institutional decay and civic disorder are the prices of the expansion of political participation.

A third source of radical praetorianism is Western colonialism. In Africa, the Middle East, and southern Asia it weakened and often completely destroyed indigenous political institutions. Even where it took the form of "indirect rule," it undermined the traditional sources of legitimacy since the authority of the native rulers was clearly dependent on the power of the imperialist state. Opposition to colonialism usually developed among the offspring of the native elite or sub-elite groups, who developed an intense commitment to modern values and were essentially middle-class in outlook, occupation, and function. Since the imperial powers were, in most cases, clearly superior militarily, the drive for independence was ideological and political in character. The intelligentsia educated in London and Paris identified themselves with national independence and popular government and attempted to develop the mass organizations to make these a reality. So long as it maintained its rule, however, the colonial power often obstructed the creation of political organizations and it then often ended its rule precipitously. The combination of colonial opposition to political organization plus colonial haste to provide national independence granted indigenous elites the latter before they had constructed the former. Even where substantial mass involvement had occurred during the years of the independence struggle, this frequently rested on very low levels of social mobilization. It was, in this sense, a somewhat artificial phenomenon and could not be organized on a permanent basis.

In either event, independence frequently left a small, modernized, intellectual elite confronting a large, amorphous, unmobilized, still highly traditional society. Africa in the 1960s was not too dissimilar from Latin America in the 1820s. In the latter case the creoles attempted to impose republican institutions inappropriate for their society; in the former case the elite attempted to impose mass institutions also inappropriate for the society. In each instance, political authority decayed and the institutions withered: the Latin American constitutions became pieces of paper; the African one-party state became a no-party state. The institutional void was filled by violence and military rule. In Latin America the low level of modernization meant a fairly sustained period of oligarchical praetorianism. In Africa the less stratified character of society and the difference in historical timing produced radical praetorianism. The "breakthrough" to middle-class political participation was thus led by the civilian nationalist intelligentsia, who were then dislodged by middle-class military officers because they lacked the continuing mobilized political support and organized political strength to fill the vacuum of authority and legitimacy left by the departing colonial rulers.

In the shift from absolute monarchy or praetorian oligarchy to radical praetorianism, in contrast, the military play a key role. The middle class makes its debut on the political scene not in the frock of the merchant but in the epaulettes of the colonel. In the praetorian oligarchy, the struggle for power frequently involves coups d'etat, but these are simply "palace revolutions" in which one member of the oligarchy replaces another. The top leadership is changed but no significant changes are made in the scope of governmental authority or the scope of political participation. Military institutions and rules lack autonomous existence. The dominant figure in an oligarchical society may well be a "general" but he is usually also a landowner, an entrepreneur, and a highly personalistic leader who, in the fashion of a Somoza or Trujillo, does not distinguish among his various roles. He, in fact, uses all the political tactics—bribery, force, cajolery, threat, popular appeal—which in a more complex praetorian society become the distinctive tactics of particular groups. The participation of the military or of military groups as collectivities in politics comes only with that differentiation of the officer corps as a semi-autonomous institution which goes with the rise of the middle class.

In due course the officer corps begins to acquire a distinctive character and esprit; its recruits are drawn more and more frequently from modest social backgrounds; its members receive unusual educational opportunities at home and abroad; the officers become receptive to foreign ideas of nationalism and progress; they develop distinctive managerial and technical skills rare elsewhere in society. Together with civilian university students, particularly those who have studied abroad, the officers are the most modern and progressive group in the society. The middle-class officers, often closely allied to such civilian groups as school teachers, civil servants, and technicians, become more and more disgusted with the corruption, incompetence, and passivity of the ruling oligarchy. In due course the officers and their civilian allies form themselves into cliques and secret societies to discuss the future of their nation and to plot the overthrow of its rulers. At some point this conspiracy revolts and overthrows the oligarchy. This coup differs from the governmental coups of the oligarchical era because its leadership normally comes from middle-ranking rather than high-ranking officers; the officers are united more by loyalty to a common purpose than as the personal following of a single leader; they normally have a program of social and economic reform and national development; and often a quantum jump occurs in the amount of violence accompanying the coup.

This change marks the shift from the oligarchical pattern of governmental coups or palace revolutions to the radical, middle-class pattern of reform coups.[7] Iraq, for instance, was firmly in the grip of oligarchical praetorianism from its independence in 1932 until 1958, its politics a politics of coup and counter-coup within the dominant military elite. The overthrow of Nuri-es-Said in 1958 did not break the prevailing pattern of praetorian politics. It did, however, mark a qualitative change in the nature of politics and the bases of legitimacy as the monarchy ended and new slogans and programs of the revolution and national development were promulgated. It also marked a significant quantitative expansion in the scope of political participation as middle-ranking and middle-class officers seized power and as the way was opened for the entry into politics of the bureaucratic and professional classes. The overthrow of the parliamentary regime in Syria in 1949 by the military involved a similar expansion of participation from a relatively small elite group to essentially middle-class elements.[8]

The shift from a traditional ruling monarchy to middle-class praetorianism is also mediated by the military. The military is typically the most modern and cohesive force in the bureaucracy of a centralized monarchy, and the monarchy typically falls victim to those it has strengthened to serve its ends. Unlike the shift from praetorian oligarchy, however, the coup which brings the middle-class military to power in a traditional monarchy is a break with previous practice and a bloody innovation in political techniques. It snaps the thread of legitimacy and ends what had previously been peaceful (if policeful) rule. Thus, the military overthrow of the Brazilian monarchy in 1889 dramatized the shift of power from the sugar planters of the northeast to the coffee and commercial elements of São Paulo and Rio de Janeiro. The Thai "Revolution of 1932" against the absolute monarchy involved the assertion of the power of essentially middle-class bureaucratic, military elements against the traditional ruling cliques associated with the court and the royal family. The coup in Egypt in 1952 similarly

7. See Huntington, *Changing Patterns*, pp. 32 ff.
8. See Caractacus, *Revolution in Iraq* (London, Victor Gollancz, 1959); Patrick Seale, *The Struggle for Syria: A Study of Post-War Arab Politics* (London, Oxford University Press, 1965).

brought middle-class military men into power, although in this case the monarchy which was overthrown did not possess much legitimacy or authority.

In these early stages of political modernization, the military officers play a highly modernizing and progressive role. They challenge the oligarchy, and they promote social and economic reform, national integration, and, in some measure, the extension of political participation. They assail waste, backwardness, and corruption, and they introduce into the society highly middle-class ideas of efficiency, honesty, and national loyalty. Like the Protestant entrepreneurs of western Europe, the soldier reformers in non-Western societies embody and promote a puritanism which, while not perhaps as extreme as that of the radical revolutionaries, is nonetheless a distinctive innovation in their societies. Military leaders and military groups played this innovating role in the larger and more complex societies in Latin America in the late nineteenth century. In Brazil, Mexico, and other countries military officers and their civilian allies adopted positivism as their philosophy of development.

In the twentieth century the professionalization of the officer corps produced a still greater commitment to modernization and to national development and also transformed the typical expression of military participation in politics from the individualistic leader to the collective junta.[9] In Chile and Brazil in the 1920s middle-class military groups pushed radical programs of social reform. During and after World War II similar programs were espoused by military officers in other Latin American countries such as Bolivia, Guatemala, Venezuela, El Salvador, Peru, and Ecuador, where traditional conservatism and oligarchy still remained strong. In the Middle East after World War II the soldiers played a similar role, modernizing middle-class military men seizing power in Syria in 1949, in Egypt in 1952, and in Iraq in 1958. The military takeovers in Pakistan and Burma in 1958 fell into a somewhat similar pattern although the differences in social background between the ousted political elites and the incoming military leaders were less than in the Middle East.

The emergence of radical praetorianism is a long and compli-

9. Johnson, *The Military and Society in Latin America*, pp. 77–79, 113–15; L. N. McAlister, "The Military," in Johnson, ed., *Continuity and Change in Latin America* (Stanford, Stanford University Press, 1964) , pp. 140–41.

cated process. It usually involves a progression of coups and other
changes as different groups struggle up over each other's backs into
positions of political power. The initial overthrow of the traditional political institution or break with the oligarchical pattern
of politics is also usually a more complex event than it may appear
simply on the surface. The actual coup itself is often preceded by
years of discussion and preparation. The Thai Promoters of 1932
grew out of the organized discussions of civilian students and
younger military officers in Paris in the 1920s. In Egypt the cadets
at the military college organized discussions on "The Social and Political Unrest in Egypt" in 1938. The 1940s saw a succession of nationalist cliques and groups forming and reforming in the military
establishment. In 1949 the Free Officers Group was formally organized; three years later it seized power.[10] Often the middle-class
officers make one or more unsuccessful efforts to seize power before
they are able to topple the regime. These "anticipatory coups" are
part of the process of sounding out sources of support and opposition, testing the strength of the ruling monarchy or oligarchy. The
suppression of these efforts by the groups in power and the execution or exile of the perpetrators of the abortive coups serve the
short-term interest of the regime by eliminating some elements of
the "counterelite" but weaken the regime in the long run by producing greater coherence, caution, and sophistication in the remaining elements of the counterelite.

The pattern of politics in the displacement of the traditional or
oligarchical rule by military coup d'etat resembles in more restrained and limited fashion the familiar Brinton model of revolution. In the construction of the coalition of military and civilian
elements to carry out the coup it is usually necessary to stress those
objectives which have the broadest appeal and to place at the head
of the coup group a moderate, conciliatory military leader who is
able to acquire the confidence of all the groups participating in
the coup and also has more ties than other members of those
groups with the old regime. The collapse of the old regime is thus
followed by the apparent accession to power of the moderates.
Soon, however, issues intensify, divisions develop among the vari-

10. See Amos Perlmutter, "Ambition and Attrition: A Study of Ideology, Poli-
tics and Personality in Nasser's Egypt" (unpublished MS), pp. 11–16; Keith
Wheelock, *Nasser's New Egypt*, The Foreign Policy Research Institute Series, 8 (New
York, Frederick Praeger, 1960), pp. 12–36.

ous participants in the coup, and in due course the more radical Jacobin elements attempt to seize power from the moderates in a consolidating coup. The consolidating coup puts the final seal on the fate of the old regime; with it the new middle-class elements establish their dominance on the political scene.

This complex pattern of anticipatory, breakthrough, and consolidating coups has characterized most of the shifts from traditional or oligarchical to middle-class praetorian regimes. In Egypt the Free Officers Group scheduled a coup for March 1952, but this was postponed. As political restiveness increased, however, the Free Officers were prompted to seize power in July. During the next eighteen months the coup moved through its consolidating phases: the Communist, Wafd, and Moslem Brethren opposition groups were successively eliminated, and in April 1954 Naguib, the popular moderate leader behind whom the more conservative elements attempted to rally, was displaced by the more radical Nasser.[11]

The overthrow of the Thai absolute monarchy followed somewhat similar lines. Thailand's first coup occurred in June 1932, when a group of civil and military individuals seized power, imprisoned the royal family, and persuaded the king to accept a limited monarchy. A fairly conservative civilian, Phya Mano, was made premier. In the spring of 1933 a crisis developed when he rejected the economic plan which had been drawn up by the civilian intellectual leader of the coup, Pridi. The military leaders resigned from the cabinet and then took action against the government. "A second, equally bloodless and successful coup was carried out—this time directed against Phya Mano and his followers, who were accused of favouring a complete Royalist comeback." This second coup completed the work of the first.

> After the first coup the Promoters had either been very modest or had cunningly played for time, for instead of pushing their people forward and filling the ranks of the old civil service, they had proclaimed that their lack of experience made it necessary to retain some of the old Royalists in their administrative jobs. The second coup saw this tactical mistake corrected: this time the Promoters replaced all officials of the

11. Here and in occasional spots in the next few pages I have drawn on my "Patterns of Violence in World Politics," in Huntington, ed., *Changing Patterns*, pp. 32–40.

old regime and put in their own men, however inexperienced they might be.[12]

Similar words have been used to describe the relationship between the March 1949 coup in Syria of Colonel Husni Za'im, which initiated the conquest of power by the new middle class in Syria by overthrowing the government of President al-Quwwatli, and the August 1949 coup of Colonel Sami Hinnawi, which ousted Za'im:

> It gradually came to light that the second coup d'etat was, in a real sense, merely the fulfillment of the original intention of the first. Those who had been Za'im's associates in the overthrow of the al-Quwwatli regime had to be rid of him before they could accomplish the original purpose of the first conspiracy, which was to unseat those who had proved themselves incompetent in the administration of the state and the conduct of the Palestine war, and to replace them in civil authority by those who had been the most upright and able critics of the old regime.[13]

The middle-class breakthrough coups in Latin America followed similar patterns. Bolivia's defeat in the Chaco War stimulated a group of young officer reformers to overthrow the old regime in May 1936 and to create a Socialist Republic headed by Colonel David Toro. This regime initiated a number of reforms, but in July 1937, "Lt. Colonel Germán Busch, who had engineered the coup which put Colonel Toro in power, overthrew Toro." Busch's government, in turn, "continued and intensified the general policies of the Toro administration." [14] Similarly, the unbroken pattern of oligarchical rule in Guatemala was challenged in the early 1940s by efforts to overthrow the traditionalist regime of General Jorge Ubico. The successful coup finally occurred in June 1944 and brought into power a moderate government led by General Ponce Valdez, "who tried to protect the old order." [15] But Ponce was unable to stop the process of change. "Young army officers, many of them made aware by wartime train-

12. John Coast, *Some Aspects of Siamese Politics* (New York, International Secretariat, Institute of Pacific Relations, 1953), p. 5.

13. Alford Carleton, "The Syrian Coups d'Etat," *Middle East Journal, 4* (Jan. 1950), 10–11.

14. Robert J. Alexander, *The Bolivian National Revolution* (New Brunswick, Rutgers University Press, 1958), pp. 25–26.

15. George Blanksten, "Revolutions," in Harold E. Davis, ed., *Government and Politics in Latin America* (New York, Ronald Press, 1958), pp. 138–39.

ing in the United States of Guatemala's need for reforms, now had their long-awaited opportunity. Together with the *ladino* (mixed blood), middle-class professional men and intellectuals of the capital, they plotted the overthrow of the generals." [16] In October 1944 a consolidating coup overthrew Ponce and eventually brought to power the radical administration of Arévalo.

In El Salvador the pattern varied somewhat in that the first step in breaking the power of *Los Catorce Grandes* (the fourteen families who supposedly controlled the country) came in the form of a general strike in April 1944 against the thirteen-year-old dictatorship of General Maximiliano Hernández Martínez. The strike was "a relatively spontaneous undertaking on the part of the middle class of the city of San Salvador." It resulted in the replacement of Martínez by a civilian moderate, Castañeda Castro. Four years later in the "Revolution of 1948" a group of junior officers ousted him from power and inaugurated a new government designed to carry out "a controlled revolution." These officers resembled those who led comparable movements in the Middle East.

The group of army officers who have controlled Salvadorian politics since 1948 share significant characteristics. Almost all come from the ranks of major and lieutenant colonel, that middle range of the officer corps where promotions come slowly and political activity appears as a promising alternative to the frustrations of immobility in the military hierarchy.

Perhaps even more significantly, these younger officers differ greatly in attitude from the older military caste which they displaced. Many of them claim lower-middle- or middle-class origins. By virtue of place of residence, education, social contacts, economic status and aspiration, and social attitudes, they identify more closely with the emergent middle class than with the economic elites. Most have spent some time in military colleges in the United States and have experienced close contact with American military missions. [17]

In the more complex societies of Latin America political institutions were more highly developed and the shift from conserva-

16. Edwin Lieuwen, *Arms and Politics in Latin America* (New York, Frederick Praeger, 1960), pp. 91–92.

17. Charles W. Anderson, "El Salvador: The Army as Reformer," in Martin C. Needler, ed., *Political Systems of Latin America* (Princeton, D. Van Nostrand Company, 1964), pp. 58–59, 61.

tive, traditional regimes to reformist middle-class governments occurred earlier historically and involved cooperation between military clubs and political parties. In Argentina, the Unión Cívica, a middle-class reform party, was organized in 1889. The next year the Logia Militar was founded by a group of progressive officers who cooperated with civilian allies in organizing unsuccessful revolts against the conservative regime in 1890, 1893, and 1905.[18] These anticipatory coups suggested that in due course the middle-class military reformers would come to power through a successful coup. This, however, proved unnecessary: Argentina was, at that point, only partially praetorian, and the radical civilian ally of the military, the Unión Cívica Radical, won control of the government through peaceful elections in 1916.

In Chile the political parties were even more highly developed, the ruling oligarchy more open to civilian middle-class penetration, and the army more highly professionalized. As a result, military intervention played only a supplementary role in the transition to a middle-class regime. The principal impetus for reform came from the Liberal Alliance, whose leader, Arturo Alessandri Palma, was elected president in 1920 "when oligarchical domination collapsed."[19] When Congress blocked Alessandri's reform program, the military intervened in politics in September 1924 and induced Congress to grant its approval. Alessandri resigned and was replaced by a Junta de Gobierno of high-ranking generals. The generals were moderate, however, and made plans to return power to more conservative civilians. As a result, in January 1925 the younger officers who had been organized in a highly reformist Junta Militar revolted and carried out a consolidating coup, which brought to power Lt. Colonel Carlos Ibáñez. His reformist and repressive dictatorship collapsed in 1931 and was briefly succeeded by another military junta which proclaimed a "Socialist Republic."[20]

RADICAL PRAETORIANISM: SOCIAL FORCES AND POLITICAL TECHNIQUES

In the mid-twentieth century oligarchical praetorianism could still be found in some of the more backward Latin American and

18. Liisa North, *Civil-Military Relations in Argentina, Chile, and Peru*, Politics of Modernization Series, 2 (Berkeley, Institute of International Studies, University of California, 1966), 26–27.

19. Federico G. Gil, "Chile: Society in Transition," in Needler, p. 361.

20. North, pp. 34–35, 74–77.

Middle Eastern societies. At the other extreme, mass praetorianism appeared in Argentina in the form of Peronism, but lay in the future for most modernizing countries. Most praetorian societies in Asia, Africa, and Latin America were in the middle stages in the expansion of political participation. The social roots of radical praetorianism lie in the gap between city and country. The former supplants the latter as the principal locus of political action and becomes the continuing source of political instability. The "stronger influence" of the city in the political life of the country leads, as Harrington predicted, to greater political turbulence.[21] In a radical praetorian society the city cannot furnish the basis for governmental stability. The extent of the instability depends upon the extent to which the government is able and willing to use the countryside to contain and to pacify the city. If the government can build a bridge to the countryside, if it can mobilize support from the rural areas, it can contain and ride out the instabilities of the city. If the countryside is passive and indifferent, if rural elite and rural masses are both excluded from politics, then the government is caught in an urban prison of instability and functions at the whim of the city mob, the capital garrison, and the central university's students. If, however, the countryside turns against the political system, if the rural masses are mobilized against the existing order, then the government faces not instability but revolution and fundamental change. The distinctive characteristic of radical praetorianism is urban instability. The stability of that instability depends upon the exclusion of the countryside from politics.

The revolt by more progressive, Western, or radical military officers which overthrows the traditional political institutions or oligarchical rule clears the way for the entry of other middle-class elements into politics. A fairly long interval may, however, separate the military overthrow of monarchy or oligarchy and the appearance of other middle-class groups on the political scene. During this initial phase of radical praetorianism, politics typically involves continuing intrigue and conflict among loosely structured groups which are primarily military in composition. Such, for instance, was the case in Turkey between 1908 and 1922 and in Thailand for three decades after the "Revolution of 1932." Such was also the case in many Latin American countries following breakthrough coups. Cliques of colonels and generals then strug-

21. See James Harrington, *Oceana*, ed. S. B. Liljegren (Heidelberg, 1924), p. 10.

gle with each other for control, but no clique is able to establish
an effective base of authority because no clique is willing to extend its appeal (and its power) beyond the ranks of the army and
mobilize other social forces to its side. Once the traditional sources
of legitimacy are discredited, however, other middle class groups
in due course supplement the military on the political scene and
strive to participate in politics in their own distinctive ways.
Among these are the professional and literary intelligentsia, merchants and industrialists, lawyers and engineers. The two most
active social forces in a praetorian system at its middle level of development are, typically, the intelligentsia and especially the students, on the one hand, and the military, on the other. A high correlation exists between student participation in politics and military participation in politics. Both are distinctive characteristics of
the radical praetorian society.

In the radical praetorian society the diversification of the political participants causes the techniques of political action to vary
markedly from one group to another. The participant groups in
the political system are much more politically specialized than
they are in a more highly developed and integrated political system. At the same time, however, these groups are less functionally
specialized and differentiated than they are in a more developed
system. The university, for instance, typically has a part-time faculty and a part-time student body. It often possesses little corporate identity and its primary functions of teaching and research
may be less developed and carry less prestige than the other social
and political functions which it performs. Respect for learning
and academic values may be low; students may expect to make
their way by relying on social status or sheer bribery; professors
may well be appointed on nonacademic grounds. Academic values
and procedures, in short, have often achieved only a low level of
institutionalization. As an academic institution with a particular
function to perform in society, the university may have little institutional autonomy.

This absence of functional autonomy, however, is often combined with a very high degree of political autonomy. In many
countries in Asia and Latin America, for instance, the university is
recognized as beyond the appropriate scope of action on the part
of the police. Activities which would be illegal and promptly
prohibited outside the campus are tolerated when carried on

within the university. "In Czarist Russia," as Lipset has noted, "university autonomy operated at times to allow the adult sections of illegal revolutionary groups to hold meetings in university precincts, without interference by the police. In Venezuela, in recent years, terrorists have exploited this tradition of university autonomy by using the university precincts as a sanctuary from the police." [22] The political autonomy of the university is, in part, the heritage of the corporate autonomy of the university and other guilds from the Middle Ages. The autonomy of the students is, in part, the product of their traditional recruitment from the upper classes. The "sons of the establishment" have more freedom to undermine the establishment than those not so well connected. "Should we turn the machine guns on them?" asked one Iranian police officer in the midst of a major student demonstration against the regime. "We cannot do that. After all they are our children." [23] The legacies of tradition in the form of corporate privileges and social status give the university and its members a political base in modernizing societies which is absent in modern societies.

The combination of functional subordination and political autonomy characteristic of the university is also, of course, even more marked in the armed forces in a praetorian society. Military professionalism is weak; military values, like academic values, are subordinated to other considerations. Social, political, economic factors intrude into the military sphere. At the same time, elaborate efforts are made to defend the political autonomy of the armed forces. The armed forces are assumed to be outside the direct authority of civilian political leaders; their budgets are typically fixed by constitution or custom; they exercise close to exclusive control over their own internal activities; and the cabinet members in charge of them are drawn from their ranks. The army, like the university, exchanges functional autonomy for political influence. The political authorities who are unable to make their writ run in the university are unlikely to be able to make it run in the army.

The prevalent forms of political action in a radical praetorian

22. Seymour Martin Lipset, "University Students and Politics in Underdeveloped Countries," *Minerva*, 3 (Autumn 1964), 20. See also pp. 43-44 for evidence of the absence of functional autonomy of universities in modernizing countries.

23. *New York Times*, December 4, 1961, p. 10.

society—bribery, strikes, demonstrations, coups—are all ways of bringing pressure upon authority rather than ways of exercising authority. They are not forms of state action or of action by primarily political bodies, but rather forms of action by bodies whose primary functions are, in theory, nonpolitical. Hence the involvement of these groups in politics varies greatly from time to time. In a highly institutionalized political system the participation of groups in politics varies with the cycle of elections and conventions and with the rise and fall of issues. The efforts by one group of political actors to win an election or to pass legislation provoke similar action by opposing groups. As a result, participation escalates; but it normally assumes similar forms and is expressed through similar institutional channels. In a praetorian society the participation of social groups in politics also tends to rise and fall simultaneously. Political action by one group, however, provokes a different form of political action by another group. These, in turn, may arouse yet a third to still other types of political behavior. Conflict intensifies and its methods diversify, producing a major political crisis which can be relieved only by a decline in political action on the part of all groups. Political activity contributes to the stability of a modern institutionalized polity, but to the instability of a praetorian society.

The "ultimate" means of bringing pressure on those in authority is to remove them from their positions of authority. The most direct means of accomplishing this end in a praetorian system is the military coup d'etat. While all social groups engage in their own forms of direct action, clearly the military form is the most dramatic and the most effective. It is, however, usually a reaction to or a product of other types of political action by other groups. In the radical praetorian society, military intervention in politics is not an isolated deviation from a normal peaceful pattern of politics. It is simply one strand in a complex pattern of direct action techniques employed by a variety of conflicting middle-class groups. In such a society, the absence of accepted institutional channels for the articulation of interests means that claims on government are advanced "by the mechanisms of civilian violence and military intervention." Resort to direct action by all social forces is not a deviation from the system's norm, rather "the persistent use of violence *is* the system, or at least a very large part of it." [24]

24. James L. Payne, *Labor and Politics in Peru* (New Haven, Yale University Press, 1965), pp. 271–72. See also Martin C. Needler's discussion of "representational

In a radical praetorian system, riots and demonstrations are a common form of political action by students and related middle-class groups. Typically, such actions bring about the downfall of the government only where they polarize the situation in such a way as to compel the military to oppose the government. In Colombia in 1957, for instance, student riots led to a general strike aimed at preventing the formal reelection and hence continuation in power of the dictator Rojas Pinilla. The military initially refused to move against Rojas, but in due course the escalation of violence induced first the church and then the army to rally to the side of the students. When this happened, Rojas was finished. In Korea in 1960 student demonstrations against the elections led to clashes in which reportedly 186 students were killed. The action by the students compelled other social forces to turn against the Syngman Rhee regime. First the United States condemned the actions of the government; then the military announced that they would remain neutral in the dispute. This withdrawal of military support brought about Rhee's downfall. In South Vietnam in 1963 the actions of the Buddhists and the students created a similar situation in which first the United States and then the military withdrew their support from the Diem government.

If the military, on the other hand, are strongly identified with the government or staunchly loyal to it, insurrectionary activities by students will not threaten the existence of the government. In 1961 and 1962, for instance, student riots in Teheran disrupted the peace, but the army remained loyal and the disorder was contained. In Caracas in the fall of 1960, student riots led to a military siege of the Central University. Here again soldier and labor groups remained loyal to the government. Similarly, in Burma student opposition to the military regime in 1962 produced another pitched battle between soldiers and students which ended with the student union building being leveled to the ground. Student demonstrations and riots thus have some, but limited, capacity to induce or to compel a government to make substantive concessions. Their power stems primarily from their ability to polarize a situation and to compel other social groups to support or to oppose the government.

In a praetorian system the expansion of political participation

---

violence," *Political Development in Latin America: Instability, Violence, and Evolutionary Change,* Chap. 3.

means the diversification of political techniques. The broadening of participation to the urban working class multiplies the types of demonstrations that are possible and introduces the strike as a major form of direct political action. In some measure, of course, political participation by labor marks the beginning of the movement of a praetorian society from its radical to its mass phase. Economically and socially, however, organized labor in a modernizing society is not entirely a lower-class movement. Those who are organized usually comprise the economic elite of the industrial labor force, and the strongest unions are often in middle-class, white-collar occupations. While the preeminent tactic of the students is the mass demonstration and riot, the distinctive tactic of labor is, of course, the strike, particularly the general strike. The ability of labor to take such action, like the ability of the military to carry through a coup, depends in part on its unity. If a reasonable degree of unity exists, the success of the political action depends upon the extent to which it precipitates coordinate or parallel action by other groups, most importantly the military. Four patterns of relationship exist.

1. *Labor vs. government and military.* In this case labor political action almost invariably fails to achieve its objective. A general strike, if it is called, is broken by the combined and cooperative action of government, police, and military. In such circumstances, indeed, the strike is often testimony to the weakness of labor (Peru, 1962; Chile, 1966).

2. *Labor plus military vs. government.* In this circumstance, the general strike performs the same function as the student riot. It polarizes the situation, and if the army already has grounds for opposing the government it may seize the opportunity so presented to engage in parallel or cooperative action with labor to bring down the government. The pattern, however, is relatively rare (Haiti, 1946; Venezuela, 1958).

3. *Labor plus government vs. military.* This situation most frequently arises when the military initiate direct action to overthrow a government which has labor support. Labor then rallies to the government by declaring a general strike to undermine the military coup. This was the pattern in Germany in the Kapp Putsch; it was also the pattern in Mexico in 1923 when labor backed Obregón against the efforts by the military rebels to overthrow him. A comparable situation occurred in Guatemala in

1949 when a military group rebelled against President Arévalo and labor came to his support by calling a general strike and by providing volunteers whom loyalist military units supplied with arms. In general, the success of the coalition of labor and government versus the military depends upon the existence of some disunity among the latter.

4. *Labor vs. government vs. military.* In this situation labor brings pressure on the government by threatening to strike and to promote civil disorder which, in turn, is likely to induce the military to overthrow the government in order to clamp down on labor and restore order. The government is thus confronted with the alternatives of changing its policies or losing office. This pattern of "democracy by violence" is prevalent in Peruvian politics. Numerous instances can be found in the politics of other Latin American states. In 1964, for instance, the strikes of the Bolivian tin miners against Paz Estenssoro's government produced civil turbulence and disorder which prompted the army to overthrow Paz. The military leaders had no particular sympathy for the workers; in a few months they too were engaged in a struggle against the miners. But the weakening of authority and the inability of the civilians to deal with the disorder had created an opportunity for the military to promote themselves into positions of political power. In Ecuador a similar pattern was thrice repeated with Velasco Ibarra: elected president, he would disenchant his followers; "his erstwhile partisans, particularly students and workers, would begin demonstrations against his government; law and order would begin to break down; and the armed forces would find it necessary to remove him." [25] In this pattern of conflict, praetorianism feeds on itself: the probability of direct action by the military encourages direct action by labor and students. The power of one social group reinforces that of another at the expense of political authority.[26]

25. Edwin Lieuwen, *Generals vs. Presidents* (New York, Praeger, 1964) , p. 48. The concept of "democracy by violence" is developed by Payne in *Labor and Politics in Peru.*

26. The vicious circle of direct action in a praetorian society is graphically illustrated by Abraham F. Lowenthal's description of Dominican politics: "There is one final aspect of the Dominican Republic's political instability on which I would like to focus: the very direct, virtually naked confrontation of social forces. The tactics employed by each group since 1961 have tended toward increasingly unrefined and undisguised displays of power, directed more often at replacing the government

In a radical praetorian society military intervention is thus usually a response to the escalation of social conflict by several groups and parties coupled with the decline in the effectiveness and legitimacy of whatever political institutions may exist. Military intervention then serves to halt the rapid mobilization of social forces into politics and into the streets (in a praetorian society the two are identical), and, by removing the target and the immediate stimulus of the escalation, to defuse the explosive political situation. Military intervention, in short, often marks the end of a se-

---

than at forcing it to take specific actions, and the use of such direct tactics has tended to produce an escalation of conflict. Students and university politicians have issued *manifiestos*, circulated leaflets, fomented repeated strikes, marched, demonstrated, rioted, physically occupied the University campus and offices to oust an entire slate of university officials on political grounds, supplied recruits for a brief guerrilla uprising, and fought in the *commandos* of the "constitutionalist" movement. Labor unions have employed public appeals, meetings, and strikes, have organized *turbas* to remove physically officials and employers they wished to replace on political grounds; they even organized an almost totally effective national general strike in 1966, and they had also formed *commandos* for the 1965 struggle. Businessmen began early with an impressive demonstration of their power in a 1961 strike against the remnants of the Trujillo regime; similar tactics were employed by a smaller group of commercial interests in order to topple Bosch in 1963 and also by a group which organized a counter-strike against the general strike of 1966. Business and commercial groups are also believed, I might add, to have organized and supported terrorist groups which have probably outdone those of the extreme left in acts of violence since 1965. Even the Church, although it has been very conscious of its standing as one of the few elements of continuity in Dominican life, has sometimes exerted its power in direct appeals. Various pastoral letters and other public appeals and even active participation in the negotiations to establish a Provisional Government in 1965 have marked overt Church actions, and the Church has also exerted an obvious influence through the campaign of *cursillos de Christianidad*—religious short-courses with political overtones—and through its support for the 1963 mass Christian Reaffirmation meetings against Bosch. Various other forces have employed not only speeches, propaganda, meetings, organization of supporters, etc. but —more importantly—subversion and conspiracy, rallying various military factions to coup and counter-coup. And the military, in turn, has acted to overthrow governments, to prevent them from executing specific policies, and also to suppress opposition. As each group in conflict exerted its power directly, the military groups were always able to prevail until the 1965 crisis. The escalation of violence in 1965, including the distribution of arms to irregular forces, produced the decision by the Air Force and the Armed Forces Training Center, wielders of the ultimately most powerful forces, to strafe their Army opponents and the civilian population. It was the effects of this decision, the ultimate step in the politics of chaos, which exacerbated the 1965 crisis and set the stage for the U.S. intervention." "Political Instability in the Dominican Republic" (Unpublished manuscript, Harvard University, May 1967).

quence of violence in politics. It is, in this sense, significantly different from the tactics employed by other social groups. Although riots, strikes, and demonstrations may directly or indirectly compel a government to modify its policies, by themselves they cannot change the wielders of governmental power. The military coup, however, is a form of direct action which changes the government in power, not just its policies. Paradoxically, the military establishment has no readily available means of direct action to achieve limited policy objectives. It can, of course, threaten a government with a coup unless the government changes its policies, but it cannot pressure the government to change its policies by carrying out a coup. In achieving this goal, civilian social forces and even the enlisted men of the armed services (who can strike or mutiny) have more suitable forms of action than the officers. The latter are, in effect, restricted to the use or threat of the use of a weapon of last resort.

The nature of the political tactics employed by the military reflects their organizational coherence and the fact that while other social forces can pressure the government, the military can replace the government. Monks and priests can demonstrate, students riot, and workers strike, but no one of these groups has, except in most unusual circumstances, demonstrated any capacity to govern. "The most serious element of chaos," one scholar has observed of Korea immediately following the overthrow of Syngman Rhee in 1960, ". . . was the fact that the student and urban forces that had initiated the action had neither the organization nor the program needed to restore social order, and the surviving political forces of the country had not been closely allied with them in the overthrow." [27] The military, in contrast, do possess some capacity for generating at least transitory order in a radical praetorian society. The coup is the extreme exercise of direct action against political authority, but it is also the means of ending other types of action against that authority and potentially the means of reconstituting political authority. In a situation of escalating conflict the military coup thus has the immediate effect of reducing the level of participation, inducing the withdrawal from the streets of the competing social forces, and producing a feeling of relief and harmony. Following the March 1962 coup in Burma, for instance, "If

27. Henderson, *Korea: The Politics of the Vortex*, pp. 175–76.

anything, there was a feeling of relief; at least, the slide downward would be stopped." [28] Similar feelings coupled with the relaxation of the intensity of conflict follow most coups which displace civilian governments in a radical praetorian society. The competitive escalation of political violence is followed by a rapid if temporary demobilization of groups from politics, as they retire from the barricades to wait upon the course of events.

The distinguishing characteristics of the coup d'etat as a political technique are that: (a) it is the effort by a political coalition illegally to replace the existing governmental leaders by violence or the threat of violence; (b) the violence employed is usually small; (c) the number of people involved is small; (d) the participants already possess institutional bases of power within the political system. Clearly a coup can succeed only (a) if the total number of participants in the political system is small, or (b) if the number of participants is large and a substantial proportion of them endorse the coup. This latter condition is rarely met; for if the number of participants is large, it will be virtually impossible to construct an effective coalition of them to support the coup. In the absence of such a coalition, the coup will either be defeated by the opposition of the other groups, as in the Kapp putsch, or it will lead to full-scale civil war, as did the uprising of the Spanish Army in 1936.

The coup which brings the military to power in a mature radical praetorian system is a political as well as a military action. It is the product of a coalition of cliques and groups, usually including both military and civilian elements, who in most cases have been preparing for it for a considerable length of time. In this period of preparation various groups of political actors have been sounded and their support assured or their opposition neutralized. If the coup comes as a result of a series of civil disorders perpetrated by intelligentsia, labor, or other civilian groups, the activities foreshadowing it have been clearly visible to all. Even where a coup is not preceded by overt violence and disorder, its appearance is almost invariably signaled in advance by shifts of political loyalties and indications of changed allegiances and alliances.

The colonel who plans a coup, if he is wise, prepares the way in much the same manner that the majority leader of the U.S. Senate prepares for a roll-call vote on a crucial bill: he trades on past favors, promises future benefits, appeals to patriotism and loyalty, attempts to distract and to divide the opposition, and when the chips are down, makes doubly sure that all his supporters are mobilized and ready to act. It is precisely this careful preparation—this painstaking construction of a political majority—which makes the coup painless and bloodless. The actual seizure of power itself may be the action of only a small group of men, but normally the support of a fairly large proportion of the total number of political actors in the society is achieved before the coup is launched. In the most successful coup, indeed, the targets offer no resistance whatsoever: they know they are beaten when the coup is announced; quietly and quickly they head for the airport. The seizure of power, in this sense, represents the end of a political struggle and the recording of its results, just as takes place on election day in a democratic country.

RADICAL TO MASS PRAETORIANISM:
VETO COUPS AND THE SOLDIER AS GUARDIAN

In the 1960s scholars spent much ink and time debating whether the military play basically a progressive or a conservative role in modernization. Most seemed to agree that in the Middle East the military were typically the proponents of change; the army, as Halpern said, is "the vanguard of nationalism and social reform"; it is the most cohesive and disciplined element in "the new middle class" whose impact on society is predominantly revolutionary. With respect to Latin America, however, no such consensus existed; proponents of both the progressive and the conservative views made impressive cases out of fact, logic, and statistics.[29]

Both cases were right. Latin America is simply more varied than the Middle East. Except for Turkey, virtually all Middle Eastern

29. Manfred Halpern, *The Politics of Social Change in the Middle East and North Africa* (Princeton, Princeton University Press, 1963), pp. 75, 253. For the modernizing argument on the military in southeast Asia, see Lucian Pye, "Armies in the Process of Modernization," in John J. Johnson, ed., *The Role of the Military in Underdeveloped Countries* (Princeton, Princeton University Press, 1962), pp. 69-90. On Latin America, the conservative interpretation is argued by Lieuwen in *Generals vs. Presidents* and by Martin C. Needler, "Political Development and Military Intervention in Latin America," *American Political Science Review*, 60 (September 1966), 616-26. A more progressive role for the military is stressed by Johnson, *The Military and Society in Latin America*.

praetorian or semi-praetorian societies were still in the process after World War II of expanding political participation from the oligarchy to the middle class. Military officers are drawn from middle-class backgrounds and perform middle-class functions in a professionalized, bureaucratic environment. Where the basic issues of politics involve the displacement of the oligarchy and the accession to power of the middle class, the military necessarily are on the side of reform. This was also true in Latin America. In the more advanced Latin American societies—Argentina, Chile, Brazil—the military played a reforming role in the early part of the twentieth century. During and after World War II military officers led or cooperated in middle-class reform movements in Bolivia, El Salvador, Guatemala, Honduras, and Venezuela. In the early 1960s they became the center of a strong middle-class reform movement in Peru and played a progressive role in Ecuador. In Brazil and Argentina in the 1950s, however, and then in Bolivia, Guatemala, and Honduras in the 1960s, the military began to play a more conservative role. This role was distinctly a function of the mobilization of the lower classes into politics.

The frequency of military coups in Latin America, José Nun has shown, has no relation to the size of the middle class.[30] Praetorian politics exists at all stages of social mobilization and the expansion of political participation. The impact and significance of military intervention in politics, however, does vary with the size of the middle class. In Latin America in the 1950s, in those countries where the middle and upper classes were very small, less than 8 per cent of the total population (Nicaragua, Honduras, Dominican Republic, and Haiti), politics was still in the personalistic, oligarchical style, and the middle-class military reformer had yet to appear on the scene. In those societies where the middle class was larger, between 8 and 15 per cent of the total population, the dominant groups in the military typically played a more modern-

30. José Nun, "A Latin American Phenomenon: The Middle Class Military Coup," in Institute of International Studies, *Trends in Social Science Research in Latin American Studies: A Conference Report* (Berkeley, University of California, 1965), pp. 68–69. Nun here reproduces the estimates of the Latin American middle class made by Gino Germani, *Política y Sociedad en una Epoca de Transición* (Buenos Aires Editorial Paidos, 1962), pp. 169–70, and I have, in turn, relied on them in my analysis in this paragraph. For other use of the same data, see Gino Germani and Kalman Silvert, "Politics, Social Structure and Military Intervention in Latin America," *European Journal of Sociology*, 2 (1961), pp. 62–81.

izing and reforming role in the 1930s and 1940s. These societies included Guatemala, Bolivia, El Salvador, Ecuador, and Peru. Panama and Paraguay, with upper and middle classes in 1950 estimated at 15 and 14 per cent respectively, were in some respects deviants from this pattern. Among those larger and more complex societies, where the middle class constituted 15 to 36 per cent of the total population, the military either abstained from politics and were primarily a professional force (Chile, Uruguay, Costa Rica, Mexico) or they intervened in politics to play an increasingly conservative political role (Argentina, Cuba, Venezuela, Colombia, Brazil).

As society changes, so does the role of the military. In the world of oligarchy, the soldier is a radical; in the middle-class world he is a participant and arbiter; as the mass society looms on the horizon he becomes the conservative guardian of the existing order. Thus, paradoxically but understandably, the more backward a society is, the more progressive the role of its military; the more advanced a society becomes, the more conservative and reactionary becomes the role of its military. In 1890 Argentine officers founded the Logia Militar to promote reform. Thirty years later they founded the Logia San Martín, which opposed reform and incubated the 1930 coup designed by its promoters to restore the "stable constitutional democracy" which was being subverted by the "massocracy" of President Yrigoyen.[31] So also, in Turkey, the Young Turks in 1908 and the Kemalists in the 1920s played highly progressive reforming roles similar to those which the military after World War II assumed in other Middle Eastern countries. By that time in Turkey, however, the military were intervening in politics to curb the rise to power of a new business class supported by the peasants. The soldiers had not changed; they still supported the reforms of the Kemalist era. But they were now unwilling to admit to power social classes which might make changes in those reforms.

The extent to which military institutions and individuals become politicized is a function of the weakness of civilian political organizations and the inability of civilian political leaders to deal with the principal policy problems facing the country. The extent to which a politicized officer corps plays a conservative or a reform

31. North, pp. 26–27, 30–33.

role in politics is a function of the expansion of political participation in the society.

The instability and coups associated with the emergence of the middle class are due to changes in the nature of the military; those associated with the emergence of the lower class are due to changes in the nature of the society. In the former case, the military are modernized and develop concepts of efficiency, honesty, and nationalism which alienate them from the existing order. They intervene in politics to bring society abreast of the military. They are the advance guard of the middle class and spearhead its breakthrough into the political arena. They promote social and economic reform, national integration, and, in some measure, the extension of political participation. Once middle-class urban groups become the dominant elements in politics, the military assume an arbitral or stabilizing role. If a society is able to move from middle class to mass participation with fairly well-developed political institutions (such as, in Latin America, Chile, Uruguay, and Mexico), the military assume a nonpolitical, specialized, professional role characteristic of systems with "objective" civilian control. Chile, Uruguay, and Mexico were, indeed, the only Latin American countries in which there were no military coups d'etat during the two decades after World War II. If, however, a society moves into the phase of mass participation without developing effective political institutions, the military become engaged in a conservative effort to protect the existing system against the incursions of the lower classes, particularly the urban lower classes. They become the guardians of the existing middle-class order. They are thus, in a sense, the door-keepers in the expansion of political participation in a praetorian society: their historical role is to open the door to the middle class and to close it on the lower class. The radical phase of a praetorian society begins with a bright, modernizing military coup toppling the oligarchy and heralding the emergence of enlightenment into politics. It ends in a succession of frustrating and unwholesome rearguard efforts to block the lower classes from scaling the heights of political power.

Military interventions of this "veto" variety thus directly reflect increasing lower-class political participation in politics. The more active role of the military in Argentina after 1930 coincided with the doubling of the industrial proletariat from 500,000 to one million workers in little over a decade. Similarly, in Brazil, "It was the clamor of the urban masses and the proliferation of politicians demagogically soliciting their votes that brought the military back into politics in 1950." In 1954 the military turned against Vargas when he moved Perón-like "to bring about a rapid resurgence of popular support for the government, with reckless promises to the workers." [32]

More specifically, veto interventions usually occur under two sets of circumstances. One is the actual or prospective victory at the polls of a party or movement which the military oppose or which represents groups which the military wish to exclude from political power. Five of the seven military coups that took place in Latin America between 1962 and 1964 had this as their objective. In Argentina in March 1962 the military intervened to remove President Frondizi from office and cancel the results of the elections in which the Peronistas won 35 per cent of the vote and elected ten of fourteen provincial governors and almost one fourth of the Chamber of Deputies. In Peru in July 1962 the military took over after an election to prevent Haya de la Torre of the Apristas or former General Manuel Odría from becoming president. In Guatemala in March 1963 the military coup was aimed at forestalling the possible election of the radical Juan Arévalo to the presidency. In Ecuador in July 1963 the military removed President Arosemena from office in part to insure against the return to power of Velasco Ibarra, whom they had removed from office in November 1961.[33] In Honduras in October 1963 the military again intervened to prevent the election of populist reformer Rodas Alvarado as President. The increasingly conservative role of the military in Latin America in vetoing the accession to power of popular, lower-class, or reform movements was reflected in the increasing extent to which military coups were associated with elections. Only 12 per cent of the coups in Latin America between 1935 and 1944 occurred during the twelve months before a scheduled election or the four months immediately after an election. From 1945 to 1954 this proportion rose to 32 per cent, and between 1955 and 1964 some 56 per cent of the coups occurred near election time.[34]

Veto coups also occur when a government in power begins to

32. Johnson, *Military and Society*, p. 217.
33. Lieuwen, *Generals vs. Presidents*, pp. 10 ff., 45–50.
34. Needler, "Political Development," pp. 619–20.

promote radical policies or to develop an appeal to groups whom the military wishes to exclude from power. This was the case in Peru in 1948, in the Dominican Republic in 1963, in Brazil in 1964, and, in a somewhat different context, in Turkey in 1960, and in Indonesia in 1965. In all these cases of both types the dominant group in the armed forces was opposed to a party or movement with substantial popular appeal—Apristas, Peronistas, Communists, Democrats, or the like—and acted to oust this group from office or to prevent it from coming to power.

In the move from a traditional or oligarchical system to one in which the middle class plays a key role, the promotion of social and economic reform goes hand-in-hand with the expansion of political participation. In the shift from a radical to a mass society the relationship is not quite as clear-cut. Almost universally, a politicized officer corps will object to the incorporation of the urban lower classes into politics. The thrust of military intervention in these circumstances has a conservative effect: it prevents the broadening of political participation to more radical groups and thus slows up the process of social-economic reform. In Middle Eastern and Asian societies, however, the masses may well be more conservative than the middle-class nationalist elites which came to power with the ebb of Western colonialism. In these circumstances, military intervention to bar the rise of new groups to political power may have a net progressive effect on governmental policies. The promotion of social-economic reform, in short, conflicts with the expansion of political participation. The ouster of the Menderes government in Turkey in 1960, for instance, was an effort to curtail the participation in politics of leaders supported by the more traditional and conservative rural masses. In such societies, politics is, so to speak, upside down rather than right side up, with the defenders of the traditional order on the bottom rather than on the top.

Even in Latin America, where a highly articulated class structure makes for a high correlation between the expansion of participation and the promotion of reform, circumstances may develop in which the military act in favor of the latter but against the former. The failure of the military to play a reform role earlier in the history of Peru, for instance, was due in large part to the development of APRA as a middle-class and working-class reform

movement and the historical incidents and accidents which alienated it from the military in the early 1930s. In effect, the middle-
class groups were divided against themselves, which redounded to
"the advantage of the upper-class groups, who consequently fomented and nursed the already existent division." [35] The result
was an "unnatural" perpetuation of oligarchical control in Peru
until a new, non-Aprista civilian reform movement developed in
the late 1950s. The military intervention in 1962, in a sense, tele-
scoped the historical process. Insofar as it was designed to block
the Apristas from coming to power, the intervention was the
manifestation of a conservative, guardian role. Insofar as it
brought into office first a reform-minded military junta and then a
reform-minded civilian regime, it fell into the older, progressive
pattern, its actions calling to mind the interventions of the Chil-
ean military in the 1920s. In some respects, indeed, the pattern of
events in 1962–63 followed the classical reform pattern. The coup
of July 1962 brought to power a three-man military junta, which
began to draw up programs for agrarian and social reform. The
chief of the junta, General Pérez Godoy, however, was more conservative; he was, as Richard Patch suggested, "among the last of
the old time generals" and he made plans for bringing back to
power the conservative General Manuel Odría. Early in 1963,
consequently, a consolidating coup eased out Godoy and replaced
him with General Nicolás Lindley López, who had been leader of
the progressive military group centered about the Centro de Altos
Estudios Militares. "The elimination of the junta chief, General
Pérez Godoy," one analyst has written, "was an additional indica-
tor of the consolidation of the reform-oriented officers." [36]

The guardian role of the military is legitimated by an impressive rationale, which is persuasive to many armies and often persuasive to American opinion leaders. Military involvement in politics
is intermittent and for limited purposes, and hence the military
view themselves neither as the modernizers of society nor as the
creators of a new political order but rather as the guardians and
perhaps the purifiers of the existing order. The army, in the words
of President (and Air Force general) Barrientos of Bolivia, should
be the country's "tutelary institution . . . watching zealously

35. North, p. 49.
36. Ibid., p. 55.

over the fulfilling of laws and the virtue of governments." [37] Military intervention, consequently, is prompted by the corruption, stagnation, stalemate, anarchy, subversion of the established political system. Once these are eliminated, the military claim that they can then return the purified polity to the hands of the civilian leaders. Their job is simply to straighten out the mess and then to get out. Theirs is a temporary dictatorship—perhaps somewhat on the Roman model.

The ideology of guardianship varies little from country to country. It is most developed, naturally enough, in Latin America, where praetorianism and political participation are both widely prevalent. The army should intervene in politics, as one Argentine general put it, to deal with "the great disasters that can imperil our national stability and integrity, leaving aside the small disasters that any attempt to repair will only serve to separate us from our mission and hamper a clear perception of our duty." Many Latin American constitutions implicitly or explicity recognize the guardian function of the military. The Peruvian military, for instance, have justified their actions in barring the Apristas from power by a constitutional provision: "The purpose of the armed force is to assure the law of the Republic, compliance with the Constitution and laws, and the conservation of public order." [38] The military in a sense assume constitutional functions analogous to those of the Supreme Court of the United States: they have a responsibility to preserve the political order and hence are drawn into politics at times of crisis or controversy to veto actions by the "political" branches of government which deviate from the essentials of that system. Yet they are also concerned about their own institutional integrity and hence divided among themselves into the military equivalents of "judicial activists" and "judicial self-restrainers."

Perhaps the most extensive and explicit manifestation of the guardian role can be found in the outlook of the Brazilian army. At the time of the military overthrow of the empire, one military intellectual defended what he described as "the undeniable right

37. Quoted by Christopher Rand, "Letter from La Paz," *New Yorker* (December 31, 1966), p. 50.

38. Major General Julio Alsogaray, *New York Times*, March 6, 1966, p. 26; Rosendo A. Gomez, "Peru: The Politics of Military Guardianship," in Needler, *Political Systems*, pp. 301–02.

of the armed forces to depose the legitimate powers . . . when the military feels that its honor requires this to be done, or judges it necessary and convenient for the good of the country." [39] The guardian role was, in some measure, written into the 1946 constitution, which provided that the function of the armed forces was to "defend the fatherland and guarantee the constitutional powers, and law and order." The prime responsibility of the army was thus to protect social peace and the Brazilian republican form of government. Consequently the army must be nonpolitical and above politics. If the army judges that the republic is in danger, that disorder is in prospect, it has the obligation to intervene and to restore the constitution. Once this is done, it then has the obligation to withdraw and to return power to the normal (conservative, middle-class) civilian leaders. "The military," President Castello Branco said, "should be ready to act in concert, opportunely, and in the face of inescapable necessity to assure a correct course in Brazil. The necessity and the opportunity would correspond not simply to a desire to be tutors to the nation, but to the recognition of a situation requiring emergency action at the service of the nation." This doctrine, once labeled "supermission," is perhaps more appropriately described as "civism." It is reflected in the army's suspicion of personalism and of a strong, popular, directly elected chief executive with a mass following, a Getulio, a Janio, a Jango, or a Juscelino. "The Army wants no Peronism, no popular party that could be organized in such a way as to threaten the Army's dominant position as interpreter and guardian of the national interest." [40] Hence the army accepts such a popular leader only until he begins to organize his own mass following with which he can challenge the army's role as arbiter of the national values.

The United States often encouraged the guardian concept. Frequently the United States was quite happy to have the military dislodge governments it disliked, then to reconcile this action with its democratic conscience by insisting that the military rulers at an early opportunity turn power over to a new—and presumably

---

39. Benjamin Constant Botelho de Bagalhaes, quoted in Charles W. Simmons, "The Rise of the Brazilian Military Class, 1840–1890," *Mid-America*, *39* (October 1957), 237.

40. *New York Times*, March 6, 1966, p. 26; Brady Tyson, "Brazilian Army 'Civism' " (unpublished MS, May 1964), p. 6.

safe—civilian government based on free elections. From the view-point of modernization and development, the second mistake simply compounded the first. For it is quite clear that while guardianship has the loftiest justifications and rationales, it also has the most debilitating and corrupting effect on the political system. Responsibility and power are divorced. Civilian leaders may have responsibility, but they know they do not have power and are not allowed to create power because their actions are subject to military veto. The military juntas may exercise power, but they know that they will not have to be responsible for the consequences of their action, for they can always turn authority back to the civilians when the problems of governance become too much for them. One might think that a system of checks and balances would develop, with the civilians attempting to do their best in order to avoid military intervention, and the military attempting to do their best in order to escape from the traumas of politics. In actuality, however, this type of system seems to bring out the worst in both sides.

The extent to which the military are locked in a middle-class outlook suggests that expectations that the military will increasingly become a force for reform are likely to be unfounded. It has, for instance, been suggested that the future will see the emergence of a Latin American Nasserism, that is, "the assumption by Latin American armed forces of the same kind of modernizing and reforming responsibilities that the military have assumed in the Near East." [41] Many Latin Americans, civilians as well as colonels, see a Nasserite solution as the most promising path toward social, economic, and political development. These hopes have little chance of realization. Most Latin American societies are beyond the possibilities of Nasserism. They are too complex, too highly articulated, too far advanced economically to be susceptible to salvation by military reform. As Latin America has modernized, the role of the military has become more conservative. Between 1935 and 1944, 50 per cent of the coups in Latin America had reformist objectives of changing the economic and social status quo; between 1945 and 1954, 23 per cent of the coups had these objectives; between 1955 and 1964, only 17 per cent did.[42] To say that

---

41. Lieuwen, *Generals vs. Presidents*, p. 138. See pp. 136–41 for a good evaluation of the possibilities of and obstacles to Latin American Nasserism.
42. Needler, "Political Development," pp. 619–20.

the Brazil of the 1960s needed a Nasser was somewhat like saying that the Russia of the 1960s needed a Stolypin. The two types of leadership were simply irrelevant to the stage of development that these societies had reached. In the 1960s, an Iran or an Ethiopia could use a Stolypin, and in Latin America there was perhaps room for a Nasser in Haiti, Paraguay, Nicaragua, or even the Dominican Republic. But the rest of the continent was simply too highly developed for such an attractively simple panacea.

As society becomes more complex it becomes more difficult for military officers, first, to exercise power effectively and then to seize power successfully. As a reasonably small, socially homogeneous, and highly disciplined and coherent group, the dominant elements in the officer corps can act reasonably effectively as a leadership cadre in a society which is still relatively uncomplex and undifferentiated. As the praetorian society becomes more complex and differentiated, the number of social groups and forces multiplies and the problems of coordination and interest aggregation become increasingly complex. In the absence of effective central political institutions for the resolution of social conflicts, the military become simply one of several relatively insulated and autonomous social forces. Their capacity to elicit support and to induce cooperation declines. In addition, of course, military officers are not necessarily skilled in the esoteric arts of negotiation, compromise, and mass appeal which are required for political action in a complex society. A more simple society can be spurred, commanded, and led toward an objective. But where social differentiation is well advanced, the political leader must be a balancer and compromiser. The tendency of the military to choose a guardian role in the more complex societies in itself indicates some awareness of the difficulties of integrating social forces.

Not only does it become more difficult for a highly specialized group to exercise political leadership in a highly complex society, but the means by which the military can acquire power also begin to lose their effectiveness. By its very nature the utility of the coup as a technique of political action declines as the scope of political participation broadens. In an oligarchical society and in the early phases of a radical praetorian society, violence is limited because government is weak and politics small. The participants in politics are few in number and often constitute a relatively closely knit group. In Burma, for instance, military and political leaders were closely linked by marriage.[43] As participation broadens, however, and society becomes more complex, coups become more difficult and more bloody. Eighty-one per cent of the coups in Latin America between 1935 and 1944 were essentially bloodless, without streetfighting and other popular participation. Between 1945 and 1954, however, 68 per cent were low in violence; and between 1955 and 1964, only 33 per cent were.[44] The increasing violence of the coups was naturally accompanied by the increased use of other more extensive forms of violence by other social forces. As society becomes more complex, other groups develop their own means of countering military action. If an effort is made to override their interests, they may retaliate with their own forms of violence or coercion. General strikes, for instance, played major roles in the overthrow of the regime in Guatemala in 1944 and in Perón's consolidating coup in Argentina in 1945.[45] When numerous groups participate in politics, he who wishes to secure power needs a broader base than is normally responsible for the classic coup. Kapp could be stopped by a general strike, but not Hitler. Similarly, the tradition of the *pronunciamiento* in Spain was broken in 1936. The revolt of the army produced not a coup but a civil war as labor, radical, Catalan, and other groups came to the support of the government. In the more extreme of the veto coups workers' militias were often created either to aid in the defense of power against elements of the regular army or to counterbalance the regular army before its seizure of power.

A succession of military coups thus eventually tends to undermine the possibility of coups. Changes in power and policy require either complex bargaining among a large number of groups or bloody civil war. As the scope of politics is broadened, violence becomes less frequent but more virulent. As Dankwart Rustow has pointed out:

> A century or two ago, vezirs might be banished or executed, sultans deposed or murdered: yet the average craftsman, villager, or nomad would scarcely notice any change.

43. Pye, "Armies in the Process of Modernization," in Johnson, *Military in Underdeveloped Countries*, pp. 234–35.

44. Needler, pp. 619–20.

45. George I. Blanksten, "The Politics of Latin America," in Gabriel Almond and James S. Coleman, eds., *The Politics of the Developing Areas* (Princeton, Princeton University Press, 1960), p. 498.

Today, by contrast, any political assassination or coup d'etat —at times even a mere election—tends to be accompanied by extensive police or even military action, by mass arrests and deportations, by the suspension of newspapers, and by political trials. Instability, once a mere ripple on the surface, now engulfs the entire society.[46]

The democratization of government in a society in which violence is a key part of government also means the democratization of violence. The coup d'etat—the limited war of domestic violence—may be replaced by the revolutionary war or other violent insurrection involving numerous elements of society. Conceivably, the conservative elements may retreat gracefully before the demands of the emerging groups, thereby permitting processes of peaceful change to develop. If they do not, the decline in the role of the military in society and government may well be accompanied by an increase in the role of violence.

The seizure of power by the military in a coup designed to veto the expansion of political participation brings only temporary relief to the political system. The groups which participate in the coup are usually united only by their desire to stop or to reverse the tendencies which they consider subversive of political order. Once the military are in power, the coup coalition begins to split. It may fragment into many small cliques, each attempting to push its own ends. More frequently, it divides into two broad factions: the radicals and the moderates, the hard-liners and the soft-liners, the *gorilas* and the *legalistas*. The struggle between the moderates and the radicals may focus on a number of issues, but typically the key issue is the return of power to civilians. Invariably, the junta which comes to power in a veto coup promises a quick surrender of power and return to normal civilian rule. The hard-liners argue, however, that the military must stay in power to bar permanently the civilian groups which they ousted from power and to impose structural reforms on the political system. The hard-liners are usually etatist in economics and authoritarian in politics. The moderates, on the other hand, usually view the aims of the coup as more limited. Once the objectionable political leaders have been removed from the scene and a few political and administrative changes introduced, they feel that they have done their job, and

46. Dankwart A. Rustow, *Politics and Westernization in the Near East* (Princeton, Center of International Studies, 1956), p. 17.

they are ready to retire to the political sidelines. As in the break-through coups which mark the rise of the middle class to political action, the moderates in the veto coups usually come to power first. They are moderate, however, not because they are willing to compromise with the existing oligarchy but because they may be willing to compromise with the emerging mass movements. The radicals, on the other hand, resist the expansion of political partic-ipation. In the breakthrough coup, the radical does not compro-mise with the oligarchy; in the veto coup the radical does not com-promise with the masses. One hastens history; the other resists it.

The division between moderates and radicals means that veto coups, like breakthrough coups, often come in pairs, the initial coup followed by a consolidating coup in which the hard-liners at-tempt to overthrow the moderates and to prevent the return of power to the civilians. In this case, however, the consolidating coup is less likely to be successful than it was in the expansion of political participation to the middle class. In Argentina in 1958 and again in 1962, for instance, the military moderates who wished to return power to civilians were able to suppress efforts by the *gorilas* to prevent this transfer. In Turkey in 1960 and 1961 General Gursel was also able to defeat attempted consolidating coups by radical colonels. In Korea after the 1961 military coup a similar struggle developed between those senior leaders more will-ing to return power to civilians or to civilianize military rule and those younger colonels who insisted that the military would have to retain power for a long period of time to purify the Korean po-litical system. In the fall of 1962 General Pak indicated that he was willing to civilianize his rule and that he would run for the presidency in open elections. In the winter of 1963, members of the military junta protested against this action. In due course, however, the moderates won out and the elections were held in the late fall of 1963. In the struggle which followed the March 1962 coup in Burma, on the other hand, the moderates lost, and their chief spokesman, Brigadier Aung Gyi, was fired from the govern-ment in February 1963 for advocating a return to civilian rule.

The basic dilemma in the guardian role involves the two as-sumptions that the army is above politics and that the army should intervene in politics to prevent changes in the political system. The guardian role of the military is based on the premise that the causes of military intervention arise from temporary and extraordinary disruptions of the political system. In fact, however, the causes are endemic to the political system and are the unavoidable consequence of the modernization of society. They cannot be removed simply by eliminating people. In addition, once the army does block the conquest of power by another social group, institutional and personal self-interest combine to make the officers deathly fearful of the retaliation which may be visited upon them if they ever withhold their veto. Hence the incentives to intervene escalate, and the army becomes irreversibly committed to insuring that the once-proscribed group never acquires office.

The army which intervenes with a veto coup confronts the choice that faced the Brazilian military after their coup in April 1964. The "Brazilian army," as Tyson wrote at the time, "must choose to be further drawn into Brazilian politics, with the consequent divisions-of-opinion that will shatter the unity of the army, or it must allow other and new groups to organize for effective political action, thus surrendering its monopoly-of-power and position as ultimate arbiter." [47] More precisely, an army which intervenes in this manner can choose among four courses of action, in terms of whether it retains power or returns it to civilians and whether it acquiesces in or resists the expansion of political participation. Each option, however, imposes costs on the military and on the political system.

1. *Return and Restrict (The Aramburu Option)*. The military can return power to civilians after a brief rule and a purge of governmental officials but continue to restrict the rise of new groups to political power. Almost invariably, however, the need to intervene recurs. In 1955, for instance, the Argentine military threw out Perón. After a struggle the soft-liners, under General P. Aramburu, defeated the hard-liners, and power was returned to civilians. Elections were held and a moderate, Frondizi, was elected President. In subsequent elections (1962) the Peronistas demonstrated that they still had the support of one third of the Argentine electorate. For this reason, Frondizi felt compelled to compromise and to attempt some forms of cooperation with them. For this reason, also, the military felt compelled to intervene again and to throw Frondizi out. New elections were held, the Peronistas were effectively barred from participation, and the centrists won with 26 per cent of the total vote, electing Arturo Illia as Presi-

47. Tyson, p. 11.

dent. The Peronistas, however, remained strong, the military remained adamant against their participation in power, and hence the political system remained in a praetorian state with the military an active veto-wielding group on the sidelines perpetually ready to intervene. When Illia's rule faltered in 1966, their reentry into politics was inevitable. The situation was comparable to that in Peru between 1931 and 1963, when the Army intervened three times to prevent the APRA from coming to power. When a situation like this develops, it is clear that guardianship becomes self-defeating. The military in effect abandon their claim to be outside, impartial guarantors of the political order. Instead they become active participants and contestants on the political scene, employing their superior organization and the threat of force to counterbalance the mass appeal and voting strength of other groups.

Another example of the limitations of this pattern is afforded by Burma. In 1958, when the ruling AFPFL party split, General Ne Win came to power, replacing the government of Premier U Nu. Ne Win made it clear, however, that he intended to return power to the civilians, and he made every effort to minimize the changes which his military regime made in the political system. In 1960 he did surrender power; elections were held, contested by two parties, and U Nu was voted back into office. Reluctantly but honestly, Ne Win returned power to U Nu. Two years later, however, conditions had deteriorated to the point where General Ne Win again felt compelled to intervene and to oust U Nu. This time Ne Win intervened for good. U Nu and his associates were jailed, and Ne Win made it clear that he intended to stay in power.

2. *Return and Expand (The Gursel Option)*. The military leaders can return power to civilians and permit the social groups which they had previously blocked to come to power under new conditions and usually with new leadership. After the 1960 coup in which the Turkish Army threw out the Menderes government, the military executed a number of its former leaders, but General Gursel also insisted on turning power back to the civilians. Elections were held in 1961. The major contestants were the Peoples Party, which the military favored, and the Justice Party, which appealed to the same groups that had previously backed Menderes. No party won a majority, but General Gursel was elected president, and the Peoples Party formed a weak coalition government.

It was clear, however, that the dominant voting groups in Turkey favored the Justice Party, and the key questions were whether the Justice Party would be moderate enough not to antagonize the military and provoke another intervention, and whether the military would be broadminded enough to permit the Justice Party to come to power through peaceful elections. Neither of these conditions had been met in Argentina in the relations between the Peronistas and the Argentine military. In Turkey, however, compromise and moderation prevailed. Efforts by military radicals to stage a second coup were squelched by the government with the support of the senior military commanders, and in the 1965 elections the Justice Party won a clear majority in Parliament and formed a government. The military acquiesced in the acquisition of power by this coalition of businessmen and peasants which previously they had barred from power when it was under the leadership of Menderes. Presumably the Turkish military will remain on the political sidelines until a new crisis of political participation develops, perhaps when the urban working class bids for a share in power. In Venezuela in 1958 and in Guatemala in 1966 the military also acquiesced in the assumption of office by social groups and political tendencies which they had previously opposed. In all such cases, the civilian leaders who assume power come to terms with and accept at least some conditions specified by the military, not the least of which is that they abjure retaliation for any actions the military may have taken when they held office.

3. *Retain and Restrict* (*The Castello Branco Option*). The military can retain power and continue to resist the expansion of political participation. In this case, despite whatever intentions they may have to the contrary, they are inevitably driven to more and more repressive measures. This was the course assumed by the Brazilian military after the coup of April 1964 which ousted the Goulart government. The coup brought to power a military regime with the support of business and technocratic elements. The state elections in Brazil in 1965, however, indicated clearly that the voting public was on the side of the opposition. These elections prompted the hard-liners in the military to demand the cancellation of the results of the elections—just as the Argentine military had done in 1962 and just as the younger Turkish military officers tried to do in 1961. In Turkey, General Gursel squelched the hard-liners' attempted coup. For several weeks in Brazil it

looked as if this scenario might be repeated. The hard-liners were expected to attempt to oust the moderate president, General Castello Branco, and to impose a more authoritarian rule to bar the opposition from political power. Many also expected that Castello Branco would be able to rally moderate opinion and defeat the hard-liners' coup. Instead of leading the successful resistance to a coup, however, Castello Branco decided to lead the coup itself, which he did by suspending parliament, abolishing political parties, and imposing new restraints on political activity and freedom of speech. Whatever the reasons for his action, its effect was to reduce the possibility that Brazil would be able to follow the Turkish pattern and work out a compromise which would permit a sanitized opposition to come to power peacefully. The situation was instead further polarized, and the Brazilian military, who had prided themselves in the past on the extent to which they adhered to a rigorous nonpolitical, guardian role, now found themselves in a situation where they could not surrender power except to groups which were completely anathema to them. To eliminate the possibility of a popular appeal to the masses, the presidential election of 1966 was made indirect and by the old congress from which the military had eliminated many opposition elements. No opposition candidate ran against the military candidate, General Costa e Silva. In the subsequent elections for a new congress many restrictions and restraints were imposed on the opposition candidates.

4. *Retain and Expand* (*The Perón Option*). The military can retain power and permit or, indeed, capitalize upon the expansion of political participation. This, of course, was the path followed by Perón and, in lesser measure, Rojas Pinilla in Colombia. In these instances, the officers come to power through a coup which deviates from the veto pattern and then alter their political base by bringing new groups into politics as their supporters. The price of this action is usually twofold. It alienates the military leader from his original source of support in the army and hence increases his vulnerability to a conservative military coup. It also tends to intensify the antagonism between the conservative middle class and the radical masses. In a sense, also, it reverses the pattern of the oligarchical praetorian society in which a poor, populist demagogue typically deserted his mass following in order to be accepted by the elite. Here a middle-class leader deserts his class

in order to win a mass following. The military commander attempts to become a populist dictator. In the end, however, he fails in the same manner and for the same reasons as his civilian counterparts. Perón goes the way of Vargas; Rojas Pinilla suffers the fate of Haya de la Torre: their efforts vetoed by their former comrades-in-arms who remain faithful to the guardian role.

Praetorianism to Civic Order:
The Soldier as Institution-Builder

In simple societies a sense of community makes possible the development of political institutions. In more complicated societies a primary, if not the primary, function of political institutions is to make the community more of a community. The interaction between the political order and the social order is thus a dynamic and dialectical one: initially the latter plays the major role in shaping the former, subsequently the former plays the more important role in creating the latter. Praetorian societies, however, are caught in a vicious circle. In its simpler forms the praetorian society lacks community and this obstructs the development of political institutions. In its more complicated forms, the lack of effective political institutions obstructs the development of community. As a result, strong tendencies exist in a praetorian society encouraging it to remain in that condition. Attitudes and behavior patterns, once developed, tend to remain and to repeat themselves. Praetorian politics becomes embedded in the culture of the society.

Praetorianism has thus tended to be more endemic in certain cultures (e.g. Spanish, Arabic) than in others and to persist in these cultures through the expansion of political participation and the emergence of a more complex modern social structure. The sources of the Latin American praetorianism lay in the absence of any inheritance of political institutions from the colonial period and then in the effort to introduce into the highly oligarchical society of early nineteenth-century Latin America the middle-class republican institutions of France and the United States. The sources of the praetorianism in the Arab world lay in the collapse of the Arab states under the Ottoman conquest, the long period of Ottoman domination, which from a high level of institutional development degenerated into a weak, alien rule, losing its legitimacy with the emergence of Arab nationalism, and then the sub-

jection of much of the Arab world to semicolonialism by France
and Great Britain. These historical experiences encouraged in the
Arab culture a continuing political weakness comparable to that
found in Latin America. Distrust and hatred among individuals
and groups produced a continuing low level of political institutionalization. When such conditions exist in a culture, the question necessarily arises: How can they be remedied? Under what
circumstances is it possible to move from a society of politicized social forces to one in which there is legitimacy and authority?
Where in such a society is there a fulcrum which can be used to
move the society out of that condition? Who or what can create
the common interests and the integrating institutions necessary
to transform a praetorian society into a civic polity?

These questions have no obvious answers. Two generalizations,
however, can perhaps be made about the movement of societies
from praetorian disunity to civic order. First, the earlier this development takes place in the process of modernization and the expansion of political participation, the lower the costs it imposes on
society. Conversely, the more complex the society the more difficult it becomes to create integrating political institutions. Second,
at each stage in the broadening of political participation the opportunities for fruitful political action rest with different social
groups and different types of political leaders. For societies in the
radical praetorian phase, the leadership in the creation of durable
political institutions obviously must come from middle-class social
forces and must appeal to such forces. Some have argued that
heroic charismatic leadership may be able to perform this role.
Where traditional political institutions are weak, or collapse, or
are overthrown, authority frequently comes to rest with such charismatic leaders who attempt to bridge the gap between tradition
and modernity by a highly personal appeal. To the extent that
these leaders are able to concentrate power in themselves, it might
be supposed that they would be in a position to push institutional
development and to perform the role of "Great Legislator" or
"Founding Father." The reform of corrupt states or the creation
of new ones, Machiavelli argued, must be the work of one man
alone. A conflict exists, however, between the interests of the individual and the interests of institutionalization. Institutionalization
of power means the limitation of power which the charismatic
leader might otherwise wield personally and arbitrarily. The

would-be institution-builder needs personal power to create institutions, but he cannot create institutions without relinquishing personal power. Institutional authority is the opposite of charismatic authority, and charismatic leaders defeat themselves if they attempt to create stable institutions of public order.

Conceivably in a radical praetorian society integrating political institutions could be the outgrowth of political organizations which originally represent narrow ethnic or economic groups but which broaden their appeal beyond the original social force responsible for their existence. The political dynamics of a praetorian society, however, militate against this. The nature of the conflict encourages political organizations to become more narrowly specialized and limited, more devoted to their own particular interests, and more reliant upon their own distinctive means of political action. The immediate rewards go to those who act aggressively in their own interests rather than to those who attempt to aggregate a number of interests.

In theory, consequently, the more effective leadership in institution-building should come from groups which are not so directly identified with particular ethnic or economic strata. In some measure, students, religious leaders, and soldiers may fall into this category. The record suggests, however, that neither students nor religious groups play a constructive role in the development of political institutions. By their very nature, students are against the existing order, and they are generally incapable of constituting authority or establishing principles of legitimacy. There are numerous cases of student and religious demonstrations, riots, and revolts, but none of student governments and few of religious ones.

The military, on the other hand, may possess a greater capacity for generating order in a radical praetorian society. There are military coups, but there are also military governments and political parties which have come out of the womb of the army. The military can be cohesive, bureaucratized, and disciplined. Colonels can run a government; students and monks cannot. The effectiveness of military intervention stems at least as much from the organizational characteristics of the military as from its control of or use of violence. The correlation between violence in politics and the military in politics is spotty at best. Most coups in most areas of the world involve only a handful of deaths. A student riot or a general strike or a religious demonstration or an ethnic protest usually produces far more casualties than a military coup. It is thus their superior organizational capacities that make intervention by the military more dramatic, more dangerous, and yet also potentially more productive than intervention by other social forces. Unlike student intervention, military intervention, which many people consider to be the source of the evil in a praetorian society, may also be the source of the cure.

The ability of the military to play this developmental role or even to play a modernizing role depends upon the combination of social forces in the society. The influence of the military in a praetorian society changes with the level of participation. In the oligarchical phase, little distinction usually exists between military and civilian leaders, and the political scene is dominated by generals or at least individuals bearing the title of general. By the time a society has moved into the radical middle-class phase, the officer corps has usually become more sharply delineated as an institution; influence is shared between military and other social forces; and a limited degree of political institutionalization may take place within the framework of a narrowly defined and non-expansible political system. Military intervention is frequently intermittent, with an alternation of military juntas and civilian ones and with the gradual emergence of more powerful, counterbalancing, civilian groups. Finally, in the mass praetorian phase, the influence of the military is circumscribed by the emergence of large, popular movements. Consequently, the opportunities for the creation of political institutions under military auspices are greatest in the early phases of a radical praetorian society.

For a society to escape from praetorianism requires both the coalescence of urban and rural interests and the creation of new political institutions. The distinctive social aspect of radical praetorianism is the divorce of the city from the countryside: politics is combat among middle-class urban groups, no one of which has reason to promote social consensus or political order. The social precondition for the establishment of stability is the reappearance in politics of the social forces dominant in the countryside. The intelligentsia has the brains; the military have the guns; but the peasants have the numbers, and the votes. Political stability requires a coalition between at least two of these social forces. Given the hostility which usually develops between the two most politically articulate elements of the middle class, a coalition of brains and guns against numbers is rare indeed. If it does come into existence, as in Turkey during the Ataturk period, it provides only a temporary and fragile stability; eventually it is overwhelmed by the entry of the rural masses into politics. A coalition between the intelligentsia and the peasants, in contrast, usually involves revolution: the destruction of the existing system as a prerequisite to the creation of a new, more stable one. The third route to stable government is by the coalescence of guns and numbers against brains. It is this possibility which offers the military in a radical praetorian society the opportunity to move their society from praetorianism to civic order.

The ability of the military to develop stable political institutions depends first upon their ability to identify their rule with the masses of the peasantry and to mobilize the peasantry into politics on their side. In many instances this is precisely what modernizing military rulers who have come to power in the early stages of radical praetorianism have attempted to do. Often the officers themselves are drawn from the rural classes or have connections with the countryside. In the late 1940s, for instance, most of the Korean officers "came from modest rural or small-town backgrounds." [48] In the early 1960s the military rulers of Korea were

> young men between the ages of 35 and 45 who come from rural backgrounds and who, in many cases, have known poverty at close range. It is natural for these men to have a rural orientation—to feel an empathy with the farmer. Such men must always regard urbanism with a certain ambivalence. Has it not bred the kind of immorality, corruption and basic selfishness characteristic of Korean politics—indeed, Korean life—in recent years? Yet they recognize that the economic realities of Korea demand more urbanism, not less. Industrialization is the key to this labor-surplus society, as the junta well knows. [49]

The leaders of the Egyptian coup in 1952 had similar backgrounds. "The army was solidly Egyptian and rural; its officers were of the rural middle class." The officer corps, Naguib affirmed,

---

48. Henderson, p. 339.
49. Robert A. Scalapino, "Which Route for Korea?" *Asian Survey, 11* (September 1962), 11.

"was largely composed of the sons of civil servants and soldiers and the grandsons of peasants." [50] In Burma, compared to the westernized political elite of the AFPFL, the military leaders were "tied more closely to the agrarian Buddhist Burmans." [51] Their rural social background often leads military regimes to give high priority to policies which benefit the more numerous elements in the countryside. In Egypt, Iraq, Turkey, Korea, Pakistan, governments born of military coups pushed land reform measures. In Burma and elsewhere military governments gave budget priority to agricultural rather than to urban programs. A substantial appeal to the most numerous and powerful elements in the countryside is the sine qua non for the stability of any government in a modernizing country, and that is as true for a military government as for any other. A military regime which is not able to mobilize such support, whose backers come only from the barracks and the city, lacks the social base upon which to build effective political institutions.

The support of rural elements is, however, only a precondition to the development of political institutions by a military regime. Initially, the legitimacy of a modernizing military regime comes from the promise it offers for the future. But eventually this declines as a source of legitimacy. If the regime does not develop a political structure which institutionalizes some principle of legitimacy, the result can only be a military oligarchy in which power is passed among the oligarchs by means of coups d'etat, and which also stands in danger of revolutionary overthrow by new social forces which it does not possess the institutional mechanisms for assimilating. Egypt and Burma may maintain an image of social change and modernization for some while, but unless they create new institutional structures, Thailand is their future. There too a modernizing military junta seized power in 1932 and embarked on a program of sweeping change. In due course, however, it ran out of steam and settled down into a comfortable bureaucratic oligarchy.

Unlike a charismatic leader or the leaders of a particular social force, the military leaders do not face an insoluble dilemma in the

50. Perlmutter, Chap. 2, pp. 25, 26; Mohammad Naguib, *Egypt's Destiny* (Garden City, Doubleday and Company, 1955) , pp. 14–15.

51. John H. Badgley, "Burma: The Nexus of Socialism and Two Political Traditions," *Asian Survey, 3* (February 1963) , 92–93.

development of political institutions. As a group, the military junta can retain power at the same time that they institutionalize it. There is no necessary conflict between their personal interests and those of political institutionalization. They can, in a sense, convert military *intervention* in politics into military *participation* in politics. Military intervention violates whatever rules of the game may exist and undermines the integrity of the political order and the basis of legitimacy. Military participation means playing the political game in order to create new political institutions. The initial intervention may be illegitimate, but it acquires legitimacy when it is converted into participation and the assumption of responsibility for the creation of new political institutions which will make impossible and unnecessary future interventions by both the military and other social forces. Intermittent military intervention to stop politics or to suspend politics is the essence of praetorianism. Sustained military participation in politics may lead a society away from praetorianism.

The principal obstacle to the military's playing this role in radical praetorian societies comes not from objective social and political conditions but from the subjective attitudes of the military toward politics and toward themselves. The problem is military opposition to politics. Military leaders can easily envision themselves in a guardian role; they can also picture themselves as the far-seeing impartial promoters of social and economic reform in their societies. But, with rare exceptions, they shrink from assuming the role of political organizer. In particular, they condemn political parties. They try to rule the state without parties, and they thereby cut off the one major way in which they could hope to move their countries out of their praetorian condition. Parties, Ayub Khan said in phrases which echo George Washington, "divide and confuse the people" and open them "to exploitation by unscrupulous demagogues." The legislature, he said, should "consist of men of high character and wisdom belonging to no party." [52] "Parties," Nasser declared, "are divisive elements, a foreign implantation, an instrument of the imperialists" which would seek "to divide us and create differences between us." [53] So also,

52. Ayub Khan, *Dawn* (Karachi), June 16, 1960, quoted in D. P. Singhal, "The New Constitution of Pakistan," *Asian Survey*, 2 (August 1962), 17.
53. Gamal Abdel Nasser, *Speeches Delivered in the Northern Region* (February–March 1961), p. 88, quoted in Perlmutter, Chap. 6, p. 37.

General Ne Win describes how after seizing power in 1958 two political leaders came to him and asked him to form and to lead a new national party, but, he says:

> I sent them away. What would be the use of forming another party? I had to stay outside politics to make sure the next elections would be fair. In Burma a political party can't win an election without being corrupt. If I had accepted the offer to form a political party of my own I would have had to become corrupt myself, and I'm not prepared to do this.[54]

Ne Win's statement is an excellent example of how the military wish to eat their cake and have it too. Politics, parties, and elections are corrupt; the military must intervene to clean them up. But they must not dirty themselves and become corrupt themselves by participating in party politics. The first action by either a reform or a guardian junta after it has seized power is usually to abolish all existing political parties. "Now there are no political parties," General Rawson proclaimed the day after his coup in 1943, "but only Argentines." The attitude is almost universal. "Politics (outside the service) is 'dissension,'" observes Lyle McAlister in summarizing the outlook of the Latin American military; "political parties are 'factions'; politicians are 'scheming' or 'corrupt'; the expression of public opinion is 'insubordination'."[55] Even more so than other groups in society, military officers tend to see parties as the agents of disunity rather than as mechanisms for consensus-building. Their goal is community without politics, consensus by command. By criticizing and downgrading the role of politics the military prevent society from achieving the community which it needs and they value.

The military leaders are thus caught in a conflict between their own subjective preferences and values and the objective institutional needs of their society. These needs are normally threefold. First, political institutions are needed which reflect the existing distribution of power but which at the same time are able to attract and to assimilate new social forces as they emerge and thus to establish an existence independent of those forces which initially gave them birth. In practice, this means that the institutions must

54. Quoted in Brian Crozier, *The Morning After* (London, Methuen and Company, 1963), p. 73.
55. McAlister, p. 152.

reflect the interests of the military groups which have come to power and yet also possess the capacity eventually to transcend the interests of those groups. Secondly, in states where the military come to power the bureaucratic, output agencies of the political system are often highly developed, in contrast to the chaos and disorganization which prevails among the input agencies presumed to perform the functions of interest articulation and aggregation. Bureaucratic agencies, chief among which are the military, assume political as well as administrative responsibilities. Consequently, political institutions are needed which can redress this balance, divorce political functions from bureaucratic agencies, and limit the latter to their own specialized tasks. Finally, political institutions are needed capable of regulating succession and providing for the transfer of power from one leader or group of leaders to another without recourse to direct action in the form of coups, revolts, or other bloodshed.

In modern, developed polities, these three functions are largely performed by the political party system. Their distaste for politics in general and for parties in particular, however, makes it difficult for military leaders to produce political institutions capable of performing these functions. In effect, they attempt to escape from politics, to sublimate politics, to assume that the problems of political conflict and consensus will be solved automatically if other more manageable problems are resolved. In some instances military leaders have taken the lead in creating political parties. But more generally their tendency is to attempt to fill the vacuum of political institutions by the creation of nonpolitical or at least nonpartisan organizations such as national associations and conciliar hierarchies. In each case, however, the inability of these organizations to perform the needed political functions has driven their military creators toward the acceptance of what in effect is some form of political party organization.

The appeal of a national association to the military lies in the universality of its membership and in its presumed utility as a means of mobilizing and organizing the population to achieve the goals of national development which they assume to be shared by all. Theirs is a "non-political model of nation-building" which fails to recognize the conflicts of interests and values inherent in any society, but particularly prevalent in one undergoing rapid social change, and which consequently makes no provision for mediating conflict and reconciling interests.[56] During their tenure in power between 1958 and 1960, for instance, the Burmese military organized a National Solidarity Association as a nonpartisan organization to promote political participation and to prevent corruption and apathy. The NSA failed to reflect either the distribution of power in the Burmese political system or the level of mass participation in that system. As a result it could neither become an institutional counterweight to the bureaucracy nor provide a framework for regulating the transfer of power.

These deficiencies led the Burmese military leaders to alter their hostility toward party organization and to follow a somewhat different path of political institution-building when they took power again in 1962. Instead of a mass organization they created what was described as a cadre party, the Burma Socialist Programme Party (BSP), designed to perform "such basic party functions as recruiting nucleus personnel called cadres, and training and testing them by assigning them duties, etc." In the words of one observer, this cadre party provided for "individual membership, a very tight code of discipline including provisions relating to factionalism, conflicts of interest, individual income, gifts, secrets, and disciplinary action, demands upon members for acquiring knowledge, self-criticism and acceptance of the 'Burmese Way to Socialism.'" [57] It was designed to be based on democratic centralism and to be the vanguard of an eventual mass party.

A similar pattern of evolution occurred in Egypt. The Free Officers coup in July 1952 was a typical military reform movement. During the two years after the coup its leaders, organized into the Revolutionary Command Council, systematically moved to eliminate competing sources of legitimacy and popular appeal. The king was sent into exile immediately and the monarchy abolished a year later. The three political parties which could have challenged the power of the officers—the Wafd, the Communists, and the Moslem Brethren—were legally abolished, their leaders prosecuted and imprisoned. In the spring of 1954 the victory of Nasser over Naguib among the Free Officers signaled the definitive

56. See James Heaphey, "The Organization of Egypt: Inadequacies of a Nonpolitical Model for Nation-Building," *World Politics, 18* (January 1966), 177–78.

57. Fred R. von der Mehden, "The Burmese Way to Socialism," *Asian Survey, 3* (March 1963), 133. On the NSA, see Richard Butwell, "The New Political Outlook in Burma," *Far Eastern Survey, 29* (February 1960), 23–24.

rejection of parliamentary institutions. By the end of 1954 all the principal sources of political legitimacy and political institutions which antedated the coup had been destroyed or discredited. The political slate, in effect, had been wiped clean. The problem now was: What sort of political institutions, if any, could be created to replace them?

In 1956 a new constitution was put into effect which provided for a popularly elected national assembly. This assembly, which was elected in 1957, and the second assembly, elected in 1964, at times criticized governmental programs and secured some modifications in them.[58] The locus of power, however, remained the military leaders of the government and particularly Nasser, who was regularly elected and reelected president with 99 per cent of the votes. Clearly the formal governmental structure was unlikely by itself to provide the mechanism for legitimizing authority and organizing popular participation. The more serious efforts to create political organizations to fill the institutional gap revolved about the efforts of the military leaders successively to create three national associations. The first, the Liberation Rally, was organized in January 1953, before the consolidation of power by the Free Officers. "The Liberation Rally," Nasser said, "is not a political party. It is a means to organize popular strength for the reconstruction of a society on a sound new basis."[59] It did, however, perform some of the functions of a political party. It served as a way for the military to mobilize and to organize popular support in its struggles with other political groups, particularly the Moslem Brethren, and to penetrate and to secure control of other mass organizations such as unions and student groups. It performed these functions reasonably well. The consolidation of power by the RCC in 1954, however, deprived the Liberation Rally of its reason for existence and at the same time promoted the tremendous expansion of its membership. It eventually came to have several million members, and, as a result, declined in effectiveness.

The new constitution of 1956 directed that "The People of Egypt shall form a National Union to accomplish the aims of the Revolution and to encourage all means to give the nation a solid foundation in the political, social, and economic realms." The

58. See P. J. Vatikiotis, *The Egyptian Army in Politics* (Bloomington, Indiana University Press, 1961), pp. 106, 284; *New York Times*, June 26, 1964, p. 2; December 15, 1965, p. 17.

59. Speech, April 9, 1953, quoted in Vatikiotis, p. 83.

Union was organized in the spring of 1957 and replaced the Liberation Rally as the means by which the regime attempted to organize mass support. The broadest possible membership was desired: the National Union, Nasser said, "is the whole nation." [60] It, too, soon acquired several million members and became too large and amorphous to be effective. In 1962, after the break with Syria, an effort was made to create yet a new organization, the Arab Socialist Union, to mobilize and organize the populace.

Significantly, the ASU was originally designed to avoid some of the weaknesses of the Liberation Rally and the National Union. Like the Burmese military, the Egyptian leaders shifted the emphasis, at least in theory, from a mass organization to an elite or cadre organization, with a division between active and inactive membership, and with its membership originally limited to ten per cent of the population. [61] In due course, however, the ASU also mushroomed in size and after two years was said to have 5,000,000 members. In 1964 Nasser reportedly attempted to supplement the ASU with yet another group, which would have only 4,000 members, and which would function as the "Government Party" within the ASU. The new organization was designed by Nasser "to enforce a peaceful transfer of power and a continuation of his policies if anything happens to him." [62]

In Burma and Egypt the military thus first attempted to create mass national associations which would include everyone and then, when these failed, redirected their efforts toward the establishment of what was officially in Burma and unofficially in Egypt a cadre party with more limited and restricted membership. The original intention of the military leaders reflects their desire to avoid politics. Other societies, as one commentator has put it, attempt to "incorporate group interests and group struggles as part of the legitimating process and the good life, whereas the Egyptian vision pictures an organization that produces efficiently and dispenses fairly to individuals *qua* individuals." [63] The union of all presupposes the unity of all. It is, however, precisely the purpose of political organization to promote this goal. Neither the Bur-

---

60. Vatikiotis, p. 139.

61. See George Lenczowski, "Radical Regimes in Egypt, Syria and Iraq: Some Comparative Observations on Ideologies and Practices," *Journal of Politics, 28* (February 1966) , 51–52.

62. *Washington Post*, February 9, 1964, p. A-17.

63. Heaphey, p. 193.

mese nor the Egyptian organizations were able to perform the functions required of political institutions. They included everyone while power remained concentrated in a few. They neither reflected the structure of social forces nor served as vehicles through which the dominant social force could extend, moderate, and legitimize its power.

Instead of starting with a group which did exist—the national junta—and attempting to organize and to institutionalize it, the Burmese and Egyptian leaders started with a group which did not exist—the national community—and attempted to organize it. They tried to breathe life into organizations not rooted in any cohesive social force. An institution is an organization which is valued for its own sake by its members and others. An organization to which everyone can belong or must belong is less likely to become an institution than one in which membership is a scarce resource. "If everyone is in the party," as Halpern asks, "why should anyone bother to be in it?" [64] In both Burma and Egypt the leading officers in the coup group constituted themselves into a body—the Revolutionary Council in Burma, the Revolutionary Command Council in Egypt—for the direction of government. Such bodies could have become the central organ of a new governmental structure. In Egypt the Free Officers were, as Vatikiotis says, "a political group approaching the proportions of a party." [65] The Free Officers, however, refused to recognize themselves for what they were, an embryonic political party, and hence denied themselves the opportunity to institutionalize their role. Instead of making the Revolutionary Command Council into the central organ of a new political structure, they disbanded it in 1956 when the new constitution was inaugurated and Nasser was elected president on the assumption that documents and plebiscites create institutions.

As a result, no organization was created in Egypt to facilitate changes in the social composition of the new ruling elite. Nasser, it is said, was anxious to replace the army as a source of top leadership in the government "by a closer alliance with civilian groups among the professional and intellectual classes." [66] The problem was to bring in new elements without disaffecting the original and

64. Halpern, *Politics of Social Change*, p. 286.
65. Vatikiotis, p. 72.
66. Ibid., p. 225.

most important sources of support in the army. A party organization is one means of performing this function: it provides a common focus of loyalty and identification for military and civilian
and hence a means for distinguishing among individuals on
grounds other than their civilian or military background. Instead
of building from the core outward, however, the military attempted to organize everyone all at once by building from the
periphery inward. "The idea of weaving from the outer edge inward, a spider's web of committees reaching to Cairo at the center
could be attractive and even useful," commented *The Economist*
on the National Union. "The trouble in the UAR is that little gets
done, and even less is understood by the people concerned. Thus
the villages, called upon to vote, voted for the same families who
have always been dominant, and the web breaks off long before it
reaches the center." [67]

In Pakistan the construction of a nonpartisan political web was
attempted through other means. Pre-1958 Pakistan, like pre-1952
Egypt, was ostensibly governed through a narrowly based parliamentary regime, the participants in which represented a small
number of oligarchical and intellectual groups. The principal
locus of power, however, was the bureaucracy. The brief phase of
popular or party government in Pakistan really came to an end in
April 1953, when the Governor General successfully dismissed a
prime minister who up to that point possessed the backing of a
sizable majority in the National Assembly. In effect, this coup created a system of co-government by bureaucrats and politicians, and
the subsequent coup of October 1958 simply transferred the leadership from inefficient civilian bureaucrats to efficient military
ones. Unlike Nasser, however, Field Marshal Mohammad Ayub
Khan fully appreciated the importance of political institutions
and had very carefully worked out ideas of the type of institutional
structure which would be appropriate for Pakistan. He had formulated these ideas in a memorandum on the "Present and Future
Problems of Pakistan," written while he was defense minister of
Pakistan in October 1954, four years before he took over control
of the government.[68] The new institutions created in Pakistan

---

67. *The Economist* (March 12, 1960), pp. 974, 977, quoted in Perlmutter, Chap. 6,
pp. 30, 31.

68. For text, see Karl von Vorys, *Political Development in Pakistan* (Princeton,
Princeton University Press, 1965), pp. 299 ff.

after 1958 were in large part the result of conscious political planning. More than any other political leader in a modernizing country after World War II, Ayub Khan came close to filling the role of a Solon or Lycurgus or "Great Legislator" on the Platonic or Rousseauian model. The new political institutions of Pakistan were created in three steps, two of which were planned by Ayub Khan and one of which was forced upon him by the necessities of political modernization. The two planned phases were in effect designed to provide for the concentration of power, on the one hand, and for the tempered expansion of power, on the other.

The Basic Democracies were the principal institutional means providing for popular participation. They were created a year after the military coup as an effort to produce a system of democratic institutions which would, in Ayub Khan's words, be "simple to understand, easy to work and cheap to run; put to the voter such questions as the voter can understand without external promptings; ensure the effective participation of all citizens to their full intellectual capacity; produce reasonably strong and stable governments." [69] A hierarchy of councils was established. At the base the Union Councils averaged ten members each with one member for every one thousand population elected by universal suffrage. Above these were Thana or Tehsil Councils composed of the chairmen of the Union Councils plus an equal number of appointed official members. Above them were the District Councils, also one half civil servants and one half Basic Democrats appointed by the Divisional Commissioner. Above these were the Divisional Councils with membership similar to the District Councils. The functions of these bodies were primarily in economic and social development, local government, administrative coordination, and elections.

Elections to the Union Councils were held in December 1959 and January 1960, with about 50 per cent of the eligible voters participating. The almost 80,000 Basic Democrats selected constituted a corps and a core of political activists for the political system. The majority of them were new to politics, and given the nature of the political structure they were relatively evenly distributed about the country in terms of population. Most of the Basic Democrats were literate and reasonably well-to-do. Over 50,000 of

69. Quoted in Richard V. Weekes, *Pakistan: Birth and Growth of a Muslim Nation* (Princeton, D. Van Nostrand and Company, 1964), p. 118.

them, however, were employed in agriculture.[70] Before 1959 Pakistan politics was almost exclusively urban politics.

> Public opinion in Pakistan is to be found in the urban middle class, the landowners and some of the religious leaders. This is a small and unstable base on which to found a durable and efficient state. . . . For the most part political activity has been confined to the very small group of active politicians based on the urban areas. The common man, especially in rural districts, has been unaware of or indifferent to the maneuvers that were taking place at the provincial or national capitals. Ordinary people have not become accustomed to regarding themselves as voters.[71]

The Basic Democracies, however, brought politics to the rural areas and created a class of rural political activists with a role to play in both local and national politics. For the first time political activity was dispersed outward from the cities and spread over the countryside. Political participation was thus broadened, a new source of support created for the government, and a major step made toward creating the institutional link between government and countryside which is the prerequisite of political stability in a modernizing country.

The corps of Basic Democrats in a sense competed with the two other social groups which had been active in Pakistani politics. On the one hand, since its locus was in the countryside, it was divorced from and had interests opposed to the middle-class intellectuals of the cities. "The entire intelligentsia," one Pakistani minister warned the Basic Democrats, "is against you." [72] On the other hand, the structure of the Basic Democracies insured a continuing struggle between bureaucratic and popular interests. Their purpose was, in Ayub Khan's words, to insure that "every village and every inhabitant in every village . . . would become an equal partner with the Administration in conducting the affairs of the state." [73] Instead of creating a completely autonomous political structure apart from the administrative structure, the effort was

70. Von Vorys, p. 201.

71. Keith Callard, *Pakistan: A Political Study* (London, Allen and Unwin, 1957), pp. 50, 52.

72. Quoted in von Vorys, p. 206.

73. Mohammad Ayub Khan, *Speeches and Statements*, 2, 35, quoted in von Vorys, p. 106.

instead to bring into existence an amalgamated structure combining bureaucratic and popular elements, with the popular element stronger at the bottom of the structure and the official or bureaucratic element stronger at the top. Inevitably this gave rise to friction between civil servants and elected leaders. The struggle between these two elements, however, was carried on within a single institutional framework and thus tended to strengthen that framework and to identify both officials and representatives with it. Both the expression of popular grievances against the bureaucracy and the bureaucratic implementation of governmental policies were channeled through the Basic Democracies structure.

Politically the Basic Democracies thus: (a) involved in the political system a new class of local political leaders throughout the country; (b) provided an institutional link between the government and the rural populace upon whose support stability depended; (c) created a popular counterweight to the dominance of bureaucratic officialdom; and (d) provided a structure through which subsequent broadening of political participation could be channeled. The Basic Democracies thus were a means of laying the framework for the expansion of the power of the political system.

The other major institutional innovation planned and implemented by Ayub Khan was primarily designed to provide for the effective concentration of power in government. This was achieved by the new constitution which was drawn up under Ayub Khan's direction and which came into force in June 1962, ending the system of martial law which had previously legitimated the concentration of power in Ayub Khan's hands. The constitution replaced the pre-1958 weak-parliament-cum-strong-bureaucracy system of rule with a strong presidential system. Although in places the constitution appeared to be modeled on the American system, in actuality the power of the executive was far greater than in the United States and even considerably greater than in the Fifth French Republic. The principal institutional curbs on the power of the president came from the judiciary rather than from the legislature, and in this respect the system approximated more the model of a *Rechtsstaat* than of a liberal democracy. The concentration of power in the presidency, however, did establish an institution which could exercise a more effective check on what had been the real center of power, the bureaucracy. The president was to be elected for a five-year term (renewable once) by an electoral college of the 80,000 Basic Democrats who, in turn, were of course elected by the people.

The Basic Democracies and the presidential constitution together provided Pakistan with a framework of political institutions. For Ayub Khan these were enough. In particular, he was, like Nasser, adamantly opposed to political parties, and parties were outlawed during the period of martial law from October 1958 to June 1962. Many leaders urged that provision be made for them in the new constitution. Ayub Khan, however, consistently rejected these demands, and the constitution banned parties unless the National Assembly decided to the contrary. As the constitution was about to go into effect and as opposition movements began to attack it, his associates made additional efforts to persuade him to accept parties as a necessary institution in a modern polity.

> Political parties regulated by law, they argued, would provide an organizational framework for mass mobilization on behalf of the government. They might further aid such development by clearly demarcating the difference between those groups which were opposed to some government policies and others which advocated the repeal of the entire constitutional structure. Finally, political parties could fragment the leadership of the Opposition.[74]

These arguments eventually persuaded Ayub Khan reluctantly to acquiesce in the legalization of political parties. Several were formed, including one by the supporters of the government. Because Ayub Khan wished to preserve a position for himself as the leader of the nation aloof from partisan activity, the party of his supporters was "a party behind the power rather than a party in power." [75] In the course of the following year, however, the need to build support for the forthcoming presidential election compelled Ayub Khan slowly to abandon his aloof position and to identify himself with the party which identified itself with him. In May 1963 he formally joined the party and a short while later was elected its president. "I have failed to play this game in accordance with my rules," he explained, "and so I have to play in

74. Ibid., pp. 256–57.

75. Mushtq Ahmad, *Government and Politics in Pakistan* (Karachi, Pakistan Publishing House, 1963) , p. 282.

accordance with their rules—and the rules demand that I belong to somebody; otherwise who is going to belong to me? So it is simple. It is an admission of defeat on my part." [76] Political participation had forced him reluctantly to an unwilling but virtually complete acceptance of party.

The presidential election in the fall of 1964 accelerated the building of links between the parties which were being developed from the top down and the Basic Democracies structure, which was being developed from the bottom up. In the first phase of the election, the people elected the 80,000 Basic Democrats in part on the basis of local issues and their personal followings and in part on the basis of their identification with one of the two major presidential candidates. In the second phase, the candidates and their parties had to mobilize support from the Basic Democrats. The campaign thus provided the need and the incentive for national political leaders to reach down, appeal to, and establish alliances with the local leaders chosen as Basic Democrats. The unwanted political party supplied the indispensable institutional link between the centralization of power provided by the constitution and the expansion of power provided by the Basic Democracies.

In Burma and Egypt the efforts by military leaders to organize mass associations to institutionalize participation and to legitimize their power came to naught. In both cases the leaders had to redirect their efforts to what was in fact if not in name a cadre party. In Pakistan Ayub Khan's institutional innovations required the reintroduction of political parties to make them operate effectively. In all three cases, the leaders resisted political parties but were eventually compelled either to accept them or to accept continued illegitimacy and instability. In other cases, military leaders have been more willing to organize political parties and to start the process of building modern political institutions which could create a basis of permanent political stability and authority.

Perhaps the most striking example of political institution-building by generals is Mexico, where at the end of the 1920s Calles and the other military leaders of the Revolution created

76. Quoted in Lucian Pye, "Party Systems and National Development in Asia," in Joseph LaPalombara and Myron Weiner, eds., *Political Parties and Political Development* (Princeton, Princeton University Press, 1966) , p. 369.

the National Revolutionary Party and in effect institutionalized the Revolution. The creation of this institution made it possible for the political system to assimilate a variety of new social forces, labor and agrarian, which rose to prominence under Cárdenas in the 1930s. It also created a political institution which was able to maintain the integrity of the political sphere against disruptive social forces. During the nineteenth century Mexico had the worst record of military interventions in politics of any Latin American country. After the 1930s, its military stayed out of politics, and Mexico became one of the few Latin American countries possessing some form of institutional immunity to military coups d'etat.

The achievement of the Mexican military was exceptional in that it was the outcome of a full-scale revolution, albeit a revolution led by middle-class generals rather than middle-class intellectuals. That achievement was, however, duplicated by Mustafa Kemal and the Turkish generals without benefit of a complete social revolution. From the very start of his political activities Kemal was sensitive to the need to create a political institution capable of governing the Turkish state. In 1909, a year after the Young Turks had taken power, he argued for the complete separation of the military from politics: those military officers who wished to pursue political careers should resign from the army; those who wished to continue military careers should not meddle in politics. "As long as officers remain in the Party," he told one meeting of the Committee for Union and Progress, "we shall neither build a strong Party nor a strong Army . . . the Party receiving its strength from the Army will never appeal to the nation. Let us resolve here and now that all officers wishing to remain in the Party must resign from the Army. We must also adopt a law forbidding all officers having political affiliations." [77] The Young Turk leaders did not follow this advice.

A decade later it was Kemal's turn as the only Turkish military hero of World War I to determine the course of events at the close of the war. In July 1919, at the beginning of the nationalist struggle against the Ottoman sultans and the French, British, and Greek interveners in Turkey, Kemal resigned from the army and thereafter almost invariably appeared in public in mufti rather

77. Quoted in Irfan Orga, *Phoenix Ascendant: The Rise of Modern Turkey* (London, Robert Hale, 1958), p. 38.

than uniform. His authority, he said, derived from his election as chairman of the Association for Defense of the Rights of Anatolia. In August 1923, when the independence of the Turkish state had been assured, this association was transformed into the Republican Peoples Party. It governed Turkey for the next 27 years. Kemal and many of his associates in founding the Turkish republic and the party were military officers. He insisted, however, that they all make a clear choice between military affairs and politics. "Commanders, while thinking of and carrying out the duties and requirements of the army," he declared, "must take care not to let political considerations influence their judgment. They must not forget that there are other officials whose duty it is to think of the political aspects. A soldier's duty cannot be performed with talk and politicking." [78]

The Turkish Republican Peoples Party and the Mexican Revolutionary Institutional Party were both founded by political generals. Calles and Cárdenas were the dominant figures in the creation of one, Kemal the dominant figure in the creation of the other. In both cases, the bulk of the leadership of the party came from the ranks of the military. In both cases also, however, the party acquired an institutional existence apart from those groups who initially created it. In both parties (although more pronouncedly in Mexico than in Turkey) the military leaders were civilianized and civilian leaders in due course replaced military ones. Both parties, as well-organized political groupings, were able to establish an effective political counterweight to the military. In Mexico the top leadership of the party and of the country was transferred from military to civilian hands in 1946. By 1958 military men accounted for only seven of twenty-nine state governors and two of eighteen cabinet ministers. "Inside the ruling party and inside the government itself civilian professionals predominate," one expert observed in the early 1960s; "they are the real policy-makers. The army is under their control. On issues that do not concern the military establishment they can act without consulting the armed forces, and they can, and do at times, oppose it on military issues." [79]

In Turkey a similar, although not quite as successful, process of

78. Quoted in Dankwart A. Rustow, "The Army and the Founding of the Turkish Republic," *World Politics, 11* (July 1959) , 546.
79. Lieuwen, *Arms and Politics,* p. 119.

civilianization also occurred through the mechanism of the ruling party. In 1924 the chief of staff was excluded from the cabinet. The number of former military officers in political positions gradually declined. In 1920, officers constituted 17 per cent of the Grand National Assembly; in 1943, 12.5 per cent; and in 1950 only 5 per cent. At the death of Mustafa Kemal in 1938, leadership was transferred to his associate Ismet Inönü, who like Kemal had come out of the army but who had functioned for two decades in civilian roles. In 1948 the first cabinet was formed which did not include any former military officers, and in 1950, of course, elections were held in which the opposition party peacefully acquired power. A decade later the efforts of the leadership of this party to suppress opposition provoked the Turkish military, in the name of the Kemalist tradition, to reenter politics and to establish a short-lived military regime, which in 1961 returned power to a freely elected civilian party regime.

In Turkey a centralized traditional monarchy ruled until 1908. At that time it was overthrown by a middle-class military coup which inaugurated a decade of praetorian politics brought to an end in the early 1920s when Mustafa Kemal stabilized his rule through the creation of an effective party organization. Mexico and Turkey are two noteworthy examples where parties came out of the womb of the army, political generals created a political party, and the political party put an end to political generals.

In the two decades after World War II the most notable effort by military men to duplicate the achievements of the Turkish and Mexican generals was made in Korea. For almost two years after he took power in South Korea in the summer of 1961, General Pak Chung Hee was under pressure by the United States to reestablish civilian rule and under pressure by the hard-liners in his own army to retain power and keep the civilians out. He attempted to resolve this dilemma by promising elections in 1963 and arranging in a Kemalist manner to shift the base of his power from the army to a political party. In contrast to the military leaders of Egypt and Pakistan, those of Korea accepted and provided for political parties in the new constitution which they drew up for their country. Far from discouraging or forbidding parties, the constitution gave them special stress. The 1962 constitution of Pakistan prohibited a candidate from identifying himself as "a member of, or as having the support of, a political party

PRAETORIANISM AND POLITICAL DECAY

or any similar organization." The 1962 constitution of Korea, in contrast, provided that each candidate "shall be recommended by the political party to which he belongs." In contrast to Ayub Khan's ideal of the high-minded, independent legislator divorced from organizational ties, the Korean constitution provided that a congressman would lose his seat "when he leaves or changes his party or when his party is dissolved."

In December 1962, Pak announced that he would run in the presidential elections scheduled for the following year. Throughout that year several members of the military junta had begun to divert funds from the national treasury to prepare for the organization of a party. Early in 1963, Pak's nephew-in-law, Brigadier General Kim Chung Pil, resigned as head of the Korean CIA and began to create a political organization, the Democratic Republican Party, to back General Pak. His intelligence work had given Kim ample opportunity to observe the organizational effectiveness of the Communist Party of North Korea, and he in part followed Leninist principles of organization in forming the Democratic Republican Party of South Korea. Kim took with him from the army some 1,200 bright and energetic officers plus allegedly substantial sums of government money. With these resources he was able to create a reasonably effective political organization. At the national level, he established a strong administrative secretariat originally supported by Korean CIA funds and staffed with able people drawn from the army, the universities, and the press. At the local level, he set up four-man secretariats in each election district and eight-man bureaus in each province, each designed to study intensely the political problems of its area, develop support, create organizations, and select candidates. The entire operation was marked by a highly professional approach.[80]

Pak's announcement of his candidacy in December 1962 precipitated an immediate reaction from those members of the military junta who believed that the army should continue in power without attempting to legitimate its rule through elections. Pak dismissed four of his opposition in the junta and was almost immediately confronted by a full-scale revolt by its remaining members. "The entire Army is against you," he was told, and he was forced to send General Kim abroad and to announce in

80. Jae Souk Sohn, "The Role of the Military in the Republic of Korea" (unpublished MS, September 1966), p. 7; Henderson, pp. 185–88, 305–06.

February that he was withdrawing as a candidate. The following month the junta formally announced that there would be no elections in 1963 and that military rule would continue for four more years. These developments in turn precipitated strong protests from the United States government and from the civilian politicians who were looking forward to the opportunity to challenge the military. For six months Pak trod a delicate path between the threat of American sanctions if he canceled the elections and the threat of a military coup if he held them. Eventually, by September, the organization of the Democratic Republican Party had progressed to the point where the fears of the officers as to the possible results of an election were reduced and the activities of the opposition groups had progressed to a point where the cancellation of the elections would have produced widespread civil violence.

The presidential election in October 1963 was weighted on the side of the government, but it was also the fairest election in the history of Korea. General Pak received 45 per cent of the vote, his principal opponent 43 per cent. In the parliamentary elections the Democratic Republicans got 32 per cent of the popular vote but won 110 of the 175 seats because of the splintering of their opponents' votes. As was to be expected, the opposition parties swept the larger cities, while the governmental party received strong support from the rural areas. In three years, a military junta had transformed itself into a political institution. In three years, military intervention in politics with power based on the praetorian use of force had been converted into military participation in politics with authority based on popular support and legitimated by electoral competition.

In the three years after it won control of the national government, General Pak's regime was able to carry out a number of reforms, the most notable of which was the consummation of a treaty normalizing Japanese-Korean relations and under which Japan would pay several hundred million dollars' reparation to Korea. The opposition to this treaty from the opposition parties and from the students was intense. Its ratification in August 1965 provoked widespread rioting and demonstrations; for a solid week 10,000 or more students protested in the streets of Seoul, demanding the overthrow of the government and the nullification of the treaty. Precisely such demonstrations, of course, had toppled

Syngman Rhee's government in 1960. General Pak, however, could rely on the loyalty of the army and the support of the countryside. With the army isolated from politics, he now insisted that students be also: the government, he said, would take "all necessary measures" to bring to an end once and for all "the evil habit of students interfering with politics." A full scale combat division was brought into Seoul; Korea University was occupied; and scores of students were hauled off to jail. In the normal politics of a praetorian society, this would not be significant, but, in the long run, creation of a system of stable party government should reduce student as well as military involvement in politics. The rising prosperity which followed upon the political stability of the regime also tended to discourage blatant student interventions in politics.

The achievements of Ayub Khan in Pakistan, of Calles and Cárdenas in Mexico, of Kemal and Inönü in Turkey, of Pak and Kim in Korea, and of others such as Rivera in El Salvador, show that military leaders can be effective builders of political institutions. Experience suggests, however, that they can play this role most effectively in a society where social forces are not fully articulated. The tragedy of a country like Brazil in the 1960s was that it was, in a sense, too developed to have either a Nasser or an Ataturk, its society too complex and varied to be susceptible to leadership by a military regime. Any Brazilian military leader would have had to find some way of striking a balance between the regional, industrial, commercial, coffee-growing, labor, and other interests which share power in Brazil and whose cooperation was necessary for the conduct of government. Any government in Brazil has to come to terms, one way or another, with the São Paulo industrialists. Nasser did not have such a problem, and hence he could be Nasser; so also Ataturk dealt with a relatively small and homogeneous elite. Modernizing military regimes have come to power in Guatemala, El Salvador, and Bolivia. But for Brazil it may be too late for military modernization and too late also for the soldier as institution-builder. The complexity of social forces may preclude the construction of political institutions under middle-class military leadership.

In those countries which are less complex and less highly developed, the military may yet be able to play a constructive role, if they are willing to follow the Kemalist model. In many of these countries, the military leaders are intelligent, energetic, progressive. They are less corrupt—in the narrow sense—and more identified with national goals and national development than most civilians. Their problem is more often subjective than objective. For they must recognize that guardianship serves only to corrupt further the society they wish to purify and that economic development without political institutionalization leads only to social stagnation. To move their society out of the praetorian cycle, they cannot stand above politics or attempt to stop politics. Instead they must make their way through politics.

At each level in the broadening of political participation certain options or possibilities for evolution may exist, which, if not acted upon, disappear quickly. At the oligarchical level of praetorianism, a viable, expansible party system depends upon the action of the aristocrats or oligarchs. If they take the initiative in the search for votes and the development of party organization, a country may well move out of its praetorian condition in that phase. If it does not, if middle-class groups begin to participate in a praetorian political milieu, the opportunity to act passes to the military. For them modernization is not enough, and guardianship is too little. What is required of the military leaders is a more positive effort to shape a new political order. In many societies the opportunity the military have for political creativity may be the last real chance for political institutionalization short of the totalitarian road. If the military fail to seize that opportunity, the broadening of participation transforms the society into a mass praetorian system. In such a system the opportunity to create political institutions passes from the military, the apostles of order, to those other middle-class leaders who are the apostles of revolution.

In such a society, however, revolution and order may well become allies. Cliques, blocs, and mass movements struggle directly with each other, each with its own weapons. Violence is democratized, politics demoralized, society at odds with itself. The ultimate product of degeneration is a peculiar reversal in political roles. The truly helpless society is not one threatened by revolution but one incapable of it. In the normal polity the conservative is devoted to stability and the preservation of order, while the radical threatens these with abrupt and violent change. But what meaning do concepts of conservatism and radicalism have in a completely chaotic society where order must be created through a positive act of political will? In such a society who then is the radical? Who is the conservative? Is not the only true conservative the revolutionary?

5. Revolution and Political Order

MODERNIZATION BY REVOLUTION

A revolution is a rapid, fundamental, and violent domestic change in the dominant values and myths of a society, in its political institutions, social structure, leadership, and government activity and policies. Revolutions are thus to be distinguished from insurrections, rebellions, revolts, coups, and wars of independence. A coup d'etat in itself changes only leadership and perhaps policies; a rebellion or insurrection may change policies, leadership, and political institutions, but not social structure and values; a war of independence is a struggle of one community against rule by an alien community and does not necessarily involve changes in the social structure of either community. What is here called simply "revolution" is what others have called great revolutions, grand revolutions, or social revolutions. Notable examples are the French, Chinese, Mexican, Russian, and Cuban revolutions.

Revolutions are rare. Most societies have never experienced revolutions, and most ages until modern times did not know revolutions. Revolutions, in the grand sense, are, as Friedrich says, "a peculiarity of Western culture." The great civilizations of the past—Egypt, Babylon, Persia, the Incas, Greece, Rome, China, India, the Arab world—experienced revolts, insurrections, and dynastic changes, but these did not "constitute anything resembling the 'great' revolutions of the West." [1] The rise and fall of dynasties in the ancient empires and the changes back and forth from oligarchy and democracy in the Greek city-states were instances of political violence but not of social revolution. More precisely, revolution is characteristic of modernization. It is one way of modernizing a traditional society, and it was, of course, as unknown to traditional society in the West as it was unknown to

1. Carl J. Friedrich, *Man and His Government* (New York, McGraw-Hill, 1963), p. 644.

traditional societies elsewhere. Revolution is the ultimate expression of the modernizing outlook, the belief that it is within the power of man to control and to change his environment and that he has not only the ability but the right to do so. For this reason, as Hannah Arendt observes, "violence is no more adequate to describe the phenomenon of revolution than change; only where change occurs in the sense of a new beginning, where violence is used to constitute an altogether different form of government, to bring about the formation of a new body politic . . . can we speak of revolution." [2]

The forerunner of the modern revolution was the English Revolution of the seventeenth century, whose leaders believed they had "great works to do, the planting of a new heaven and a new earth among us, and great works have great enemies." [3] Their semantics were religious but their purpose and effect were radically modern. By legislative action men would remake society. In the eighteenth century the image was secularized. The French Revolution created the awareness of revolution. It "cracked the modern consciousness and made men realize that revolution is a fact, that a great revolution may occur in a modern, progressive society. . . . after the French Revolution we find a conscious development of revolutionary doctrines in anticipation of revolutions to come, and the spread of a more active attitude toward conscious control over institutions in general." [4]

Revolution is thus an aspect of modernization. It is not something which can occur in any type of society at any period in its history. It is not a universal category but rather an historically limited phenomenon. It will not occur in highly traditional societies with very low levels of social and economic complexity. Nor will it occur in highly modern societies. Like other forms of violence and instability, it is most likely to occur in societies which have experienced some social and economic development and where the processes of political modernization and political development have lagged behind the processes of social and economic change.

2. Hannah Arendt, *On Revolution* (New York, Viking, 1963) , p. 28.

3. Stephen Marshall, 1641, quoted in Michael Walzer, *The Revolution of the Saints* (Cambridge, Harvard University Press, 1965) , p. xiv. Walzer's analysis persuasively illumines the modernizing, revolutionary nature of the Puritans.

4. George S. Pettee, *The Process of Revolution* (New York, Harper, 1938) , p. 96.

Political modernization involves the extension of political consciousness to new social groups and the mobilization of these groups into politics. Political development involves the creation of political institutions sufficiently adaptable, complex, autonomous, and coherent to absorb and to order the participation of these new groups and to promote social and economic change in the society. The political essence of revolution is the rapid expansion of political consciousness and the rapid mobilization of new groups into politics at a speed which makes it impossible for existing political institutions to assimilate them. Revolution is the extreme case of the explosion of political participation. Without this explosion there is no revolution. A complete revolution, however, also involves a second phase: the creation and institutionalization of a new political order. The successful revolution combines rapid political mobilization and rapid political institutionalization. Not all revolutions produce a new political order. The measure of how revolutionary a revolution is is the rapidity and the scope of the expansion of political participation. The measure of how successful a revolution is is the authority and stability of the institutions to which it gives birth.

A full-scale revolution thus involves the rapid and violent destruction of existing political institutions, the mobilization of new groups into politics, and the creation of new political institutions. The sequence and the relations among these three aspects may vary from one revolution to another. Two general patterns can be identified. In the "Western" pattern, the political institutions of the old regime collapse; this is followed by the mobilization of new groups into politics and then by the creation of new political institutions. The "Eastern" revolution, in contrast, begins with the mobilization of new groups into politics and the creation of new political institutions and ends with the violent overthrow of the political institutions of the old order. The French, Russian, Mexican, and, in its first phases, Chinese Revolutions approximate the Western model; the latter phases of the Chinese Revolution, the Vietnamese Revolution, and other colonial struggles against imperialist powers approximate the Eastern model. In general, the sequence of movement from one phase to the next is much more clearly demarcated in the Western revolution than in the Eastern type. In the latter all three phases tend to occur more or less simultaneously. One fundamental difference in sequence, however, does exist between the two. In the Western revolution, political mobilization is the consequence of the collapse of the old regime; in the Eastern revolution it is the cause of the destruction of the old regime.

The first step in a Western revolution is the collapse of the old regime. Consequently, scholarly analysis of the causes of revolution usually focuses on the political, social, and economic conditions which existed under the old regime. Implicitly, such analyses assume that once the authority of the old regime has disintegrated, the revolutionary process is irreversibly underway. In fact, however, the collapse of many old regimes is not followed by full-scale revolution. The causes of the collapse of the old regime are not necessarily sufficient to trigger off a major revolution. The events of 1789 in France led to a major social upheaval; those of 1830 and 1848 did not. The fall of the Manchu and Romanov dynasties was followed by great revolutions; the fall of the Hapsburg, Hohenzollern, Ottoman, and Qajar dynasties was not. The overthrow of traditional dictatorships in Bolivia in 1952 and in Cuba in 1958 set loose major revolutionary forces; the overthrow of traditional monarchies in Egypt in 1952 and in Iraq in 1958 brought new elites to power but did not completely destroy the structure of society. The downfall of the Syngman Rhee regime in Korea in 1960 might have marked the beginning of a great revolution, but it did not. In virtually all these instances, the same social, economic, and political conditions existed under the old regimes whose demise was not followed by revolution as existed under the old regimes whose demise was followed by revolution. Old regimes—traditional monarchies and traditional dictatorships with concentrated but little power—are continually collapsing but only rarely is this collapse followed by a major revolution. The factors giving rise to revolution, consequently, are as likely to be found in the conditions which exist after the collapse of the old regime as in those which exist before its downfall.

In the "Western" revolution very little overt action by rebellious groups is needed to overthrow the old regime. "The revolution," as Pettee says, "does not begin with the attack of a powerful new force upon the state. It begins simply with a sudden recognition by almost all the passive and active membership that the state no longer exists." The collapse is followed by an absence of authority. "Revolutionists enter the limelight, not like men on horseback, as victorious conspirators appearing in the forum, but like fearful children, exploring an empty house, not sure that it is empty." [5] Whether or not a revolution develops depends upon the number and the character of the groups entering the house. If there is a marked discrepancy in power among the remaining social forces after the old regime disappears, the strongest social force or combination of forces may be able to fill the vacuum and to reestablish authority, with relatively little expansion of political participation. The collapse of every old regime is followed by some rioting, demonstrations, and the projection into the political sphere of previously quiescent or suppressed groups. If a new social force (as in Egypt in 1952) or combination of social forces (as in Germany in 1918–19) can quickly secure control of the state machinery and particularly the instruments of coercion left behind by the old regime, it may well be able to suppress the more revolutionary elements intent on mobilizing new forces into politics (the Moslem Brotherhood, the Spartacists) and thus fore-stall the emergence of a truly revolutionary situation. The crucial factor is the concentration or dispersion of power which follows the collapse of the old regime. The less traditional the society in which the old regime has collapsed and the more groups which are available and able and inclined to participate in politics, the more likely is revolution to take place.

If no group is ready and able to establish effective rule following the collapse of the old regime, many cliques and social forces struggle for power. This struggle gives rise to the competitive mobilization of new groups into politics and makes the revolution revolutionary. Each group of political leaders attempts to establish its authority and in the process either develops a broader base of popular support than its competitors or falls victim to them.

Following the collapse of the old regime, three social types play major roles in the process of political mobilization. Initially, as Brinton and others have pointed out, the moderates (Kerensky, Madero, Sun Yat-sen) tend to assume authority. Typically, they attempt to establish some sort of liberal, democratic, constitutional state. Typically, also, they describe this as the restoration of an earlier constitutional order: Madero wanted to restore the constitution of 1856; the liberal Young Turks the constitution of

5. Ibid., pp. 100–01.

1876; and even Castro in his initial moderate phase held that his goal was the restoration of the constitution of 1940. In rare cases, these leaders may adapt to the subsequent intensification of the revolutionary process: Castro was the Kerensky and the Lenin of the Cuban Revolution. More frequently, however, the moderates remain moderate and are swept from power. Their failure stems precisely from their inability to deal with the problem of political mobilization. On the one hand, they lack the drive and the ruthlessness to stop the mobilization of new groups into politics; on the other, they lack the radicalism to lead it. The first alternative requires the concentration of power, the second its expansion. Unable and unwilling to perform either function, the liberals are brushed away either by counterrevolutionaries who perform the first or by more extreme revolutionaries who perform the second.

In virtually all revolutionary situations, counterrevolutionaries, often with foreign assistance, attempt to stop the expansion of political participation and to reestablish a political order in which there is little but concentrated power. Kornilov, Yuan Shih-kai, Huerta, and, in a sense, Reza Shah and Mustafa Kemal all played these roles in the aftermath of the downfall of the Porfirian regime and of the Romanov, Ch'ing, Qajar, and Ottoman dynasties. As these examples suggest, the counterrevolutionaries are almost invariably military men. Force is a source of power, but it can have longer range effectiveness only when it is linked to a principle of legitimacy. Huerta and Kornilov had nothing but force and failed in the face of the radicalization of the revolution and the mobilization of more social groups into politics. Yuan Shih-kai and Reza Shah both attempted to establish new, more vigorous traditional systems of rule on the ruins of the previous dynasty. Many similarities existed between the two countries: the old dynasty had decayed and collapsed; foreign powers were openly and competitively intervening and preparing themselves for the possible dismemberment of the country; warlordism and anarchy were rampant; the principal hope for stability seemed to lie in the commanders of the new military forces which had been brought into existence in the last years of the decaying dynasty.

That Yuan Shih-kai failed to establish a new dynasty while Reza Shah Pahlevi succeeded is due primarily to the fact that political mobilization had gone much further in China than it had in Persia. The middle-class in the Chinese cities was sufficiently well developed to have supported a nationalist movement since the 1890s. Students and intellectuals played a crucial role in Chinese politics while they were almost absent from the Persian scene. The lower level of social mobilization in Persia made it possible to give new vigor to traditional forms of rule. Indeed, in a sense, Reza Shah had no alternative: reportedly he was anxious to establish a Kemalist style republic in Iran but the opposition to the abandonment of the traditional forms of legitimacy was so strong that he dropped the idea. In part because of this lower level of social mobilization, Reza Shah was able to identify himself with Persian nationalism. He became a symbol of Persian independence from Russian and British influence. In China, on the other hand, Yuan Shih-kai notably failed to respond vigorously to the Twenty-One Demands from Japan in 1915. This failure completed his isolation from the middle-class nationalist groups and deprived him of the authority necessary to counterbalance the disintegrative forces of warlordism.

The radical revolutionaries are the third major political group in a revolutionary situation. For ideological and tactical reasons, their goal is to expand political participation, to bring new masses into politics, and thereby to increase their own power. With the breakdown of the established institutions and procedures for co-opting groups into power and socializing them into the political order, the extremists have a natural advantage over their rivals. They are more willing to mobilize more groups into politics. Hence the revolution becomes more radical as larger and larger masses of the population are brought into the political scales. Since in most modernizing countries the peasants are the largest social force, the most revolutionary leaders are those who mobilize and organize the peasants for political action. In some instances, the appeals to the peasants and other lower class groups may be social and economic; in most instances, however, these will be supplemented by nationalist appeals. This process leads to the redefinition of the political community and creates the foundations for a new political order.

In Western revolutions the symbolic or actual fall of the old regime can be given a fairly precise date: July 14, 1789; October 10, 1911; May 25, 1911; March 15, 1917. These dates mark the beginning of the revolutionary process and the mobilization of new groups into politics as the competition among the new elites struggling for power leads them to appeal to broader and broader masses of the people. Out of this competition one group eventually establishes its dominance and reestablishes order either through force or the development of new political institutions. In Eastern revolutions, in contrast, the old regime is modern, it has more power and legitimacy, and hence it does not simply collapse and leave a vacuum of authority. Instead it must be overthrown. The distinguishing characteristic of the Western revolution is the period of anarchy or statelessness after the fall of the old regime while moderates, counterrevolutionaries, and radicals are struggling for power. The distinguishing characteristic of the Eastern revolution is a prolonged period of "dual power" in which the revolutionaries are expanding political participation and the scope and authority of their institutions of rule at the same time that the government is, in other geographical areas and at other times, continuing to exercise its rule. In the Western revolution the principal struggles are between revolutionary groups; in the Eastern revolution they are between one revolutionary group and the established order.

In terms of our twin concerns of institutions and participation, the Western revolution moves through the collapse of the established political institutions, the expansion of participation, the creation of new institutions. More elaborately, in Brinton's terms, it evolves from the fall of the old order, through the revolutionary honeymoon, the rule of the moderates, the efforts at counterrevolution, the rise of the radicals, the reign of terror and of virtue, and, eventually, the thermidor.[6] The pattern of the Eastern revolution is quite different. The expansion of political participation and the creation of new political institutions are carried on simultaneously and gradually by the revolutionary counterelite and the collapse of the political institutions of the old regime marks the end rather than the beginning of the revolutionary struggle. In the Western revolution the revolutionaries come to power in the capital first and then gradually expand their control over the countryside. In the Eastern revolution they withdraw from central, urban areas of the country, establish a base area of control in a remote section, struggle to win the support of the

6. Crane Brinton, *The Anatomy of Revolution* (New York, Vintage, 1958).

peasants through terror and propaganda, slowly expand the scope of their authority, and gradually escalate the level of their military operations from individual terroristic attacks to guerrilla warfare to mobile warfare and regular warfare. Eventually they are able to defeat the government troops in battle. The last phase of the revolutionary struggle is the occupation of the capital.

In the Western revolution the fall of the old regime which marks the beginning of the revolutionary struggle can be given a precise date, but the end of the struggle is virtually impossible to identify; the revolution, in a sense, peters out as one group gradually establishes its preeminence and restores order. In the Eastern revolution, in contrast, it is impossible to date precisely the beginning of the revolution in the local attacks by small bands of insurrectionaries on village chiefs, governmental officials, and police patrols. The origins of the revolt are lost in the obscurity of jungle and mountain. The end of the revolutionary process, on the other hand, can be precisely dated symbolically or actually by the final conquest of power by the revolutionaries in the capital of the regime: January 31, 1949, January 1, 1959.

In the Western revolution, the revolutionaries fight their way out of the capital to capture control of the countryside. In the Eastern revolution they fight their way in from the remote areas of the countryside and eventually capture control of the capital. Hence, in the Western revolution the bloodiest fighting comes after the revolutionaries have seized power in the capital; in the Eastern revolution it comes before they capture the capital. In a Western revolution the capture of the central institutions and symbols of power is usually very rapid. In January 1917 the Bolsheviks were a small, illegal, conspiratorial group, most of whose leaders were either in Siberia or in exile. Less than a year later they were the principal, although far from undisputed, political rulers of Russia. "You know," Lenin observed to Trotsky, "from persecution and a life underground, to come so suddenly into power. . . . *Es schwindelt!*" [7] The Chinese Communist leaders, in contrast, experienced no such exhilarating and dramatic change in circumstances. Instead they had to fight their way gradually and slowly to power over a 22-year period from their retreat into the countryside in 1927, through the fearsome battles of

7. Leon Trotsky, *My Life* (New York, Scribner's, 1930), p. 337, quoted in Merle Fainsod, *How Russia Is Ruled* (Cambridge, Harvard University Press, 1953), p. 84.

Kiangsi, the exhaustion of the Long March, the struggles against the Japanese, the civil war with the Kuomintang, until finally they made their triumphal entry into Peking. There was nothing "dizzying" about this process. During most of these years the Communist Party exercised effective political authority over substantial amounts of territory and numbers of people. It was a government attempting to expand its authority at the expense of another government rather than a band of conspirators attempting to overthrow a government. The acquisition of national power for the Bolsheviks was a dramatic change; for the Chinese 'Communists it was simply the culmination of a long, drawn-out process.

One major factor responsible for the differing patterns of the Western and Eastern revolutions is the nature of the prerevolutionary regime. The Western revolution is usually directed against a highly traditional regime headed by an absolute monarch or dominated by a land-owning aristocracy. The revolution typically occurs when this regime comes into severe financial straits, when it fails to assimilate the intelligentsia and other urban elite elements, and when the ruling class from which its leaders are drawn has lost its moral self-confidence and will to rule. The Western revolution, in a sense, telescopes the initial "urban breakthrough" of the middle class and the "green uprising" of the peasantry into a single convulsive, revolutionary process. Eastern revolutions, in contrast, are directed against at least partially modernized regimes. These may be indigeneous governments that have absorbed some modern and vigorous middle-class elements and that are led by new men with the ruthlessness, if not the political skill, to hang on to power, or they may be colonial regimes in which the wealth and power of a metropolitan country gives the local government a seemingly overwhelming superiority in all the conventional manifestations of political authority and military force. In such circumstances no quick victory is possible and the urban revolutionaries have to fight their way to power through a prolonged rural insurrectionary process. Western revolutions are thus precipitated by weak traditional regimes; Eastern revolutions by narrow modernizing ones.

In the Western revolution the principal struggle is usually between the moderates and the radicals; in the Eastern revolution it is between the revolutionaries and the government. In the Western revolution the moderates hold power briefly and insecurely between the fall of the old regime and the expansion of participation and conquest of power by the radicals. In the Eastern pattern, the moderates are much weaker; they do not occupy positions of authority; and as the revolution gets under way, they are crushed by the government or the revolutionaries or they are forced by the polarization process to join one side or the other. In the Western revolution, terror occurs in the latter phases of the revolution and is employed by the radicals after they come to power primarily against the moderates and other revolutionary groups with whom they have struggled. In the Eastern revolution, in contrast, terror marks the first phase of the revolutionary struggle. It is used by the revolutionaries when they are weak and far removed from power to persuade or to coerce support from peasants and to intimidate the lower reaches of officialdom. In the Eastern pattern, the stronger the revolutionary movement becomes the less it tends to rely on terrorism. In the Western pattern the loss of the will and the ability to rule by the old elite is the first phase in the revolution; in the Eastern model it is the last phase and is a product of the revolutionary war waged by the counterelite against the regime. Emigration, consequently, reaches its peak at the beginning of the revolutionary struggle in the Western model but at the end of the struggle in the Eastern pattern.

INSTITUTIONAL AND SOCIAL CIRCUMSTANCES OF REVOLUTION

Revolution, as we have said, is the broad, rapid, and violent expansion of political participation outside the existing structure of political institutions. Its causes thus lie in the interaction between political institutions and social forces. Presumably revolutions occur when there is the coincidence of certain conditions in political institutions and certain circumstances among social forces. In these terms, the two prerequisites for revolution are, first, political institutions incapable of providing channels for the participation of new social forces in politics and of new elites in government, and, secondly, the desire of social forces, currently excluded from politics, to participate therein, this desire normally arising from the group's feeling that it needs certain symbolic or material gains which it can achieve only by pressing its demands in the political sphere. Ascending or aspiring groups and rigid or inflexible institutions are the stuff of which revolutions are made.[8]

The many recent efforts to identify the causes of revolution have given primary emphasis to its social and psychological roots. They have thus tended to overlook the political and institutional factors which affect the probability of revolution. Revolutions are unlikely in political systems which have the capacity to expand their power and to broaden participation within the system. It is precisely this fact that makes revolutions unlikely in highly institutionalized modern political systems—constitutional or communist—which are what they are simply because they have developed the procedures for assimilating new social groups and elites desiring to participate in politics. The great revolutions of history have taken place either in highly centralized traditional monarchies (France, China, Russia), or in narrowly based military dictatorships (Mexico, Bolivia, Guatemala, Cuba), or in colonial regimes (Vietnam, Algeria). All these political systems demonstrated little if any capacity to expand their power and to provide channels for the participation of new groups in politics.

Perhaps the most important and obvious but also most neglected fact about successful great revolutions is that they do not occur in democratic political systems. This is not to argue that formally democratic governments are immune to revolution. This is surely not the case, and a narrowly based, oligarchical democracy may be as incapable of providing for expanded political participation as a narrowly based oligarchical dictatorship. Nonetheless, the absence of successful revolutions in democratic countries remains a striking fact, and suggests that, on the average, democracies have more capacity for absorbing new groups into their political systems than do political systems where power is equally small but more concentrated. The absence of successful revolutions against communist dictatorships suggests that the crucial distinction between them and the more traditional autocracies may be precisely this capacity to absorb new social groups. If a democracy acts in an "undemocratic" manner by obstruct-

8. Cf. Chalmers Johnson, *Revolution and the Social System* (Stanford, Hoover Institution, 1964), pp. 3–22; Harry Eckstein, "Internal War: The Problem of Anticipation," in Ithiel de Sola Pool et al., *Social Science Research and National Security* (Washington, Smithsonian Institution, 1963), pp. 116–18.

ing the expansion of political participation, it may well encourage revolution. In the Philippines, for instance, the Hukbalahap movement of the tenant farmers of Luzon first attempted to achieve its goals by exploiting the opportunities for participation offered by a democratic political system. The Huks participated in the elections and elected several members of the Philippine legislature. The legislature, however, refused to seat these representatives, and, as a result, the Huk leaders returned to the countryside to precipitate revolt. The revolution was subdued only when the Philippine government under the leadership of Magsaysay undercut the Huk appeal by providing symbolic and actual opportunities for the peasantry to identify themselves with and to participate in the existing political institutions.

Revolution requires not only political institutions which resist the expansion of participation but also social groups which demand that expansion. In theory, every social class which has not been incorporated into the political system is potentially revolutionary. Virtually every group does go through a phase, brief or prolonged, when its revolutionary propensity is high. At some point, the group begins to develop aspirations which lead it to make symbolic or material demands on the political system. To achieve its goals, the group's leaders soon realize that they must find avenues of access to the political leaders and means of participation in the political system. If these do not exist and are not forthcoming, the group and its leaders become frustrated and alienated. Conceivably this condition can exist for an indefinite period of time; or the original needs which led the group to seek access to the system may disappear; or the group may attempt to enforce its demands on the system through violence, force, or other means illegitimate to the system. In the latter instance, either the system adapts itself to accord some legitimacy to these means and thus to accept the necessity of meeting the demands which they were used to support, or the political elite attempts to suppress the group and to end the use of these methods. No inherent reason exists why such action should not be successful, provided the groups within the political system are sufficiently strong and united in their opposition to admitting the aspiring group to political participation.

Frustration of its demands and denial of the opportunity to

participate in the political system may make a group revolutionary. But it takes more than one revolutionary group to make a revolution. A revolution necessarily involves the alienation of many groups from the existing order. It is the product of "multiple dysfunction" in society.[9] One social group can be responsible for a coup, a riot, or a revolt, but only a combination of groups can produce a revolution. Conceivably, this combination might take the form of any number of possible group coalitions. In actuality, however, the revolutionary alliance must include some urban and some rural groups. The opposition of urban groups to the government can produce the continued instability characteristic of a praetorian state. But only the combination of urban opposition with rural opposition can produce a revolution. In 1789, Palmer observes, "Peasant and bourgeois were at war with the same enemy, and this is what made possible the French Revolution."[10] In a broader sense, this is what makes possible every revolution. To be more precise, the probability of revolution in a modernizing country depends upon: (a) the extent to which the urban middle class—intellectuals, professionals, bourgeoisie—are alienated from the existing order; (b) the extent to which the peasants are alienated from the existing order; and (c) the extent to which urban middle class and peasants join together not only in fighting against "the same enemy" but also in fighting for the same cause. This cause is usually nationalism.

Revolutions are thus unlikely to occur if the period of the frustration of the urban middle class does not coincide with that of the peasantry. Conceivably, one group might be highly alienated from the political system at one time and the other group at another time; in such circumstances revolution is improbable. Hence a slower general process of social change in a society is likely to reduce the possibility that these two groups will be simultaneously alienated from the existing system. To the extent that social-economic modernization has become more rapid over time, consequently, the probability of revolution has increased. For a major revolution to occur, however, not only must the urban middle class and the peasantry be alienated from the existing order, but they must also have the capacity and the incentive

9. Pettee, pp. 12, 100; Brinton, pp. 100 ff.; Johnson, pp. 5 ff.
10. R. R. Palmer, *The Age of the Democratic Revolution, I,* 484.

to act along parallel, if not cooperative, lines. If the proper stimulus to joint action is missing, then again revolution may be avoided.

THE CITY AND REVOLUTION

Lumpenproletariat

What groups are most likely to be revolutionary in the city? Three obvious possibilities are: the lumpenproletariat, the industrial workers, and the middle-class intelligentsia.

On the surface, the most promising source of urban revolt is clearly the slums and the shantytowns produced by the influx of the rural poor. In many Latin American cities during the 1960s from 15 to 30 per cent of the population lived in the appalling conditions which prevailed among the *favelas, ranchos,* and *barriadas.* Similar slum towns were emerging in Lagos, Nairobi, and other African cities. The rise in urban population in most countries clearly exceeded the rise in urban employment. Unemployment rates in the cities frequently amounted to 15 or 20 per cent of the labor force. Clearly these social conditions would seem to be ripe to generate not only opposition but revolution, and in the 1960s American policymakers became increasingly concerned about the probability of violence and insurrection sweeping the cities of many countries to whose economic and political development the United States was committed. "The city," Lady Jackson warned, "may be as lethal as the bomb." [11]

Yet the striking thing in the mid-1960s was the extent to which the shantytowns and slums had not become a major locus of either opposition or revolution. Throughout Latin America and in much of Asia and Africa the slums grew larger in size and little better in living conditions, and yet with rare exceptions the expected social violence, riots, and insurrections did not materialize. The gap between the obvious social and economic evil and the absence of political action to protest or correct that evil was an astonishing phenomenon in the politics of modernizing countries.

Not only was there a general infrequency of political and social violence, but there were also patterns of orthodox political behavior which often seemed strangely incongruous with their social

11. Barbara Ward, " 'The City May Be as Lethal as the Bomb,' " *New York Times Magazine,* April 19, 1964, p. 22.

setting. In theory the *favelas* ought to have been a strong source of support for communist and other radical left-wing movements. In actual fact, this was infrequently the case. Where the shanty-towns voted for opposition parties, they often voted for right-wing rather than left-wing groups. In 1963, in Peru, for instance, the slums of Lima were carried by General Odría, the most conservative of the four candidates running for president. In the same year in Caracas, Uslar Pietri, the conservative candidate, polled a majority of the shantytown vote. In Chile in 1964 the slums of Santiago and Valparaíso voted for the more moderate Frei rather than the more radical Allende.[12] Similar patterns have been observed in São Paulo and other Latin American cities.

How can this apparent conservatism and acquiescence be explained? Four factors seem to play a role. First, rural migrants to the city have demonstrated geographical mobility, and in general they have undoubtedly improved their living conditions by their move to the cities. Comparing his urban economic status with that of his past gives the migrant a "feeling of relative reward. This may happen even though he is at the bottom of the urban stratification ladder." [13] Secondly, the rural migrant brings with him rural values and attitudes including well-established behavior patterns of social deference and political passivity. A low level of political consciousness and political information pervades most urban slums. Politics is not a serious concern: less than one fifth of a sample of Rio slum dwellers engaged in a serious political discussion over a six-month period. Rural patterns of dependence persist in the city, and the levels of political aspiration and expectation consequently also remain low. Various studies show that "the urban and rural poor in Latin America do not seriously expect their government to do anything to alleviate the situation." In Panama City 60 per cent of working-class students believed that "what the government does won't affect my life very much." These attitudes of indifference to and detachment from politics

12. Ernst Halperin, "The Decline of Communism in Latin America," *Atlantic Monthly*, 215 (May 1965), 65.

13. Glaucio A. D. Soares, "The Political Sociology of Uneven Development in Brazil," in Irving L. Horowitz, ed., *Revolution in Brazil* (New York, Dutton, 1964), p. 191; Andrew Pearse, "Some Characteristics of Urbanization in the City of Rio de Janeiro," in Philip Hauser, ed., *Urbanization in Latin America* (Paris, UNESCO, 1961), p. 196.

and from the possibility of political change form the basis of the conservatism of the poor. Nor should this conservatism be surprising. In the United States also, "people in the lower social strata register as substantially more conservative than do people of higher status." [14]

A third factor responsible for the weakness of political radicalism among the slum dwellers is their natural concern for immediate benefits in food, jobs, and housing which can only be secured by working through rather than against the existing system. Like the European immigrant to nineteenth-century urban America, the rural migrant to the modernizing city today is fodder for political machines and bosses who deliver the goods rather than for ideological revolutionaries who promise the millennium. The slum dwellers are, in Halperin's words, "realists on the lookout for material improvement, and in politics they tend to support the man who is in a position to provide such improvement even if he is a dictator or a politician with an unsavory record." [15] The *barriadas* of Lima voted for General Odría because of the employment he had furnished in his extensive public works program during his previous presidential term. The slumdweller lives on a low margin; the payoff that counts is in the here and now. He who is concerned about eating is unlikely to be concerned about revolting.

Finally, the patterns of social organization in the slums may also discourage political radicalism. In Latin America, a high level of mutual distrust and antagonism exists in many urban slums and this consequently makes difficult any sort of organized cooperation to articulate demands and engage in political action. These feelings are more prevalent in the urban slums than in the

14. Angus Campbell et al., *The American Voter* (New York, John Wiley, 1960), pp. 209–10; Frank Bonilla, "Rio's Favelas," *American Universities Field Staff Report Service* (East Coast South America Series, Vol. 8, No. 3, February 1, 1961), 12; John P. Harrison, "The Role of the Intellectual in Fomenting Change: The University," in John J. TePaske and Sydney N. Fisher, eds., *Explosive Forces in Latin America* (Columbus, Ohio State University Press, 1964), p. 34; Daniel Goldrich, "Toward an Estimate of the Probability of Social Revolutions in Latin America: Some Orienting Concepts and a Case Study," *Centennial Review*, 6 (Summer 1962), 400. See also Daniel Goldrich, Raymond B. Pratt, and C. R. Schuller, "The Political Integration of Lower Class Urban Settlements in Chile and Peru: A Provisional Inquiry" (paper presented at Annual Meeting of the American Political Science Association, New York, September 6–10, 1966).

15. Halperin, p. 66.

rural communities from which the migrants came: in Peru, for instance, 54 per cent of the slum dwellers said they always felt distrust even among their friends compared to only 34 per cent in the rural areas.[16] The difficulties of forming new associations to press for their needs are complemented by the persistence of more traditional forms of social structure. The family continues to play a major role, and the local political boss takes the place of the landlord or estate manager. To the extent that these traditional patterns of authority meet the minimum needs of the slum-dwellers, they also minimize the incentives to form new associations with broader political and community goals. In Africa, in contrast, immigrants to the cities apparently very quickly form themselves into voluntary associations with a tribal or regional basis. Performing a variety of mutual benefit and welfare functions, these associations would appear to furnish some basis for movement toward a more highly developed politics of organized interest groups.

Politically, the slumdweller may support the government or he may vote for the opposition. But he is no protagonist of revolution. Reforms that bring immediate material benefits to the slum-dweller in terms of jobs and housing are likely to have a stabilizing effect at least in the short run. At some point, however, this situation is likely to change, and improvement in the conditions of the slumdwellers will in all probability generate more political unrest and violence. The first generation of slumdwellers imports into the slum traditional rural attitudes of social deference and political passivity. Their children grow up in an urban environment and absorb the goals and aspirations of the city. While the parents are content with the geographical mobility, the children demand vertical mobility. If the opportunities are not forthcoming, radicalism in the slums is likely to increase significantly.

The relationships between length of urban residence, occupational mobility, and political radicalism are graphically illustrated by Soares' data from Rio. The percentages of skilled workers supporting the PTB or labor party were the same (37–38%) for those who had lived in Rio for more than twenty years and those who had lived there for less than twenty years. Among unskilled migrants to the city, however, the duration of urban residence ac-

16. H. Rotondo, "Psychological and Mental Health Problems of Urbanization Based on Case Studies in Peru," in Hauser, p. 255.

counted for significant differences in voting patterns. Only 32 per cent of those who had lived in Rio less than twenty years supported the PTB, while 50 per cent of those who had lived there twenty years or more supported the PTB.[17] Prolonged urban residence coupled with little or no occupational mobility, in short, produced political radicalism. Similarly, in Calcutta, the *goondas* or professional rowdies who furnish the leaders and many of the members of rioting mobs are drawn much more heavily from the one third of the population native to the city than from the two thirds composed of immigrants and refugees from the countryside. The rural connections of the latter reduce the probability that they will engage in anomic and illegal activity. "Contrary to popular belief, the migrant's ties to the village and to his family, his uncertainty and perhaps even distrust of the big city, lead to a kind of orderliness; it is the settled urban dweller, dependent upon the city for income and security, who turns more easily against authority and joins the underworld. The rural immigrant needs to be acculturated to urban life before he turns to professional crime. The villager must be taught not to fear authority, but to be contemptuous of it, before he or his descendants will become criminals." [18]

These patterns are confirmed by American experience. In the process of European immigration, the tensions and discontent of adjustment were most notable in the second generation born or bred in America. "The second generation was," in Handlin's words, "an unstable element. . . . As it grew in prominence, it created troublesome problems precisely because it had not a fixed place in the society." [19] Similarly, in the United States the increasing criminal and mob violence in the northern Negro slums in the 1960s was the product of the city-born children of the first generation migrants from the rural south who had moved north

17. Soares, pp. 191–92; Alfred Stepan, "Political Development Theory: The Latin American Experience," *Journal of International Affairs, 20* (1966), 229–31; Joseph A. Kahl, "Social Stratification and Values in Metropoli and Provinces: Brazil and Mexico," *América Latina, 8* (Jan.–Mar. 1965), 33. Cf. John C. Leggett, "Uprootedness and Working-Class Consciousness," *American Journal of Sociology, 68* (1963), 682 ff.

18. Weiner, *The Politics of Scarcity*, pp. 205–06 (footnotes omitted), and Weiner, "Urbanization and Political Protest," *Civilisations, 17* (1967), 44–50.

19. Oscar Handlin, *The Uprooted* (Boston, Little Brown, 1951), p. 267; Will Herberg, *Protestant-Catholic-Jew* (Garden City, N.Y., Doubleday, 1956), pp. 28–35; Marcus L. Hansen, *The Immigrant in American History* (Cambridge, Harvard University Press, 1940), pp. 92–96.

during the Great Depression and World War II. The first generation held to rural ways and attitudes; the second generation drew its dreams from the city, and to realize those dreams turned first to crime and then to anomic action. Forty-four per cent of Detroit Negroes participating in the July 1967 riot had been born in Detroit, but only 22 per cent of those Negroes not rioting were native to the city. Similarly, 71 per cent of the rioters but only 39 per cent of the non-rioters had grown up in the North rather than the South. "The older generation," Claude Brown told Robert Kennedy in 1966,

> subscribed to the myth that they were inferior and they weren't supposed to get any more than the white society was giving them. This generation doesn't believe that any more, because of TV, because of the upbringing they have had, because of the exposure to the popular magazines and this sort of thing, and this generation wants its share. It demands its share. And you know something, Senator? Perhaps no one has taken time to notice it, but the only thing that has really brought any meaningful concession from the white society in the Negro communities has been the riots. Nobody knew that Watts existed prior to the '65 Watts riot.[20]

In Asia and Latin America, as well as North America, urban violence, political and criminal, is due to rise as the proportion of natives to immigrants in the city rises. At some point, the slums of Rio and Lima, of Lagos and Saigon, like those of Harlem and Watts, are likely to be swept by social violence, as the children of the city demand the rewards of the city.

Industrial Labor

A less likely source of revolutionary activity is the industrial proletariat in late modernizing countries. In general the gap between the mobilization of social forces for political and social action and the creation of institutions to organize that action is much greater in the later modernizing countries than in those which modernized earlier. Just the reverse relationship, however,

20. Claude Brown, Testimony, *Hearings on Federal Role in Urban Problems,* U.S. Senate, Subcommittee on Executive Reorganization of the Committee on Government Operations, 89th Congress, 2d Session (1966), Part V, p. 1106; Philip Meyer, *A Survey of Attitudes of Detroit Negroes After the Riot of 1967* (Detroit, Detroit Urban League and Detroit Free Press, 1967).

is true in the field of labor. In the nineteenth century in Europe
and America industrial labor was radical and at times revolutionary because industrialization preceded unionization, the dominant
groups in society often vigorously opposed unions, and employers
and governments did what they could to resist the demands of
labor for higher pay, shorter hours, better working conditions,
unemployment insurance, pensions, and other social benefits. In
these countries, the mobilization of labor easily outran the organization of labor, and consequently radical and extremist
movements often gained support among the alienated working
class before unions became strong. When unions were organized
they were organized to protest and to struggle with the existing
order on behalf of this new class. Communist and other radical
groups were strongest in labor movements which were denied legitimacy and recognition by the political and economic elites.
"Greater discontinuities," as Kornhauser observes, "tend to occur
in the *early* period of industrialization, and that is the time when
mass movements flourish. The mitigation of mass tendencies
depends on the creation of new social forms, especially trade
unions, to mediate between the industrial labor force and the
national society. This takes time." [21]

All these conditions are much less prevalent among countries
industrializing later. In twentieth-century societies with traditional political systems (such as Saudi Arabia), labor unions were
often proscribed. In other later modernizing societies, however,
the gap between the mobilization of workers and the institutionalization of workers' organizations was drastically reduced if
not eliminated. In some instances, indeed, the organization of the
labor force all but preceded the formation of the labor force. In
many modernizing countries of Africa and Latin America in the
mid-twentieth century more than 50 per cent of the nonagricultural workers were organized into unions. In 14 of 23 African
countries and 9 of 21 Latin American-Caribbean countries union
members made up more than a quarter of nonagricultural workers. In the Middle East and Asia labor organization was less extensive, but even in these areas it reached very respectable proportions in some countries. All in all, in the 1950s and 1960s,
some 37 Asian, African, and Latin American countries had higher

---

21. Kornhauser, *The Politics of Mass Society*, pp. 150–51; italics in original.

proportions of their labor force organized into unions than did
the United States. Thus the radicalizing and destabilizing tendencies associated with the introduction of rural migrants into factory discipline were greatly reduced. The labor movement in these
countries is, in general, a much more conservative force than it
was in the early stages of industrialization in the West.

TABLE 5.1. Extent of Labor Organization

Countries	Ratio of Labor Union Membership to Nonagricultural Employment				
	.50 and over	.25–.49	.10–.24	Less than .10	Total
African	7	7	5	4	23
Latin American and Caribbean	6	3	5	7	21
Middle East– North African	1	5	1	9	16
Asian	1	6	2	8	17
Communist	10	2	1	0	13
Western	7	11	1	1	20
Total	32	34	15	29	110

Source: Ted Gurr, New Error-Compensated Measures for Comparing Nations: Some
Correlates of Civil Violence (Princeton, Princeton University, Center of International Studies, Research Monograph No. 25, 1966), pp. 101–10.

Here, indeed, is a dramatic instance of organization slowing social and economic change. In the West the relatively later development of unionism permitted greater exploitation of industrial
workers in the early phases of the industrialization process, facili-
tating capital accumulation and investment. Among the early
industrializers real wages also rose slowly during these initial intensive phases of industrialization. The earlier spread of unionization among the later industrializers, on the other hand, has meant
higher wages and more welfare benefits during the initial phases
of industrialization, but also a slower rate of capital investment.
More organization has produced greater industrial peace and political stability, but slower economic development.

Not only is labor less radical because unions are formed early,
but the unions themselves also tend to be less radical because they
are often outgrowths of the establishment rather than protests
against the establishment. Perhaps the greatest source of social

conflict and industrial strife in the early industrializers was the reluctance of the authorities to recognize the right of labor to organize and to accept the legitimacy of unions. These principles
had to be established through struggles in the nineteenth century.
The more intense and persistent a government was in refusing to
recognize the legitimacy of labor organization, the more radical
the unions became. Unionization was interpreted as a challenge
to the existing order and this interpretation tended to make it a
challenge to the existing order. In the twentieth century, however, labor organization is generally accepted as a natural feature
of an industrial society. All the advanced countries have large and
well-organized labor movements, hence the backward countries
want them also. A national labor federation is as essential to national dignity as an army, an airline, and a foreign office.

Labor unions in Asia, Africa, and Latin America, it is often remarked, are much more "political" than they are in the United
States and some other Western countries. The implication of this
comment is often that the unions are concerned with the pursuit
of long-range comprehensive political and social objectives. In
fact, however, this is not the case. The unions are political usually
because they are part of the political establishment. Their organization and growth have been aided and abetted by the government or political parties. British and French colonial governments in general followed permissive policies toward labor organization. Unions were often permitted where political parties
were not, and once national independence movements did come
into existence, close ties usually existed between them and the
unions. Nehru, Gandhi, Mboya, Adoula, Nkomo, U Ba Swe,
Touré, are only a few of the nationalist leaders of Asia and Africa
who also played prominent roles in the labor movements of their
countries. Indeed, the achievement of independence for some
countries posed significant problems for the labor unions because
of the heavy movement of labor leaders into governmental office.
In Latin America, also, unions were closely connected with political parties, and in the largest countries, such as Brazil, Argentina,
and Mexico, the organization of unions has been actively promoted by the government. In some instances, as in Brazil, a distinct class of labor union officials, the *pelegos*, emerged, who were
also government employees, and who in many respects functioned

more as bureaucrats of the state than as representatives of the workers.[22]

The fostering of labor organization from above has been paralleled by promotion of labor welfare from above. In the nineteenth century English coal miners developed their own independent organizations and methods of protest; in contrast, "German miners enjoyed a state-protected status and special economic advantages during the pre-industrial period but inherited legacies of submissiveness and of dependence on the state."[23] Such also is the case with much of labor in the modernizing countries of the twentieth century. The benefits their relatively small industrial labor forces enjoy are, in large part, the result not of the pressure they have exerted through the political process but rather of the initiative of the political elite. In Latin America, the dominant pattern has been "for labor as a whole, or some neglected sector of it, to make its crucial first gains well before it is really established as a powerful pressure group. Rather, these early gains are often handed to it on a silver platter, in order to build it up as a source of support, or to forestall the growth of discontent."[24] Similarly, in South Asia, it is reported that "Because of the control of trade union rank and file from above, whether by government officials, political leaders, or employers, the governments of South Asia exhibit a tendency to protect the workers through extensive social legislation (which is often difficult to enforce) rather than to permit them to develop independently their own protective devices."[25] The industrial worker, in most modernizing countries, is almost a member of the elite; he is economically far better off than the rural population, and he is usually in a favored position from governmental policy. In the

22. See George E. Lichtblau, "The Politics of Trade Union Leadership in Southern Asia," *World Politics*, 7 (1954), 89–99; Arnold Zack, *Labor Training in Developing Countries* (New York, Praeger, 1964), p. 12; Bruce Millen, *The Political Role of Labor in Developing Countries*, pp. 49–52; Robert J. Alexander, *Organized Labor in Latin America* (New York, Free Press, 1965), p. 13; Marshall R. Singer, *The Emerging Elite* (Cambridge, M.I.T. Press, 1964), pp. 128–36.

23. Gaston V. Rimlinger, "The Legitimation of Protest: A Comparative Study in Labor History," *Comparative Studies in Society and History*, 2 (April 1960), 342–43.

24. Henry A. Landsberger, "The Labor Elite: Is It Revolutionary?" in Seymour Martin Lipset and Aldo Solari, eds., *Elites in Latin America* (New York, Oxford University Press, 1967), p. 260.

25. Lichtblau, p. 100.

288 POLITICAL ORDER IN CHANGING SOCIETIES

modernizing countries of today, Fallers has observed, the worker enters the industrial environment

> under circumstances rather less productive of all those frustrations and anxieties that Marx subsumed under the term "alienation" than did the Western pioneers of industrial labor. There is an ample supply of alienated people in the new states; but industrial workers are not the most prominent among them, both because the industrial sector remains small and because workers tend to be relatively secure and prosperous in relation to their countrymen.[26]

Lenin may well have been right that political consciousness could only come to labor from outside groups. In most of the modernizing countries today, however, that consciousness has been brought to labor not by revolutionary intellectuals but by political leaders or governmental bureaucrats. As a result, the goals of labor have been fairly concrete and immediate economic ones, rather than the transformation of the political social order. In the competition for the leadership of Latin American labor, "ideologically less extreme elements triumph over more extreme ones, provided they are vigorously progressive."[27] Labor organizations were created by politics and are active in politics: their goals, however, are not political but economic. They differ from American unions not in the ends which they seek, but in the means they use to achieve those ends. These means reflect their own origins and the nature of the political system in which they operate.

Middle-Class Intelligentsia

At times, both the industrial proletariat and the lumpenproletariat may oppose the government. Eventually, the slumdwellers may erupt into riots and political violence. In general, however, they are not the stuff out of which revolution is made. The former has too much at stake in the status quo; the latter is too

26. Lloyd Fallers, "Equality, Modernity, and Democracy in the New States," in Clifford Geertz, ed., *Old Societies and New States* (New York, The Free Press, 1963), p. 188. See also Theodore Draper's comment that the Cuban trade unions "had over the years gained enough concessions and benefits to make their members a relatively privileged class." *Castroism: Theory and Practice* (New York, Praeger, 1965), pp. 76–77.

27. Landsberger, p. 271.

preoccupied with immediate ends. The true revolutionary class in most modernizing societies is, of course, the middle class. Here is the principal source of urban opposition to government. It is this group whose political attitudes and values dominate the politics of the cities. What Halpern has observed of the Middle East is true of most other rapidly modernizing areas: "the thrust toward revolutionary action on the part of the new middle class is overwhelming." The revolutionary character of the middle class is underlined by the differences in political outlook of white collar and blue collar unions in modernizing countries. Typically the former are more extreme and radical than the latter. In Latin America unions of bank employees, for instance, have been strongholds of left-wing and communist support. In Venezuela the bank employees union played a leading role in the left-wing efforts to bring down the reform-minded Betancourt government in 1960. Similarly in Cuba, under Batista, "As a rule, the more 'middle class' the union, the stronger was the Communist influence in it, a notable example of which was the union of bank employees." [28]

The image of the middle class as a revolutionary element clashes, of course, with the stereotype of the middle class as the keystone of stability in a modern polity. The relation of the middle class to stability, however, is not unlike that of affluence to stability. A large middle class, like widespread affluence, is a moderating force in politics. The creation of a middle class, like economic growth, however, is often a highly destabilizing event. The evolution of the middle class, indeed, can be traced through several phases. Typically the first middle-class elements to appear on the social scene are intellectuals with traditional roots but modern values. They are then followed by the gradual proliferation of civil servants and army officers, teachers and lawyers, engineers and technicians, entrepreneurs and managers. The first elements of the middle class to appear are the most revolutionary; as the middle class becomes larger, it becomes more conservative. All or most of these groups may at times play a revolutionary role, but in general it is the nonbureaucratic and the nonbusiness segments which are most prone to opposition, to violence, and to revolu-

28. Halpern, *The Politics of Social Change in the Middle East and North Africa*, p. 75; Draper, p. 79.

tion. And of all segments of the middle class those most inclined in these directions are the intellectuals.

The desertion of the intellectuals is, Brinton and others have argued, a forerunner of revolution. In fact, however, it is not the desertion of the intellectuals but rather their emergence as a distinct group which may be the harbinger of revolt. In most cases, the intellectuals cannot desert the existing order because they have never been a part of it. They are born to opposition, and it is their appearance on the social scene rather than any transfer of allegiance which is responsible for their potentially revolutionary role.

The revolutionary intellectual is a virtually universal phenomenon in modernizing societies. "No one is as inclined to foster violence as a disgruntled intellectual, at least within the Indian context," Hoselitz and Weiner have observed. "It is these persons who compose the cadres of the less responsible political parties, who make up the narrower entourage of demagogues, and who become leaders of millenarian and messianic movements, all of which may, when the opportunity is ripe, threaten political stability." In Iran extremists of both the left and the right were more likely than moderates to be products of the city, to come from the middle economic strata, and to be better educated.[29] This syndrome of characteristics is the prevalent one. The ability of the intellectuals to carry out a revolutionary role depends upon their relations with other social groups. Initially they are likely to be the dominant middle-class group; their ability to instigate a revolution at this time depends upon their ability to arouse mass support from other elements in the population, such as the peasants.

The city is the center of opposition within the country; the middle class is the focus of opposition within the city; the intelligentsia is the most active oppositional group within the middle class; and the students are the most coherent and effective revolutionaries within the intelligentsia. This does not necessarily mean of course that the majority of students, like the majority of the general population, are not politically apathetic. It does mean, however, that the dominant activist group in the student bodies in most modernizing countries is against the regime. It is here, in the university, that the most consistent, extreme, intransigent opposition to the government exists.

Peasants and Revolution

The middle-class intelligentsia is revolutionary, but it cannot make a revolution on its own. Confined within the city, it can oppose the government, it can stimulate riots and demonstrations, it can at times mobilize support from the working class and the lumpenproletariat. If it can also win the cooperation of some elements within the military, it can bring down the government. The overthrow of a government by urban groups, however, does not normally mean the overthrow of the political and social system. It is a change within the system, not of the system. Except in rare instances, it does not herald the beginning of the revolutionary reconstruction of society. By themselves, in short, the opposition groups within the city can unseat governments but they cannot create a revolution. That requires the active participation of rural groups.

The role of the dominant groups in the countryside hence becomes the critical factor determining the stability or fragility of the government. If the countryside supports the government, the government has the potential to isolate and contain the urban opposition. Given the proclivity of the dominant urban groups, any government, even one which follows a government overthrown by those groups, must find sources of support in the countryside if it is to avoid the fate of its predecessor. In Turkey, for instance, the Menderes regime was overthrown in 1960 by urban student, military, and professional groups. The succeeding military government of General Gursel and the subsequent Republican Party regime under Inönü had substantial support from these groups but could not command the support of the mass of the peasantry in the countryside. Only in 1965 when the Justice Party won a clear victory, as a result of its massive support from the peasantry, did a stable government emerge. This government was still challenged by important urban opposition, but in a system which makes any pretense to democracy a government with the support of the countryside and the opposition of the city will be more stable than one whose principal source of support is the volatile groups in the city. If no government can come to power which can win the support or the acquiescence of the countryside, then little basis exists for political stability. In South Vietnam, for instance, after the Diem regime was overthrown by the urban opposition of students, monks, and military officers, elements of these groups opposed each of the succeeding regimes. Deprived of support from the countryside by the Viet Cong, the successor regimes could find few stable sources of support in the quagmire of urban politics.

The countryside thus plays the crucial "swing" role in modernizing politics. The nature of the Green Uprising, the way in which the peasants are incorporated into the political system, shapes the subsequent course of political development. If the countryside supports the political system and the government, the system itself is secure against revolution and the government has some hope of making itself secure against rebellion. If the countryside is in opposition, both system and government are in danger of overthrow. The role of the city is constant: it is the permanent source of opposition. The role of the countryside is variable: it is either the source of stability or the source of revolution. For the political system, opposition within the city is disturbing but not lethal. Opposition within the countryside, however, is fatal. He who controls the countryside controls the country. In traditional society and during the early phases of modernization, stability rests on the dominance of the rural landowning elite over both countryside and city. As modernization progresses, the middle class and other groups in the city emerge as political actors challenging the existing system. Their successful overthrow of the system, however, depends upon their ability to win rural allies, that is, to win the support of the peasants against the traditional oligarchy. The ability of the political system to survive and of its government to remain stable depends upon its capacity to counter this revolutionary appeal and to bring the peasants into politics on the side of the system. As political participation expands, those groups dominant in the political system must shift their basis of support within the countryside and win the allegiance of the peasants. In a system with only restricted political participation, the support of the traditional rural elite is sufficient for political stability. In a system in which political consciousness and political participation are broadening, the peasantry becomes the critical group. The basic political competition becomes the competition between the government and the urban revolutionary intelligentsia for the support of the peasantry. If the peasantry acquiesces in and identifies with the existing system, it furnishes that system with a stable foundation. If it actively opposes the system, it becomes the carrier of revolution.

The peasantry may thus play either a highly conservative role or a highly revolutionary one. Both images of the peasantry have been prevalent. On the one hand, the peasantry has often been held to be an extremely traditional conservative force, resistant to change, loyal to church and to throne, hostile toward the city, involved with family and village, suspicious of, and at times, hostile to even those agents of change, such as doctors, teachers, agronomists, who come to the village solely and directly to improve the peasants' lot. Reports of the murder of such agents by suspicious and superstitious peasants are found in virtually all modernizing areas.

This image of a highly conservative peasantry coexists with a more recent one of the peasantry as a force for revolution. Each of the major revolutions in Western, as well as non-Western societies, was in large part a peasant revolution. This was true in France and in Russia as it was in China. In all three countries, the peasants more or less spontaneously acted to overthrow the old agrarian political and social structure, to seize the land, and to establish a new political and social system in the countryside. Without this peasant action, not one of these revolutions would have constituted a revolution. In France during the summer of 1789, while the National Assembly debated in Versailles, the peasants produced the revolution in the countryside.

> Agrarian insurrection raged throughout the country. Peasants refused taxes, tithes, and manorial payments. They invaded chateaux and burned the legal papers on which their obligations rested. What they intended was no less than a social revolution, in that they meant by their own action to destroy the manorial or "feudal" system and the forms of property and income that this system represented. . . . The peasants in destroying the manorial system were destroying the economic foundations of the nobility.[30]

30. Palmer, *1*, 483–84.

Faced with this condition in the countryside which in large part was not to its liking, the middle-class-majority in the National Assembly "decreed what it could not prevent." In the resolutions of August 4th it "abolished feudalism" and in effect gave its legislative imprimatur to the changes which the peasants were wreaking on the countryside.

In Russia the situation was not substantially different. As the Provisional Government delayed action on land reform, the peasants deserted the army and returned home to seize the land for themselves. In the spring their actions were generally peaceful and cloaked in a semilegality. They simply refused, as in France, to pay rents and taxes and proceeded to make illegal use of the estates for pasture and other purposes. By the summer and fall, however, violence and disorder became widespread. In May in the two most important agricultural areas, 60 per cent of the peasant actions represented pseudolegal seizures of property, while open seizures accounted for 30 per cent, and cases of destruction 10 per cent. In October, only 14 per cent of the cases were pseudolegal; open seizures still accounted for 30 per cent; but 56 per cent now involved destruction and devastation. By October the agrarian revolution had turned into a primitive, ferocious campaign to eliminate every trace of the old order. "Libraries, works of art, bloodstock, conservatories, and experimental stations were in many cases destroyed, animals hamstrung, houses burned, and masters or agents sometimes murdered. It was now far more than a mere seizure of estates and property." [31] During this period, despite the opposition of the Provisional Government, local peasant committees and soviets took over control of the land. By not identifying itself with this movement, the Provisional Government insured its own downfall. This fact was quickly grasped by Lenin. Unable to call for support from the countryside, the Provisional Government would be unable to defend itself in the cities. The agrarian uprising, as Lenin accurately said at the time, is the "biggest fact in contemporary Russia" and made the case for insurrection "stronger than a thousand pessimistic evasions of

31. John Maynard, *The Russian Peasant and Other Studies* (London, Victor Gollancz, 1947), pp. 74–75; Launcelot Owen, *The Russian Peasant Movement, 1906–1917* (New York, Russell and Russell, 1963), p. 139. On these developments, I have been greatly aided by an unpublished paper by JoClayre Marvin, "The Political Role of the Russian Peasantry, 1890–1921" (Cambridge, Mass., Harvard University, 1965).

a confused and frightened politician." More importantly, the peasant uprising made possible the success of the Bolshevik insurrection. "Without the peasant," Owen has observed, "it is certain that his effort to emulate the Paris Commune of 1871 would have suffered the same fate as that of the socialists of Montmartre and it would have gone down in history as a similar event." [32]

The initial phases of the Chinese Communist Revolution were not substantially different. Like other revolutionary groups before them, the Chinese Communists focused on the cities, not on the countryside. The potentialities of the peasant as a revolutionary went virtually unnoticed until the Northern Expedition of the combined Nationalist-Communist forces in 1926–27. One participant in this movement was Mao Tse-tung who was charged as a rural commissar with restraining peasant rebellions in Hunan and Hopeh. Mao, however, found the peasant revolution to be the real revolution. The peasants in Hunan and Hopeh were seizing property and dispossessing landlords just as the French and the Russians had done in 1789 and 1917. "In force and momentum, the attack is just like a tempest or hurricane; those who submit to it survive, those who resist perish," Mao reported. "What Mr. Sun Yat-sen wanted to but failed to accomplish in the forty years he devoted to the national revolution, the peasants have accomplished in a few months." This spontaneous peasant uprising in an area where land inequalities were great and peasant conditions abominable produced a new appreciation of the key role of the peasantry as a revolutionary force. Since the victory of the Chinese Communists, their revolutionary potential has, of course, become obvious to almost everyone. The basic truth about revolution was, however, well stated by Mao in 1927.

> To give credit where due, if we allot ten points to the accomplishments of the democratic revolution, then the achievements of the urban dwellers and the military rate only three points, while the remaining seven points should go to the peasants in their rural revolution . . . Without the poor peasants there can be no revolution. To reject them is to reject the revolution. To attack them is to attack the revolu-

32. Owen, p. 138; Lenin, quoted in William Henry Chamberlin, *The Russian Revolution, 1917–1921* (New York, Macmillan, 1952), *1*, 294.

tion. From beginning to end, the general direction they have given the revolution has never been wrong.[33]

Revolutionaries have learned this lesson well. The peasants, as Furtado has observed in Brazil, are "much more susceptible to revolutionary influences of the Marxist-Leninist kind than the urban classes, although the latter, according to orthodox Marxism, should be the spearhead of the revolutionary movement." [34] Such is the case for modernizing countries generally.

If there is no revolution without the peasantry, the key question then becomes: What turns peasants into revolutionaries? If the conditions which make for peasant revolt can be ameliorated by reforms rather than exacerbated by them, a possibility exists for more or less peaceful social change rather than for violent upheaval. Clearly, in traditional societies, the peasants are generally a static conservative force, wedded to the status quo. Modernization typically has two significant impacts upon the peasant. Its initial impact is to worsen the objective conditions of peasant work and welfare. In the traditional society land is often owned and farmed communally either by the village or by the extended family. Modernization—and particularly the impact of Western concepts of land ownership—undermines this system. As in southern Italy and the Middle East the nuclear family replaces the extended family: the plots which collectively had been a viable economic unit are replaced by small and often scattered individual lots which are barely sufficient to support a family and which greatly extend the risks that the family may suffer total economic catastrophe. Where many individuals and groups have exercised rights and privileges with respect to the same piece of land, Western rulers typically break this pattern and insist upon the single ownership of land. In practice this means that those with more wealth and social status acquire exclusive rights to the land, while those with less wealth and status lose their traditional privileges in the land. In the Middle East, for instance, the law of the nation-state undermined the old communal systems of land ownership, made the sheikhs the sole land owners, and thus created

33. Mao Tse-Tung, "Report of an Investigation into the Peasant Movement in Hunan," reprinted in Stuart R. Schram, ed., The Political Thought of Mao Tse-tung (New York, Praeger, 1963), pp. 180–82, 184; italics in original.

34. Celso Furtado, quoted in Thomas F. Carroll, "Land Reform as an Explosive Force in Latin America," in TePaske and Fisher, pp. 119–20.

inequalities which had not existed previously. Typically, the new laws

> expressly forbade the registration of any kind of joint rights or special rights over a landowner by others. This prevented any legal protection of the rights of tenants, or of the rights of tribesmen to communally owned land, against the sheikhs. In practice, in almost all areas, land passed into the hands of members of the literate class—existing owners, tax collectors, officials, political heads of tribes or sections of tribes.[35]

In India, similarly, the British in many areas assigned effective sole ownership of the land to the zamindars, who previously had simply functioned as tax collectors. In Latin America, communal ownership of land prevailed in the Inca, Maya, and Aztec civilizations. The impact of Western civilization, however, replaced these communal systems of land ownership with the hacienda, and the Indian farmer was reduced to peonage or forced to eke out a bare existence on a minifundio. The shift from communal to individual ownership was often viewed as an essential step for progress. Thus in Mexico the Ley Lerdo (1856) of the Juárez regime required corporate bodies (such as the church) and communal groups (such as the Indian villages) to sell their lands. The purpose of the law was to create a system of individual peasant proprietors. Its effect, however, was to hasten the reduction of the peasant to peonage. Only those already wealthy were able to purchase the land liberated from collective ownerships and restraints, and the next half century witnessed the increasing concentration of land ownership in fewer and fewer hands.

The impoverishing effect that modernization has upon the peasant would not be politically significant if it were not also for the elevating effect it eventually has upon his aspirations. The time lag between the one and the other may be substantial, in some cases, indeed, amounting to several centuries. In due course, however, the enlightenment of the cities becomes available in the

35. Paul Stirling, "Structural Changes in Middle East Society," in Philip W. Thayer, ed., *Tensions in the Middle East* (Baltimore, Johns Hopkins Press, 1958), p. 145. See also Douglas D. Crary, "The Villager," in S. N. Fisher, ed., *Social Forces in the Middle East* (Ithaca, Cornell University Press, 1955), p. 52. On this point, I am also in debt to Steven Dale's unpublished paper, "The Anatomy of La Miseria: A Critique of Banfield's Theory of the Moral Nature of Underdeveloped Societies" (Cambridge, Mass., Harvard University, 1966).

countryside. The barriers to communication and transportation are broken down; roads, salesmen, and teachers reach the villages. The radio makes its appearance. The peasant comes to realize not only that he is suffering but that something can be done about this suffering. Nothing is more revolutionary than this awareness. The peasant's dissatisfaction stems from the realization that his material hardships and sufferings are much worse than those of other groups in society and that they are not inevitable. His lot can be improved. His goals, which are typically the ones stressed by revolutionary movements, are to improve his immediate material conditions of life and work.

The concern of the peasants with their immediate economic and social conditions does not distinguish them significantly from the industrial workers of the cities except insofar as the peasants are normally worse off than the workers. The primary differences between the two lie in their relationship to economic development and in the avenues of action open to them. Like the entrepreneur, the worker is a newcomer to the modernizing society. He participates in the production of new economic wealth. His struggles with the employer revolve about: (a) the ability of the worker to organize collectively so as to make an effective claim for his share of the new product; and (b) the actual distribution of that product among worker, owner, and consumer. If the owners accept the right of the worker to organize and thus substantially remove the first ground of contention, the second set of issues can normally be resolved through collective bargaining supplemented by strikes, lockouts, and the other instruments of industrial conflict between management and labor. The worker thus has little or no incentive to be revolutionary; he is simply interested in asserting his claim to an appropriate share of the economic product and, if unions and collective bargaining are accepted as legitimate, recognized procedures and methods exist for resolving these issues.

The peasant, however, is in a very different situation. The common interest of capitalist and worker in a larger economic product does not exist between landlord and peasant. The relationship of social structure to economic development in the countryside is just the reverse of what it is in the city. In industrial society, a more equitable distribution of *income* is the result of economic growth; in agrarian society, a more equitable distribution of *ownership* is the prerequisite to economic growth. It is precisely for this reason that modernizing countries find it so much more difficult to increase agricultural output than to increase industrial output, and it is precisely for this reason that the tensions of the countryside are potentially so much more revolutionary than those of the city. The industrial worker cannot secure personal ownership or control of the means of production; this, however, is precisely the goal of the peasant. The basic factor of production is land; the supply of land is limited if not fixed; the landlord loses what the peasant acquires. Thus the peasant, unlike the industrial worker, has no alternative but to attack the existing system of ownership and control. Land reform, consequently, does not mean just an increase in the economic wellbeing of the peasant. It involves also a fundamental redistribution of power and status, a reordering of the basic social relationships which had previously existed between landlord and peasant. The industrial worker participates in the creation of an entirely new set of economic and social relationships which had not previously existed in the society. Peasant and landlord, however, coexist in the traditional society, and the destruction or transformation of their existing social, economic, and political relationship (which may be of centuries' standing) is the essence of change in the agrarian order.

The cost of economic improvement for the peasant in the countryside is thus far greater than the cost of economic improvement for his counterpart in the city. Consequently, it is hardly surprising that the more active and intelligent individuals in the countryside move to the city. They are driven there by the comparative advantages of the opportunities for economic and social mobility in the city versus the rigidities of the class structure in the countryside. The resulting rapid urbanization leads to social dislocation and political instability in the cities. These, however, are minor social and political ills compared to what would result in the countryside in the absence of such urbanization. Urban migration is, in some measure, a substitute for rural revolution. Hence, contrary to common belief, the susceptibility of a country to revolution may vary inversely with its rate of urbanization.

In addition, no recognized and accepted means exist through which the peasant can advance his claims. The right of labor to organize is accepted in most countries; the rights of peasants to organize are much more dubious. In this respect, the position of peasants in the modernizing countries of Asia and Latin America in the latter half of the twentieth century is not too different from the position of the industrial worker in Europe and North America in the first half of the nineteenth century. Any form of collective action tends to be viewed as inherently revolutionary by the powers that be. To take but one example: in Guatemala, labor unions among urban workers were organized in the 1920s. Unions among agricultural workers, however, were prohibited. Not until 1949 was this provision repealed. During the next five years the Confederation of Guatemalan Peasants came into existence with over 200,000 members. In 1954, after the overthrow of the left-wing Arbenz regime, one of the first actions of the new government under the leadership of Col. Castillo Armas was to again make agricultural unions illegal. Peasant unions and peasant movements are thus still enveloped in the nineteenth century. The result is, of course, to encourage their revolutionary propensities. As Celso Furtado has acutely observed in commenting on the campesino movement in Brazil:

> Ours is an open society for the industrial worker, but not for the peasant. In effect, our political system permits the urban groups to organize in order to press their claims within the rules of the democratic game. The situation of the *campesinos* is totally different. Since they have no rights whatsoever, they cannot have *legal* claims or bargaining power. If they organize, it is assumed that they do so with subversive ends in mind. We get to the necessary conclusion that Brazilian society in its important rural sector is very rigid.[36]

THE REVOLUTIONARY ALLIANCE AND NATIONALISM

The urban middle-class intelligentsia is the most constantly revolutionary group in modernizing societies. But to produce a revolution, the intelligentsia must have allies. One potential source is the lumpenproletariat in the cities, which is for many years not a very revolutionary group. Its revolutionary proclivities are, however, likely to increase, and hence at some point in most

36. Celso Furtado, quoted in Carroll, "Land Reform," p. 120; see also Royal Institute of International Affairs, *Agrarian Reform in Latin America* (London, Oxford University Press, 1962) , p. 15.

modernizing countries the alliance of the *cidade universitaria* and the *favela*, of the students and slumdwellers, may pose a major challenge to political stability. The conditions for the success of this revolutionary combination are, however, in some measure the conditions for its failure. If the society remains primarily agricultural, the intelligentsia and urban poor may be able to overthrow the government, but they cannot destroy the basic social structure of the society since their action is limited to the urban area. They would still have to add the peasants to their alliance to effect a fundamental change in social structure. On the other hand, if urbanization has reached the point where much of the population is concentrated in one or a few large cities, urban revolutionary action might be able to wreak a fundamental transformation of the society.

The very process of urbanization which makes this possible, however, also is likely to create counterbalancing forces supporting political stability. Sustained urbanization not only increases the number of slumdwellers, but it also expands and diversifies the middle class, bringing into existence new, more conservative middle-class strata which will, in some measure, restrict and dilute the revolutionary fervor of the middle-class intelligentsia. As was pointed out earlier, the first middle-class groups to appear on the scene are the most radical ones. Subsequent elements are likely to be more bureaucratic, more technical, more business-oriented, and, hence, more conservative. While the lumpenproletariat goes through a process of radicalization with its second generation more revolutionary than the first, the middle class goes through a process of conservatization, with each addition to that class shifting the balance from revolution toward stability. At some point, conceivably, the balance of forces might be right to produce a major social-political upheaval solely in the city, but the likelihood of this occurring seems relatively low.[37] The probability of revolution, consequently, depends primarily upon parallel or cooperative action by the middle-class intelligentsia and the peasantry.

The rarity of revolution is in large part due to the difficulties of parallel action by intelligentsia and peasants. The gap between

37. For a useful succinct discussion of the prospects of a university intellectual-urban poor alliance, see Harrison, "The University," in TePaske and Fisher, pp. 34–36.

city and countryside is the crux of politics in modernizing societies. The difficulties which governments have in bridging this gap
are almost matched by the difficulties which revolutionaries have
in bridging it. The obstacles to the formation of the revolutionary alliance stem from the differences in background, in perspectives, and in purposes between the two groups. The social distance between the urban, middle- or upper-class, educated, Westernized, cosmopolitan intelligentsia, on the one hand, and the
rural, backward, illiterate, culturally traditional, provincial peasants, on the other, is about as great a gap as can be imagined between any two social groups. The problems of communication
and understanding between them are tremendous. They speak
different languages, often quite literally. The opportunities for
mistrust and misunderstanding are immense. All the natural sus-
picions of the earthy, practical peasant for the articulate urban
dweller and of the latter for the narrowminded provincial peasant
must be overcome.

The goals of peasants and intelligentsia are also different and
often conflicting. Peasants' demands tend to be concrete but also
redistributive, and it is the latter quality which makes peasants
into revolutionaries. The demands of the intelligentsia, in contrast, tend to be abstract and openended; both qualities make
revolutionaries out of intellectuals. The substantive concerns of
the two groups often differ significantly. The urban intelligentsia
is usually more concerned with political rights and goals than
with economic ones. The peasantry, in contrast, is at least initially concerned primarily with the material conditions of land
tenure, taxes, and prices. Although "land reform" is a familiar
and obvious revolutionary slogan, urban revolutionaries have in
fact been rather hesitant to inscribe it on their banners. Products
of the urban and the international environment, they tend to
formulate their goals in much more sweeping political and ideological terms. In Iran, Peru, Brazil, Bolivia, and elsewhere the
revolutionary intellectuals were slow to pay attention to peasant
needs. In Iran the urban middle-class nationalists allowed themselves to be outmaneuvered by the Shah and placed in the position of opposing the government's land reform program. At the
beginning of the 1952 revolution in Bolivia, the Communist
Party opposed land reform.[38] In Middle Eastern countries, the

38. See Edmundo Flores, *Land Reform and the Alliance for Progress* (Princeton,
Center of International Studies, 1963), p. 13.

radical intelligentsias have opposed the extension of the suffrage to the rural poor on the assumption, often valid, that their passivity and indifference will simply add to the votes of the landlord. At worst, the urban intellectual sees the peasant as a brute, and the peasant sees the intellectual as an alien.

The differences in the mobility and enlightenment of the two groups impose upon the intellectual primary responsibility for taking the initiative in creating the revolutionary alliance. Conscious efforts by the intelligentsia to arouse the peasants have in general, however, met with little success. The failure of the prototype of such efforts, the attempt of the Narodniki to "go to the people" in 1873 and 1874, is typical. In Latin America, the efforts of urban intellectuals to arouse the peasants to guerrilla warfare in the 1950s and 1960s generally failed, with the notable exception of Cuba. In most of these instances, the social distance between the two groups and the active efforts by the government to blunt the intelligentsia's appeal blocked the creation of a revolutionary alliance. In Guatemala, for instance, the leftist intellectuals were at first unable even to speak the language of the Indian peasant.

Efforts by intellectuals to arouse peasants almost invariably fail unless the social and economic conditions of the peasantry are such as to give them concrete motives for revolt. The intelligentsia can ally themselves with a revolutionary peasantry but they cannot create a revolutionary peasantry. In the Russian Revolution, Lenin thoroughly recognized the crucial role of the peasants and adapted the Bolshevik program and tactics to the need to win peasant support. The Bolsheviks, however, remained primarily an urban and intellectual group, and they were more successful in the cities than in the countryside. The Chinese Communists, on the other hand, were defeated in the cities because the social base and organization for coming to power in the urban areas of central China were wanting. Consequently, Mao and those who followed him, acting on Mao's own observation of the revolutionary character of the peasantry, moved out to reconstitute the Communist movement in the countryside after their defeat in the cities. At that point, for the first time in history, the peasant uprising which accompanies every revolution became organized, disciplined, and led by a group of highly conscious and articulate professional revolutionary intellectuals. What distinguishes the Chinese Revolution from earlier revolutions is not the behavior of the peasants but the behavior of the intellectuals. The Chinese Communists succeeded where the Left S.R.'s failed and forged a revolutionary alliance which gave coherence, direction, and leadership to the peasant uprising. For the two decades after the failure of the revolution in the cities they kept it alive in the countryside.

A peasant or rural-based revolutionary movement may have equal difficulty in appealing to the urban intelligentsia. In South Vietnam, for instance, urban middle-class elements opposed the government of Ngo Dinh Diem and then caused continuing instability in the years immediately following his downfall. Yet the peasant-oriented Viet Cong was unable to capitalize upon this discontent and to create an alliance with the revolutionary elements in the cities. Indeed, in the early 1960s the only social-political fact in Vietnam more striking than the failure of the government to elicit support from the peasants was the failure of the Viet Cong to build up significant support among urban groups. Both failures were testimony to the gap which can separate urban from rural society in a modernizing country.

The differences in background, perspective, and purpose between intelligentsia and peasants render revolution unlikely if not impossible in the absence of some additional common cause produced by an additional catalyst. Yet revolutions do occur. The common cause which produces the revolutionary alliance or revolutionary parallelism is usually nationalism and the catalyst is usually a foreign enemy. It is possible, as in the United States, to have a nationalist war of independence which is not also a social revolution. But it is impossible to have a social revolution which is not also a nationalist revolution. It is typically the process of appealing to nationalist sentiments which mobilizes large numbers of people into politics and furnishes the basis for collaboration between urban intelligentsia and peasant masses.

The stimulus to nationalist mobilization may be furnished either by a foreign political, economic, and military presence in a country before the collapse of the old order or by foreign political and military intervention after that collapse. In Mexico, China, Vietnam, Cuba, Guatemala, the presence of foreign business, foreign bases, or foreign rule, furnished a target against which the masses could be aroused. All these countries except Vietnam were formally independent when their revolutions began but all of them also were economically and militarily subordinate to foreign powers. In Porfirian Mexico tax laws and economic regulations discriminated in favor of the foreigner; British investments doubled, French quadrupled, American quintupled in the decade or so before the Revolution. Americans purportedly had more capital invested in Mexico than the Mexicans, owning 75 per cent of the mines and 50 per cent of the oil fields and sugar, coffee, and cotton plantations. The legal system was designed to favor the foreigners, and a popular saying had it that "only generals, bullfighters, and foreigners" were assured of favorable decisions in the courts. So also in China in the first decade of the twentieth century, unequal treaties, economic concessions, and outright territorial grants and other surrenders of sovereignty gave Germany, Japan, Britain, Russia, and France special positions and their citizens special privileges. In Cuba in the 1950s American investments totaled just under a billion dollars. Americans owned 90 per cent of the telephone and electric power systems, 50 per cent of the railways, 40 per cent of the raw sugar production, and banks which held 25 per cent of Cuban deposits. On a per capita basis American investments in Cuba were three times as large as they were in Latin America as a whole. Over 70 per cent of Cuban exports went to the United States, and over 75 per cent of Cuban imports came from the United States. The United States had a major naval and marine base at Guantanamo. Politically, culturally, economically, and militarily, Cuba was an American satellite.[39]

A foreign presence undoubtedly plays some role in stimulating revolution. But revolutions have occurred in countries (e.g., France, Russia) where the foreign presence was neither significant nor obvious. No revolution, however, is likely to run its full course without the spur of foreign intervention. The pattern was set in the French Revolution where the Prussian invasion during the summer of 1792 coincided with and was in large part responsible for radicalizing the Revolution as the *sans culottes* and the émigré intellectuals in Paris broadened the scope of popular participation in the revolution, completed the destruction of feudalism, and proclaimed the French Republic. "The war revolution-

39. On Mexico, see Henry Bamford Parker, *A History of Mexico* (rev. ed. Boston, Houghton Mifflin, 1950), p. 309. On Cuba, see Leland L. Johnson, "U.S. Business Interests in Cuba and the Rise of Castro," *World Politics, 17* (April 1965), 440–59.

ized the Revolution . . . making it more drastic at home and more powerful in its effects abroad."[40] Foreign intervention also played a major role in revolutionizing the Mexican, Chinese, Russian, Yugoslav, Vietnamese, and Cuban revolutions. The absence of hostile foreign intervention in the Bolivian Revolution, on the other hand, may have helped undermine the political achievements of that revolution. No society can carry out a revolution in isolation. Every revolution is, in some measure, against not only the dominant class at home but also against the dominant system abroad.

In Mexico the diplomatic intervention of the United States helped produce Huerta's accession of power, which, in turn, led to the assassination of Madero and the uprisings against Huerta under the leadership of Carranza, González, and Pancho Villa. It was this second wave of mobilization, triggered by the counter-revolutionary triumph of Huerta and U.S. Ambassador Henry Lane Wilson, which expanded the Mexican Revolution from the limited middle-class affair it had been under Madero into a mass upheaval in which peasants and labor played a decisive role under a new group of leaders who in large part came from humble backgrounds: Zapata and Obregón were peasants; Calles a country school teacher; Villa an illiterate bandit.

In China the role of foreign intervention in galvanizing the revolution and in keeping it going was even more striking. In 1915 Japan's Twenty-One Demands served to undermine Yuan Shih-kai's government, and broaden the process of popular mobilization. In 1919 the announcement from Versailles of the transfer of Germany's concessions in Shantung to Japan produced the May 4th Movement with student demonstrations in Peking and other cities and the emergence of a new group of leaders drawn neither from the traditional ruling class nor from the regional warlords but from students, intellectuals, workers, and merchants. In 1925 the failure of the Peking government to act positively against police killing of students in Shanghai led to more mass demonstrations against the British and other foreigners, undermined the authority of the Peking government, and prepared the way for the Nationalist-Communist march northward. The Japanese occupation of Manchuria in 1931 and her subsequent invasion of China produced the stimuli for the full-scale mobilization

40. Palmer, 2, 4.

of the peasant masses into the war against the invader. Finally, the American presence in China after World War II and the identification of the Nationalist regime with the United States helped to bolster the legitimacy and the appeal of the Chinese Communists in the last years of the revolution and civil war. At each of these moments—1919, 1925, 1937, 1946—foreign intervention served to give new impetus to the revolutionary forces and to enable them to broaden their mass appeal.

In a revolutionary situation the identification of any government with a foreign regime creates the basis for undermining the legitimacy of that government. At the end of World War I the Sultan's government in Constantinople was discredited by its association with the British and French occupation forces, and thereby contributed strength to Kemal's Anatolian nationalist movement. The Wafd regime in Egypt in the 1930s succumbed to British demands and the resulting riots in the streets against the "unfair treaty" mobilized new groups into politics which, through the Moslem Brotherhood and then the Nasserite movement, produced the end of the parliamentary regime in Egypt. So also, the Kuomintang which started out as a nationalist movement became tinged with anti-nationalism by its failure to prosecute the war against the Japanese and by its close association with the United States. In Iran in the late 1940s both the Shah and the radical middle-class intelligentsia in the National Front struggled for the nationalist mantle. To compete with Mossadeq, the Shah had not only to oppose Russian designs on his country but also to assert Iranian national interest against the Anglo-Iranian oil company and to develop his doctrine of "positive nationalism" against the "negative nationalism" of Mossadeq. He was aided in this struggle by the fact that it coincided with the changing balance of foreign interests in Iran. Iranian nationalism at that point was directed primarily against its traditional enemies: Russia and Britain. The opposition of the Shah to both in some measure obscured his cooperation with the United States. In this instance a traditional ruler competed with the radical intelligentsia for the nationalist mantle and, at least temporarily, won.[41]

41. See Perlmutter, "Ambition and Attrition," Chap. 3, pp. 10, 11; Chalmers Johnson, *Peasant Nationalism and Communist Power* (Stanford, Stanford University Press, 1962), pp. 22–26; Richard Cottam, *Nationalism in Iran* (Pittsburgh, University of Pittsburgh Press, 1964), p. 291.

Foreign intervention may be sufficiently powerful, as in Guatemala, to suppress the revolutionary movement. Normally, however, the greater the successes of intervention the greater the opposition it arouses and the more extensive the mass mobilization it provokes. In addition, the intervening powers normally have no viable political alternative to the revolutionary movement. The intervention itself is almost always carried on in collaboration with and perhaps even led by émigrés and exiles whose primary purpose is to restore the old regime. That regime, however, has already been fundamentally undermined by the expansion of political participation and of the amount of power in the political system. In every revolution participation peaks at one point and then declines somewhat, but it is never stably restored to the prerevolutionary level. The distribution of power is much more flexible than the amount of power in the system. Conceivably power once dispersed can again be concentrated, but power which has been dramatically expanded cannot then be dramatically reduced. Once led out of the cave, the masses cannot again be permanently denied the sunlight. The principal impetus to this movement is foreign war and foreign intervention. Nationalism is the cement of the revolutionary alliance and the engine of the revolutionary movement.

POLITICAL DEVELOPMENT BY REVOLUTION

Community and Party

Scholars often attempt to distinguish "great" or social and economic revolutions from those more limited upheavals which are "only" political. In fact, however, the most significant results of the great revolutions are either precisely in the political sphere or directly related to that sphere. A full-scale revolution involves the destruction of the old political institutions and patterns of legitimacy, the mobilization of new groups into politics, the redefinition of the political community, the acceptance of new political values and new concepts of political legitimacy, the conquest of power by a new, more dynamic political elite, and the creation of new and stronger political institutions. All revolutions involve modernization in the sense of the expansion of political participation; some revolutions also involve political development in the sense of the creation of new patterns of political order.

The immediate economic results of a revolution are almost

entirely negative. Nor are they simply the result of the violence and destruction caused by the revolution. These may be responsible for some of the economic collapse, but the disruption of the social and economic structures may cause even more. The Bolivian Revolution produced little bloodshed but almost total economic disaster. So also in Cuba the violence was relatively small but its economic consequences were relatively severe. It takes a society many years and perhaps decades to reach again the level of economic production it had achieved immediately before the outbreak of the revolution. The achievement of a new rate of economic growth, moreover, is almost always dependent upon the stabilization of the new institutions of political order. The industrialization drives of the Soviet Union had to wait for a decade until the Bolsheviks had firmly established their pattern of rule. The rapid growth of the Mexican economy did not begin until the 1940s, after the political structures created by the revolution had assumed a stable and highly institutionalized form.

Conservatives invariably point to the economic collapse produced by revolution as a sign of total failure of the revolution. In the 1950s and 1960s, for instance, the economic shortages and hardships produced by the Bolivian, Vietnamese, and Cuban revolutions were regularly cited as evidence of the imminent collapse of the revolutionary governments in those countries. But the same economic phenomena appear in all revolutions: food shortages, neglect of maintenance, failure to coordinate production plans, wastefulness, and inefficiency are all part of what Trotsky called "the overhead expenses of historic progress" involved in any revolution.[42] One can go even further. Economic success is immaterial to revolution, while economic deprivations may well be essential to its success. The conservative predictions that food shortages and material hardships will lead to the overthrow of the revolutionary regime are never fulfilled for one very simple reason. Material deprivations, which would have been insufferable under the old regime, are proof of the strength of the new one. The less their food and material comfort the more people come to value the political and ideological accomplishments of the revolution for which they are sacrificing so much. "As the regime becomes more firmly entrenched," one journalist observed of Cas-

42. Leon Trotsky, *History of the Russian Revolution* (New York, Simon and Schuster, 1932), 2, 46.

tro, "the older Cubans learn to live with their hardships and the younger Cubans to love them as a symbol of the revolution." [43] Revolutionary governments may be undermined by affluence; but they are never overthrown by poverty.

Economics is relatively unimportant to both revolutions and revolutionaries, and economic disaster is a small price to pay for the broadening and redefinition of the national community. The revolution destroys old social classes, the old bases, usually ascriptive, of social differentiation, and the old social cleavages. It produces a new sense of community and a common identity for the new groups which acquire political consciousness. If the problem of identity is a crucial one in the process of modernization, revolution furnishes a conclusive, although costly answer to that problem. It means the creation of a national or political community of equals. It means a fundamental shift from a political culture in which subjects view the government as "they" to one in which citizens view the government as "we." No aspect of political culture is more significant than the scope and intensity of the identification of the people with the political system. The most dramatic accomplishment of a revolution is this rapid change in political values and attitudes. The masses which were previously excluded from the system now identify with it; the elites which may have previously identified with the system are now ejected from it.

The decimation of the old elites and their emigration may be encouraged by the revolutionary leaders. The goal of the revolution is a new homogeneous community, and forcing dissident or unassimilable elements into exile is one means of producing that community. Consequently, what is often viewed by conservative foreigners as a weakness of the revolutionary system is actually a means of strengthening it. Mustafa Kemal created a stronger state by limiting its scope to ethnic Turks and excluding Armenians, Arabs, Greeks, and other groups which had played key roles in the Ottoman Empire. Communist revolutionary leaders especially have learned the lesson well. The exodus of 900,000 refugees, principally Catholic, from North Vietnam in 1954 and 1955 greatly strengthened the North Vietnamese political community at the same time that it introduced a disrupting and divisive force into the politics of South Vietnam. The acquiescence prior to

43. Edwin Reingold, *Time, 84* (August 14, 1964) , 28.

1961 of the East German government in the relatively free emigration of its citizens to West Germany laid the foundations for a more stable political order in East Germany. The willingness of Castro to permit the departure of substantial numbers of unhappy Cubans served to enhance the long-run stability of his regime. In the prerevolutionary society those who are alienated are the many and the poor to whom migration is impossible. In the postrevolutionary society the alienated are the few and the affluent who can more easily be eliminated either by decimation or by migration.

The disaffection of some groups is more than matched by the new sense of identity acquired by other, more numerous, groups and by the new sense of political community and unity that results. In part, this new sense of community is reflected in the emphasis on equality and unity in forms of dress and address: *sans culottes* and *tutoiment* become the order of the day; everyone is a brother or a comrade. Revolutions produce little liberty, but they are history's most expeditious means of producing fraternity, equality, and identity. This identity and sense of community legitimize the economic shortages and material burdens. "Thanks to Fidel," one unskilled Cuban worker declared in 1965, "there is real equality now. . . . Even if food is scarce, I don't mind, because now I am part of my country. Now the fight for Cuban survival is my fight. If this is communism, I'm all for it." [44]

Political development, we have argued, involves the creation and institutionalization of public interests. Nowhere is this more dramatically revealed than in the process of revolution. The society existing before the revolution is typically one with little sense of the common good. It is usually characterized by the decay and breakdown of political institutions, the fragmentation of the polity, the assertion of local and provincial claims, the pursuit of private ends, the dominance of loyalties to the family and other immediate groupings. The revolution destroys the old social order with its classes and pluralism and limited loyalties. New, more general sources of morality and legitimacy come into existence. These are national rather than parochial, political rather than social, revolutionary rather than traditional. The slogans, the mystique, and possibly the ideology of the revolution provide the new criteria of political loyalty. Loyalty to the revolution and

44. Quoted by C. K. McClatchy, *Washington Post*, September 26, 1965, p. E4.

the dominant formulation of its goals replaces loyalty to the more limited and traditional social groupings of the old society. The public interest of the old order had declined into a welter of conflicting parochial interests. The public interest of the new order is the interest of the Revolution.

Revolution thus involves moral renewal. The manners and accepted patterns of behavior of the previously corrupt society are replaced by an initially highly Spartan and Puritan regimen. In its negative phase, revolution completes the destruction of an already disintegrating code of morals and set of institutions. In its positive phase, revolution gives rise to new, more demanding sources of morality, authority, and discipline. Every revolutionary regime sets higher and broader and crueler standards of public morality than those of the regime which it replaces. The "Protestant discipline" of the first major revolutionary movement in Western society astounded seventeenth-century Europe.[45] Since then it is striking how the word "discipline" recurs in the language of revolutionaries and in the descriptions of revolutions. National discipline, proletarian discipline, party discipline, revolutionary discipline are constantly invoked in the revolutionary process. If a praetorian society is one lacking authority, honesty, discipline, legitimacy, and a concept of the public interest, a revolutionary society is one which has all these things, often to an oppressive degree. Just as the Puritans may be persuasively described as the first Bolsheviks, so also may the Bolsheviks and their twentieth-century compatriots be described as latter-day Puritans. Every revolution is a Puritan revolution.

Revolutions occur where political participation is limited and political institutions are fragile. "The peoples erect scaffolds," as de Jouvenel put it, "not as the moral punishment of despotism, but as the biological penalty for weakness." [46] The negative phase of revolution, however, involves the destruction of the old social order as well as the remnants of the old political institutions. This leaves a vacuum. Society is no longer the basis of community. In the processes of political development and modernization the differentiation and increasing complexity of society gradually make community dependent on politics. In a revolution, this change occurs drastically. Political ideologies and political in-

45. See Walzer's brilliant interpretation, *Revolution of the Saints*, passim.
46. Bertrand de Jouvenel, *On Power* (Boston, Beacon Press, 1962), p. 218.

stitutions become crucially important in providing community not as a result of the growth of society but as a result of its destruction. Every revolution strengthens government and the political order. It is a form of political development which makes society more backward and politics more complex. It is a way of reestablishing violently and destructively but also creatively the balance between social and economic development, on the one hand, and political development, on the other.

Revolutions, it has often been argued, replace weak governments with strong governments. These governments are the product both of the concentration of power and, even more significantly, the expansion of power in the political system. The "true historical function of revolutions," in de Jouvenel's words, "is to renovate and strengthen Power." [47] The completion of the political work of the revolution, however, depends upon the creation of new political structures to stabilize and to institutionalize the centralization and expansion of power. The successful revolution requires, in short, the creation of a political party system.

Historically revolution has led to either: (a) the restoration of traditional structures of authority; or (b) military dictatorship and the rule of force; or (c) the creation of new authority structures, reflecting the fundamental changes in the amount and the distribution of power in the political system produced by the revolution. Charles II and Louis XVIII represent the restoration of traditional rulers and traditional structures of authority. Cromwell was the military dictator attempting, unsuccessfully, to find a new basis of legitimacy. Napoleon was the military dictator attempting, unsuccessfully, to establish a new, imperial dynasty drawing its legitimacy from military success, popular approval, and monarchial mystique. In a sense, this was an effort to combine traditional and military sources of legitimacy. Chiang Kaishek and the Kuomintang, on the other hand, attempted to combine military and modern sources of legitimacy. The Nationalist government was part party rule and part military dictatorship. It failed, however, to create in the Kuomintang an institution capable of adapting itself to the changing patterns of participation.

In Mexico, on the other hand, the revolution first produced rule by the successful generals, thinly disguised in constitutional

47. Ibid.

forms. In 1929, however, the combination of circumstances, selfish interests, and statesmanship on the part of Calles led to the creation of the revolutionary party, and the system of quasilegitimate rule by an oligarchy of generals was transformed into the institutionalized and legitimate system of authority of the PRI. This framework then provided the institutional mechanism through which Cárdenas broadened the appeal of the revolution and the identification of the masses of the people with the new political system. Calles' creation of the party of the revolution made possible Cárdenas' extension of the revolution by the party. Thus, while the Chinese Nationalists reverted from efforts at party rule to military dictatorship, the Mexican Revolution evolved in the opposite direction from almost pure military dictatorship to pure party rule.

Historians have called many ages the age of revolution. But the twentieth century is peculiarly the century of revolution because only in the twentieth century have revolutionary processes given birth to revolutionary institutions. In this sense, both the English and the French revolutions were failures. Their agony and travail purchased only military dictatorship and the restoration of traditional authority, a Protector and an Emperor, neither of whom institutionalized his rule and who were in due course replaced by a Stuart and a Bourbon. The English Revolution ended in compromise, the French in a bifurcated political tradition which divided France against itself for a century and a half. In France the revolution produced no consensus; in England it produced a consensus which was not revolutionary. Both revolutions, in a sense, occurred too early, before men became aware of and accepted political parties as organizations. Both revolutions expanded political participation but failed to give rise to new political structures to institutionalize that participation.

Contrast these "incomplete" revolutions with those of the twentieth century. Since the first organization of continuing political parties in the United States in the late eighteenth century, the revolutionary expansion of political participation has been indissolubly linked with the creation of revolutionary political parties. In contrast to the English and French revolutions, the Russian Revolution escaped both military dictatorship and monarchial restoration. It instead produced an entirely new system of party supremacy, "democratic centralism," and ideological legitimacy, which effectively consolidated and institutionalized the concentration of power and the expansion of power produced by the revolution. Every major revolution of the twentieth century has led to the creation of a new political order to structure, to stabilize, and to institutionalize the broadened participation in politics. It has involved the creation of a political party system with deep roots in the population. In contrast to all previous revolutions, every major twentieth-century revolution has institutionalized the centralization and the expansion of power in a one-party system. However else they may differ, this is the common legacy of the Russian, Chinese, Mexican, Yugoslav, Vietnamese, and even Turkish revolutions. The triumph of the revolution is the triumph of party government.

Mexico

Not all revolutions end in triumph, however, and not all triumphs are irreversible. Revolution is one means of political development, one way of creating and institutionalizing new political organizations and procedures, of strengthening the political sphere in relation to social and economic forces. Political development by revolution is clearly visible where communist parties have come to power through insurrection and civil war. It can also be seen in other cases, such as Mexico, whose revolution produced major changes in political culture and political institutions. On the other hand, however, it is possible, even in the twentieth century, for a society to suffer the agonies of revolutionary dislocation without achieving the stability and integration that revolution can bring. A comparison of the successes and failures of revolution in terms of political development in the Mexican and Bolivian cases may afford some grounds for evaluating the probable course of revolution in other, as yet unresolved, instances.

The twenty years before 1910 in Mexico witnessed phenomenal economic development. Mineral production quadrupled; scores of textile mills were built; sugar mills were constructed, quadrupling sugar production; a steel mill was built; oil production became a major industry; an extensive railroad net was laid. Foreign trade and tax revenues increased ten times during the Porfirian era. "The whole apparatus of a modern economy was dropped into place within a generation: railroads, banks, heavy

industry, stable currency, and gilt-edged national credit abroad."
This economic expansion, however, was accompanied by a growing gap between rich and poor. Control over the new financial
and industrial wealth was concentrated in foreign hands and in
the closely knit oligarchy. The nouveaux riches bought up the
private and communal lands of the Indians, so that by 1910 one
per cent of the population owned 85 per cent of the arable land
and 95 per cent of the ten million people engaged in agriculture
owned no land whatsoever. The peasants were reduced to virtual
serfdom: the real wages of the peon in 1910, it has been estimated, amounted to about 25 per cent of what they were in
1800.[48]

This rapid economic growth and growing inequality took place
in a political system ill-equipped to moderate the impact of these
changes or to provide opportunities for political expression and
release of tension. Power was concentrated in the hands of the
ruthless and aging dictator surrounded by a small and aging creole oligarchy. By 1910 the men at the top of the political system
were often in their seventies and eighties and many had held office
for twenty years or more. The new, literate, middle-class groups
in the cities were denied opportunities to participate in the political system. The government actively discouraged labor unions
and prohibited strikes, thereby generating labor violence and encouraging the development of labor along radical, anarcho-syndi-
calist lines. The political system was one of uninstitutionalized
personal and oligarchical rule, lacking autonomy, complexity, coherence, and adaptability. Power was concentrated, but there was
little of it and it was employed increasingly for personal ends.
The economic development for which Díaz was responsible generated social forces which could not be accommodated within the
political system he insisted on maintaining. When the dictator
was finally overthrown, the stage was set for the bloody struggle
for power among the emancipated elites and the rapid mobilization into politics of the worker and peasant masses.

The resulting revolution produced a major change in Mexican
political culture and the innovation of entirely new political institutions. In the two decades before 1910 Mexico had undergone
rapid economic development and modernization. In the three

48. See Howard F. Cline, *The United States and Mexico* (2d ed. Cambridge, Harvard University Press, 1963) , p. 52; Parkes, p. 308.

decades after 1910 Mexico went through equally if not more
rapid political development and political modernization. The
weak, personal, uninstitutionalized system of rule which had prevailed before the revolution, in which personal interests and social forces dominated, was replaced by a highly complex, autonomous, coherent, and flexible political system, with an existence of
its own clearly apart from social forces and with a demonstrated
capacity to combine the reasonably high centralization of power
with the expansion of power and the broadened participation of
social groups in the political system. The costs of these achievements were considerable: one million Mexicans were killed or
starved to death; nearly all the original leaders of the revolution
were murdered at some point in its proceedings; the economy of
the country was completely dislocated. Yet these costs were, at
least, not in vain. The political system which emerged out of the
revolution furnished Mexico with a political stability unprecedented in Latin America and the political framework necessary
for a new period of rapid economic growth in the 1940s and 1950s.

The revolution enhanced the coherence of the Mexican political system by breaking down the rigid class stratification and by
ending the traditional cleavage in Mexican society between the
aristocratic, creole, military, religious tradition which came down
from colonial times and the liberal, middle-class, individualistic,
civilian political strand which had developed in the nineteenth
century. In effect, the revolution produced something like a
Hegelian synthesis. The conservative colonial pattern was corporate in form and feudal in content; the nineteenth-century pattern of Juárez and Madero was individualistic in form and liberal
in content. The revolution neatly mixed the two into a political
culture which was pluralistic in form and populist and even socialist in content. This ended the great fault which had divided
Mexican society, and eventually even those groups alienated by
the revolution—landowners, the church, the army—became reconciled to coexistence on its terms. The revolution also provided a
new unifying social myth and basis for legitimacy. It gave Mexico
a national epic, national heroes, and national ideals by which to
formulate purposes and to judge results. The ideals of the revolution, defined in part in the 1917 Constitution—the first socialist
constitution in the world—became the basis of the Mexican consensus much as the ideals of the Constitution and the Declaration

of Independence had in the United States. "Every major public topic," Scott observes, "is approached, considered, accepted, or rejected in terms of what the Revolution is supposed to stand for, and no serious proponent of just about anything would dream of forgetting to claim legitimacy for his particular point of view by labeling it the authentic voice, perhaps the only authentic voice, of the Revolution." [49]

The revolution not only created new political institutions but it also enabled them to establish their autonomy from and their authority over social forces. The party furnished an effective framework for both the articulation and the aggregation of group interests. Before the revolution Mexican politics had fallen into the typical Latin American "Mediterranean" style of corporate politics in which hierarchically organized social forces—primarily the church, the military, and the landowners—competed with each other and dominated the weak political institutions. [50] As Mexican society became more modern, these traditional social forces were supplemented by business, labor, and professional groupings. The problem of the revolution was to subordinate autonomous social forces to an effective political institution. This was accomplished in the 1930s by the incorporation of these organized social forces into the revolutionary party and by the organization of the party into four sectors: agrarian, labor, popular, and military. Each sector, in turn, was composed of a variety of groups and interests drawn from the appropriate social forces.

The conflicts between the sectors now had to be resolved within the framework of the party and under the leadership of the president and the central leadership of the party. Offices within each district were allocated to the sectors in terms of their relative strength in the district and each sector was obligated to support the candidates nominated by the other sectors. A system of institutionalized bargaining and compromise within the party framework replaced the earlier praetorian politics of open conflict and violence. The sectoral organization of the party also tended to strengthen the central leadership by reducing the influence of local bosses and regional caudillos. The interests of the sectors

49. Robert E. Scott, *Mexican Government in Transition* (Urbana, University of Illinois Press, 1959) , p. 96.

50. See Kalman Silvert, ed., *Expectant Peoples* (New York, Random House, 1963) , pp. 358–61.

were subordinated to and aggregated into the interests of the party. The combination of an authoritative political institution with the continued representation of the organized group structures of Mediterranean politics in effect created a new type of political system which might best be described, in Scott's phrase, as *corporate centralism.*

The subordination of previously autonomous social forces to the governing political institution was nowhere more dramatically revealed than in the changing role of the military in Mexican politics. Before 1910 the politics of Mexico was both the politics of the military and the politics of violence. "Probably no country in Latin America," Lieuwen observes, "has suffered longer and more deeply than Mexico from the curse of predatory militarism. More than one thousand armed uprisings plagued this unfortunate republic in its first century of nationhood." [51] The revolution brought this pattern to an end. In Mexican history presidential elections and military revolts had gone hand in hand. The last successful military uprising against a presidential election occurred in 1920. In the 1923 revolt, half the officer corps sided with the rebels, and the military revolt was put down with the assistance of armed battalions of workers and peasants. Participation of these groups demonstrated that the ability of the military to monopolize violence and the capacity for coercive political action was drawing to an end. Mexican politics was becoming too complex to be dominated simply by military force. Less than a quarter of the officers supported the 1927 military uprising, and in 1938 the last military revolt of the post-revolutionary era found little support and was easily suppressed.

The elimination of the military from politics was aided by the introduction of more highly professionalized systems of training during the 1920s and by fairly drastic policies concerning the assignment and retirement of officers, which were designed to prevent any general from building up a local political machine. The crucial factor forcing the withdrawal of the military from politics, however, was the organization in 1929 of the revolutionary party and the insistence of its two first leaders, Calles and Cárdenas (both of whom had been generals), that the allocation of office and the determination of policy take place within the party struc-

51. Edwin Lieuwen, *Arms and Politics in Latin America*, p. 101.

ture. When the party was reorganized in 1938, a military sector
was created to provide for the representation of the military
within the party. This action was designed not to enhance the
role of the military in Mexican politics but rather to adapt that
role from the techniques of violence to those of elections and
bargaining. In defending the military sector, Cárdenas declared
that "We did not put the Army in politics. It was already there.
In fact, it had been dominating the situation, and we did well to
reduce its influence to one vote out of four." [52] Three years later
President Avila Camacho disbanded the military sector, broke up
the military bloc in Congress, and retired many of the remaining
revolutionary generals. Political offices and political roles were increasingly assumed by civilian bureaucrats and politicians rather
than generals.

The political system created by the revolution also reflected a
high degree of institutional complexity. As in the other post-
revolutionary states, the basic institutional distinction was between the party and the government. The former monopolized
the "input" functions of the political system, the latter played a
crucial role in the "output" functions. Within the party, the
sectoral organization provided a pattern of cleavage which cut
across class and region. Thus, the agrarian sector was divided between peasants' organizations, rural workers' organizations, and
those of agronomists and technicians. The labor sector was split
between the dominant rightist bloc and a smaller leftist one. The
popular sector encompassed a heterogeneous collection of groups
representing civil servants, small business, professionals, women,
and other groups. This structure fractionated conflict and eased
the aggregation of political interests. The traditional bases of political conflict in Mexico—family, clique, and region—were now
supplemented by rivalries between sectors and rivalries among
groups within sectors.

Finally, the revolutionary political system also demonstrated its
adaptability. Perhaps the most obvious achievement of the Mexican party system was the extent to which it solved the problem of
peaceful succession. The original slogan of the revolution was
"No Re-election" and the revolutionary party transformed this
slogan into a foundation for political stability. Presidents were

52. Lázaro Cárdenas, quoted in Lieuwen, p. 114. See above, pp. 256–57, for the
civilianization of Mexican political leadership.

elected for a single six-year term. They were selected through a complex and somewhat mysterious intraparty process of *"auscultación,"* of recommendation, consultation, discussion, and consensus-building in which the incumbent president played a leading and perhaps dominant role. Once selected by this informal process, the candidate was nominated by the party convention and elected over weak opposition from the splinter parties in the system. During his six years in office he had substantial power, but no hope of reelection. This practice contributed significantly to the stability of the system. If a president were able to stay in power indefinitely, other presidential aspirants would have every incentive to attempt to oust him from power illegally. With each president limited to a single term, ambitious politicians can look forward to several opportunities of possible presidential election, until the point is reached where they are too old to be selected but also too old to protest effectively against their being passed over.

The Mexican political system also manifested significant adaptability in terms of policy innovation. In 1933 Calles announced that the revolution was failing to achieve its objectives, that corruption and ignorance were undermining its progress. The election of Cárdenas the following year demonstrated the ability of the political system to produce new purposes, to assimilate new groups, and to inaugurate a whole series of sweeping new reforms. In terms of policy the regime of Cárdenas was the second Mexican Revolution. Land reform was reinvigorated, the railroads and oil wells nationalized, education expanded, new social welfare programs established. That the leadership to produce these changes could be produced by the system and that the changes themselves could be produced by working within the system are significant testimony both to the wisdom of the political leaders and to the adaptability of the political system. Cárdenas himself was only 39 years old when elected president and his accession represented the emergence within the party structure of a new generation of younger, more radical, more intellectual political leaders. The accession to power of this generation was a peaceful revolution in the history of the Mexican political system, comparable in many ways to the coming to power of the Jacksonian Democrats in the American political system.

At the close of his term Cárdenas used his influence to secure the election as president of a much more conservative figure, Avila Camacho. Camacho was followed in 1946 by the more radical Alemán, who was succeeded in 1952 by the more conservative Cortines, who was followed in 1958 by the more radical López Mateos, who was succeeded in 1964 by the more conservative Díaz Ordaz. Flexibility was thus built into the system through the informal but effective process of alternating radical and innovating presidents with more conservative ones. The system thus achieved through the conscious choice of its leaders that alternation of reform and consolidation which more competitive party systems acquire through the shifts in voter preferences.

The high degree of institutionalization of the Mexican political system enabled it to deal effectively with the problems of modernization in the middle of the twentieth century. The creation of the revolutionary party in 1929 was followed during the 1930s by both the centralization of power necessary for the promotion of social reform and the expansion of power involved in broadening the identification of people with the political system. The key man in this process was Cárdenas who institutionalized the party, centralized power in the presidency, inaugurated social reforms, and broadened political participation. The centralization of power had been done initially on an informal basis by Calles during the 1920s. In the 1930s, after the creation of the revolutionary party, the centralization of power was institutionalized in the presidency. After his election as president Cárdenas effectively challenged Calles' informal power and established his own authority throughout the party. The reorganization of the party on a sectoral rather than geographical basis broke the power of the regional caudillos. The flow of party funds was from the sectoral organizations to the national organization and thus the latter was able to exercise control over party activities on the local level.

Under Cárdenas power was expanded as well as centralized. Cárdenas actively pushed the organization of labor and agriculture, sponsoring the formation of the National Peasant Confederation (CNC) and of the Mexican Workers Confederation (CTM). These organizations were brought into the party structure, and the membership of the party itself greatly expanded, with the dominant element now being workers and peasants rather than governmental employees. By 1936 the party had over 1,000,000 members. Subsequently, professional organizations, youth groups, cooperative societies, and other social organizations were brought into the party framework. This process, in effect, mobilized new groups into the party and thus into politics at the same time that it strengthened the organization of those groups. Mobilization and organization were carried out simultaneously. Equally important, Cárdenas provided the symbols for popular identification with the system. In his presidential campaign in 1934 he inaugurated the practice, duplicated by subsequent candidates, of a prolonged, 16,000-mile presidential campaign tour to build up popular support and to arouse popular interest. Once in office he made every effort to dramatize his closeness to the people and his accessibility (even to the point of ordering the National Telegraph Service to take free for one hour every day any messages addressed to the President).[53] Like Castro or Magsaysay subsequently, he spent much of his time traveling about the country, visiting villages, listening to complaints, and impressing upon the people the feeling that the government was *their* government.

The significance of this process of extending political participation in the system and popular identification with the system can be dramatically seen in Almond and Verba's comparative analysis of political values and attitudes in the United States, Great Britain, Germany, Italy, and Mexico.[54] On virtually all indices of social and economic development, Mexico and Italy rank behind the other three countries and Mexico considerably behind Italy. Yet in terms of political culture, striking differences appear between Mexico and Italy, and even between Mexico and the other much more highly modernized countries. The Mexicans manifested less pride in their politics and government than did Americans and British, but far more pride than did Germans and Italians. Mexicans had little recognition of the role of government in their lives, but a solid majority took an interest in politics. Even those Mexicans who perceived little governmental impact on their lives still manifested a high exposure to politics.

Perhaps most significantly, Mexicans, like Americans, had a much higher citizen competence than subject competence. Here, as Almond and Verba suggest, is a prime difference between revolutionary societies and non-revolutionary societies. Rephrased

53. On Cárdenas, see Scott, p. 127.
54. Gabriel A. Almond and Sidney Verba, *The Civic Culture*

somewhat, this difference may provide social science data to support de Tocqueville's insight that the United States benefited from the results of a democratic revolution without ever having had to go through one. Thirty-three per cent of the Mexicans in comparison to 27 per cent of the Italians showed citizen competence, and 45 per cent of the Mexicans compared to 63 per cent of the Italians were classified as alienated in terms of the input aspects of the political system. Normally, as Almond and Verba point out, people develop competence as subjects before they do as citizens. In Mexico, however, the Revolution reversed this process. Mexicans thus say that they receive few benefits from their political system, but they have hopes that they will receive more. Theirs is a politics of aspiration. Mexican political culture is distinguished by "the promise of the Revolution," and the legitimacy of the political system rests on the hopes and the aspirations which that event produced.[55]

Political development is never complete, and no political system ever solves the problems confronting it. Judged in comparison to other revolutions, however, the Mexican Revolution was highly successful in political development, that is, the creation of complex, autonomous, coherent, and adaptable political organizations and procedures, and it was reasonably successful in political modernization, that is, the centralization of power necessary for social reform and the expansion of power necessary for group assimilation. Thirty-five years after the creation of the revolutionary party, many questioned the continued ability of the political system to meet the needs of Mexico's rapidly changing social and economic scene. Conceivably, major changes would be necessary in the political system to enable it to deal with these problems. Conceivably, also, the system might be unable to adapt to the new levels of economic development and social complexity. Whatever its subsequent fate, however, the system produced by the revolution gave Mexico political stability, popular identification with government, social reform, and economic development unparalleled in the earlier history of the country, and unique in Latin America.

55. Sidney Verba and Gabriel A. Almond, "National Revolutions and Political Commitment," in Harry Eckstein, ed., *Internal War* (New York, The Free Press, 1964), p. 230; Almond and Verba, *Civic Culture*, pp. 99, 219. Cf. Robert E. Scott, "Mexico: The Established Revolution," in Pye and Verba, eds., *Political Culture and Political Development*, pp. 330–95.

Bolivia

No such record of achievement resulted from the Bolivian Revolution. In contrast to Mexico, Bolivia shows that while revolution may be the road to political stability under some circumstances, it does not necessarily lead there. On the surface many similarities existed between the Bolivian and the Mexican revolutions. Prerevolutionary Bolivia was ruled by a small, white elite which dominated the mass of illiterate, non-Spanish-speaking Indian peasants. Three tin companies and 200 families, it was said, owned the country. In 1950 10 per cent of the landowners did own 97 per cent of the land.[56] Here was an almost perfect two-class oligarchical society. In the 1930s, however, Bolivia became engaged in the Chaco War with Paraguay, which required the mobilization of a substantial peasant army. Bolivia's defeat in the war, in turn, led to a military coup by a group of colonels bent on creating a more efficient and progressive government. In 1939 this military junta was replaced by a more conservative regime. In the following years several political parties were organized, including the Movimiento Nacionalista Revolucionario (MNR) by a group of intellectuals. In 1943 a military coup brought to power a group of army officers in coalition with the MNR. This regime embarked on a program which was semi-fascist, semi-radical, and semi-bloodthirsty. In 1946 it was overthrown in an urban upheaval, a conservative government was again installed in power, and the leaders of the MNR went into exile. In 1951 elections were held, purportedly won from exile by Paz Estenssoro, a leader of the MNR. The army, however, canceled the elections. A period of disorder followed.

Finally in April 1952 the MNR launched its drive to overthrow the government. This succeeded with relatively little bloodshed; the revolutionaries came to power; Paz Estenssoro returned from exile to become president of the new revolutionary regime. The MNR government nationalized the tin mines and established universal suffrage. Although its leaders had been moderates on agrarian issues, the peasants in 1952 formed their own organizations and began to seize the land for themselves. Confronted with this

56. Russett et al., *World Handbook of Political and Social Indicators,* p. 239; Cornelius H. Zondag, *The Bolivian Economy, 1952–1965* (New York, Praeger, 1966), p. 144.

upheaval from below, the MNR leaders, like the National Assembly in 1789 and the Bolsheviks in 1917, took the only possible revolutionary course and legalized the peasant action. The regime also abolished the old army and organized the peasants and miners into militia units. During the next twelve years Bolivia had in effect a one-party system in which the MNR monopolized power against various dissident and splinter groups to the left and the right. In 1956 another founder of the MNR, Hernán Siles, was elected president and followed more moderate and cautious policies than his predecessor. In 1960 Paz was again chosen president and, after amending the constitution to make it possible, was reelected in 1964. Throughout the 1950s there were various attempted coups and revolts, mostly from the right, and all of which were suppressed. In 1961, however, the government became involved in a series of armed clashes with tin miners as a result of its efforts to modernize the mines. These mounted in intensity until October 1964 when the country became engulfed in virtual civil war as the army and the peasants fought students and miners. The first week of November the top commanders of the army and air force deposed President Paz, sent him off into exile, and established a military regime. The following year this regime also became involved in a series of bloody battles with the miners. In 1966 the leader of the military, General René Barrientos, was elected president over no serious opposition.

This sequence of events poses fascinating and important questions. Like the Mexican Revolution, the Bolivian Revolution produced immediate results in terms of social equality, political mobilization, and economic chaos. Why, unlike the Mexican Revolution, did it not also produce long-term results in terms of political stability? What went wrong with the Bolivian Revolution? Why was the MNR, unlike the PRI, unable to institutionalize itself effectively? Why did militarism and the military coup reappear on the Bolivian scene?

Four factors would appear to share responsibility. First, the Bolivian Revolution had many characteristics of a major revolution: displacement and emigration of a traditional social-economic elite; a revolutionary alliance between middle-class intellectuals and peasants; nationalization of property and virtual expropriation of land; massive extension of political participation; establishment of one-party rule. But it lacked one feature of the complete revolution. The seizure of power itself involved relatively little violence. The old regime collapsed in April 1952, the army split, and the armed partisans of the MNR in cooperation with labor and the insurrectionary portion of the army easily asserted their control. In Mexico between 1910 and 1920 something like one million people lost their lives through violence or starvation, almost ten per cent of the population. In the Bolivian Revolution of 1952 perhaps 3,000 people were killed, less than one tenth of one per cent of the population, and once in power the MNR regime established a reasonable degree of order and security. There was scattered violence in the countryside during the next year or two, but all in all the revolution was, as revolutions go, a fairly peaceful affair. "The revolution," as Richard Patch has said, "did not follow the rules. There was no class struggle. There was little loss of life. There was little fighting outside of La Paz. There was no accession of the extremists, no reign of terror, no Thermidor." [57] In the months after the MNR came to power, there was considerable peasant and worker mobilization but it was not a competitive mobilization. The violent struggle over the succession which normally takes place among revolutionary elements after the fall of the old regime was notably absent in the Bolivian case. In this sense, the conquest of power by the MNR resembled more the conquest of power by Nasser in Egypt than it did the bloody struggle for ascendancy which was required by the *norteños* in Mexico, the Bolsheviks in Russia, or the Communists in China.

The relatively peaceful character of the conquest in Bolivia adversely affected subsequent political stability in at least two ways. First, sustained violence produces physical, human, and moral exhaustion which eventually leads a society to accept any sort of order so long as it is order. One reason why extremely violent revolutions are followed by peace and stability is that people are simply exhausted by the violence and are ready to acquiesce in the rule of any government which seems able to prevent its renewal. The Mexicans in 1920, the Russians in 1922, the Chinese in 1949, like the Spanish in 1939, had had enough of civil war to last them for awhile. The Bolivians, in contrast, were not exhausted by their revolution, and the Bolivian appetite for violence was

57. Richard Patch, "Bolivia: The Restrained Revolution," *Annals*, *334* (March 1961), 127.

unabated. Secondly, one function of the violent competition for power among revolutionary groups is to eliminate rival claimants to leadership of the revolution. In the first decade of the Mexican Revolution the killing of Madero, Villa, Zapata, and Carranza made it possible for the partnership of Obregón and Calles to establish order in the 1920s. The subsequent murder of Obregón left Calles in solitary command of the postrevolutionary scene. Such struggle, as de Jouvenel has observed, "supplants a weary and sceptical set of rulers with the political athletes who have just emerged bloody but victorious from the eliminating contests of the revolution." [58] In Bolivia this violent struggle and elimination of the revolutionary contestants for power did not take place in the early phases of the revolution.

The failure to eliminate the revolutionary contestants for power in the early phases of the revolution would not have disrupted subsequent political stability if the political leaders had been able to resolve the differences among themselves by compromise. Paz Estenssoro, the dominant figure of the revolution, was, however, highly reluctant to share power with his colleagues. His insistence on running for a second term as president in 1960 alienated a cofounder of the MNR, Walter Guevara Arze, who assumed it was his turn to be president and who ran on a splinter ticket. To bolster himself, Paz made an alliance with the left wing of the MNR, whose leader, Juan Lechín, was nominated and elected vice-president on the Paz ticket. In 1964 Lechín assumed it was his turn to be president, but Paz amended the constitution to permit his own reelection, and alienated Lechín and the left wing of the MNR. Thus, by his efforts to monopolize the presidential office, Paz antagonized virtually all the other major leaders of the party. As a result his own position was gravely weakened, and when the army turned against him in November 1964 he could find little support from among his former party associates.

The contrast between this course of events and that in Mexico demonstrates the importance of statesmanship in providing for political stability and the institutionalization of power. The cardinal rule of the Mexican Revolution was "no reelection" and, despite the temptations to remain in office, the leaders of the revolution adhered to this principle. When Carranza attempted to get around it by promoting a henchman into the presidency,

58. De Jouvenel, p. 219.

he was deposed from office. In the 1920s Obregón and Calles alternated in the presidency, and when Obregón was assassinated in 1928 Calles adhered to the principle of no reelection and refused to succeed himself. Instead he declared that the revolution must be institutionalized and took the lead in creating the Mexican Revolutionary Party. Similarly, five years later, Calles had the wisdom to recognize that the revolution was stagnating, that new younger leadership was necessary, and to acquiesce in the nomination of Cárdenas as President. In contrast, Paz Estenssoro undermined the political stability of his country by attempting to perpetuate his own hold on political office. Political stability is in part the product of historical conditions and social forces, but it is also in part the result of choices and decisions made by political leaders. A second reason for the differences in political stability produced by the Mexican and Bolivian Revolutions is the differences in statesmanship between Calles and Paz Estenssoro.

A third crucial difference between the two revolutions does concern the relationship of social forces to political institutions. One result of the Mexican Revolution was to subordinate autonomous social forces to the authority of an integrating political party. Traditional social institutions, such as the military and the church, which were initially hostile to the revolution were excluded from politics and then gradually reincorporated into the political system in ancillary or subordinate roles. The new social groupings, such as workers and peasants, which moved into politics as a result of the revolution were, in large part, also organized by the revolution. In 1918 President Carranza and the government sponsored the organization of a labor union confederation. In the 1920s the labor union movement under Luis Morones became closely associated with President Calles. In the 1930s, Cárdenas as president helped organize new peasant and labor associations, which were, in turn, directly integrated into the structure of the revolutionary party when Cárdenas reorganized it along sectoral lines in 1938. The distinguishing characteristics of Mexican labor were its close association with the governmental party, the active participation by labor leaders in the leadership of the party, and the correspondingly great influence of the party over organized labor.

In Bolivia also organized labor and the organized peasants were crucial forces in politics. Largely because the Bolivian Revolution occurred forty years after the Mexican Revolution, however, the organization of labor in Bolivia was far more advanced at the time of the revolution than it had been in Mexico. For two decades before 1910 the Díaz regime in Mexico had opposed and suppressed labor organization. In the 1930s, however, the Toro and Busch regimes in Bolivia actively encouraged labor organization, and during the 1940s the MNR, other leftist parties, and the government all competed for control of the labor movement. Thus in Mexico the elements of a more fragmented labor movement competed for access to the political leaders and for influence within the revolutionary party, whereas in Bolivia the political parties competed for influence in and control over the central labor organization. Indeed, between 1952 and 1958, the government was in theory a "co-government" of the MNR and the central labor organization, with the latter choosing four members of the cabinet.[59] Thus, in contrast to Mexico, the organization of labor in Bolivia in large part preceded the revolution and after the revolution proceeded independently of the control of the political authorities.

In even more striking fashion, peasant organization in Bolivia also proceeded independently of political parties and the national political leadership. The first peasant syndicates were organized in the Cochabamba area after the Chaco War. During the next fifteen years peasant organization spread gradually, and then after the 1952 revolution very rapidly. Immediately after its assumption of power in April 1952 the MNR attempted to create its own peasant organization, but it had to give way to the movement which had been organized independently by the peasants. These *campesino* organizations took the lead in the land seizures in late 1952 and 1953, thus compelling the government to enact an agrarian reform law.[60] As a result, the MNR came to be closely identified with the peasant movement, and subsequently several leaders associated with the peasants came to play important roles in the government. The peasant organizations, however, always had an independent existence apart from the party.

59. On the patterns of Mexican and Bolivian labor organization, see Alexander, *Organized Labor in Latin America*, pp. 102–10, 197–98.
60. Richard W. Patch, "Bolivia: U.S. Assistance in a Revolutionary Setting," in Richard Adams, ed., *Social Change in Latin America Today* (New York, Vintage, 1960), pp. 119–24.

Organized social forces such as the peasants and the workers thus had greater influence vis-à-vis the dominant political party in Bolivia than they did in Mexico. The MNR, as one observer said, "was not the nation's principal arena of mass political action: The center of grass-roots politics was rather the miners' and peasants' unions. The populace was thus mobilized into action by essentially class organizations, and ones which did not demand or produce loyalty to the political establishments." [61] This situation would not necessarily have led to political disruption if it were not for the intense conflicts which developed over the mines. The principal sources of support for the MNR at the time of the revolution had been the urban students and intellectuals, the miners and other workers. During the 1950s, however, after the mines were nationalized, production declined rapidly and efficiency even faster. At the same time rampant inflation led the government, under President Siles, to embark on a fairly rigid stabilization program in 1957. This was resisted by the miners' organization under Juan Lechín. In the showdown which followed the miners acquiesced in the government's policy, but Lechín retained his control of the miners' organization. Subsequently, Paz Estenssoro, after being reelected president in 1960, inaugurated with foreign assistance and guidance a program to modernize the mines. This created a new confrontation between miners and government, characterized by strikes, rioting and violence.

By this time the principal sources of support for the government had shifted from the urban intelligentsia, who oppose most governments, and the miners, who were alienated by government policies, to the peasants, who had been the beneficiaries of the land reform and other government actions. In theory Paz should have mobilized the peasants and the peasant militia in his struggle with the miners. During his second term, however, he rebuilt a new professional army. Between 1960 and 1963 the Bolivian military budget doubled, thus bringing into existence a new social force with the capacity for independent action. The political strength of the military was apparent in the spring of 1964 when Paz was forced to reverse an earlier decision and to make the Air Force chief of staff, General René Barrientos, his running mate for vice-president. After his reelection, the dispute with the

61. Richard Weinert, "Bolivia's Shaky Truce," *The New Leader*, 48 (July 5, 1965), 8.

miners intensified, and Paz had to send the army into action to put down the miners' uprising. At the same time, teachers and other urban groups were also on strike and opposed to the regime. Confronted with the prospects of civil war, General Barrientos led the coup which deposed Paz.

By splitting the MNR in his struggles with Lechín, Guevara, and Siles, Paz had isolated himself from his urban middle-class and working-class supporters and had retained only the allegiance of the peasants. By creating a new army to support his authority, however, he also brought into existence what he later accurately described as a "military Frankenstein monster." [62] When the showdown came, the intelligentsia and the workers were against the regime, the peasants were unwilling or unable to act, and the army, consequently, was able rather easily to depose him from power. In 1923 in Mexico President Obregón had put down a military revolt by rallying peasant militia and labor battalions. In 1964 in Bolivia the labor battalions were on the other side, and the peasant militia was too weak and too indifferent to be quickly mobilized to the support of the President. The alignment of social forces more closely resembled that in Turkey in 1960 and suggests that while peasant support is a necessary condition for political stability, it is not a sufficient one. The cooperation of at least one of the major urban elements—intelligentsia, workers, or army—is also required.

The fourth factor which may be linked to the failure of the Bolivian Revolution to produce political stability is the curious absence of antiforeign nationalism. Every other major revolution has involved at one stage or another the mobilization of the masses in a struggle against a foreign enemy. This feature was markedly absent in the Bolivian case. The foreign presence in Bolivia before the revolution was relatively moderate; the three great tin mine owners—Patiño, Hochschild, and Aramayo—were all Bolivians. The nationalization of the mines produced no significant foreign protest, much less any intervention. In an isolated, landlocked country far removed from the centers of world power, the Bolivian Revolution lacked any immediate and obvious target which could serve as a generator of mass participation, hatred, and nationalism.

62. *The Daily Journal* (Caracas), June 4, 1965, p. 24.

The Bolivian Revolution thus raises the issue of whether a complete revolution is possible in the absence of both a significant prerevolutionary foreign presence and a significant postrevolutionary foreign intervention. It raises the question but does not answer it. For not only was there no foreign intervention against the revolution, but there was also substantial foreign support for the revolution. The Bolivian Revolution was in effect financed by the United States. It was, in fact, financed by the same American Administration which suppressed one revolution in Guatemala and prepared to overthrow another in Cuba. From 1953 through 1959 Bolivia received $124 million in direct U.S. economic and technical assistance and $30 million in loans. Per capita aid far exceeded that granted to any other Latin American nation. Even after the inauguration of the Alliance for Progress Bolivia still remained one of the major recipients of U.S. aid, the total through 1964 amounting to about $400 million.

The question then is: To what extent did U.S. support for the revolutionary system contribute to the eventual instability of that system? This may have occurred in at least two ways. First, the dependence of the government upon U.S. financial support enabled the United States to compel or to induce the government to pursue policies it would not have undertaken in the same way if it had been dependent upon purely domestic sources of political support. The Bolivian government followed a conservative policy in paying the former tin mine owners and in servicing its foreign debt. At U.S. insistence, President Siles in 1957 inaugurated a highly unpopular stabilization program which attempted to freeze wages at levels far below the relative increase in prices since 1952. The U.S. also insisted on the postponement or abandonment of some social welfare and development programs. "We had to tell the Bolivian Government," one U.S. official said, "that they couldn't put their money into it and we weren't going to put ours into it." [63] In 1962–63 the U.S., along with West German interests and the Inter-American Development Bank, extended aid for the rehabilitation of the tin mines on condition that the government take drastic action to reduce costs and dispose of ex-

63. Roy R. Rubottom, Jr., Assistant Secretary of State for Inter-American Affairs, *Hearings on Mutual Security Act of 1960*, U.S. House of Representatives, Committee on Foreign Affairs, 86th Cong., 2d Sess. (1960), p. 847, quoted in Patch, "U.S. Assistance," p. 159. In general I have relied on Patch for the impact of U.S. aid programs in Bolivia.

cess labor. Apparently the U.S. also influenced the selection of political leaders. It stoutly backed Siles while he was president and consistently supported Paz Estenssoro. In 1964 the U.S. ambassador toured the country with Paz in his election campaign. At that time and subsequently, the U.S. apparently did all it could to head off a military coup against Paz. Earlier, in 1955, it was reported that the leftist trade union leader, Juan Lechín, was forced out of his cabinet position as minister of mines as a result of U.S. insistence.[64] Virtually all these actions tended to exacerbate the relations between the government and the tin miners. A government not dependent on American aid would have had little choice but to follow a much more conciliatory policy toward the miners. U.S. intervention in Bolivia contributed significantly to the polarization of Bolivian politics.

The second major destabilizing effect of that intervention was to encourage and to help bring into existence the political force which played the decisive role in the overthrow of the government that the U.S. supported. This, of course, was the Bolivian army. Bolivia received almost no military assistance from the United States before 1960. From 1960 to 1965, however, Bolivia received $10.6 million in U.S. military assistance. Without this assistance, the army as an organized force and political institution would probably have been too weak to overthrow Paz. In 1944, eight years before the revolution, Paz Estenssoro declared that, "In an economically dependent country like ours, an extremist revolution cannot be accomplished." [65] He may well have been right. It would appear that one major contributory factor to Bolivian political instability was the dependence of the Bolivian revolutionary government upon American assistance. That aid may have contributed significantly to social welfare and economic development. But its political effects were destabilizing. By assisting the revolution, the United States may have corrupted it.

LENINISM AND POLITICAL DEVELOPMENT

Different motives have led both communists and noncommunists to stress the revolutionary character of communism. But the communists did not invent the idea of revolution; there were modernizing revolutions long before there were communists. The

64. Patch, "U.S. Assistance," p. 133.
65. Paz Estenssoro, New York Times, Oct. 26, 1963, p. 9.

communist theory of revolution is simply a generalization of the experience of the French Revolution subsequently modified by the experiences of the Russian and Chinese revolutions. Few traditional regimes have been overthrown by communist movements. The distinctive communist achievement has, instead, been the creation after revolutions of modern governments based on widespread mass participation in politics.

Societies which move into the modern world bereft of traditional principles of legitimacy and traditional institutions of authority are peculiarly susceptible to the communist appeal. Before the Bolshevik revolution no revolution was politically complete because no revolutionary leaders had formulated a theory explaining how to organize and to institutionalize the expansion of political participation which is the essence of revolution. Lenin solved this problem, and in doing so made one of the most significant political innovations of the twentieth century. His followers elaborated the political theory and practice for mating the mobilization of new groups into politics to the creation and institutionalization of new political organizations. Many different types of groups—religious, nationalist, class—can bring new participants into politics. But only the communists have consistently demonstrated the ability to organize and structure that participation and thus to create new institutions of political order. Not revolution and the destruction of established institutions, but organization and the creation of new political institutions are the peculiar contributions of communist movements to modern politics. The political function of communism is not to overthrow authority but to fill the vacuum of authority.

The efficacy and stability of communist political systems, moreover, are only partially dependent upon the way in which they are established. Six of the fourteen communist governments (Soviet Union, China, Yugoslavia, Albania, North Vietnam, Cuba) came to power through essentially domestic social and national revolution. The other eight (Poland, East Germany, Hungary, Bulgaria, Roumania, Czechoslovakia, North Korea, Mongolia) were largely imposed by foreign (i.e. Soviet) power. Communist legitimacy was obviously weaker in the latter states than in the former ones, because less identity existed between communism and nationalism. Indeed, the interests of communism and nationalism may well conflict, as they did at times in the eastern European countries. The eight communist "occupation" systems are thus less stable than the six communist "revolutionary" systems. The "occupation" regimes may well be able to overcome their initial handicap, however, by identifying themselves with nationalist sentiments in their countries and asserting their national independence (as Roumania and North Korea did in the 1960s) against foreign control. Indeed, the occupation regimes are under more domestic pressure to do this than the revolutionary regimes which may feel that they can ally themselves and even subordinate themselves to foreign powers without compromising the independence of their country or the standing of their regime as a spokesman for national interests. Communist states of both types, moreover, demonstrate high levels of political stability and institutionalization in comparison to the political systems of most other countries at similar levels of social and economic development.

The strength of communism is found not in its economics —which is hopelessly antiquated—nor in its character as a secular religion, where it can be easily outclassed by the appeals of nationalism. Its most relevant characteristic is its political theory and practice, not its Marxism but its Leninism. In the socialist intellectual tradition, Marx is usually thought of as the peak: before Marx there were precursors, such as the utopian socialists; after Marx there were disciples and interpreters, such as Kautsky, Bernstein, Luxemburg, Lenin. In terms of the political theory of Marxism, however, this is quite inappropriate—Lenin was not a disciple of Marx, rather Marx was a precursor of Lenin. Lenin made Marxism into a political theory and in the process stood Marx on his head. The key to Marx is the social class; the key to Lenin is the political party. Marx was a political primitive. He could not develop a political science or a political theory, because he had no recognition of politics as an autonomous field of activity and no concept of a political order which transcends that of social class. Lenin, however, elevated a political institution, the party, over social classes and social forces.

More specifically, Lenin argued that the proletariat could not, by itself, achieve class consciousness. Such consciousness had to be brought by intellectuals from without. Revolutionary consciousness is a product of theoretical insight, and a revolutionary movement is a product of political organization. The Social Democrats,

Lenin said, must aim "to create *an organization of revolutionaries,* which leads the struggle of the proletariat." [66] This organization must "divert" the working class from a preoccupation with purely material gains and create a broader political consciousness. The loyalties of the members of the potentially revolutionary social forces must transcend the immediate interests of those social forces. These classes must acquire an "all-sided political consciousness" and "learn to apply practically the materialist analysis and the materialist estimate of *all* aspects of the life and activity of *all* classes, strata and groups of the population." [67] Lenin's constant emphasis on the achievement of a true revolutionary political consciousness as distinct from a limited immediate "trade union" or economic consciousness was a practical recognition of the broader scope and needs of politics and of the transcendence of political goals over economic ones.

The organization of revolutionaries, moreover, may be drawn from all social strata. It "must be comprised first and foremost of people whose profession is that of revolutionists. . . . As this is the common feature of the members of such an organization, *all distinctions between workers and intellectuals,* and certainly distinctions of trade and profession, must be dropped." [68] The criterion of party membership was shifted from the ascriptive test of Marx (class background) to the achievement test of Lenin (revolutionary consciousness). The distinctive characteristic of Communist party members, in this sense, is that they are classless. Their devotion is to the party, not to any social group. The prominent role accorded intellectuals simply derives from the fact that intellectuals are less attached than most other members of society to any particular social group.

Marxism, as a theory of social evolution, was proved wrong by events; Leninism, as a theory of political action, was proved right. Marxism cannot explain the communist conquest of power in such industrially backward countries as Russia or China, but Leninism can. The decisive factor is the nature of political organization not the stage of social development. The Leninist party required for

66. Lenin, quoted in Bertram D. Wolfe, *Three Who Made a Revolution* (Boston, Beacon Press, 1955) , p. 225.

67. V. I. Lenin, *What Is To Be Done?* (New York, International Publishers, 1929) , pp. 41, 67–68, 81–82.

68. Ibid., pp. 105–06.

the conquest of power is not necessarily dependent upon any particular combination of social forces. Lenin thought mostly in terms of intellectuals and workers; Mao showed that Lenin's theory of political development was equally relevant to a coalition of intellectuals and peasants. The Chinese Communist Party, as Schwartz says, was "an elite corps of politically articulate leaders organized along Leninist lines but drawn on its top levels from various strata of Chinese society." Trotsky was wrong when he said, "Classes decide and not parties." [69] Lenin and Mao were right when they stressed the primacy of a political organization independent of social forces and yet manipulating them to secure its ends. The party must, indeed, appeal to all groups in the population.

> To bring political knowledge to the workers the Social-Democrats must *go among all classes of the population,* must despatch units of their army *in all directions.* . . . We must take upon ourselves the task of organizing a universal political struggle under the leadership of *our party* in such a manner as to obtain the support of all opposition strata for the struggle and for our party. We must train our Social-Democratic practical workers to become political leaders.[70]

The broadening of the appeal of communism from the proletariat to other social groups goes hand in hand with the stress on the party as the engine of political change.

Lenin thus substituted a consciously created, structured, and organized political institution for an amorphous social class. By stressing the primacy of politics and the party as a political institution, by emphasizing the need to build a "strong political organization" based on a "broad revolutionary coalition," Lenin laid down the prerequisites for political order. The parallels between Lenin and Madison, between *The Federalist* and *What Is To Be Done?,* are in this respect rather striking. Both are works of practical political scientists analyzing social reality and formulating principles upon which a political order can be constructed. Lenin deals with classes as Madison deals with factions. Madison finds his

69. Benjamin Schwartz, *Chinese Communism and the Rise of Mao* (Cambridge, Harvard University Press, 1951), pp. 193, 198.

70. Lenin, *What Is To Be Done?,* pp. 76–77, 82.

basis for political order in the institutions of representative government and the inherent limits on the power of majorities in an extensive republic. Lenin finds his basis for political order in the supremacy of party over all social forces.

A political organization, the party, thus becomes the summum bonum, an end in itself, its needs overriding those of individual leaders, members, and social groups. For Lenin ultimate loyalty belongs not to the family, the clan, the tribe, the nation, or even the class: it belongs to the party. The party is the ultimate source of morality, *partiinost'* the highest loyalty, party discipline the supreme sanction. The interest of all other groups and individuals must be sacrificed, if necessary, to insure the survival and success of the party and its victory. "The Party in the last analysis is always right," Trotsky admitted when charged with error, "because the Party is the single historic instrument given to the proletariat for the solution of its fundamental problems. . . . One can be right only with the Party, and through the Party, for history has created no other road for the realization of what is right." [71] In Leninism the party is not just institutionalized; it is deified.

Here, indeed, is a marked paradox. Most revolutionaries attack organization; Lenin glorified it. "The most serious sin we commit," he said, "is that we *degrade* our political and organizational tasks to the level of immediate, 'palpable,' 'concrete' interests of the everyday economic struggle." "Our fighting method is organization," he said again. "We must organize everything." [72] Lenin's stress on organization was reflected in Bolshevik and communist practice and echoed in the thinking of later communist leaders. In the early history of the Chinese Communist Party, Mao distinguished himself by his emphasis on the importance of organization. In the modernizing countries of Asia and Africa, the stress on organization has been the crucial characteristic differentiating communist from other nationalist movements. Both groups, as Franz Schurmann has said, have shown "themselves capable of eliciting great response from the people on whom they have acted. But in regard to one essential mechanism of political action, the

71. Leon Trotsky, quoted in Fainsod, p. 139.

72. Lenin, *What Is To Be Done?*, p. 100, and quoted in Alfred G. Meyer, *Leninism* (Cambridge, Harvard University Press, 1957), p. 54. See also Sheldon Wolin, *Politics and Vision* (Boston, Little Brown, 1960), pp. 421–29, for a brilliant interpretation of Lenin as the pioneer of twentieth-century organization theory.

nationalists have shown themselves far weaker and less adept than the Communists. That mechanism is *organization*." From the Bolsheviks in Russia in the early 1900s to the Viet Cong in Indochina in the 1960s, organization has been the distinctive source of communist strength.[73]

The Bolshevik concept of the political party, moreover, provides a conscious and explicit answer to the problem of mobilization vs. institutionalization. The communists actively attempt to expand political participation. At the same time they are the most energetic and intense contemporary students of de Tocqueville's "art of associating together." Their specialty is organization, their goal the mobilization of the masses into their organizations. For them mobilization and organization go hand in hand. "There are only two kinds of political tasks," a leading Chinese Communist theorist has said: "one is the task of propaganda and education, and the other is the task of organization."[74] The party is initially a highly select group of those who have achieved the proper degree of revolutionary consciousness. It expands gradually as it is able to win the support and participation of others. Peripheral organizations and front groups provide an organizational ladder for the gradual mobilization and indoctrination of those who in due course become full-fledged party members. If the political struggle takes the form of revolutionary war, mobilization occurs on a gradual territorial basis as village after village shifts in status from hostile control to contested area to guerrilla area to base area. The theory is selective mobilization; the political involvement of masses who have not reached the proper level of revolutionary consciousness can only benefit reaction. The "opportunist" Menshevik, Lenin warned, "strives to proceed from the bottom upward, and, therefore, wherever possible and as far as possible, upholds autonomism and 'democracy.'" The Bolshevik, on the other hand, "strives to proceed from the top downward, and upholds an extension of the rights and powers of the center in relation to the parts."[75]

73. Schwartz, p. 35; Franz Schurmann, "Organisational Principles of the Chinese Communists," *China Quarterly*, 2 (April–June 1960), 47; Douglas Pike, *Viet Cong* (Cambridge, The M.I.T. Press, 1966), passim.

74. Ai Ssu-chi, quoted in Frederick T. C. Yu, "Communications and Politics in Communist China," in Pye, ed., *Communications and Political Development*, pp. 261–62.

75. V. I. Lenin, *One Step Forward, Two Steps Back* (*The Crisis in Our Party*), in *Collected Works* (London, Lawrence and Wishart, 1961), pp. 396–97.

Lenin held to the traditional Marxist theory of the state as an organ of class domination and hence lacking autonomous existence as a political institution. In bourgeois society the state is a creature of the capitalist class. The organization of revolutionaries, however, does have an autonomous existence; it is, thus, a higher form of political organization. The subordination of the state contrasts with the autonomy of the party. Lenin's theory of the party was, of course, formulated initially for the party out of power. It is, however, equally, if not more, relevant to the role of the party in power and the definition of the relations between political authority and social forces. The party consists of the political elite; it is autonomous from and yet in touch with the masses. It provides the will and the direction. The party is "the vanguard" of the proletariat; it "cannot be a real Party if it limits itself to registering what the masses of the working class think or experience." It maintains contact with the masses through a system of transmission belts: unions, cooperatives, youth groups, soviets. The state apparatus becomes simply the administrative subordinate of the party. The "dictatorship of the proletariat is *in essence* the 'dictatorship' of its vanguard, the 'dictatorship' of its Party, as the main guiding force of the proletariat." [76] Western scholars interpret this famous passage from Stalin as a warning of and legitimation of the ruthless dictatorship its author was shortly to establish. But it can also be seen as another manifestation of Lenin's constant theme of the primacy of politics and of the political realism of the Bolsheviks. Government is by political institutions, not social forces. Parties rule and not classes: a dictatorship must be the dictatorship of a party even if it is in the name of a class.

In adhering to the Marxist theory of the state, Lenin, of course, flew in the face of fifty years' evidence that the political systems of Western Europe and North America were not simply creatures of the bourgeoisie. He refused to concede to the liberal democratic state the political virtues which, in different form, he held to be the essence of the professional revolutionary organization. This blindness explains why his theory of political development has been irrelevant to the most highly industrialized Western societies and why the communist parties in these societies have had so little

76. Joseph Stalin, *Problems of Leninism* (New York, International Publishers, 1934) , p. 34, and *Foundations of Leninism* (New York, International Publishers, 1932) , pp. 105–06; italics in original.

success. Marx's theory of the growth and pauperization of the proletariat was undermined by Western economic development which limited the class appeal of the communist parties to a minority and eventually declining sector of society. Lenin's theory of the subordination of the state to the capitalist class was undermined by the Western political development which limited the political appeal of the communist parties because of the adaptability and effectiveness of the existing political institutions. The absence of a proletariat such as existed in Europe makes Marxism irrelevant to the modernizing countries of Asia, Africa, and Latin America. The absence of political institutions such as existed in Europe, however, makes Leninism peculiarly relevant.

A curious parallel exists between Lenin's efforts to broaden and politicize Marxism and those of the political reformers in nineteenth-century Europe to broaden and to adapt their own political institutions. The aristocratic classes in most European countries were no more willing to accept parliaments, bureaucracies, and officer corps not dominated by wealth and birth than the economists and Mensheviks were willing to accept a party not dominated by the immediate interests of the proletariat. In each case, however, the forces attempting to create broader-based, more autonomous political institutions were able to score at least partial victories.

Marxism is a theory of history. Leninism is a theory of political development. It deals with the bases of political mobilization, the methods of political institutionalization, the foundations of public order. The theory of party supremacy is, as we have suggested earlier, the twentieth-century counterpart of the seventeenth-century theory of absolute monarchy. The modernizers of the seventeenth century canonized the king, those of the twentieth the party. But the party is a far more flexible and broad-gauged institution for modernization than the absolute monarchy. It is capable not only of centralizing power but also of expanding it. This is what makes the Leninist theory of political development relevant to the modernizing countries of Asia, Africa, and Latin America.

The relevance of the Leninist model of political development is perhaps most dramatically illustrated by China. Surely one of the most outstanding political achievements of the mid-twentieth century was the establishment in China in 1949 for the first time in a hundred years of a government really able to govern China. The undoing of that government, in turn, came when its leader abandoned Lenin for Trotsky and subordinated the interests of the party to those of revolutionary renewal.

The effectiveness of the Leninist model can also be seen comparatively in the two instances where it and alternative approaches were applied side-by-side to the same people with the same culture, with roughly the same level of economic development, and in adjoining territory: Korea and Vietnam. The economic arguments here can be turned one way or another. With more resources, North Korea initially advanced faster economically than South Korea. Before it became convulsed by insurrection, South Vietnam was advancing economically more rapidly than North Vietnam. One can make an economic case for either communism or its absence. In terms of politics, however, North Korea and North Vietnam early achieved a level of political development and political stability which was long absent in South Korea and still longer absent from South Vietnam. Political stability here means real political stability, not just the long tenure in office of Ho Chi Minh and Kim Il-song, but institutional stability, which led one to have confidence that when Ho and Kim passed from the scene neither country would suffer the political disruption and violence which followed the departure from office of Syngman Rhee and Ngo Dinh Diem. The differences in political experience between the northern halves and the southern halves of these two countries cannot be attributed to different cultures or significant differences in economic development. Nor can one fob them off by saying simply that political stability is the other side of the coin of political dictatorship. Diem did create a political dictatorship in South Vietnam; Rhee tried to create one in South Korea. Neither achieved political stability. The difference between north and south in both countries was not the difference between dictatorship and democracy but rather the difference between well-organized, broadly based, complex political systems, on the one hand, and unstable, fractured, narrowly based personalistic regimes, on the other. It was a difference in political institutionalization.

6. Reform and Political Change

Revolutions are rare. Reform, perhaps, is even rarer. And neither is necessary. Countries may simply stagnate or they may change in ways which could not be called either revolution or reform. While the line between the two may at times be hazy, they can be distinguished in terms of the speed, scope, and direction of change in the political and social systems. A revolution involves rapid, complete, and violent change in values, social structure, political institutions, governmental policies, and social-political leadership. The more complete these changes, the more total is the revolution. A "great" or "social" revolution means significant changes in all these components of the social and political system. Changes limited in scope and moderate in speed in leadership, policy, and political institutions may, in turn, be classed as reforms. Not all moderate changes, however, are reforms. The concept of reform implies something about the direction of change as well as something about its scope and rate. A reform, as Hirschman says, is a change in which "the power of hitherto privileged groups is curbed and the economic position and social status of underprivileged groups is correspondingly improved." [1] It means a change in the direction of greater social, economic, or political equality, a broadening of participation in society and polity. Moderate changes in the opposite direction are better termed "consolidations" than reforms.

The way of the reformer is hard. In three respects, his problems are more difficult than those of the revolutionary. First, he necessarily fights a two-front war against both conservative and revolutionary. Indeed, to be successful, he may well have to engage in a multi-front war with a multiplicity of participants, in which his

1. Albert O. Hirschman, *Journeys Toward Progress* (New York, Twentieth Century Fund, 1963), p. 267.

enemies on one front are his allies on another. The aim of the revolutionary is to polarize politics, and hence he attempts to simplify, to dramatize, and to amalgamate political issues into a single clear-cut dichotomy between the forces of "progress" and those of "reaction." He tries to cumulate cleavages, while the reformer must try to diversify and to disassociate cleavages. The revolutionary promotes rigidity in politics, the reformer fluidity and adaptability. The revolutionary must be able to dichotomize social forces, the reformer to manipulate them. The reformer, consequently, requires a much higher order of *political skill* than does the revolutionary. Reform is rare if only because the political talents necessary to make it a reality are rare. A successful revolutionary need not be a master politician; a successful reformer always is.

The reformer not only must be more adept at the manipulation of social forces than is the revolutionary, but he also must be more sophisticated in the control of social change. He is aiming at some change but not total change, gradual change but not convulsive change. The revolutionary has some interest in all types of change and disorder. Presumably anything which disrupts the status quo is of some value to him. The reformer must be much more selective and discriminating. He has to devote much more attention to the methods, techniques, and timing of changes than does the revolutionary. Like the revolutionary he is concerned with the relation between types of change, but the consequences of these relationships are likely to be even more significant for the reformer than they are for the revolutionary.

Finally, the problem of priorities and choices among different types of reforms is much more acute for the reformer than it is for the revolutionary. The revolutionary aims first at the expansion of political participation; the politically relevant forces which result are then employed to generate changes in social and economic structure. The conservative opposes both social-economic reform and expanded political participation. The reformer has to balance both goals. Measures promoting social-economic equality usually require the concentration of power, measures promoting political equality the expansion of power. These goals are not inherently contradictory, but, as the experiences of the modernizing monarchs suggest, too great a centralization of power in institutions inherently incapable of expanding power can lead a political system up a blind alley. The reformer thus has to balance changes in social-economic structure against changes in political institutions and to marry the one to the other in such a way that neither is hampered. Leadership and institutions which facilitate one type of reform may be less capable of providing for the other. The military reformer—Mustafa Kemal, Gamal Abdel Nasser, Ayub Khan—is, for instance, notably more successful at promoting social-economic changes than at organizing the participation of new groups in the political system. The Social Democratic or Christian Democratic party leader—Betancourt, Belaunde, Frei—on the other hand, may be better able to identify previously outcast groups with the political system than to bring about social and economic changes.

In theory two broad strategies are open to the reformer who desires to bring about a number of significant changes in social-economic structure and political institutions. One strategy would lead him to make known all his goals at an early time and to press for as many of them as he could in the hope of obtaining as much as possible. The alternative strategy is the foot-in-the-door approach of concealing his aims, separating the reforms from each other, and pushing for only one change at a time. The former is a comprehensive, "root," or blitzkrieg approach; the latter is an incremental, "branch," or Fabian approach.[2] At various times in history reformers have essayed both methods. The results of their efforts suggest that for most countries subjected to the strains and dissensions involved in modernization, the most effective method of reform is the combination of a Fabian strategy with blitzkrieg tactics. To achieve his goals the reformer should separate and isolate one issue from another, but, having done this, he should, when the time is ripe, dispose of each issue as rapidly as possible, removing it from the political agenda before his opponents are able to mobilize their forces. The ability to achieve this proper mix of Fabianism and blitzkrieg is a good test of the political skill of the reformer.

In terms of an overall reform program, one can, however, make a logical case for a blitzkrieg strategy. Why should not the reformer make clear his total set of demands immediately, arouse and mobilize the groups which favor change, and through a pro-

2. See Charles E. Lindblom, "The Science of 'Muddling Through,'" *Public Administration Review, 19* (Spring 1959), 79–88.

cess of political conflict and political bargaining settle for as much as the balance of forces between change and conservatism permit? If he asks for 100 per cent of what he wants, will he not be sure of getting at least 60 per cent? Or, even better, if he asks for 150 per cent of what he wants, will he not be able to settle for just about everything he can really hope to achieve? Is not this a general strategy of bargaining observable in diplomatic negotiations between states, in labor-management relations, and in the politics of the budgetary process?

The answer to these questions in terms of reform-mongering in a modernizing society is, in general, negative. The comprehensive or blitzkrieg strategy is effective only if the parties to the process are relatively given and unchangeable, if, in short, the structure of the bargaining context is highly stable. The essence of reform-mongering in a modernizing country, however, is to structure the situation so as to influence if not to determine the participants in the political arena. The nature of the demands and the nature of the issues formulated by the reformer in large part shape the allies and the opponents who will play roles in the political process. The problem for the reformer is not to overwhelm a single opponent with an exhaustive set of demands, but to minimize his opposition by an apparently very limited set of demands. The reformer who attempts to do everything all at once ends up accomplishing little or nothing. Joseph II and Kuang Hsu are perfect cases in point. Both attempted simultaneously to push a large number of reforms on a wide variety of fronts, in order to change comprehensively the existing traditional order. They failed because their efforts to attempt so much mobilized so many opponents. Virtually all the social groups and political forces with a stake in the existing society felt themselves threatened; the blitzkrieg or all-out attack simply served to alert and to activate the potential opposition. Here then is the reason why comprehensive reform, in the sense of a dramatic and rapid "revolution from above," never succeeds. It mobilizes into politics the wrong groups at the wrong time on the wrong issues.

The failures of Joseph II and Kuang Hsu contrast markedly with the successful Fabian strategy employed by Mustafa Kemal in the early days of the Turkish Republic. Kemal faced almost all the usual problems of modernization: the definition of the national community, the creation of a modern secular political organization, the inauguration of social and cultural reform, the promotion of economic development. Instead of attempting to solve all these problems simultaneously, however, Kemal carefully separated them one from the other and won acquiescence or even support for one reform from those who would have opposed him on other reforms. The sequence in which the problems were tackled was designed to move from those where Kemal had the greatest support to those which might arouse the greatest controversy. First priority had to be given to the definition of the national community and the delimitation of the ethnic and territorial boundaries of the state. Once a relatively homogeneous ethnic community had been established, the next step—as in the sequels to the Mexican, Russian, and Chinese revolutions—was to create effective modern political institutions for the exercise of authority. It was then possible for those in control to work through the institutions to impose religious, social, cultural, and legal reforms on society. Once traditional forms and customs had been weakened or eliminated, the way was then open for industrialization and economic development. Economic growth, in short, required cultural modernization; cultural modernization required effective political authority; effective political authority had to be rooted in a homogeneous national community. The sequences in which many countries have tackled the problems of modernization have been the products of accident and history. The sequence of change in Turkey, however, was consciously planned by Kemal, and this pattern of unity-authority-equality is the most effective modernization sequence.[3]

Kemal's success in achieving these reforms depended upon his ability to deal with each separately and in effect to suggest at the time that he was handling one that he had no intention of tackling the others. His grand design and ultimate purposes he kept to himself. The first necessity was to create a Turkish national state in Anatolia out of the collapse of the Ottoman Empire. In his struggle to define the national community, Kemal carefully di-

---

3. Dankwart A. Rustow, *A World of Nations*, pp. 126–27. On Kemal's strategy and tactics of reform-mongering, see Rustow, "The Army and the Founding of the Turkish Republic," *World Politics, 11* (July 1959), 545 ff.; Bernard Lewis, *The Emergence of Modern Turkey* (London, Oxford University Press, 1961), p. 254; Richard D. Robinson, *The First Turkish Republic* (Cambridge, Harvard University Press, 1963), pp. 65–66, 69, 80–81; Lord Kinross, *Ataturk* (New York, William Morrow, 1965), p. 430.

vorced the issue of a limited, integral, homogeneous Turkish
nation-state from the type of political authority which would exist
in that state. Between 1920 and 1922 the sultan remained in Constantinople while the nationalist movement, under Kemal's leadership, gained strength in the interior. By his successful battles
against the Armenians, French, and Greeks, Kemal developed a
substantial following. The sultan and the sultanate, however, still
retained widespread popular support and sympathy. Kemal consequently separated the struggle for a national state from opposition
to the sultanate. He instead proclaimed one aim of the nationalist
movement to be the liberation of the sultan from the control of
the British and French forces which had occupied Constantinople.
He attacked the sultan's ministers for their collaboration with the
foreigners but not the sultan himself. As Kemal subsequently said,
"We chose Ferid Pasha's cabinet alone as our target and pretended
that we knew nothing about the complicity of the Padishah [Sul-
tan]. Our theory was that the Sovereign had been deceived by the
Cabinet and that he himself was in total ignorance of what was
really going on." [4] Through this means Kemal was able to align
with the nationalist cause those conservatives who still gave primary allegiance to the traditional authority of the sultan.

Once the nationalist victory was assured, Kemal turned his attention to the problem of the political organization of the new
state. The nationalists had earlier declared their loyalty to the sovereign, but at the same time they had also proclaimed the sovereignty of the people. Just as earlier he had separated the national
issue from the political issue, so now Kemal took pains to separate
the political issue from the religious issue. The Ottoman ruler
combined the political office of sultan with the religious office of
caliph. Kemal knew there would be serious opposition to tamper-
ing with the latter position: it gave Turkey special status among
Islamic nations. "[If] we lose the Caliphate," one newspaper observed in November 1923, "the State of Turkey, with its five or
ten million inhabitants, would lose all importance in the world of
Islam, and in the eyes of European politics we would sink to the
rank of a petty and insignificant state." [5] Conscious of the strength
of the religious feelings attached to the caliphate, Kemal in this

4. Mustapha Kemal, *A Speech Delivered by Ghazi Mustapha Kemal, President of the Turkish Republic, October 1927* (Leipzig, K. F. Koehler, 1929) , p. 119.

5. Quoted in Lewis, p. 257

phase of his reform-mongering limited himself to the elimination of the political elements of traditional authority. In November 1922 the Grand National Assembly abolished the sultanate, but provided for the caliphate to be continued in a member of the Ottoman ruling house chosen by the Assembly. The following summer the Republic People's Party was organized and a new national assembly elected. Shortly thereafter, in October 1923, the capital of the state was transferred from Istanbul—with its multitudinous associations with the Ottoman and, indeed, Byzantine past—to the small town of Ankara in the midst of the Anatolian heartland. A few weeks later the national assembly completed the work of political reconstruction by formally proclaiming Turkey a republic and providing for the election of a president by the assembly. Through this carefully delimited series of steps the imperial political institutions of Ottoman rule were replaced by the modern political structures of a secular republic and a nationalist party.

The political basis of the new society having been laid, Kemal then turned to the problem of religious and cultural reform. Support for these reforms would come primarily from the modernized and Western-oriented bureaucratic and intellectual elite. The principal sources of opposition would be the religious bureaucracy and, potentially, the peasants. To put through the desired social and cultural reforms, it would be necessary to insure the passivity and relative indifference of the latter. Consequently, Kemal carefully divorced this phase of his reforms from any efforts at economic development and change which might tend to stimulate peasant political consciousness and activity. In January 1924 Kemal moved to inaugurate the phase of secularization and two months later he persuaded the national assembly to abolish the caliphate and the religious ministries, to banish all members of the Ottoman house, to close the separate religious schools and colleges and thus to unify public education, and to abolish the special religious courts which applied Islamic law. To replace the Islamic law, a commission was appointed to draw up a new code, and early in 1926 the assembly approved its recommendation for an adaptation of the Swiss civil code. New codes of commercial, maritime, and criminal law, new civil and criminal procedures, and a new judicial system were also introduced. In 1925 Kemal launched his campaign against the fez as a symbol of religious traditionalism.

and its use was prohibited. Also in 1925 the old calendar was abolished and the Gregorian calendar adopted. In 1928 Islam was formally disestablished as the state religion, and in the fall of the same year the shift from Arabic to Roman script was decreed. This latter reform was of fundamental importance: it made it virtually impossible for the new generations educated in the Roman script to acquire access to the vast bulk of traditional literature; it encouraged the learning of European languages; and it greatly eased the problem of increasing literacy.

The accomplishment of these social reforms in the late 1920s prepared the way for an emphasis on economic development in the 1930s. A policy of etatism was proclaimed, and a five year plan adopted in 1934. Throughout the decade great stress was placed on industrial development, particularly in the textile, iron and steel, paper, glass, and ceramics industries. Between 1929 and 1938, national income increased 44 per cent, per capita income by 30 per cent, mining production by 132 per cent, and "industry made even more impressive progress." [6]

This sequence of reforms—national, political, social, and economic—reflected a conscious strategy on the part of Kemal. In April 1923 Kemal had issued a manifesto for the Republic People's Party which stressed the political reforms that he was then attempting to put through: the abolition of the sultanate, popular sovereignty, representative government, fiscal and administrative reforms. Commenting on this program in 1927 after most of his social-religious reforms had been introduced, Kemal specifically articulated his strategy of attempting only one thing at a time, while maintaining a discreet veil over his long-range goals. The program of 1923, he said,

> contained essentially all that we had carried through up to that day. There were, however, some important and vital questions which had not been included in this programme, such as, for instance, the proclamation of the Republic, the abolition of the Caliphate, the suppression of the Ministry of Education, and that of the Medressas [clerical schools] and Tekkas [religious orders], and the introduction of the hat.

6. Peter F. Sugar, "Economic and Political Modernization: Turkey," in Robert E. Ward and Dankwart A. Rustow, eds., *Political Modernization in Japan and Turkey* (Princeton, Princeton University Press, 1964), p. 174; Z. Y. Hershlag, *Turkey: An Economy in Transition* (The Hague, Van Keulen, 1958), Chaps. 11, 14, 15.

I held the opinion that it was not appropriate to give into the hands of ignorant men and reactionaries the means of poisoning the whole nation by introducing these questions into the programme before the hour had come to do so, because I was absolutely sure that these questions would be settled at the proper time and that the people in the end would be satisfied.[7]

By dealing with each set of issues separately Kemal minimized the opposition to each set of reforms. The opponents of one reform were separated from their potential allies opposed to other reforms. "Those whom the *Gazi* would destroy," Frey accurately observes, "he would first isolate." [8]

A Fabian strategy of isolating one set of issues from another thus tends to minimize the opposition which the reformer confronts at any one time. Similar considerations lead the reformer to employ blitzkrieg tactics in handling each individual issue or set of issues. Then the problem is to enact and to implement legislation embodying a specific reform policy. Celerity and surprise—those two ancient principles of war—here become tactical necessities. The existing amount of power in the political system is normally fairly heavily concentrated in the hands of the reforming leader. His need is to put through his reforms before the opposition can mobilize its supporters, expand the number of participants and the amount of power in the system, and thus block the changes. "Both experience and reason," Richelieu observed, "make it evident that what is suddenly presented ordinarily astonishes in such a fashion as to deprive one of the means of opposing it, while if the execution of a plan is undertaken slowly the gradual revelation of it can create the impression that it is only being projected and will not necessarily be executed." [9]

The most successful and rapid racial desegregation in the United States, it has been observed, frequently occurred where those in power introduced abrupt, firm, and irreversible policies without much prior preparation. Such policies brought about effective changes in behavior without attempting to alter attitudes

7. Kemal, p. 598.

8. Frederick W. Frey, "Political Development, Power and Communications," in Pye, ed., *Communications and Political Development*, pp. 314–15.

9. Cardinal Richelieu, *Political Testament* (tr. H. B. Hill, Madison, University of Wisconsin Press, 1961) , p. 75.

and values. Changes in the latter, however, are likely to follow changes in behavior. A more gradual approach to desegregation did not, on the other hand, increase the likelihood of its acceptance by those in the community opposed to integration. *"Opportunity and time for preparation of public for change is not necessarily related to 'effectiveness' and 'smoothness' of change.* An interval of time for change not only may be used for positive preparation, but may also be used as opportunity to mobilize overt resistance to change." [10]

Again Mustafa Kemal demonstrates the effectiveness of blitzkrieg tactics on individual issues. Typically, in introducing reform, he first held some general discussions of the problem, sounding out in a cautious way the attitudes of different groups. He next had his aides secretly prepare a plan for reform. This plan was shown to a few top leaders in politics and society and their support for it secured. At the politically most propitious time, Kemal would then dramatically announce the need for the reform to the party and the national assembly, unveil his plan for change, and demand its immediate approval. The legislation enacting the reform would be promptly passed by the assembly before the opposition could rally its forces and prepare a counterattack. Plans for the proclamation of the Turkish Republic, for instance, were worked out by Kemal and a few of his closest advisers during the summer of 1923. The announcement of this revolutionary idea, "wholly at odds with that of the traditional Moslem state," caused a tremendous "commotion, both in the press of Istanbul and in the lobbies of Parliament, where no serious republican movement had yet existed. Kemal realized that a debate on it might be fatal. The Republic must be forced through by other means before the Opposition had time to unite." [11] At the time, various groups wanted a continuation of traditional rule, the establishment of a constitutional monarch, with or without the Caliph as the monarch, or a multiparty parliamentary democracy. To secure approval of the Republic before these groups could combine their opposition, Kemal arranged a ministerial crisis, plunged the government into seeming anarchy for several days, and then dramat-

---

10. Kenneth Clark, "Desegregation: An Appraisal of the Evidence," *Journal of Social Issues, 9* (1953), 43; italics in original. See also Ronald Lippitt et al., *The Dynamics of Planned Change* (New York, Harcourt, Brace, 1958), pp. 58–59.

11. Kinross, p. 431.

ically presented the proposed constitutional change to the party caucus and the assembly, which could do little but to approve it despite the resentment and muttered opposition of many of their members.

Similar tactics were employed by Kemal in putting through his other major reforms. In January 1924, for instance, Kemal determined that the time had come to abolish the Caliphate. He invited the top leaders of the government to go on military maneuvers with him, at which time he secured their agreement to this proposal, to the abolition of the Ministry of Seriat, and to the changes in religious education. Included in the conference were the editors of leading newspapers, who were locked up with the President for two days, during which time he persuaded them to begin to attack the government for its inaction on the caliphate issue. Hardly a month later, on March 1, Kemal presented his proposals in his opening speech to the Grand National Assembly, arguing that the changes were necessary to safeguard the republic, to unify the national system of education, and to cleanse and elevate the Islamic faith. Again the conservative and religious opposition was given little time to oppose: legislation to accomplish the Gazi's goals was approved on March 3.

Other modernizing reformers have duplicated, sometimes consciously, Kemal's tactics. In Pakistan, for instance, Ayub Khan attempted in many respects to model himself on Mustafa Kemal and, in particular, emulated this blitzkrieg pattern of reform-mongering. "When he is faced with a problem," one observer reported, "he sets up an expert commission to find a solution, and once it has reported he implements the solution rapidly." [12] Such was, for instance, the tactic employed in 1958 to put through land reform. Legislation was drafted by a commission of inquiry, and five days after the commission reported, the legislation was enacted into law.

As this discussion of Fabian strategy and blitzkrieg tactics suggests, the key question for the reformer concerns the rate and the sequence of the mobilization of new groups into politics. The reformer has to attempt to control and to guide this process, to insure that at each time and on each issue his supporters will be stronger than his opponents. Both the revolutionary and the con-

12. Guy Wint, "The 1958 Revolution in Pakistan," *St. Anthony's Papers* (No. 8, 1960) , 79.

servative, on the other hand, operate under much less restraint in mobilizing new political participants. Revolution is itself the process of the mobilization of previously excluded groups into politics against the existing political institutions and social-economic structure. Clearly, under some circumstances the limited mobilization which is necessary for reform could lead to the runaway mobilization which is the essence of revolution. At the same time, however, mobilization could threaten the reformer from the conservative side. Since reforms involve movements toward greater social, economic, and political equality, they are necessarily opposed by the "vested interests" which benefit from the inequalities of the existing order. Surmounting these interests presents many difficulties to the reformer, but these can usually be overcome so long as the vested interests are unable to mobilize substantial apathetic groups into politics on their side. Such groups usually have little material stake in the existing order, and indeed they would often benefit materially from the proposed reforms. They do have a symbolic stake in the existing society, however, and their values and attitudes are often highly conservative and resistant to change. They may well identify with social and religious institutions whose reform would be to their advantage. It is precisely this which makes the task of the reformer so difficult. There is, as Machiavelli said,

> nothing more difficult to carry out, nor more doubtful of success, nor more dangerous to handle, than to initiate a new order of things. For the reformer has enemies in all those who profit by the old order, and only lukewarm defenders in all those who would profit by the new order, this lukewarmness arising partly from fear of their adversaries, who have the laws in their favour; and partly from the incredulity of mankind, who do not truly believe in anything new until they have had actual experience of it. Thus it arises that on every opportunity for attacking the reformer, his opponents do so with the zeal of partisans, the others only defend him half-heartedly, so that between them he runs great danger.[13]

The dialectic of change is such that the proposals for reform frequently activate previously apathetic groups who now see their

13. Niccolò Machiavelli, *The Prince and the Discourses* (New York, The Modern Library, 1940), pp. 21–22.

important interests threatened. In some measure, the aristocratic resurgence against the rise of the middle class in the late eighteenth century was a movement of this nature. So also was the so-called "backlash" in the twentieth century from lower income white groups against the rise of the Negro in the United States. These developments tend to dichotomize politics and to undermine the position of the reformer. The combination of Fabian strategy and blitzkrieg tactics is designed to reduce this danger and lessen the likelihood that the opponents of reform will have the incentive or the capability to mobilize the masses against change. The mobilization of the masses to political action before the modernization of their values and attitudes constitutes the greatest potential obstacle to the reformer. The competitive mobilization of the masses by both revolutionary and conservative groups also tends, of course, to polarize politics and thus to reduce the support for the reformer. Whoever wins this struggle, the reformer cannot hope to benefit from it. The German communists were notoriously wrong when in 1932 they confidently predicted "Nach Hitler kommen wir"; they were not so wrong, however, in directing their attacks against the middle and thus creating a choice of "Hitler or us."

The effects of broadening political participation vary from one situation to another. In Kemalist Turkey, political activity was largely limited to urban, bureaucratic, elite groups. Within this narrow circle of politics, the modernizing elements in the army and the civil service could exercise a preponderant influence. Consequently, the interests of reform ran counter to the interests of more widespread political participation. The broadening of political participation would have brought more conservative groups into politics and turned the balance against the reformers. Eventually in the 1950s this was precisely what happened, but by then the foundations of the Kemalist state were so strong that only relatively minor movements in the direction of tradition were possible. Foreseeing this danger in the 1920s, however, Kemal did little then to expand political participation. Indeed, as Frey says: "It is the essence of the Ataturk Revolution that it *exploited* the communications bifurcation existing in Turkish society rather than lamenting it or immediately attacking it, as a number of other nationalist movements have done. . . . The lack of communications between elite and mass was a vital factor which he used to simplify his task and equate it with his resources." [14] A tension existed in Turkey between the achievement of social and economic equality, on the one hand, and the achievement of political equality, on the other. Progress toward the former depended upon the limitation of the latter, and it was precisely this function which was performed by the one-party political system that existed in Turkey through World War II. The shift to a competitive party system after World War II, in turn, expanded political participation, made politics more democratic, but also slowed down and in some areas even reversed the process of social-economic reform.

The situation confronting reformers in many Latin American countries was just the opposite of that which faced Kemal. In these countries, politics was "right side up," and the political arena was dominated by conservative and oligarchical groups. Consequently, social-economic reform was associated with the broadening of political participation rather than with its limitation. This cumulation of issues and cleavages made politics in Latin America more intense and violent than it was in Turkey and made social revolution seem a much more imminent potentiality. In Turkey the reformer could create political institutions and promote social-economic change without broadening political participation. In Latin America, however, the broadening of political participation was not a brake on social change but a prerequisite to such change. Consequently, in Latin America the conservative seemed more reactionary because he opposed both, while the reformer seemed more revolutionary (and threatening to the conservative) because he had to support both.

In no society do significant social, economic, or political reforms take place without violence or the imminent likelihood of violence. Relatively decentralized and spontaneous violence is a common means through which disadvantaged groups call attention to their grievances and their demands for reform. The active participants in such violence are usually far removed from the centers of power, but the fact of such violence may be effectively used by reformers to push through measures which might otherwise be impossible. Such violence, indeed, may well be encouraged by leaders who are completely committed to working within the existing system and who view the violence as a required stimulus

14. Frey, pp. 313–14 (italics his).

for reforms within that system. The history of reform in the United States—from the Jeffersonians down through abolitionists, populists, the labor movement, and the civil rights movement—is studded with instances of violence and other forms of disorder which helped to trigger changes in governmental policy. In England in the early 1830s riots and other violence played a significant role in consolidating Whig support for the Reform Act of 1832. In India in the 1950s middle-class groups typically employed demonstrations, riots, *satyagraphas,* and other forms of mass protest (usually accompanied by violence) to wrest concessions from the government.[15]

In modernizing countries generally, perhaps the most significant form of illegal and often violent activity for promoting reform is the land invasion. For many reasons discussed below, land reform is of crucial importance to the maintenance of political stability. The achievement of such reform, however, frequently requires the disruption of stability. In Colombia in the late 1920s and early 1930s, for instance, peasants began to occupy private lands. Some haciendas were seized in toto and turned into cooperatives run with the help of communist functionaries. The landowners insisted upon the police and the army acting to restore their property rights. The government, however, refused to become actively engaged on either side of these local struggles, and instead capitalized on the rural violence to force through parliament—which like most parliaments in modernizing countries was dominated by landlords—a land reform law which legalized the invasions and in effect made property rights dependent upon effective working of the property. Somewhat similarly, in Peru the land invasions which occurred in 1963 at the time of the election of the Belaunde government furnished the trigger necessary to rally support for the reform measures promoted by that government. In both these cases, however, the decentralized violence coincided with the presence in power of a sympathetic and reform-minded administration, just as did the civil rights violence in the mid-1960s in the United States. In most societies, civic peace is im-

15. Joseph Hamburger, *James Mill and the Art of Revolution* (New Haven, Yale University Press, 1963) , pp. 277–78; Myron Weiner, *The Politics of Scarcity,* Chap. 8. On the role of violence in reform in general, see Hirschman, pp. 256–60, and H. L. Nieburg, "The Threat of Violence and Social Change," *American Political Science Review, 56* (Dec. 1962) , 865–73.

possible without some reform, and reform is impossible without some violence.

The effectiveness of violence in promoting reform stems directly from the extent to which it appears to herald the mobilization into politics of new groups employing new political techniques. In addition, the effectiveness of violence depends upon the existence of feasible policy alternatives, the implementation of which are likely to reduce the disorder. If the violence appears to be a purely anomic response to a general situation and to have diffuse or uncertain targets, it will do little to promote reform. For the latter, both reformers and conservatives must perceive the violence as directly related to action on a particular policy issue. The violence, then, shifts the debate from the merits of the reform to the need for public order. The case for reform, indeed, is never stronger than when it is couched in terms of the need to preserve domestic peace. Its effect then is to swing to the side of reform conservatives interested in the maintenance of order. Since the early days of Vargas in the 1930s, Brazilian elites have often quoted the phrase: "We must make the revolution before the people do." Following the Birmingham riots in 1963, President Kennedy, in somewhat similar fashion, declared that passage of his civil rights bill was necessary "to get the struggle off the streets and into the courts." Failure to pass the bill, Kennedy warned, would lead to "continued, if not increased, racial strife—causing the leadership on both sides to pass from the hands of reasonable and responsible men to the purveyors of hate and violence." Underscored by the racial violence and disorder which did exist, predictions like this caused even conservative Republicans and Democrats to support civil rights legislation.

The effectiveness of violence and disorder in stimulating reform, however, does not lie in its inherent character. It is not violence per se but rather the shock and the novelty involved in the employment of an unfamiliar or unusual political technique that serves to promote reform. It is the demonstrated willingness of a social group to go beyond the accepted patterns of action which gives impetus to its demands. In effect, such action involves the diversification of political techniques and a threat to existing political organization and procedures. Riots and violence, for instance, were familiar phenomena in England in the early nineteenth century. The scope and intensity of the violence in 1831, however, were new. Commenting on riots at Nottingham and Derby, Melbourne observed that, "Such violence and outrage are I believe quite new and unprecedented in this Country; at least I never remember to have heard of Country homes being attacked, plundered, and set on fire in any former times of political ferment." [16] It was the seemingly unprecedented nature of the violence which drove Melbourne to reform. So also in the United States the sit-down strikes of the 1930s and the sit-ins of the 1960s were new tactics whose novelty underwrote the seriousness of the demands of labor and the Negroes. In South Vietnam in 1963 riots and demonstrations were familiar occurrences. The self-immolation of the Buddhist monks, however, represented a dramatic escalation in the level of domestic violence which undoubtedly played a significant role in leading American officials and Vietnamese officers to decide on the need for a change in regime.

That it is the novelty of the technique rather than its inherent character which stimulates reform is demonstrated by the fact that repeated use of the technique depreciates its value. In 1963 racial riots in the United States and monkish self-immolations in Vietnam helped to produce significant changes in governmental policy and political leadership. Three years later similar events failed to produce similar consequences. What had once seemed a shocking departure from the political norm now seemed a relatively conventional political tactic. In many praetorian political systems, of course, violence becomes an endemic form of political action and consequently completely loses its capacity to generate significant change. In addition, in nonpraetorian systems novel or unusual forms of protest may well be incorporated into the recognized bounds of legitimate political action. As Arthur Waskow has perceptively observed:

> To the degree that the politics of disorder is aimed at bringing about change, it is generally invented by people who are "outside" a particular system of political order, and want to bring change about so that they can enter. In doing so, they tend to use new techniques that make sense to themselves out of their own experience, but that look disorderly to people who are thinking and acting inside the system. The Negroes

16. Quoted in Hamburger, p. 278.

were by no means the first to initiate this process. For example, in the seventeenth and eighteenth centuries, urban lawyers and merchants who could not get the entrenched politicians to pay attention to their grievances (and who were scarcely represented in Parliament) used the illegal and disorderly device of political pamphleteering against the established order. In the same way, nineteenth-century workers who could not get their employers or the elected legislators to pay attention to their demands used unionization and the strike—which at first were illegal—to call attention to their grievances. In both these cases, using the politics of disorder not only got the users accepted into the political order and got their immediate grievances looked after, but also got the new techniques accepted into the array of authorized and approved political methods. In short, the system of "order" was itself changed. Thus the "criminal libel" of political pamphleteering was enshrined as freedom of the press, and the "criminal conspiracy" of striking was enshrined in the system of free labor unions. One century's disorder became the next century's liberty under ordered law.[17]

One test of the adaptability of a political system, indeed, may well be its ability to assimilate, to moderate, and to legitimate new techniques of political action employed by groups making new demands upon the system.

The effectiveness of violence or any other novel technique in promoting reform may also decline with its success in stimulating such reforms. If disorder and violence by a group lead the government to make concessions, the propensity of the group to resort to disorder and violence may well increase. The repeated use of the same tactics reduces their impact. At the same time, the willingness of the government to make further concessions presumably decreases. On the one hand, the government undoubtedly argued earlier that its reforms would reduce violence rather than intensify it, and it can understandably be expected to react angrily when this does not turn out to be the case. In addition, the fact that it has made the concessions which it thought desirable and necessary

17. Arthur I. Waskow, *From Race Riot to Sit-In, 1919 and the 1960s* (Garden City, N.Y., Doubleday, 1966), pp. 278–79.

means that the new violence for additional concessions is, in its view, of decreasing legitimacy since it is support of "irresponsible" rather than "reasonable" demands. Consequently, the situation polarizes, with the government feeling that it "must draw the line" against groups "which have gone too far," and the groups feeling that the government has "sold them short" and has "no interest in fundamental change." It is at this point that the impact of reform on the prospects for revolution becomes of decisive significance.

REFORM: SUBSTITUTE OR CATALYST?

At the beginning of the 1960s social reform became an explicit goal of American policy. The Alliance for Progress embodied the idea that democratic reform leading to a more equitable distribution of material and symbolic resources in Latin America would provide a substitute for violent revolution. The pressures for social change which were building up in societies still dominated by narrow oligopolistic groups would have to be relieved gradually, or they would develop to the point where they would break through all at once, overwhelming and destroying the entire structure of society. A continuing succession of small-scale changes in leadership and policies would avert the drastic, rapid, violent changes in institutions, social structure, and values which are associated with revolution.

This policy assumption was well grounded in political theory and historical experience. "Succession, programmatic reform, and palace revolution," say Lasswell and Kaplan, "function as substitutes for political and social revolution." In a like vein, Friedrich suggests that "many small revolutions prevent a big one; for as various factors of the social order are 'revolutionized' by way of the functioning political process, the tensions which would make the forcible 'overthrow' of the political order necessary are alleviated by being 'channeled' into constructive operations." Similarly, R. R. Palmer concludes his great two-volume work on the French Revolution with this observation: "No revolution need be thought of as inevitable. In the eighteenth century there might have been no revolution, if only the old upper and ruling classes had made more sagacious concessions, if, indeed, the contrary tendencies toward a positive assertion of aristocratic values had not been so strong."[18] Surely this seems a reasonable proposition. What other evidence of its validity is required than the frustration of Marxist hopes in western Europe, as country after country defused the revolutionary dynamite of the industrial revolution by suffrage extension, factory legislation, union recognition, wages and hours laws, social security, and unemployment insurance?

There is, however, a counter-proposition. Reform, it can be argued, may contribute not to political stability but to greater instability and indeed to revolution itself. Reform can be a catalyst of revolution rather than a substitute for it. Historically, it has often been pointed out, great revolutions have followed periods of reform, not periods of stagnation and repression. The very fact that a regime makes reforms and grants concessions encourages demands for still more changes which can easily snowball into a revolutionary movement. De Tocqueville, indeed, in his analysis of the French Revolution, came to a famous and oft-quoted conclusion which is just the opposite of Palmer's:

> the social order overthrown by a revolution is almost always better than the one immediately preceding it, and experience teaches us that, generally speaking, the most perilous moment for a bad government is one when it seeks to mend its ways. Only consummate statecraft can enable a King to save his throne when after a long spell of oppressive rule he sets to improving the lot of his subjects. . . . [Reforms in France] prepared the ground for the Revolution not so much because they removed obstacles in its way but far more because they taught the nation how to set about it.[19]

The catalyst theory is undoubtedly a minority viewpoint among American thinkers. The American assumption that reform contributes to domestic political stability, however, contrasts rather strikingly with the opposing approach which appears dominant in American thinking about international affairs. Americans tend to assume that concessions produce stabilizing results in the face of

18. Harold D. Lasswell and Abraham Kaplan, *Power and Society* (New Haven, Yale University Press, 1950), p. 276; Carl J. Friedrich, *Man and His Government* (New York, McGraw-Hill, 1963), p. 641; Palmer, *The Age of the Democratic Revolution*, 2, 574.

19. Alexis de Tocqueville, *The Old Regime and the French Revolution*, pp. 176–77, 188.

domestic demands for change but destabilizing results in the face of international demands for change. Have-not classes are assuaged, have-not governments only aroused. Domestic concessions are good; they are called reforms. International concessions are bad; they are called appeasement. Here again, it would appear, American policy assumptions are shaped by historical experience, and, more particularly, by the fact that Franklin Roosevelt's domestic policy worked but Neville Chamberlain's foreign policy did not. Obviously, however, in both the international and the domestic spheres, neither assumption about gradual change is universally valid.[20] Domestically and internationally, in some cases gradual change or reform may produce greater stability, and in other cases it may promote disorder and violent fundamental change.

TABLE 6.1. Attitudes Toward Political Change

Attitude toward revolution	Assumptions on reform in relation to revolution	
	Catalyst	Substitute
For	Orthodox Revolutionary	Left Deviationist
Against	Stand-patter	Reform-monger

The relation between reform and revolution is of crucial significance to all groups involved in the process of political change. The "reform-monger" believes that reform is a substitute for revolution and precisely for this reason attempts to achieve greater social and economic equality through peaceful means. The extreme radical, or "left deviationist," also usually adheres to the substitute theory and for that reason opposes reform. The "orthodox revolu-

20. Unfortunately, little theoretical work seems to have been done on the question of when interstate appeasement appeases and when it incites. A useful brief discussion is George A. Lanyi, "The Problem of Appeasement," *World Politics, 15* (Jan. 1963), 316–29. A few items in the large literature on peaceful change are also relevant. See, particularly, Bryce C. Wood, *Peaceful Change and the Colonial Problem* (New York, Columbia University Press, 1940) and Lincoln Bloomfield, *Evolution or Revolution?* (Cambridge, Harvard University Press, 1957). The parallels and/or analogies between domestic politics and international politics cannot be pressed too far. The domestic scene usually includes conservatives, reformers, and revolutionaries, the international scene status quo powers and have-not powers. Revolutionaries are usually committed to revolution as a necessary means and deny the possibility of securing the results of a revolution without having a revolution. Have-not powers, on the other hand, are more often happy to achieve the results of war without going to war.

tionary" and the "stand-patter," on the other hand, both hold to the catalyst theory, which leads the latter to oppose any modification of the status quo, while the former hopes to use small changes as the entering wedge for more fundamental ones.

The principal debates take place not between those who put differing values on the desirability of revolution, but rather between those who have different prognostications on the relation between revolution and reform. The reform-monger tells the stand-patter that some concessions are necessary to avoid the deluge; the stand-patter warns that any concession will lead to the undermining of the established order. A parallel controversy goes on between the orthodox revolutionary and the left deviationist. Indeed, historically, the most interesting, informative, and perceptive debates on this issue have been carried on in Marxist circles. Perhaps the most prolific writer on the subject was Lenin himself who, at one time or another, seems to have argued almost every conceivable position on it. In general, however, his views most frequently approximated those of the "orthodox" revolutionary; he believed that reforms extracted from a regime hastened revolution, although reforms voluntarily initiated by a regime might delay it. "Reforms," Lenin argued in 1894 against the revisionist, i.e. reform-mongering, tendencies of Peter Struve, "are not to be contrasted to revolution. The struggle for reforms is but a means of marshaling the forces of the proletariat for the struggle for the final revolutionary overthrow." Similarly, he argued on his other flank, against the Boycottists and the Otzovists in 1906 and the " 'Left' Communists" in 1920, that reforms wrung from the existing system were good and would lead to revolution: "Semivictories in revolutions, those forced, hasty concessions on the part of the old regime, are the surest token of new, far more decisive, sharper civil disturbances which will involve broader and broader masses of the people." [21]

Twentieth-century revolutionaries, however, have become increasingly dubious about Lenin's modified catalyst theory of reform. The failure of Marxist expectations in the developed societies of the West has made it difficult to believe that revolutionaries can

21. Lenin, quoted in Bertram D. Wolfe, *Three Who Made a Revolution* (Boston, Beacon Press, 1955), p. 120, and in Alfred G. Meyer, *Leninism* (Cambridge, Harvard University Press, 1957), p. 73. See below, p. 377, for Lenin's somewhat different evaluation of land reforms.

have reforms and their revolution also. The traditional revolutionary orthodoxy has declined, and acceptance of the substitute theory divided its former supporters between those who follow the path of Bernstein and those who follow the path of Mao.

Social scientists—like social revolutionaries—cannot have it both ways. If the substitute theory is generally right, the catalyst theory is generally wrong, and vice versa. More probably, one is right under some conditions and the other is right under other conditions. The relevant conditions include the *prerequisites* for reform and revolution and the *consequences* of reform for revolution. Undoubtedly, the single most important connection between reform and revolution is that the centralization of power in the political system appears to be a precondition for both. The centralization of power, particularly in a system where there is little power, is, as we have pointed out, an essential prerequisite for policy innovation and reform. It is also a prerequisite for revolution. At least in the early stages of modernization, the vulnerability of a regime to revolution varies directly with the capability of the regime for reform.

The dilemma which confronts the modernizing monarch in a traditional political system is only the clearest manifestation of a more pervasive characteristic of polities undergoing political change. In the eighteenth century, the physiocrat Letronne argued that: "The present situation in France is vastly superior to that of England, for here reforms changing the whole social structure can be put through in the twinkling of an eye, whereas in England such reforms can always be blocked by the system of party government." [22] But the same conditions which made reform easy in France also made revolution possible, and "the system of party government" which obstructed reform in England also protected it against revolution. So also, in 1861, Alexander II successfully decreed the abolition of serfdom, while the simultaneous accomplishment of the comparable reform in the United States required four years of bloody conflict. Yet the same centralized power which made possible the Russian reforms of the 1860s also made possible the revolutions of 1917.

More generally, as we have seen, centralized traditional systems, and particularly bureaucratic empires such as the Manchu, Ro-

22. Quoted in de Tocqueville, pp. 161–62.

manov, and Ottoman, are most likely to end in revolution. In these societies the monarch monopolizes legitimacy, and the system is thus unable to adapt peacefully to the expansion of political power and the emergence of other sources of social initiative and political authority. The emergence of such sources requires the overthrow of the system. In countries, on the other hand, with more complex and dispersed political systems, with vigorous local government, with autonomous states or provinces, the path of reform and the probability of revolution are both more uncertain. Social forces opposed to the groups dominating the central government may still control regional and local governments and thus will be identified with some elements of the existing political system instead of alienated from the entire system. "If anything definitive can be said about political revolutions," argues Tannenbaum, "it is that they do not and cannot take place in countries where political strength is dispersed in a thousand places, and where myriads of men feel personally involved in the continuing problems of a self-governing parish or township and participate in making the rules for the larger unit, county, state or nation." [23]

The dependence of both reform and revolution on centralized power often makes for a dramatic race between the two. In these circumstances, the effects of reform on the probability of revolution may depend upon the nature of the reforms, the composition of the revolutionaries, and the timing of the reforms. Policy reforms, for instance, may make revolution more likely, because they arouse expectations of further gain at the same time that they imply weakness in the existing regime. Leadership reforms, on the other hand, may drain away the dynamic elements in the revolutionary movement and join them to the Establishment, thereby making revolution less likely. The differences in political stability between Great Britain, on the one hand, and France and Germany, on the other, may, in some measure, be related to these differing patterns of reform. [24] In addition, some policy reforms (but not others) and some leadership reforms (but not others) may tend to divide the revolutionary forces, to moderate their

23. Frank Tannenbaum, "On Political Stability," *Political Science Quarterly*, 75 (June 1960), 169.

24. See Seymour Martin Lipset, "Democracy and the Social System," in Harry Eckstein, ed., *Internal War* (New York, The Free Press, 1964), pp. 296–302; de Tocqueville, pp. 81–96.

fervor, to reduce their appeal to potential allies, and to rally to the forces of reform groups which will oppose further concessions to the revolutionary forces. In particular, reforms can themselves alter the balance of power among the various revolutionary groups opposed to the existing order. Reforms in response to the demands of the more moderate revolutionary leaders strengthen those leaders and their policies in relation to the more extremist revolutionaries. Reforms in response to violence and direct action sponsored by radical groups within the revolutionary movement strengthen these leaders and persuade others of the correctness of their tactics and goals. For the governments in many modernizing countries, however, these are often precisely the preconditions necessary for reform. The governments are too weak, too apathetic, too conservative, or too blind to the divisions within the revolutionary movement to produce reforms which will have the effect of strengthening the moderate tendencies in that movement. Instead, riots, demonstrations, and violence are necessary to spur them to action; in these circumstances reform is only an incentive, as Lenin suggested, to more riots, demonstrations, and violence.

The timing of reforms may also be important in a more general sense. Counterelites, Lasswell and Kaplan have suggested, are more likely to make revolutionary demands in their phases of minimal power and of maximal power.[25] In the former phase, they have little incentive to accept reforms and concessions because the latter are so small in comparison to their aspirations for the total reconstruction of society. In the latter phase, on the other hand, their willingness to accept reforms or concessions is small because of their closeness to the acquisition of total power: they are in a position to demand unconditional surrender. With intermediate power, however, the counterelite may be interested in acceptance into the existing power structure. Its members may well want to share in the rule—to achieve some gains immediately— rather than to hold to the hope of overthrowing the entire system. Leadership reforms, consequently, may well be effective in this phase while they may be futile when the revolutionaries are either markedly weaker or markedly stronger.

More specifically, the effects of reforms on the probability of revolution depend on the social composition of the groups de-

---

25. Lasswell and Kaplan, p. 267.

manding change and the nature of the aspirations of those groups. The two critical groups are the urban middle-class intelligentsia and the peasantry. These groups and their demands differ fundamentally. As a result, reforms directed at the urban middle class are a catalyst of revolution: reforms directed at the peasantry are a substitute for revolution.

The Urban Intelligentsia: Reform as a Catalyst

The opposition of the urban intelligentsia to the government is a pervasive characteristic not only of praetorian societies, but of almost every type of modernizing society. In praetorian societies students are typically the most active and important civilian middle-class political force. In non-praetorian societies, their opportunities for political action are restricted by the strength of the political institutions and the prevailing concepts of legitimacy. Their attitudes and values, however, fall into the same oppositional syndrome which exists in the praetorian societies. In traditional political systems the university in the capital city is typically the center of hostile attitudes and plotting against the regime. In Iran and Ethiopia, Teheran and Haile Selassie Universities are the principal centers of anti-monarchial sentiments. The cities in Morocco and Libya have been disrupted by student riots and demonstrations. At the opposite extreme, in communist political systems, the universities have also been centers of criticism and opposition to the regime. In the Soviet Union, in China, in Poland, and elsewhere in eastern Europe, the voice of the student is the voice of dissent: in these cases less dissent from the ideological premises of society than from the political institutions and practices of government.[26] In the independent states of Africa— but apparently particularly in the former French colonies—students have also been frequent opponents of the regime.

The student opposition to government represents the extreme middle-class syndrome of opposition because it is so constant. Student opposition can only be marginally influenced by reforms or ameliorative government actions. It exists virtually independent of the nature of the government in the society and of the nature of the policies which the government pursues. In Korea, for instance,

26. See Seymour Martin Lipset's summary, "University Students and Politics in Underdeveloped Countries," in Lipset, ed., "Special Issue on Student Politics," *Comparative Education Review, 10* (June 1966), 132 ff.

the growing number of students in Seoul became the center of opposition to the Syngman Rhee regime in the late 1950s. Student
demonstrations and riots in April 1960 started the chain of events
which led to the overthrow of the Rhee dictatorship. This regime
was replaced by the liberal government of John Chang, which in
its goals, policies, leadership, and sources of support represented
virtually everything the students had demanded. A few months
after the Chang government came to office, however, it too was
rocked by student demonstrations, and a survey of student attitudes indicated that less than four per cent of Korean students
gave their full support to the government.[27] Six months later,
when the Chang regime was ousted by the military, student opposition almost immediately manifested itself against the new government headed by General Pak. In the following years, on the
anniversary of the "April Revolution" against Rhee and frequently at other times also, the Pak regime was confronted by massive riots and demonstrations on the part of the college and university students in Seoul. Authoritarian dictatorship, liberal democracy, military rule, party government: the Korean students
opposed them all.

Similar patterns are found in other societies. In 1957, Colombian students played a key role in overturning the dictatorship
of Rojas Pinilla and making possible a return to electoral democracy. A few years later, however, 90 per cent of the students at
Bogotá National University said that they had no confidence in the
political system and in the social values of the government. Countries which have turned communist are similar. The University of
Havana was the center of opposition to Batista; it became the
center of opposition to Castro. In 1920 Peking University was the
birthplace of the Chinese Nationalist movement and of the Chinese
Communist party; in 1966 it was, according to the Central Committee of that party, "a stubborn stronghold of reaction." [28] In
some modernizing countries support for the government comes
primarily from the wealthy classes, in other countries primarily
from the masses of the poor. In some countries, the government
appeals to the more modern elements, in others it relies on the

27. Henderson, *Korea: The Politics of the Vortex*, p. 181.

28. John P. Harrison, "The Role of the Intellectual in Fomenting Change: The
University," in TePaske and Fisher, eds., *Explosive Forces in Latin America*, p. 33;
Red Flag, quoted in *Boston Globe*, July 5, 1966, p. 14.

backing of traditional groups. In some countries, governmental support is organized through bureaucratic structures, in others through associational or ascriptive groupings. But in virtually all modernizing countries no government can count for long on support from the intellectual community. If there is any cleavage which is virtually universal in modernizing countries, it is the cleavage between government and university. If the presidential palace is the symbol of authority, the student union building is the symbol of revolt.

This pattern of urban middle-class, intelligentsia, and student opposition suggests that it is the sort which reforms will not moderate and may well exacerbate. This opposition does not stem, in most cases, from any material insufficiency. It is an opposition which stems instead from psychological insecurity, personal alienation and guilt, and an overriding need for a secure sense of identity. The urban middle class wants national dignity, a sense of progress, a national purpose, and the opportunity for fulfillment through participation in the overall reconstruction of society. These are utopian goals. They are demands which no government can really ever meet. Consequently these elements of the urban middle class cannot be appeased by reforms. They are indeed, in most cases, vigorously opposed to reforms, which they tend to view as a sop in lieu of a change. This may in fact often be the case, but there is also another side to the issue. For if the cry of reform may become an excuse for incomplete action, the demand for revolution often is the excuse for complete inaction. Latin American coffeehouses and bars are filled with intellectuals who dismiss with disdain opportunities to improve their societies because the proposed changes are not fundamental, revolutionary, or, to use their favorite phrase, structural in character.

The student, in particular, becomes exposed to the modern world and to the advanced nations of the West. In his mind two great gaps exist, one between the principles of modernity—equality, justice, community, economic well-being—and their realization in his own society, and a second between the actual conditions which exist in the advance nations of the world and those prevailing in his own society. "In all countries, of course," Lipset has written, "reality is usually at variance with principles, and young persons, especially those who have been indulged in adolescence, . . . feel this strongly. Educated young people everywhere, consequently tend disproportionately to support idealistic movements which take the ideologies of the adult world more seriously than does the adult world itself." [29] The student thus becomes ashamed of and alienated from his own society; he becomes filled with the desire to reconstruct it completely to bring it into "the front rank of nations." Divorced from his family and from traditional norms and behavior patterns, the student identifies all the more completely with the abstract standards and principles of modernity. These become the absolute standards by which he judges his own society. No goal is sufficient short of the total reconstruction of society.

The modernizing efforts of students and intellectuals in nineteenth-century Russia are, in many respects, a prototype for their twentieth-century counterparts in Asia, Africa, and Latin America. The behavior of the Russian intellectuals also neatly illustrates how reform can be the catalyst of more radical extremism. The "Great Reforms" of Alexander II directly stimulated revolutionary organization and revolutionary activity by students and other members of the intelligentsia. In response to student disorders in the late 1850s Alexander followed a policy of leniency and liberalizing concessions. Discontent simply increased, however, reaching its peak in the years immediately after the abolition of serfdom and culminating in the attempt to assassinate Alexander in 1866. The "modest extension of freedom permitted by the new Tsar," Mosse notes, "inevitably produced a pressing demand for more. Restraints accepted almost without murmur under Nicholas were suddenly felt to be irksome; the public, hitherto largely excluded from state affairs, now protested that the relative freedom given by Alexander was inadequate." [30] In some measure, the Russian revolutionary movement in the latter half of the nineteenth century was the product of the "Great Reforms" by Alexander in the middle of the century.

In somewhat similar fashion, in many countries the revolutions of 1848 followed hard upon efforts of governments to inaugurate reforms designed to meet some at least of the demands of the

29. Lipset, pp. 140–41.
30. Mosse, *Alexander II and the Modernization of Russia,* pp. 125–26; Franco Venturi, *Roots of Revolution* (New York, Grosset and Dunlap, 1966), pp. 222–26; Michael Karpovich, *Imperial Russia, 1801–1917* (New York, Holt, Rinehart and Winston, 1932), p. 46.

middle class. In the Papal territories, for instance, Pius IX between 1846 and 1848 extended freedom of the press, established a municipal government for the city of Rome, modernized provincial administration, created a consultative assembly, and brought into existence a Civil Guard, "thereby arming the middle class whose demand of reform was strongest." Pius's reforms, however, did not satisfy the middle-class elements; revolution broke out; the Civil Guard sided with the insurgents; and Pius was forced to flee to Naples.[31]

In a completely different situation in the twentieth century, the Reid Cabral government in the Dominican Republic was overthrown by an urban middle-class insurrection just after it began to inaugurate a number of reforms. These included the revitalization of the economy, the expansion of political liberties, the reduction of corruption, the enforcement of austerity measures, the scheduling of elections and the purge of "some of the most oppressive and corrupt elements from the armed forces." Yet it was "precisely at this moment of moderate upswing and slow, gradual improvement that the revolution of April, 1965, broke out; and it seems ironic that Reid was ousted at least partially because of the reforms he began to carry out."[32]

Programs catering to the demands of the radical middle class only increase the strength and radicalism of that class. They are unlikely to reduce its revolutionary proclivities. For the government interested in the maintenance of political stability, the appropriate response to middle-class radicalism is repression, not reform. Measures which reduce the numbers, strength, and coherence of the radical elements of this class contribute significantly to the maintenance of political order. Governmental actions designed to restrict the development of universities may well reduce the influence of revolutionary groupings. On the other hand, programs designed to provide benefits to students will not lessen their revolutionary tendencies. They may, indeed, simply intensify the latent guilt feelings which frequently exist among middle- and upper-class students and thus intensify oppositional tendencies.

31. Nicholas S. Timasheff, *War and Revolution* (New York, Sheed and Ward, 1965), pp. 179–80.

32. Howard J. Wiarda, "The Context of United States Policy toward the Dominican Republic: Background to the Revolution of 1965" (unpublished paper, Harvard University, Center for International Affairs, 1966), pp. 30–31.

The National University of Bogotá, for instance, was a center of political agitation and antigovernment and anti-American activity. In the mid-1960s the university inaugurated, with substantial AID assistance, a broad program to reduce this discontent. Included in the program were the "provision of better dormitory and other facilities, enlargement of the faculty and revision of the curriculum." [33] Such reforms, however, are likely to facilitate and to encourage student political agitation. In terms of political stability, the Ethiopian government followed a wiser course when in 1962 and 1963 it closed dormitories at Haile Selassie University and thus compelled many students to return home.

The Peasantry: Reform as a Substitute

Someone once said that the glory of the British Navy was that its men never mutinied, or at least hardly ever mutinied, except for higher pay. Much the same can be said of peasants. They become revolutionary when their conditions of land ownership, tenancy, labor, taxes, and prices become in their eyes unbearable. Throughout history peasant revolts and jacquieries have typically aimed at the elimination of specific evils or abuses. In Russia as well as elsewhere they were almost invariably directed at the local landlords and officials, not at the authority of tsar or church nor at the overall structure of the political or social systems. In many instances, the economic conditions of the peasantry drastically declined shortly before the outbreak of the revolution. The unrest of the 1780s in rural France, Palmer observes, "was due not merely to poverty but to a sense of pauperization." [34] The economic depression of 1789 aggravated these conditions, and the price of bread reached its highest point in a hundred years. These material sufferings combined with the political opportunity opened by the calling of the Estates General furnished the fuel and the draft for the peasant explosion. Peasant action in all the great revolutions was directed primarily to the prompt, direct, and, if necessary, violent rectification of the immediate material conditions which had become intolerable. Revolutionary intellectuals proclaim the death of the old order and the birth of a new society; revolutionary peasants kill the tax collector and seize the land.

33. Eugene B. Mihaly and Joan M. Nelson, "Political Development and U. S. Economic Assistance" (unpublished paper, 1966), p. 8.
34. Palmer, *1*, 482.

The material basis of peasant dissatisfaction is of crucial importance in providing an alternative to revolution. No government can hope to satisfy the demands of rioting students. But a government can, if it is so minded, significantly affect the conditions in the countryside so as to reduce the propensity of peasants to revolt. While reforms may be the catalyst of revolution in the cities, they may be a substitute for revolution in the countryside.

The material sources of peasant unrest help to explain the conflicting images of peasant behavior. The urban middle-class intellectual has aspirations which can never be realized and he hence exists in a state of permanent volatility. There is no mistaking his role. The peasantry, on the other hand, may be the bulwark of the status quo or the shock troops of revolution. Which role the peasant plays is determined by the extent to which the existing system meets his immediate economic and material needs as he sees them. These needs normally focus on land tenure and tenancy, taxes, and prices. Where the conditions of land-ownership are equitable and provide a viable living for the peasant, revolution is unlikely. Where they are inequitable and where the peasant lives in poverty and suffering, revolution is likely, if not inevitable, unless the government takes prompt measures to remedy these conditions. No social group is more conservative than a landowning peasantry, and none is more revolutionary than a peasantry which owns too little land or pays too high a rental. The stability of government in modernizing countries is thus, in some measure, dependent upon its ability to promote reform in the countryside.[35]

Intellectuals are alienated; peasants are dissatisfied. The goals of intellectuals, consequently, tend to be diffuse and utopian; those

35. The phrases "land reform" and "agrarian reform" can be distinguished by "what" and "how." In terms of substance or "what," the phrase "land reform" will be used to refer to the redistribution of land ownership and hence of income from land. Agrarian reform refers to improvements in farming techniques, farm equipment, fertilizers, soil conservation, crop rotation, irrigation, and marketing which have the effect of increasing agricultural productivity and efficiency. The principal focus here will be on land reform, since it is most directly related to political stability. Agrarian reform without land reform, indeed, may increase economic productivity and rural instability. Land reform without agrarian reform may increase political stability and decrease agricultural production. In terms of "how," the phrase "land reform" when used without other qualification will mean changes in land tenure brought about by methods short of revolution. Since all revolutions also produce changes in land tenure, these latter will be referred to as "land reform by revolution" to distinguish them from land reform through more peaceful means.

of peasants concrete and redistributive. This latter characteristic makes peasants potential revolutionaries: the landlord must be dispossessed if the peasant is to be benefited. The situation is a zero-sum conflict; what one loses the other gains. On the other hand, the fact that peasant goals are concrete means that if the government is strong enough to compel some redistribution of land, such action will immunize the peasant against revolution. Material concessions to the middle-class intellectual foster resentment and guilt feelings; material concessions to peasants create satisfaction. Land reform carried out by revolution or by other means thus turns the peasantry from a potential source of revolution into a fundamentally conservative social force.

Land reform in Japan after World War II inured Japanese peasants to the appeals of socialism and made them the strongest and most loyal supporters of the conservative parties. In Korea the American-sponsored distribution of formerly Japanese lands in 1947 and 1948 "did much to reduce rural instability, undermine Communist influence, actual or potential, among the peasants, increase their cooperation with the election process, and arouse expectation, later fulfilled, that Korean landlord-held lands would be disposed of similarly." In India the immediate post-independence land reforms by the Congress Party made "the land owners and landed peasants seem more likely to play a role akin to their post-revolutionary French than to their Russian or Chinese counterparts, providing a broad base of small proprietors who have a vested interest in the present system rather than a source for exploitation for rapid industrialization." In Mexico the land reforms following the Revolution were a major source of the political stability which prevailed in that country after the 1930s. In Bolivia the land reforms carried out after 1952 made the peasants into a fundamentally conservative force supporting the government in its struggles with revolutionary groups. "The reform," as one study noted, "despite its initial revolutionary excesses, has not tended to promote the Communization of the country. It appears rather that the peasantry, whose possession of land now gives them a stake in the prosperity and stability of the state, serves as a check on the more radically-minded workers." On occasion the Bolivian government mobilized armed peasants to suppress urban uprisings and violence. In Venezuela as in Mexico and Bolivia land reform made the political climate "more conservative" and increased "the political influence of a basically conservative sector of the population." [36]

That land reform could have this conservatizing effect was foreseen by Lenin in his comments on the changes which Stolypin attempted to make in Russian land tenure between 1906 and 1911. Stolypin's goal was to reduce the role of the peasant commune or *mir*, to promote individual land ownership, and to bring into existence a class of satisfied peasant proprietors who would provide a stable source of support for the monarchy. "Individual ownership," Stolypin argued, ". . . is the guaranty of order, because the small proprietor is the basis on which stable conditions in the state can rest." [37] Lenin directly challenged those revolutionaries who argued that these reforms would be meaningless. The Stolypin Constitution and the Stolypin agrarian policy, he declared in 1908,

> mark a new phase in the breakdown of the old semi-feudal system of tsarism, a new movement toward its transformation into a middle-class monarchy. . . . If this should continue for very long periods of time . . . it might force us to renounce any agrarian program at all. It would be empty and stupid democratic phrase-mongering to say that the success of such a policy in Russia is "impossible." It is possible! If Stolypin's policy is continued . . . then the agrarian structure of Russia will become completely bourgeois, the stronger peasants will acquire almost all the allotments of land, agriculture will become capitalistic, and any "solution" of the agrarian problem—radical or otherwise—will become impossible under capitalism.

Lenin had good reason to be worried. Between 1907 and 1914, as a result of the Stolypin reforms, some 2,000,000 peasants with-

36. For these quotations, see respectively, Henderson, pp. 156–57; Lloyd I. Rudolph and Susanne Hoeber Rudolph, "Toward Political Stability in Underdeveloped Countries: The Case of India," *Public Policy* (Cambridge, Graduate School of Public Administration, 1959), *9*, 166; Royal Institute of International Affairs, *Agrarian Reform in Latin America* (London, Oxford University Press, 1962), p. 14; Charles J. Erasmus, "A Comparative Study of Agrarian Reform in Venezuela, Bolivia, and Mexico," in Dwight B. Heath, Charles J. Erasmus, Hans C. Buechler, *Land Reform and Social Revolution in Bolivia* (unpublished manuscript, University of Wisconsin, Land Tenure Center, 1966), pp. 708–09.

37. Stolypin, quoted in William Henry Chamberlin, "The Ordeal of the Russian Peasantry," *Russian Review, 14* (October 1955), 297.

drew from the *mir* and became individual proprietors. By 1916, 6,200,000 families, out of about 16,000,000 eligible families had applied for separation; in 1915 about half the peasants in European Russia had a hereditary tenure in land. Lenin, as Bertram Wolfe observes, "saw the matter as a race with time between Stolypin's reforms, and the next upheaval. Should an upheaval be postponed for a couple of decades, the new land measures would so transform the countryside that it would no longer be a revolutionary force. . . . 'I do not expect to live to see the revolution,' said Lenin several times toward the close of the Stolypin period." [38] That this expectation turned out to be incorrect was in some measure due to the assassin's bullet which felled Stolypin in September 1911.

Land reform, it would appear, thus has a highly stabilizing effect on the political system. Like any reform, however, some violence may be necessary to produce the reform, and the reform itself may produce some violence. The emancipation of the serfs, for instance, stimulated some local uprisings and acts of insubordination in rural Russia. Unlike the reform-stimulated extremism of the intelligentsia, however, this violence decreased rapidly with time. In 1861, when the emancipation edict was issued, acts of insubordination occurred on 1,186 properties. In 1862 only 400 properties were affected by insubordination and in 1863 only 386. By 1864 the disorders produced by the reform had been virtually eliminated.[39] This sequence of a sharp but limited and brief rise in violence and disorder followed by a steady decline and relatively early return to tranquility appears to be the typical pattern produced by land reforms. Land reform, as Carroll has remarked, "when seriously undertaken is an explosive and unpredictable business, but may be much more explosive when left undone." [40] In terms of political stability, the costs of land reform are minor and temporary, the gains fundamental and lasting.

The advantages and disadvantages of land reform in terms of other criteria are not perhaps so clear-cut. The immediate impact of land reform, particularly land reform by revolution, is usually

38. Quotations and data from Wolfe, pp. 360–61.

39. Mosse, p. 60; Jerome Blum, *Lord and Peasant in Russia* (Princeton, Princeton University Press, 1961), p. 592.

40. Thomas F. Carroll, "Land Reform as an Explosive Force in Latin America," in TePaske and Fisher, p. 84.

to reduce agricultural productivity and production. In the longer run, however, both usually tend to increase. After the Bolivian land reform of 1953 the new peasant owners apparently felt no incentive to produce more food than they could consume and agricultural production dropped seriously, rising again in the 1960s. In Mexico, agricultural productivity also dropped immediately after the revolution but subsequently rose, and during the 1940s Mexico had the highest agricultural growth rate in Latin America.

The economic argument for land reform is, of course, that it gives the individual farmer a direct economic interest in the efficient use of his land and thus tends to increase both agricultural productivity and agricultural production. Clearly, however, land reform by itself will not necessarily produce economic benefits. It has to be supplemented by various other types of agrarian reforms designed to facilitate the efficient use of land. So long as the bulk of the population of a country is on the land, obviously the growth of industry will in large part reflect the ability of that population to consume the products of industry. By creating a class of small proprietors and thus significantly raising the median income level in the rural areas, land reform, it is said, enlarges the domestic market and hence creates additional incentives for industrial development. It can, on the other hand, also be argued that insofar as land reform reduces the average size of the agricultural unit, it tends also to reduce the possibilities for large-scale efficiency in agricultural production, and this has a restraining effect on economic growth as a whole.

In some measure land reform probably does contribute to economic development as well as to social welfare and political stability. As with other aspects of modernization, however, these goals may at times conflict with each other. In Egypt, for instance, the land reform of 1952 was designed to produce fundamental social changes in the countryside and to be "a lever in the overthrow of the former ruling class." In the years after the reform many improvements took place in the welfare of the rural population, and the agricultural production index rose from 105 in 1951 (1935–39 = 100) to 131 in 1958. These ends, however, were achieved at a cost of the social goals. The reform "evolved into a useful instrument for the fulfillment of the Five Year Plan; and in the process the original conception of reform as a broad measure of income redistribution had evaporated. The authentic social impetus had been overlaid by the drive for economic efficiency." Despite the reform's technical achievements, the hopes of the peasants "had been disappointed by the small scale of redistribution and cynicism fostered by evasion of rent control." [41] In order to restore the revolutionary impetus and the social goals of land reform, a new law was passed in 1961 further restricting the acreage which landlords might retain and tightening up other provisions of the old law. The purpose of the law, Nasser declared, was to complete the suppression of feudalism, and the law was one element in the significant turn to the left which the Nasser regime took at that time. Five years later, in 1966, the attack on the "feudalists" was again pressed with a new drive to enforce the law more rigorously. This Egyptian experience suggests that insofar as the implementation of land reform is left to the bureaucracy, economic and technical goals tend to achieve preeminence over political and social ones. To keep the latter to the forefront, the political leadership has to act periodically through political processes to give renewed impetus to the reform.

THE POLITICS OF LAND REFORM

Patterns of land tenure obviously vary greatly from country to country and from region to region. In general, in Latin America, a relatively small number of latifundia have encompassed a large proportion of the total farm land while a large number of minifundia covered a small proportion of the total farm land. Neither large estate nor small plot has been typically farmed efficiently, and, of course, the disparity in income between the owner of one and the owner of the other has been very great. In Asia land ownership typically has not been as concentrated as in Latin America, but tenancy, absentee landlordism, and high population densities have been more prevalent. Near Eastern countries have been characterized by a high concentration of land ownership in some instances (Iraq, Iran) and by high tenancy rates in others. With the exception of tropical Africa, in one form or another the objective conditions likely to give rise to peasant unrest are common in much of the modernizing world. If, as appears likely, modernization will in due course arouse peasant aspirations to the point where these conditions are no longer tolerable, then the

41. Doreen Warriner, *Land Reform and Development in the Middle East,* (2d ed. London, Oxford University Press, 1962) , pp. 208–09.

alternatives of revolution or land reform are very real ones for many political systems.

The saliency of land reform to politics in different countries is suggested by the data in Table 6.2. On the horizontal axis this table gives a rough idea of the importance of agriculture to a country's economy; on the vertical axis, it classifies countries by inequality in land distribution, the data for which are for different years for different countries and in some cases two different years for the same country. Underneath the names of most countries on the table are figures on farm tenancy and their date.

From these data it would appear that land reform is not a pressing issue in four types of countries. First, in countries which have reached a high level of economic development, agriculture has a relatively minor role, and consequently even highly inequitable patterns of land ownership do not pose substantial problems of social equality and political stability. Such is the case with virtually all the countries in the left-hand column of Table 6.2. Even in a country like Argentina, characterized by both great inequality in land ownership and a high tenancy rate, the land issue is relatively secondary since less than 30 per cent of the labor force is employed in agriculture. Italy also combines unequal ownership and high tenancy, but the problem there is, of course, largely concentrated in the southern region, and reasonably effective actions have been taken by the government to cope with it. For countries in this category land reform is only a secondary issue in politics.

Second, many countries have had or achieved long ago reasonably equitable patterns of land ownership. Many of the countries of western Europe in groups G and J fall into this category as well as into the first category of countries where agriculture is of minor importance in economic life. While accurate and comparable figures are not readily available, at least some modernizing countries not listed in the table may also fit this pattern, among them possibly Cyprus, Lebanon, Turkey, Thailand, and Indonesia.

A third category consists of those countries, mostly in tropical Africa, where traditional communal patterns of land ownership are just beginning to give way to individual proprietorship. These countries are, in a sense, one phase behind those other modernizing countries where traditional communal patterns of ownership, if they ever existed, were replaced some time ago by individual ownership and then by the concentration of ownership in rela-

TABLE 6.2. Vulnerability to Agrarian Unrest

Distribution of agricultural land: Gini Index of Inequality	*Percentage of labor force employed in agriculture*		
	0–29%	30–59%	60% and over
	A	**B**	**C**
	Australia-93(48) *	Mexico-96(30)	Bolivia-94(50)
	Argentina-86(52)	Chile-94(36)	20(50)
	33(52) **	13(55)	Iraq-88(58)
	Italy 80-(46)	Venezuela-91(56)	Peru-88(50)
	24(30)	21(50)	Guatemala-86(50)
		Costa Rica-89(50)	17(50)
		5(50)	Brazil-84(50)
.800 and over		Ecuador-86(54)	9(50)
		15(54)	El Salvador-83(50)
		Columbia-(86)60	15(50)
		12(60)	Egypt-81(52)
		Jamaica-82(43)	12(39)
		10(43)	
		Uruguay-82(50)	
		35(51)	
	D	**E**	**F**
	New Zealand-77(49)	Dominican Rep.-79(50)	Honduras-76(52)
	22(50)	21(50)	17(52)
	Puerto Rico-74(59)	Cuba-79(45)	Nicaragua-76(50)
	4(59)	54(45)	Libya-70(60)
.700–.799	United Kingdom-71(50)	Spain-78(29)	9(60)
	45(50)	44(50)	
	United States-71(50)	Greece-75(30)	
	20(59)	18(39)	
		Austria-74(51)	
		11(51)	
		Panama-74(61)	
		12(61)	
	G	**H**	**I**
	West Germany-67(49)	Mexico-69(60)	S. Vietnam-67(35)
	6(49)	Taiwan-65(30)	20(50)
	Norway-67(59)	40(48)	Egypt-67(64)
	8(50)	Finland-60(50)	Iran-65(60)
	Luxembourg-64(50)	2(50)	India-63(54)
	19(50)	Ireland-60(60)	53(31)
	Netherlands-61(50)	3(32)	W. Pakistan-61(60)
.500–.699	53(48)	Philippines-59(48)	India-59(61)
	Belgium-59(59)	37(48)	E. Pakistan-51(60)
	62(50)	Philippines-53(60)	
	France-58(48)		
	26(46)		
	Sweden-58(44)		
	19(44)		
	J	**K**	**L**
	Switzerland-49(39)	Japan-47(60)	Yugoslavia-44(50)
	19(44)	3(60)	
.499 and	Canada-49(31)	Taiwan-46(60)	
below	7(51)	Poland-45(60)	
	Denmark-46(59)		
	4(49)		

Source: Bruce M. Russett et al., *World Handbook of Political and Social Indicators* (New Haven, Yale University Press, 1964), Tables 50, 69, 70; Hung-chao Tai, "Land Reform in Developing Countries: Tenure Defects and Political Response" (Unpublished Paper, Harvard University, Center for International Affairs, 1967).

* Gini index and date.
** Farms on rented land as percentage of total farms and date.

tively few hands. Depending upon the nature of the processes of individualization of land, these African countries may avoid the problems of its inequitable distribution which now plague so many other modernizing countries.

A final, fourth category of countries where land reform is not a salient problem includes those where effective, thoroughgoing reforms have been carried out by revolution or otherwise in recent years. These include all the communist countries which have collectivized agriculture plus Poland and Yugoslavia, which have created highly equitable patterns of individual land ownership. Among the noncommunist countries, the post-World War II reforms in Japan and Taiwan at least temporarily removed the land question as a major political issue. In some measure the same result has been obtained through revolution in Mexico and Bolivia, although the problems of the inefficiency of the *ejido* and tendencies toward the reconcentration of ownership continue to plague the former country.

In the remainder of the modernizing world, land reform has a high saliency to politics. Land reform problems, it may be predicted, are likely to be most critical in those seven countries in group C which combine high inequalities of land ownership with substantial agricultural labor forces. In 1950 Bolivia had what was probably the highest Gini index of inequality in land ownership in the world and also substantial tenancy; in 1952 Bolivia had its agrarian revolution. In 1958 Iraq also had a highly unequal pattern of land ownership; the same year a modernizing military junta overthrew the old regime and instituted a program of land reforms. In El Salvador and Peru, with similar inequality, reform governments, with the active support of the United States, made major efforts to introduce land reforms in 1961 and 1964. The governments of Guatemala and Brazil also attempted to inaugurate major land reforms in 1954 and 1964, respectively, only to be overthrown by military insurrections. In Egypt the Nasser reforms reduced the index from .81 in 1952 to .67 in 1964. In all six countries apart from Bolivia land reform remained a major issue in the mid-1960s.

Much the same was also true for the countries in groups B and F as well as for those other countries where 30 per cent or more of the labor force was employed in agriculture and where 20 per cent or more of the farms were on rented land (i.e. Dominican Republic, Cuba, Taiwan, Philippines, South Vietnam, and India). Significantly, two of these countries—Cuba and Taiwan—have carried out substantial reforms, Taiwan's index of inequality dropping from .65 in the 1930s to .46 in 1960. The remaining twenty countries with highly unequal ownership and/or high tenancy rates (groups B, C, and F minus Bolivia, plus the Dominican Republic, Spain, Philippines, South Vietnam and India) are presumably those countries on the chart where land reform is peculiarly relevant to politics. To these must also be added countries (such as Morocco, Syria, Ethiopia) for which no data on land ownership were available but either where land ownership is known to be highly inequitable or where land reform has been a major issue in politics. In all these countries, the long-run stability of the political system may well depend upon the ability of the government to carry through land reforms.

Under what conditions, then, does land reform become feasible? Like other reforms, changes in land tenure require the concentration and expansion of power in the political system. More specifically, they involve, first, the concentration of power in a new elite group committed to reform and, second, the mobilization of the peasantry and their organized participation in the implementation of the reforms. Analysts of land reform processes have at times attempted to distinguish "reform from above" from "reform from below." In actuality, however, a successful land reform involves action from both directions. The efficacy of land reform by revolution, of course, is that it does involve both elements: the rapid centralization of power in the revolutionary elite and the rapid mobilization into politics of the peasantry. In a case like Bolivia the peasants seize the land and organize themselves into national peasant leagues; the new governing elite enacts a land reform law confirming their rights and creating the administrative structures necessary for the implementation of the reforms.

If it is assumed that the traditional elite in the society is a landowning elite the initiative for reform from above must come from some new elite group which is able to displace the landed interests in the political system and arrogate to itself sufficient power to secure the adoption and implementation of land reform despite the opposition of substantial elements among the landowners. By its very nature land reform involves some element of confiscation.

This may take the form of the outright expropriation of the land by the state with no pretence of compensation, as in revolutions; or taking the land at its assessed value for tax purposes which is, of course, normally far below its market value; or providing compensation through bonds or other forms of deferred payment, whose value typically is drastically reduced by inflation and the instability of the government which makes the promises. The only real exceptions to partial or complete confiscation by one of these means occur in those lucky countries, like Venezuela or Iran, which are able to carry out what might be termed "land reform by petroleum" and provide substantial compensation to owners from their oil revenues. Except in these instances land reform means the forceful taking away of property from one group of people and giving it to another. It is precisely this character of land reform, which makes it the most meaningful—and the most difficult—of reforms for a modernizing government.

The willingness of landowners to lose their property through land reforms short of revolution varies directly with the extent to which the only alternative appears to be to lose it through revolution. In addition, the ability of the government to carry out land reforms may well vary directly with the degree of concentration of ownership. If land ownership is highly concentrated, a substantial amount of land can be made available for redistribution by the expropriation of a small, highly affluent minority which may well be able to afford the loss of the land. If, on the other hand, land reform requires the dispossession of a much larger class of medium-sized land owners or kulaks, the problems confronting the government are much greater.

Displacement of the traditional landholding elite may occur in a variety of ways and with new elite groups drawn from a variety of sources. In land reform by revolution, the peasant uprisings normally eliminate much of the landowning elite by violence and death or by fear and emigration. The radical intelligentsia of the city assumes the political leadership roles in the society, brings into existence new political institutions, and ratifies the actions of the peasants by land reform decrees. More land reform has taken place by revolution than by any other means.

The second most effective means of bringing about land reform is by foreign action. Foreigners, like revolutionaries, have no stake in the existing social order, and while the decrees of revolutionaries legitimate the actions of rebellious peasants, those of foreigners are themselves legitimated by their armies of occupation. In each case, reform is made possible by the intrusion of new elites and new masses into the formerly restricted political arena. The foreigners typically do not displace the traditional elite completely from positions of power but instead subordinate it either through colonial rule or through military occupation. Changes in land tenure under colonialism have usually involved the replacement of traditional communal ownership patterns by Western-style individual freeholds. As was pointed out previously, this frequently facilitates the concentration of land ownership in a relatively few hands. Only rarely, as was in part true with the United States in the Philippines in the 1930s, have colonial governments expressed much interest in securing a more equal ownership of land.

Such has not been the case with military occupation. After World War II the United States promoted in Japan one of the most effective land reforms of modern times. The percentage of tenants and tenant-owners (i.e. farmers renting 50 per cent or more of the lands they cultivate) was reduced from 43.5 to 11.7; the portion of farm income coming from rent, interest, and wages was reduced to less than 4 per cent; the landlords were compensated for their land at its 1938 value which, because of the drastic postwar inflation, amounted to virtual confiscation. In South Korea the American Military Government carried out one land reform involving the distribution of Japanese-owned land, and the ROK government then inaugurated a second one directed at Korean owners. In 1945 full or half tenants constituted 67.2 per cent of the total farm population; by 1954 they made up only 15.3 per cent of that population. As in Japan, the wealthy landowning class was virtually eliminated and a high degree of economic equality spread throughout the countryside. Paradoxically, the most comprehensive land reforms after World War II were produced either by communist revolution or by American military occupation.

A somewhat similar pattern was also followed in Taiwan. There the "occupying power" was the Chinese Nationalist elite which fled to the island after the Communist conquest of the mainland. The reform reduced tenant-cultivated land from 41.1 per cent of the total farm land in 1949 to 16.3 per cent in 1953 and significantly improved rents and security of tenants.[42] The participation of the peasants in the implementation of this program was encouraged by American advisors and supported by the Sino-American Joint Commission on Rural Reconstruction, financed from American sources.

In some instances land reforms may be inaugurated by traditional leaders working within the existing structures of authority. The prerequisite here is a high concentration of power within the traditional system. Typically an absolute monarch supported by elements from his bureaucracy attempts to impose reforms on a recalcitrant landowning aristocracy. Alexander II's emancipation of the serfs, Stolypin's reforms, and the Amini-Arsanjani reforms of 1961–62 in Iran are examples of changes imposed through traditional political institutions. These instances are the most extreme versions of "land reform from above," and consequently the major problem of such reforms is the mobilization of the peasantry for the sustained action and participation necessary to insure their success.

Other traditional systems lack not only the ability to mobilize power from below but also the capacity to concentrate for purposes of reform whatever limited power there is within the system. In these circumstances reform requires either a full-scale revolution or the overthrow of the traditional landlord-based regime by a modernizing military elite. The latter pattern is particularly typical of the Middle East, as exemplified in Egypt, Iraq, Pakistan, and, in part, Syria. The Egyptian case neatly illustrates many of the common features of agrarian development. Prior to the nineteenth century land was in large part owned by the state or by religious foundations. The modernizing reforms of Muhammed Ali, however, encouraged private ownership and the eventual concentration of landholdings in large estates. As a result, "a thin stratum of large landowners had become sharply differentiated from the mass of fellahs by the end of the century." [48] From World War I until 1952 the Egyptian parliament and the Egyptian government were

42. See Sidney Klein, *The Pattern of Land Tenure Reform in East Asia After World War II* (New York, Bookman, 1958), pp. 230, 250; R. P. Dore, *Land Reform in Japan* (New York, Oxford University Press, 1959).

43. Gabriel Baer, *A History of Landownership in Modern Egypt, 1800–1950* (London, Oxford University Press, 1962), pp. 13 ff. My discussion of Egypt is based primarily on this book.

dominated by the large landowning interests, the largest single landowner being the king himself. The peasants were quiescent, and the absence of an indigenous bourgeoisie and autonomous urban middle class meant that there were no other social groups which could challenge the landowners' dominance. Even extreme radical groups did not give an overriding role to the land reform issue. Egyptian Communists, for instance, endorsed the elimination of large estates, but "the agrarian question as a whole did not occupy an important place in their political and social struggle. Even during the 1940s, when Communist activity was legal, the principal Communist periodical, *al-Fajr al-Jadid*, hardly touched on it at all. Unlike most of the other parties, the Communists had no roots in the Egyptian villages." During the 1940s, however, other groups and reformers began to bring the land issue to the forefront of public consciousness. The military revolution of 1952, in turn, was preceded by what looked like the beginnings of a true agrarian revolution in the countryside. "In 1951, for the first time in modern Egyptian history, a number of rebellions broke out in which fellahs made common cause against their landlords." For the first time on any scale, the fellah resorted to land invasions and violence.[44] The military regime came to power in July 1952; in September it enacted a land reform law.

Finally, it is at least conceivable that land reforms may be introduced by the leadership of a political party which has won power through democratic means. Land reform measures have been passed by democratically elected governments in India, the Philippines, Venezuela, Chile, Peru, Colombia, and a few other countries. Land reform through democratic processes, however, is a long, frustrating, and often impossible task. Pluralistic politics and parliamentary rule are often incompatible with effective land reforms. In particular, a parliamentary system without a dominant party provides no means by which the modernizing elite can effectively displace the landowning conservatives. In modernizing countries, legislatures are more conservative than executives, and elected parliaments are usually dominated by landowning interests.

A basic incompatibility exists between parliaments and land reform. In Pakistan, for instance, land reform made no progress for a decade under the parliamentary regime but was swiftly adopted

44. Ibid., pp. 214–15, 220–22.

and implemented once General Ayub Khan assumed supreme power. In Iran, similarly, the great landowners dominated the Majlis. To make land reform into a reality, parliament had to be suspended and the reform issued by decree subsequently confirmed by a popular referendum. "Parliaments good or bad," growled reform prime minister Amini, "are an obstacle to reform." [45] In Egypt, as in Pakistan, land reform legislation got nowhere until the traditional regime with its king and its parliament was replaced by Nasser and his military elite. In Ethiopia the Land Reform Bill of 1963, proposed by the government, was defeated in the Senate.

Latin American legislatures have also traditionally been the graveyards of land reform measures. In the early 1960s the Brazilian Congress, for instance, consistently refused to pass the land reform measures recommended by President Goulart, and they were eventually issued by decree in 1964. At the same time in Ecuador, the congress "was unwilling to give serious consideration to the fundamental reforms urged by President Arosemena, such as tax revision and agrarian reform." [46] Similarly, the Peruvian Congress in the early 1960s refused to pass land reform legislation and thus willingly forfeited a $60 million loan from the United States, payment of which had been made conditional upon the passage of such legislation.[47] In Syria in the mid-1950s, the Ba'ath Party's relatively modest proposals for agrarian reform were stopped in the legislature which was dominated by landowning interests.

In Korea, the Interim Legislative Assembly which operated under the American military government in the 1940s failed to take action on land reform proposals. As a result, "After long KILA debate unproductive of satisfactory legislation, [General] Hodge had to issue a land reform ordinance unilaterally." Subsequently, after the Republic of Korea was established, the Assembly, in which landlords were a major influence, nonetheless passed a land-reform measure in order to assert its power against the executive. The bill was vetoed by President Rhee, but subsequently another bill was passed and approved by the President. In the Assembly,

45. Prime Minister Ali Amini, quoted in Donald N. Wilber, *Contemporary Iran* (New York, Praeger, 1963), p. 126.
46. Edwin Lieuwen, *Generals vs. Presidents*, pp. 47, 74–84.
47. Tad Szulc, *The Winds of Revolution* (New York, Praeger, 1964), pp. 182–83.

"Landlords were a dominant minority; their common interests were reflected in the land-reform and even the law on public officials." [48]

The tendency for landed elements to dominate the legislature in modernizing societies with electoral competition reflects the absence of effective political organizations. The bulk of the population is in the countryside, and hence the nature of the regime is determined by the nature of the electoral process in the countryside. In the absence of effective parties, peasant unions, or other political organizations, the crucial resources are economic wealth and social status, and the traditional elites capitalize upon their possession of these to secure election to the parliament in overwhelming numbers. In some instances, of course, the electoral procedures themselves help to insure this. In Brazil, Peru, and other Latin American countries parliamentary seats were apportioned on the basis of population but suffrage was limited to those who were literate. Consequently, a small number of upper-class rural voters controlled a large number of rural seats. On the other hand, in some Middle Eastern countries, almost the reverse situation has existed. Conservative, landowning groups pushed for the extension of suffrage to the illiterate peasants because of their confidence that their economic and social influence would control this vote and bring it into the political arena on their side.

Democratic governments are able to enact land reforms where there are vigorous and popular executive leadership and strong party organizations with a corporate interest in winning the peasant vote. In Venezuela Rómulo Betancourt plus the strong organization of the Acción Democrática and its close affiliation with the *campesino* unions resulted in the passage of a land reform law in 1960. Even under these favorable circumstances, however, parliament remained the major focus of opposition, and recourse had to be had to semi-extraparliamentary procedures. A nonparliamentary land reform commission was created which after extensive hearings, consultations, and investigation, drew up the proposed bill which was then submitted to the legislature and forced through by the government's majority with little or no significant change. "The Commission was, at the outset, an aggrega-

48. Gregory Henderson, "Korea: The Politics of the Vortex (Unpublished manuscript, Harvard University, Center for International Affairs, 1966), pp. 413, 425–26, 447.

tive body, comprised of representatives of all political parties and philosophies, and most Venezuelan interest groups concerned with agriculture. Thus it was that all political factions could be brought to a consensus on the final version of the Commission's proceedings." [49] In effect, the legislative process was performed in the more favorable environment of the land reform commission rather than in the less favorable environment of the legislature. The success of this land reform measure produced an active competition among the political parties appealing to the peasant on the land reform issue. "Vote-buying," as one Venezuelan agrarian reform official said, "is good politics. There is no better kind." [50] Somewhat similarly, the Colombian land reform law of 1961 was also drafted by an extraparliamentary commission; unlike the Venezuelan law, however, the bill also received extensive consideration and further amendments in the legislature.

In India land reform legislation was the product of the historical commitment of the Congress Party and its leadership. The first phase of the reforms, the elimination of the zamindars, moreover, was viewed as part of the process of independence. The land titles of the zamindars had been created by the British in the nineteenth century and hence their abolition could be held to be a necessary element in the completion of independence from British rule. Just as foreign rulers can, with relative ease, dispossess local landlords, so also local rulers can, with relative ease, dispossess foreign landlords or those whose property rights seem to stem from foreign sources (provided the foreign landlords cannot sponsor foreign intervention to restore those rights). Subsequently, however, land reform in India moved very slowly. It was within the jurisdiction of the state legislatures, and throughout the 1950s, with the notable exception of Uttar Pradesh, no state legislature enacted effective land reform legislation. Those laws which were enacted were often filled with substantial loopholes which made it difficult for the peasants to secure their rights and easy for the landlords to escape their obligations.

In the other principal democratic country in southern Asia, the Philippines, land reform suffered a similar and perhaps worse fate. The Hukbalahap rebellion and the dynamic leadership of Magsay-

---

49. John Duncan Powell, "The Politics of Agrarian Reform in Venezuela: History, System and Process" (Ph.D. thesis, University of Wisconsin, 1966), pp. 176–77.
50. Quoted in Erasmus, p. 725.

say induced the Philippine legislature to pass a land reform law in 1955. The law was, however, shot full of loopholes. Some suggestion of its ineffectiveness is perhaps furnished by the guarded comments of a 1962 UN report: "Even if the law were fully applied, the large area which landlords are allowed to retain would still maintain high tenancy rates. The provisions are in fact regarded as inadequate, and tenants tend to prefer good relationships with the landowning families to the benefits which they might obtain under the law." [51] The weakness of this law led President Macapagal to press for passage of another law in 1963.

In any political system enactment of effective land reforms requires some other elite group to break with the landed oligarchy and to support such legislation. In an authoritarian system either a monarch, a dictator, or a military junta must take the initiative in bringing about land reforms. In a democratic system with strong political parties, the leadership of the dominant party may play this role. In the absence of strong parties with a commitment to land reform, the enactment of such legislation normally requires a break in the ranks of the economic upper class and the support for land reform by industrialists, commercial interests, and "progressive" landowners. The passage of the Philippine land reform law of 1963, for instance, was made possible by industrial and middle-class groups who backed the legislation as a necessary element in a general program of economic development. President Macapagal, indeed, formulated his appeal for this measure designed to eliminate tenancy more in terms of its contributions to economic development than in terms of its contribution to social justice. The bill still met substantial resistance in the legislature, but was eventually passed. "Congressional resistance to changes in the land tenure pattern," it was observed, "has weakened as new industrial groups have come to share power with the landed interests." [52]

A similar pattern has manifested itself in Latin America. Differences between industrialists and "progressive farm owners and operators," on the one hand, and the "semi-feudal" landowners, on the other, facilitated passage of the Colombian land reform law of 1961. In Peru a similar division helped passage of the land reform bill of 1964. In the Brazilian state of São Paulo the agrarian

51. United Nations, Department of Economic and Social Affairs, *Progress in Land Reform: Third Report* (United Nations, 1962), p. 22.

52. Jean Grossholtz, *Politics in the Philippines* (Boston, Little Brown, 1964), p. 71.

transformation law of 1961 was in part the result of the fact that "the new middle and upper classes in the city can have a strong influence on land policies." [53] In the absence of a strong political organization capable of forcing through land reform legislation despite the opposition of the landowning group, it would appear that industrial and commercial leaders may be necessary partners in securing the approval of land reform legislation.

"In the beginning of any undertaking," Mustafa Kemal once said, "there is a need to go from above downward; not from below upward." Many students of land reform argue to the contrary that reform can only be inaugurated by the positive action and demands of the peasantry. In actuality, however, so far as the inauguration of land reforms is concerned, neither extreme position would seem to be correct. Land reforms may result from the initiative of either governmental elite or peasant mass. Short of revolution, rural unrest and violence and the organization of peasant leagues capable of making effective and coordinated demands on the government usually serve to hasten land reform legislation. The Hukbalahap rebellion of the late 1940s and early 1950s made possible the Philippine law of 1955. Peasant land seizures in the Cuzco area and the growth in strength of peasant organizations helped the passage of the Peruvian land reform law of 1964. In Venezuela land invasions in the late 1950s eased the passage of a land reform law in 1960. In Colombia the agrarian reform law which was passed in the 1930s was, like the typical action of revolutionary governments, primarily designed to legitimize peasant land seizures which had already occurred. The formation of national peasant organizations in Chile and Brazil in 1961 gave an impetus to those elements in both governments interested in pushing reform.

On the other hand, land reform is not only the result of push from below. In most countries, tenants and landless peasants lack the skills and the organization to make themselves an effective political force. They are more likely to take advantage of the weakness of government and to attempt to seize land for themselves than they are likely to take advantage of the strength of government and to attempt to induce political leaders to use governmental power on their behalf. Even in a country like the Philippines, the poor farmers and tenants lacked effective organization

53. Hirschmann, pp. 155–56; Carroll, pp. 107–08.

in the early 1960s and played little role in securing passage of the 1963 land reform law. As a result, in many instances elite elements may take the initiative in dealing with land reform in the absence of any immediate peasant demand, but in anticipation of future demands. In Colombia, in the early 1960s the "social group which stood to benefit most from the law—Colombia's small tenant farmers, sharecroppers, minifundio holders and landless laborers —took only a small and indirect part in its adoption." Some land invasions did occur, but only on a relatively small scale. In Venezuela the ideological commitment and political leadership of Betancourt were the necessary complement to the mild land invasions. In Iran there was no peasant violence or extra legal activity at all. In this case, like Colombia, the leaders pushing reform were more concerned about the possible major violence in the future than actual minor violence in the past. "I do not wish to be a prophet of doom," one Colombian legislator declared: "but if the next Congress fails to produce an Agrarian Reform, revolution will be inevitable." "Divide your lands or face revolution—or death," Prime Minister Amini warned the Iranian elite.[54]

"Land reform," Neale has observed, "does not make new men of peasants. New men make land reforms." [55] In the absence of revolution, the new men are initially usually from the non-peasant classes. The effectiveness of land reform, however it is initiated, nonetheless depends upon the active and eventually organized participation of the peasants. Mobilization of peasants is not necessary to start land reform, but land reform, to be successful, must stimulate the mobilization and organization of the peasants. Reform laws only become effective when they are institutionalized in organizations committed to making them effective. Two organizational links between government and peasants are necessary if land reform is to become a reality.

First, in almost all cases, the government has to create a new and adequately financed administrative organization well-staffed with expert talent committed to the cause of reform. In most countries where land reform is a crucial issue, the Ministry of Agriculture is a weak, lethargic entity, with little commitment to modernization

54. Hirschman, pp. 142, 157; Prime Minister Amini, quoted by Jay Walz, *New York Times*, May 30, 1961, p. 2.

55. Walter C. Neale, *Economic Change in Rural India* (New Haven, Yale University Press, 1962) , p. 258.

and reform, and often quite subservient to the established agricultural interests. An indifferent bureaucracy can make reform a nullity. The failure of land reform in several districts in India, for instance, was ascribed in one survey to two causes: "one is faulty legislation itself, and the second is the negative attitude of the government officials at state, district, block or village levels. With the exception of Aligarh, no serious attempt was made to enforce the enacted land reform legislation." [56] Virtually all effective land reforms thus involve the creation of an agrarian reform institute. Where such institutes are not created, as was generally the case in India, the reforms tend to become ineffective. In addition, it is also often necessary to mobilize a substantial bureaucratic force to implement the reform in the countryside. The Japanese land reform required the assistance of some 400,000 people to purchase and transfer 2,000,000 hectares and to rewrite 4,000,000 leases. The reform in Taiwan required an administrative force of some 33,000 officials. In the Philippines and in Iran the army has been employed to help implement the reform. [57] In India, in contrast, in the early 1960s only about 6,000 full-time workers were concerned with land reform.

The second organizational requirement of land reform is the organization of the peasants themselves. Concentrated power can enact land reform decrees, but only expanded power can make those decrees into reality. While peasant participation may not be necessary to pass legislation, it is necessary to implement legislation. In democratic countries, in particular, land reform laws may be passed in deference to public opinion or ideological commitment. They often remain unenforced because of the absence of peasant organizations to participate in their implementation. "The clue to the failure of rural development," it was argued in India, "lies in this, that it cannot be administered, it has to be organized. While administration is something which the civil service can take care of, rural development is a political task, which the administration cannot undertake." [58] Peasant leagues, peasant as-

56. Wolf Ladejinsky, *A Study on Tenurial Conditions in Packaya Districts* (New Delhi, Government of India Press, 1965), p. 9.

57. J. Lossing Buck, "Progress of Land Reform in Asian Countries," in Walter Froehlich, ed., *Land Tenure, Industrialization and Social Stability: Experience and Prospects in Asia* (Milwaukee, Marquette University Press, 1961), p. 84.

58. *The Economic Weekly* (Bombay), Feb. 1964, p. 156, quoted by Wayne Wilcox, "The Pakistan Coup D'Etat of 1958," *Pacific Affairs, 38* (Summer 1965), 153.

sociations, peasant cooperatives are necessary to insure the continued vitality of land reform. Whatever their declared functions, the fact of organization creates a new center of power in the countryside. De Tocqueville's democratic science of association brings a new political resource into rural politics, counterbalancing the social status, economic wealth, and advanced education which had been the principal sources of power of the landowning class.

The creation of peasant associations, consequently, is a political act, and it is most often and most effectively performed by political parties, who have an interest in mobilizing peasant support and firmly binding the peasants to their party through the mechanisms of peasant organizations. Virtually every strong political party in a modernizing country is closely affiliated with a peasant organization. Such organization clearly serves the interests of the party leaders, but it also serves the interests of the peasants.

> Whatever power the peasants gain [one comparative analysis has concluded], it will tend with time to exert a conservative influence on the national government, for, as small proprietors they have a high regard for private property. But most important to the growth of power among the rural masses is the phenomenon of peasant syndicate organizations which tend to accompany agrarian reform. The formation of these interest groups may well prove to be the most important outcome of many agrarian reform movements.[59]

Reform, in short, becomes real only when it becomes organized. Peasant organization is political action. Effective peasant organization comes with effective political parties.

---

59. Erasmus, p. 787.

7. Parties and Political Stability

MODERNIZATION AND PARTIES

Political Community in Modern Society

By mobilizing new people into new roles modernization leads to a larger and more diversified society which lacks the "natural" community of the extended family, the village, the clan, or the tribe. Because it is a larger society, whose boundaries are often determined by the accidents of geography and colonialism, the modernizing society is often a "plural" society encompassing many religious, racial, ethnic, and linguistic groupings. Such communal groupings may exist in the traditional society, but the society's low level of political participation reduces the problems they pose for integration. As the scope of social mobilization in such communal groups extends downward, however, the antagonisms between them intensify. The problem of integrating primordial social forces into a single national political community becomes more and more difficult. Modernization also brings into existence and into political consciousness and activity social and economic groups which either did not exist in the traditional society or were outside the scope of politics in traditional society. Either these groups are assimilated into the political system or they become a source of antagonism to and of revolution against the political system. The achievement of political community in a modernizing society thus involves both the "horizontal" integration of communal groups and the "vertical" assimilation of social and economic classes.

The common factor giving rise to the problems of national integration and political assimilation is the expansion of political consciousness and participation produced by modernization. Polities which have a stable balance between participation and institutionalization at low levels of both face the prospect of future instability unless the development of political institutions keeps pace with the expansion of political participation. Since the prospects for this are relatively low, such societies are presumptively unstable. On the other hand, societies which have created large-scale modern political institutions with the capability of handling much more extensive political participation than exists at present are presumptively stable. Societies where participation already exceeds institutionalization are, clearly, unstable, while societies with a balance between the two at high rates of both may be said to have validated stability. These political systems are both politically modern and politically developed. They have institutions with the demonstrated capability to absorb into the system new social forces and the rising levels of participation produced by modernization.

The future stability of a society with a low level of political participation thus depends in large part on the nature of the political institutions with which it confronts modernization and the expansion of political participation. The principal institutional means for organizing the expansion of political participation are political parties and the party system. A society which develops reasonably well organized political parties while the level of political participation is still relatively low (as was largely the case in India, Uruguay, Chile, England, the United States, and Japan) is likely to have a less destabilizing expansion of political participation than a society where parties are organized later in the process of modernization. In the 1960s, the presumptive stability of Malaya, where traditional leaders had woven a plurality of ethnic groups into a single party framework, was higher than the presumptive stability of Thailand, where the virtual absence of political parties left the polity with no institutional mechanisms for assimilating new groups.

In most countries in Latin America in the 1960s peasants manifested low levels of involvement in and identification with the political system. Presumably, however, the ability of a comprehensive party system like that in Mexico to deal with this problem was far higher than that of an uninstitutionalized dictatorship like that in Paraguay. Societies with a low level of participation and a partyless absolute monarchy (like Saudi Arabia, Libya, or Ethiopia in the 1960s) were presumptively unstable. Similarly, societies such as Haiti under Duvalier, the Dominican Republic under Trujillo, or, at an earlier time, Mexico under Díaz, which lack both effective traditional and effective modern political institutions, faced highly unstable futures. The problems faced by the American political system in the 1960s of assimilating into the system the Negro minority did not differ significantly from those faced by many political systems in modernizing countries. The American political system and American parties in the past, however, had demonstrated an institutional capability for precisely such assimilation. The successful absorption of the Karens, the Tamils, the Kurds, or the Negroes into the Burmese, Ceylonese, Iraqi, or Sudanese political systems was far more problematical simply because the political elites of those countries had no such highly developed and institutionalized procedures for handling these problems.

Societies with highly developed traditional political institutions may evolve to higher levels of political participation through the adaptation of those institutions. At some point, political parties become necessary to organize and to structure the expanded participation, but these parties play a secondary role supplementing institutional strength rather than filling an institutional vacuum. Most later modernizing countries, however, lack traditional political institutions capable of successful adaptation to the needs of the modern state. Hence minimizing the likelihood of political instability resulting from the expansion of political consciousness and involvement requires the creation of modern political institutions, i.e. political parties, early in the process of modernization.

The distinctive problem of the later modernizing countries is that they confront simultaneously the problems which the early modernizers faced sequentially over fairly long historical periods. Simultaneity, however, is an opportunity as well as a challenge. It at least enables the elites of those countries to select the problems to which they will give priority. What for the early modernizers was determined by history can for the later modernizers be a matter of conscious choice. The experience of both early and later modernizers suggests that early attention to the problems of political organization and the creation of modern political institutions makes for an easier and less destabilizing process of modernization. "Seek ye first the political kingdom and all things will be added unto it." The political decay in Ghana highlighted the consequences of Nkrumah's failure to follow his own precept. The political kingdom, however, cannot be found; it must be created.

The relative success of communist states in providing political order in large part derives from the priority they have given to the conscious act of political organization. In the Soviet Union, one function of the NEP was to permit the reconstruction and strengthening of the party, the reinvigoration of its cadres, before the major effort to industrialize Soviet society and to collectivize Soviet agriculture was launched in the 1930s. The Bolsheviks appropriately gave first attention to the perfection of the political organization through which they would rule Russia. As a result, as early as 1923

> the basis for the control by the party over national life had been laid: the perfected system of control over appointments which enabled the central apparatus to place trusted and well-screened nominees in key positions in all the party organizations; strict party discipline, which ensured both that the nominees would obey the centre and that the rank and file members of local party organizations would obey the central nominee; and finally, the establishment of party supremacy over state institutions.[1]

During the remainder of the 1920s the control of the party over industry and culture was extended simultaneously with the expansion of the control of the apparatus over the party. By 1930 a political organization had been created which could prosecute industrialization, collectivization, and war, and survive their consequences. A similar course was followed by the Communist Party of China in the years after 1949. First priority was given to the extension of party control throughout China and the refurbishing of the party organization. Only in the late 1950s did economic development move to the forefront among party objectives. The sequence followed in North Korea did not deviate from this pattern: "the development of Korean economic institutions took place more slowly than the political, particularly in the areas of trade and agriculture. While the adoption of Soviet political forms was virtually complete by 1948, the sovietization of the economy did not near completion until 1957, the private sector having by then been reduced to insignificant proportions."[2]

1. Leonard B. Schapiro, *The Communist Party of the Soviet Union* (New York, Random House, 1960), p. 258.
2. Philip Rudolph, *North Korea's Political and Economic Structure* (New York, Institute of Pacific Relations, 1959), p. 61.

The more successful efforts at modernization by noncommunist one-party states have also given first priority to political objectives. In Turkey Mustafa Kemal consciously laid first the national and then the political basis for his society before turning to social reform and economic development. Similarly in Mexico the period from the Revolution of 1910 to 1940

> was an era in which Mexico was developing the essential preconditions for the new role of the state. During those thirty years, the state regained physical control over the nation; it began to shape and define a new philosophy for its existence and a new role in the performance of its goals; it manufactured a new set of powers and generated a new crop of institutions; and it began to flex its muscles by attempting new programs and new approaches to the old problems of credit, transportation, water resources, and land tenure in the country.[3]

The strengthening of the state and the development of the party organization in the 1930s laid the foundation for the tripling of the Mexican gross national product during the 1940s and 1950s.

So also in Tunisia the Neo-Destour government gave first priority to promoting national integration and developing political institutions before turning in 1961 to a program of economic and social development. A similar pattern of priorities was set for Tunisia's western neighbor. "For Algeria as for China, economic development is not priority number one, but priority number three. The prime objective is the building of the State; the second, the formation of the national ruling class. To achieve them, the second especially, it may be advantageous to regress with regard to the third."[4] In modernizing society "building the state" means in part the creation of an effective bureaucracy, but, more importantly, the establishment of an effective party system capable of structuring the participation of new groups in politics.

Parties organize political participation; party systems affect the rate at which participation expands. The stability and the strength

3. Raymond Vernon, *The Dilemma of Mexico's Development* (Cambridge, Harvard University Press, 1963), p. 59.

4. M. Corpierre, "Le totalitarisme africain," *Preuves, 143* (January 1963), 17, quoted in Immanuel Wallerstein, "The Decline of the Party in Single-Party African States," in LaPalombara and Weiner, eds., *Political Parties and Political Development*, p. 204.

of a party and of a party system depend upon both its level of institutionalization and its level of participation. A high level of participation combined with low levels of political party institutionalization produces anomic politics and violence. Conversely, however, a low level of participation also tends to weaken political parties vis-à-vis other political institutions and social forces. It is in the interest of party leaders to expand political participation so long as they are able to organize the participation within the framework of their party. A party with mass support is obviously stronger than a party with restricted support. So also a party system with mass participation is stronger than a party system in which increased political participation leads to the gradual separation of the party from its presumptive supporters and the conversion of what was once a broad-based organization into a handful of rootless politicians. Participation without organization degenerates into mass movements; organization lacking participation degenerates into personalistic cliques. Strong parties require high levels of political institutionalization and high levels of mass support. "Mobilization" and "organization," those twin slogans of communist political action, define precisely the route to party strength. The party and the party system which combine them reconcile political modernization with political development.

Unlike elections and representative assemblies or parliaments, parties and party systems thus perform dynamic as well as passive functions in the political system. Elections and parliaments are instruments of representation; parties are instruments of mobilization. Parliaments or other types of elected councils are hence quite compatible with a relatively static traditional society. The strength of the dominant groups in the social structure is reproduced within the parliament. The existence of an elected assembly is, in itself, an indication of neither the modernity of a political system nor of its susceptibility to modernization. The same is true of elections. Elections without parties reproduce the status quo; they are a conservative device which gives a semblance of popular legitimacy to traditional structures and traditional leadership. They are, indeed, usually characterized by a very low turnout. Elections with parties, however, provide a mechanism for political mobilization within an institutional framework. The political parties direct political participation out of anomic paths and into electoral channels. The stronger the political parties involved in the elections, the larger the voting turnout. A half dozen individual candidates furiously competing with each other without benefit of party produce a far smaller turnout of voters than one strong party lacking any effective opposition. The 99 per cent turnouts in communist states are testimony to the strength of the political parties in those states; the 80 per cent turnouts in western Europe are a function of the highly developed organization of parties there; the 60 per cent turnouts produced by American parties reflect their looser and less highly articulated organization.

The Fragility of the No-Party State

Traditional polities do not have political parties; modernizing polities need them but often do not want them. The opposition to political parties in such societies comes from three different sources. Conservatives oppose parties because they see them, quite appropriately, as a challenge to the existing social structure. In the absence of parties political leadership derives from position in the traditional hierarchy of government and society. Parties are an innovation inherently threatening to the political power of an elite based on heredity, social status, or land ownership. The conservative attitude toward parties is well reflected in Washington's warning in 1794 that the "self-created societies" were "labouring incessantly to sow the seeds of distrust, jealousy, and of course discontent" about the country and that if not stopped they would destroy the government of the country.[5]

Inevitably a ruling monarch tends to view political parties as divisive forces which either challenge his authority or greatly complicate his efforts to unify and modernize his country. Efforts to mix monarchial rule and party government almost always end in failure. The choice has to be made between Bolingbroke and Burke; and for the individual or group wishing to combine conservative authority and modernizing policies the former is far more attractive than the latter. The modernizing monarch necessarily sees himself as the "Patriot King" who is "to espouse no party, but to govern like the common father of his people." [6] The conservative nonroyal leader—Sarit, Ayub Khan, Franco, Rhee—

5. George Washington, Letter to Jay, November 1, 1794, *Writings* (W. C. Ford ed., New York, Putnam's, 1891) , *12*, 486.

6. Lord Bolingbroke, "The Idea of a Patriot King," *Works* (London, Hansard and Sons, 1809) , *4*, 280–81.

shares similar sentiments opposed to party development, although he may well be forced to compromise with the need for parties. For a state without parties is also a state without the institutional means of generating sustained change and of absorbing the impact of such change. Its ability to modernize politically, economically, socially is drastically limited. "A regime without parties is of necessity," as Duverger says, "a conservative regime." [7]

The conservative opposition to parties in a modernizing state is frequently joined by an administrative opposition. The pure conservative rejects both the rationalizing and the participant aspects of political modernization. The administrator opposed to parties accepts the need to rationalize social and economic structures. He is unwilling, however, to accept the implications of modernization for broadening the scope of popular participation in politics. His is a bureaucratic model; the goal is efficiency and the elimination of conflict. Parties simply introduce irrational and corrupt considerations into the efficient pursuit of goals upon which everyone should be agreed. The administrative opponent of parties may wear any dress, but he is less likely to be in mufti than in uniform.

The third source of opposition to parties comes from those who accept participation but not the necessity to organize it. Theirs is a populistic, Rousseauian belief in direct democracy. The conservative opponent of parties believes that the existing social structure is sufficient to link people to government. The administrative opponent sees the bureaucratic structure meeting these needs. The populist opponent denies the need for any intervening structure between the people and its political leaders. He wants a "partyless democracy." Jayaprakash Narayan joins Gamal Abdel Nasser and Haile Selassie in denying the relevance of parties to political modernization.

The conservative sees party as a challenge to the established hierarchy; the administrators see it as a threat to rationalized rule; the populists as an obstacle to the expression of the general will. Yet all the critiques share certain common themes. These were, perhaps, most cogently and eloquently stated by Washington when he warned of "the baneful effects of the Spirit of Party" on the American system of government. Party, Washington said:

7. Maurice Duverger, *Political Parties* (New York, John Wiley, 1954), p. 426.

serves always to distract the Public Councils, and enfeeble the Public administration.—It agitates the community with ill-founded jealousies and false alarms, kindles the animosity of one part against another, foments occasionally riot and insurrection.—It opens the doors to foreign influence and corruption, which finds a facilitated access to the Government itself through the channels of party passions. Thus the policy and will of one country are subjected to the policy and will of another.[8]

Washington's remarks neatly express the four principal charges against parties which are made today. Parties promote corruption and administrative inefficiency. They split society against itself and promote conflict: parties, as Ayub Khan said, "divide and confuse the people." They encourage political instability and political weakness. They lay the state open to influence from and penetration by external powers: if freedom is given to party development, as one leader in a modernizing country said, at least one party will become the instrument of the CIA.

The arguments against parties betray the circumstances of their historical origin in the early phases of political modernization. They are, in fact, less arguments against parties than they are arguments against *weak* parties. Corruption, division, instability, and susceptibility to outside influence all characterize weak party systems rather than strong ones. They are, indeed, features of weak political systems generally, which lack stable and effective institutions of rule. Parties may indeed furnish incentives to corruption, but the development of a strong party substitutes an institutionalized public interest for fragmented private ones. In their early stages of development, parties appear as factions and seemingly exacerbate conflict and disunion, but as they develop strength parties become the buckle which binds one social force to another and which creates a basis for loyalty and identity transcending more parochial groupings. Similarly, by regularizing the procedures for leadership succession and for the assimilation of new groups into the political system, parties provide the basis for stability and orderly change rather than for instability. Finally, while weak parties may indeed become. the instruments of foreign powers, strong parties provide in large measure the institutional

8. Washington, "Farewell Address," in Ford, ed., *13*, 304.

mechanisms and defenses for insulating the political system against such external influence. The evils attributed to party are, in reality, the attributes of a disorganized and fragmented politics of clique and faction which prevails when parties are nonexistent or still very weak. Their cure lies in political organization; and in a modernizing state political organization means party organization.

The widespread suspicion of parties, however, means that anti-party policies of prevention or suppression prevail in many modernizing states. In a highly traditional political system, the elites normally attempt to prevent the emergence of parties. Party organizations, like labor unions and peasant associations, are illegal. At times, in such systems, a relaxation of restrictions may allow certain forms of political association to come out in the open. But in most cases, the traditional ruler and traditional elite attempt to limit political groupings to intra-elite factions and cliques func tioning within the parliamentary assembly, if such exists, or within the bureaucracy. Thus in the 1960s parties still did not exist in Ethiopia, Libya, Saudi Arabia, Jordan, Kuwait, and a few other generally minuscule surv'ving potentatedoms. In other traditional systems, such as Thailand and Iran, parties had had a frag ile existence at one point but were either currently illegal (Thailand) or severely restricted (Iran). In all these systems, as modernization progresses the need to organize political participation also increases. These systems, in some cases, display all the signs of contemporary stability, but the efforts of their governments to prevent the development of political parties make them presumptively unstable. The longer the organizational vacuum is maintained, the more explosive it becomes.

In most modernizing countries the government at one time or another follows a policy of suppression vis-à-vis parties. At some point, parties are allowed to be formed either within a traditional parliament or by groupings among the people. Or parties may develop in the struggle against colonial rule. At a subsequent stage, an effort may be made to reduce the amount of political power in the system and to restrict both political participation and the organizations associated with that participation. In a traditional system, such as Morocco, a monarch may reassert his authority after a period of fairly intense party development. More frequently, a military dictator assumes power after parties have become weakened or fragmented and outlaws them, attempting to rule through purely administrative means. In most Latin American countries parties have been illegal at one time or another. In African and Asian countries where military coups overthrew civilian national-ist leaders after independence, parties were also generally pro-scribed. The suppression of parties usually accompanies substan-tial efforts to decrease the level of political consciousness and polit-ical activity. In Spain, for instance, the Falange was a useful means of mobilizing and organizing support for the rebel cause during and immediately after the Civil War. Subsequently, however, the Franco regime wished to promote political passivity rather than political participation and the Falange declined in importance as a result.

In countries where parties are suppressed, the social base usually exists for parties which are somewhat more than cliques or factions and which have roots in large and at times self-conscious social forces. Prolonged periods of party suppression hence generate forces which, when the authoritarian rule comes to an end, burst forth with explosive energy. A rapid escalation in political partici-pation occurs with hitherto submerged or underground parties coming forth into daylight. The more unexpected the end of re-pressive rule, the more extensive and variegated the expansion of political participation.[9] This expansion then typically leads to a rightist reaction and the renewed efforts by conservative authori-tarian groups to reduce political participation and restore a narrow-based political order.

The no-party state is the natural state for a traditional society. As society modernizes, however, the no-party state becomes in-creasingly the antiparty state. Conscious and coercive effort is re-quired to prevent or to suppress political parties. Increasingly efforts are made to furnish party substitutes, to find techniques for organizing political participation in such a way as to minimize its expansive and disruptive consequences. The more hostile a gov-ernment is toward political parties in a modernizing society, how-ever, the greater the probable future instability of that society. Military coups are far more frequent in no-party states than in any other type of political system. A partyless regime is a conservative

9. See Myron Weiner and Joseph LaPalombara, "The Impact of Parties on Polit-ical Development," in LaPalombara and Weiner, p. 400.

regime; an antiparty regime is a reactionary regime. The progress of modernization increases the fragility of the no-party system.

TABLE 7.1. Coups and Coup Attempts in Modernizing Countries
Since Independence

Type of Political System	Number of Countries	Countries with Coups Number	Countries with Coups Per cent
Communist	3	0	0
One-party	18	2	11
One-party dominant	12	4	33
Two-party	11	5	45
Multiparty	22	15	68
No effective parties	17	14	83

Source: Fred R. von der Mehden, *Politics of the Developing Nations* (Englewood Cliffs, N.J., Prentice Hall, 1964), p. 65.

Strong Parties and Political Stability

The stability of a modernizing political system depends on the strength of its political parties. A party, in turn, is strong to the extent that it has institutionalized mass support. Its strength reflects the scope of that support and the level of institutionalization. The modernizing countries which achieve high levels of actual and presumptive political stability possess at least one strong political party. Congress, Neo-Destour, Acción Democrática, Partido Revolucionario Institucional, Mapai, Partido Popular Democrático, Republican People's Party, TANU: each was at one time a model of effective political organization in a modernizing society. The differences in political stability between India and Pakistan in the 1950s were measured by the differences in organizational strength between the Congress Party and the Moslem League. The differences in political stability between North and South Vietnam during the decade after Geneva were measured by the differences in organizational strength between the Lao Dong Party, on the one hand, and the Dai Viet, VNQDD, and Can Lao, on the other. The differences in political stability in the Arab world between Tunisia, on the one hand, and the eastern Mediterranean, on the other, were in large measure the difference between the broad scope and high institutionalization of Neo-Destour and the high institutionalization but narrow scope of the Ba'ath.

The susceptibility of a political system to military intervention varies inversely with the strength of its political parties. Countries like Mexico and Turkey which developed strong political parties also found the road to reducing military involvement in their politics. The decline in party strength, the fragmentation of leadership, the evaporation of mass support, the decay of organizational structure, the shift of political leaders from party to bureaucracy, the rise of personalism, all herald the moment when colonels occupy the capitol. Military coups do not destroy parties; they ratify the deterioration which has already occurred. In the Dominican Republic, for instance, Juan Bosch's party "had begun to disintegrate" after the elections in which he was chosen president. As a result, the party "presented no challenge to the police and the armed forces. Most of the PRD leaders, it seems, had become bureaucrats, occupying themselves with technical and administrative functions essential to the reform program." [10] So also, violence, rioting, and other forms of political instability are more likely to occur in political systems without strong parties than in systems with them.

Most non-communist modernizing countries after World War II lacked both strong political parties and strong party systems. Most parties were too young to have demonstrated any real adaptability. The principal exceptions were several Latin American parties and the Congress Party in India. Otherwise, most parties were not only young but also still led by their founders. The institutional strength of a political party is measured, in the first instance, by its ability to survive its founder or the charismatic leader who first brings it to power. The adaptability of the Congress Party was reflected in its changing leadership from Banerjea and Besant to Gokhale and Tilak to Gandhi and Nehru. Similarly the shift in leadership from Calles to Cárdenas set the National Revolutionary Party on the road to successful institutionalization, signaled by its subsequent change in name to the Institutional Revolutionary Party. The institutional strength of Mapai was measured by the fact that it was able to survive not only Ben Gurion's desertion but also his active opposition. Here clearly was a case where the party was stronger than its leader. In Puerto Rico Muñoz Marin, in contrast to Ben Gurion, consciously chose to retire from the leadership of the PPD in part to promote its institu-

10. Edwin Lieuwen, *Generals vs. Presidents*, p. 61.

tionalization: "The election was a beginning," he said. "I've begun to prove that the Island can get along without me. The people will get used to the idea of an institutionalized party and they will learn to work with Sánchez just as they have worked with me." [11] On the other hand, weak parties depend upon their leaders. The deaths shortly after the independence of their countries of Senanayake in Ceylon, of Jinnah and Ali Khan in Pakistan, and of Aung San in Burma directly hastened the disintegration of their political parties. That the deaths of Gandhi and Patel in India had no such effect on the Congress was not due just to Nehru.

A second aspect of party strength is organizational complexity and depth, particularly as revealed by the linkages between the party and social-economic organizations such as labor unions and peasant associations. In Tunisia, Morocco, Venezuela, India, Israel, Mexico, Jamaica, Peru, Chile, and a few other countries, such linkages greatly extended the appeal and bolstered the organization of the major parties. They also created the usual problems in the relations between functional organizations and political ones, and the degree of association between party and union or league varied from almost complete integration to loose ad hoc alliances. To the extent, of course, that the party became identified with the organized expression of only a single social force, it tended to lose its own identity and to become the creature of that social group. In the stronger parties, the leadership of unions and other functional groups was subordinated to the leadership of the party, and the area of political decisions was carefully reserved for the party leadership. Most parties in modernizing countries, however, did not have such supporting organizational links. In most cases they were unable to develop mass appeals to workers and peasants; in some instances, the parties or individual leaders within the parties did have such appeals, but they did not develop the organizational and institutional framework for organizing mass support.

A third aspect of party strength concerns the extent to which political activists and power seekers identify with the party and the extent to which they simply view the party as a means to other ends. The party's competitors for the loyalty of political actors

11. Luis Muñoz Marín, *New York Times*, Dec. 27, 1964, p. 43.

may be traditional social groupings, the bureaucracy, or other parties. Conservative parties, for instance, typically place greater reliance on social structure and ascriptive relationships and hence develop a less autonomous and less highly articulated organization than more radical parties which reject or attack the existing social structure. There is, as Philip Converse has suggested, "an increasingly *overt* stress on group loyalty and cohesion *per se* as one moves from right to left across party spectra in most political systems." [12]

In many modernizing countries after independence political leaders may transfer their loyalty from nationalist party to governmental bureaucracy. In effect this represents their ideological subversion by colonial norms and their political conversion from popular to administrative rule. In many African countries the nationalist party was the single important modern organization to exist before independence. The party "was generally well organized. The conditions of the political struggle and the dedication of the top elite to the party as the prime instrument of political change led the elite to give the major portion of their energies and resources to building a solid, responsive organization capable of disciplined action in response to directives from the top and able to ferret out and exploit feelings of dissatisfaction among the masses for political ends." [13] After independence, however, the dominant political party is often weakened by the many competing demands on organizational resources. A marked dispersion of resources means a decline in the overall level of political institutionalization. "Talents that once were available for the crucial work of party organization," one observer has warned, "may now be preoccupied with running a ministry or government bureau. . . . Unless new sources of loyal organizational and administrative talents can be found immediately, the party's organization—and, therefore, the major link between the regime and the masses—is likely to be weakened." [14] In these situations identification with

12. Philip E. Converse, "The Nature of Belief Systems in Mass Publics," in David Apter, ed., *Ideology and Discontent* (New York, The Free Press, 1964), pp. 248–49; italics in original.
13. William J. Foltz, "Building the Newest Nations: Short-Run Strategies and Long-Run Problems," in Karl W. Deutsch and William J. Foltz, eds., *Nation-Building* (New York, Atherton Press, 1963), p. 121.
14. Ibid., pp. 123–24.

the party was only a transitory phenomenon, undermined by the attraction of governmental office.

In highly developed political systems it is rare for a political leader to shift from one party to another and the movement of social groups and classes from one party to another is usually a complex and lengthy historical process. In some modernizing systems, however, the interparty movement of individuals and groups is highly prevalent. In the Philippines, for instance, political leaders regularly shift back and forth between the two major parties. Local leaders typically join the party which wins the national election, and national leaders shift from one party to the other party in terms of their own electoral prospects. "You know how it is here," as one leader said, "It is not the same as in Great Britain or the United States. We have only private interests, no party loyalties. We change parties when it suits our interests. Everybody does it." [15] The constancy of the party name thinly veils constantly changing coalitions of political leaders operating beneath it.

Processes of Party Development

A strong political party system has the capability, first, to expand participation through the system and thus to preempt or to divert anomic or revolutionary political activity, and, second, to moderate and channel the participation of newly mobilized groups in such a manner as not to disrupt the system. A strong party system thus provides the institutionalized organizations and procedures for the assimilation of new groups into the system. The development of such party institutions is the prerequisite for political stability in modernizing countries. The process of party development usually evolves through four phases: factionalism, polarization, expansion, and institutionalization.

Factionalism. In the first phase both political participation and political institutionalization are low. Individuals and groups break out of the traditional patterns of political behavior, but they have not yet developed modern political organizations. Politics involves a small number of people competing with each other in a large number of weak, transitory alliances and groupings. The groupings have little durability and no structure. They are typically the

15. Quoted in Caridad C. Semaña, "Some Political Aspects of Philippine Economic Development After Independence" (Ph.D. dissertation, Harvard University, 1965), p. 166.

projections of individual ambitions in the context of personal and family rivalries and affiliations. These political groupings may be called parties, but they lack the continuing organization and social support which are the essence of party. Reports that 42 parties exist in Korea or 29 in South Vietnam or 18 in Pakistan are false on their face. Such groupings are, in fact, factions, and they closely resemble the political cliques, juntos, factions, and family groupings which dominated eighteenth-century politics in Europe and America. In American state politics in the 1780s,

> a faction appeared as a portion of an electorate, political elite, or legislature whose adherents were engaged in parallel action or coordination of some consistency but limited durability in conflict with other portions. A clique . . . was a factional group whose relationships depended upon a family, a commanding individual, or a close coterie of personal associates: generally the demise or retirement of the focal person led to the collapse of the clique. . . . Such politics depended heavily on personalities and personal ties and was subject to abrupt, kaleidoscopic change.[16]

Similar patterns predominated in most twentieth-century modernizing countries. In the 1950s, for instance, in Pakistan,

> The political party . . . became the vehicle for politicians' personal political careers. New parties were formed when a career seemed to be making no progress in an old party. A party would be founded by a leader or group of leaders who then tried to organize a following. Some parties were formed almost entirely from among members of legislatures and constituted, in effect, a temporary grouping within an assembly for the purpose of making or breaking a ministry.[17]

Similarly, in Thailand, the parties, when they exist, "have little or no extra-parliamentary organization. In general, each member must get elected through his own efforts in his own province. Party labels are incidental. Parties have never represented sub-

16. William N. Chambers, *Political Parties in a New Nation* (New York, Oxford University Press, 1963), p. 26.

17. Keith Callard, *Political Forces in Pakistan, 1947–1959* (New York, Institute of Pacific Relations, 1959), pp. 24–25.

stantial social forces but only cliques and individuals within the
top level of the ruling class." [18]

In political systems with legislatures the factions are oriented to
maneuvering in the legislature rather than to campaigning in the
constituency. They are parliamentary not electoral organizations.
Typically they are formed within the legislature by successful candidates after they are elected rather than in the constituency by
aspiring candidates in order to get elected. Candidates are elected
as individuals on the basis of their social or economic status and
appeal. The legislative faction or clique then becomes a means of
linking them to other political activists, not a means of linking political activists to the masses. In Korea after World War II, for instance, candidates were elected as individuals and joined parties
after they arrived in Seoul for the national assembly. The parties
"originated in the capital as factions providing alternate—and
opportunistically shifting—ladders to executive power." Even in
a country like Nigeria, with the colonial stimulus to party development, most candidates elected to the legislatures in the 1951 elections ran as independents and only joined the NCNC or the Action
Group after they took their seats.[19]

The legislative clique is thus one form of preparty faction typical of the early phases of modernization. In the absence of legislatures and elections the dominant form of preparty faction becomes
the revolutionary conspiracy. As with the legislative cliques, these
conspiracies are small in size, weak in viability, and many in number. Like the cliques they are also initially divorced from ties with
any substantial social force. The intellectuals and others in them
form and re-form in a confusing series of permutations and com-
binations which are no less factions for being equipped with
ponderous names and lengthy manifestos. They are the civilian
equivalents of the secret juntas and clubs formed by military
officers intent on challenging the existing traditional order. If
eighteenth-century England furnishes the prototype of the politics
of legislative factions, nineteenth-century Russia furnishes the
prototype of the politics of revolutionary factions. And the differ-

18. David A. Wilson, *Politics in Thailand* (Ithaca, Cornell University Press, 1962),
p. 68.

19. Henderson, *Korea: The Politics of the Vortex*, p. 288; David Abernethy, "Education and Politics in a Developing Society: The Southern Nigerian Experience"
(Ph.D. dissertation, Harvard University, 1965), p. 331.

ences between the two, while great, are not fundamental. In one case factions function within the existing system, in the other outside it. But in both cases the amount of power in the factional pattern is very limited and what there is is highly fragmented.

Like no-party politics, factional or preparty politics is inherently conservative. The revolutionary factions may talk of the masses and may, indeed, make some efforts to mobilize mass support. But the conditions are simply not yet ripe. Like the Narodniki they are rebuffed by the very groups whose interests they wish to further. Consequently they remain as isolated in their cellars as the legislative factions are in their chambers. In and of itself the competition of factions—legislative or revolutionary—tends to be a closed system, an endless round of interminable maneuvering in which the actors continually shift partners and antagonists without ever enlarging the number of participants.

Polarization. A crucial turning point in the evolution of a political system occurs when politics breaks out of the closed circle of revolutionary or legislative factionalism, political participation broadens, new social forces appear on the political scene, and political parties are formed by the organized linking of political faction to social force. Before this "breakout" or "take-off" in party development can occur, however, the pattern of factional politics itself has to change so as to produce the incentives for factional leaders to expand political participation. So long as a multiplicity of groups compete with each other, little reason exists for any one of them to attempt to expand political participation. The key to success in the struggle between one faction and another lies in the appeal to other factions. Without an overriding cleavage to bifurcate the political arena, each faction tries to overcome its opponents of today by alliances with its opponents of yesterday. A multiplicity of groups and a multiplicity of cleavages leads the actors to devise strategies for the redistribution of power within the system rather than for the expansion of the power of the system.

The accomplishment of the latter depends upon factional coalescence and polarization, which, in turn, depend upon either the cumulation of cleavages in such a manner as to divide the factions into two reasonably stable groupings or the emergence of a single dominant issue which overshadows all others and consequently also tends to polarize the political participants. Once all the principal actors in the political system are committed to one side or another of a two-sided struggle, the leaders of each side are under strong compulsion to expand the scope of the struggle and to mobilize additional social forces into politics on their side.

The crucial issue then becomes: Under what situations does a closed system of multiple cleavages shift to an expansible system of polarized cleavage? Clearly the strongest incentives toward polarization exist where some factions are intent on the complete destruction of the existing system. Once the opposition or revolutionary factions themselves cease to struggle with each other and instead direct their attention to the existing political system, the stage is set for a polarization of politics between the revolutionaries and the establishment. It is also possible, however, for dominant cleavages to appear among legislative factions. These may well have their roots in attitudes toward the traditional sources of authority: Whig versus Tory, the king's men reacting to the proponents of popular rule. In addition, as society modernizes, the demands on government increase, and the proper economic policies to be followed by the government in response to these demands tend to become the dominant issue of politics. The introduction of a Hamiltonian program of economic modernization into a politics of legislative factionalism can hardly help but provoke a polarization of opinion and a coalescence of factions. The coalition of factions within the political system may also be prompted by the emergence of a social force outside the system and demanding entrance into it. In this case the dominant issue of politics becomes the relation of the new social force to the political system.

Writers on politics make much of the desirability of crosscutting cleavages which moderate the intensity of conflict within a society. Such a pattern is, indeed, a condition of political stability. And the polarization of politics, we have argued in Chapter 5, is the goal of the revolutionary. It involves the intensification of political conflict. In a modernizing society, however, this intensification of conflict may be the precondition to the creation of a broader based political system. If it can be handled through the extension of the competition of groups already within the system, the revolution may be a peaceful one. A broadly mobilized system with fairly widespread popular participation requires cross-cutting cleavages to prevent it from being torn apart by the struggle between two overpowering mass movements who between them command the allegiance of almost the entire population. In a society where only a small proportion of the population is politically active, however, the polarization of opinion and the cumulation of cleavages play a much more functional role. They promote the extension of political participation and the establishment of links between the political factions and rising social forces. In one form or another, the polarization of opinion is a prerequisite for the shift from factional politics to party politics.

Expansion. A strong party appeals to large masses of the population and binds those masses to it through an effective organization. Political leaders are motivated to develop such appeals and to create such organizational bonds only when these actions are necessary to achieve highly desired goals. These goals are normally the conquest of power and the reordering of society. The expansion of participation and the organizing of that participation in parties is thus the product of intense political struggle. This struggle normally involves the efforts of political leaders either to overthrow the existing system, to control the existing system, or to enter the existing system.

In the revolutionary or nationalist pattern the aim of the political activists is to destroy the established order or to oust the imperial power. The revolutionary or nationalist leaders are driven to the continual broadening of their political appeal in their effort to build up popular support against the existing regime. They are similarly driven to organize that support and as a result they create a political party or parties. All revolutions, as we have seen, involve the expansion of political participation and successful revolutions produce strong political parties to organize that participation. Prolonged struggles for national independence have similar results. The nationalist leaders initially function simply as a number of factions on the outskirts of the imperial administration. In this stage they are frequently beset by a variety of alternative and conflicting goals: assimilation, participation, home-rule, the restoration of traditional authority, full-scale independence, all compete with each other. In due course, however, the issues simplify, the factions coalesce, and the now "unified" nationalist movement begins to develop a broader popular appeal. The factions which are unwilling to appeal to the masses are brushed aside by those who are. Through nationalist struggle participation is expanded and organization developed. This period of incubation of parties during colonial rule requires an imperial power which is willing to permit and to contend with a nationalist movement for many years, thus furnishing the time, the struggle, and the slowly increasing responsibility which are the ingredients of institution-building. In general, however, colonial governments tend to suppress nationalist movements for as long as possible, and then when they see independence as inevitable to bring it about as quickly as possible. National independence, in short, may abort political development.

In the pattern of party development more typical of the West, parliamentary factions operating within the political system coalesced into broader groupings and then began to mobilize new supporters into politics. The shift from factional politics to party politics and the increasing competition between parties was directly related to the increases in political participation.[20] This pattern in which two groups of leaders within the existing system take the lead in expanding the system involves the least discontinuity in political evolution. The entry of new social forces into the system is made more acceptable by the proper sponsorship under which it occurs. The expansion of participation can be lasting, however, and the organizations which are established effective, only if they are the product of competitive struggle. Strong one-party systems are always the product of nationalist or revolutionary movements from below which had to fight for power. In contrast, efforts to establish one-party systems from above, as in the case of Nasser, lead nowhere: mobilization and organization are processes for acquiring or building power. Authoritarian leaders in power normally lack the need to do either. Precisely for this reason, General Pak succeeded in doing in Korea what Colonel Nasser failed to do in Egypt. Paradoxically, two-party systems can be built from the top down; one-party systems only from the bottom up.

The competitive struggle to expand participation and organize parties may also develop from the efforts of a social force to enter the political system. In this case, the social force normally creates a political party which functions initially outside or on the fringes of the political system and then attempts to penetrate the system. Many of the socialist parties in western Europe followed this pat-

20. See, e.g., the American experience discussed in Chambers, pp. 32–33.

tern as have several parties in Latin America. This challenge to the existing system often stimulates the factional leaders and traditional leaders to coalesce in opposition to the new threat. Organization from below stimulates organization above, the result consequently tending to be a multi-party system in which each major social force has its own political vehicle. Since members of the political elite play a less significant role in promoting the expansion of political participation, the process is likely to involve more violence and conflict than in the case where established leaders compete among themselves in expanding participation.

Institutionalization. The way in which political participation is expanded obviously shapes the party system which subsequently develops. The antisystem revolutionary or nationalist process eventually results in the displacement of the former political system and the establishment of a new one with typically a one-party or dominant-party system. The intrasystem process most often leads to the early institutionalization of a two-party system, while the into-system process is likely to eventuate in the emergence of a multiparty system. Once these patterns are established in the early phases of party development, they tend to become institutionalized. Subsequent changes in the nature of the party system usually occur only as result of a major crisis or fundamental change in the nature of the society.

In a one-party system the processes determining governmental policy and political leadership function almost exclusively through the framework of a single party. Minor parties may exist but they are so minor as not to exert any significant influence upon what goes on within the major party. In the mid-twentieth century one-party systems included the communist states, authoritarian regimes like Franco's Spain and Nationalist China, Tunisia, Mexico, and at one point or another almost all the African states south of the Sahara. In a dominant-party system only one party has the capacity to govern, but two or more opposition parties, usually representing more specialized social forces, are sufficiently strong so that they can affect the political process which goes on within the dominant party. The dominant party, in short, does not monopolize politics; it must, in some measure, be responsive to other groups of political actors. At one time or another dominant-party systems existed in India, Burma, Malaya, Singapore, South Korea, Pakistan, and several African states.

A two-party system may have majority and minority parties, but it differs from a dominant-party system in that the minority party commands enough of the opposition to constitute a feasible alternative government. The dominant party in a dominant-party system may well command the support of less than a majority of the electorate, but fragmentation of other political groups leaves it in a dominating position. In the 1950s the Christian Democrats in Germany usually got a larger proportion of the total vote than the Congress Party got in India. Yet the Indian system was a dominant-party system because there was no major alternative to the Congress Party, while the SPD did constitute a feasible alternative to the Christian Democrats. Minor parties usually exist in two-party systems and, indeed, their existence is encouraged by the possibility of achieving a balance-of-power position between the two major parties. The distinctive characteristic of such a system, however, is that only two parties are capable of constituting a government.

Finally, in a multiparty system no party by itself is able either to form a government or to stand head and shoulders above its rivals. Some parties are bigger than others but the creation of a government requires a coalition of several parties and several different coalitions conceivably could be the basis of a government. In this situation parties may move back and forth from government to opposition as a result not of any change in their standing with the electorate but of changes in the attitudes and ambitions of their leaders. The line between a multiparty system and a dominant-party system often is hazy, and one reasonably common intermediate pattern is where one party is sufficiently larger than the others and located sufficiently in the center of the political spectrum so that it must be included in the government coalition. This was for years the case with Mapai in Israel and with the Christian Democrats in Italy.

Adaptability of Party Systems

Writers on politics have spent much time and many words arguing about the relative merits of one-party systems and competitive party systems for modernizing countries. In terms of political development, however, what counts is not the number of parties but rather the strength and adaptability of the party system. The precondition of political stability is a party system capable of assimilating the new social forces produced through modernization. From this viewpoint, the number of parties is important only insofar as it affects the ability of the system to provide the institutional channels necessary for political stability. The question consequently is: What connection, if any, is there between party number and party strength in modernizing countries?

On a global basis little relationship appears to exist between party number and party strength. As Table 7.2 suggests, strong parties and weak parties may exist in each type of numerical party system. The rough and impressionistic classification of this table is apparently confirmed in Table 7.3 by the Banks and Textor breakdown of party stability in relation to party number. The absence of unstable one-party systems might well have been corrected if allowance had been made for the African states which fell victims to military coups in the 1960s.

This apparent evidence of no significant correlation between party number and party strength does not, however, tell the entire story. The relation between the two varies with the level of modernization. At high levels of modernization, any number of parties

TABLE 7.2. Party Strength and Party Number

Strength of Parties	Number of Parties			
	ONE	DOMINANT	TWO	MULTI
Strong	Communist Tunisia Mexico	India	Great Britain Germany	Low Countries Scandinavia Italy
	Taiwan	Malaya South Korea	United States	Israel Chile Venezuela
			Uruguay Jamaica	Peru
	Guinea Tanganyika Liberia		Ceylon	Argentina
			Philippines	Brazil
		Somalia? Bolivia?	Colombia Honduras	Other Central American
Weak	Other African			

may be compatible with strong parties. At lower levels of modernization, one-party systems may be either strong or weak. Multiparty systems, however, are invariably weak. The eleven stable multiparty systems in the Banks and Textor accounting, for instance, include Israel plus ten Western European countries; the two moderately stable multiparty systems are Italy and Costa Rica; the thirteen unstable multiparty systems include nine from Latin America, two from Asia, and one each from the Middle East and Africa. In short, no stable multiparty system existed in a modernizing country with the questionable exception of Israel.

TABLE 7.3. Party Stability and Party Number

Number of Parties	Degree of Stability			
	STABLE	MODERATELY STABLE	UNSTABLE	TOTAL
One party	19	4	0	23
Dominant party	2	4	3	9
One-and-a-half party	2	0	0	2
Two party	7	0	2	9
Multiparty	11	2	13	26
Total	41	10	18	69

Source: Arthur S. Banks and Robert B. Textor, *A Cross-Polity Survey* (Cambridge, M.I.T. Press, 1963), pp. 97–98, 101.

In modernizing states one-party systems tend to be more stable than pluralistic party systems. Modernizing states with multiparty systems are, for instance, much more prone to military intervention than modernizing states with one party, with one dominant party, or with two parties. In 1965 and 1966, to be sure, many African states succumbed to military coups. These did not, however, alter the basic picture of the inverse relationship between party number and party stability. As the data in Table 7.4 indicate, as of 1966, one-party modernizing states still were least likely to suffer successful coups and multiparty modernizing states were most likely. Clearly a one-party system is no guarantee against a military coup; but multiparty systems are almost sure to produce a coup. The only exceptions were one borderline case (Morocco) which did suffer a royal coup d'etat in 1965 reinstituting monarchial rule and two highly Europeanized countries (Israel, Chile) in which recent or past emigration plus historical tradition reproduced the more stable multiparty patterns of continental Europe.

One rough measure of the adaptability of a party system is to be found in the average age of its constituent parties. The higher the average age of the parties, presumably the more institutionalized and stable is the party system. In general, of course, the average age of the principal parties in a multiparty system is lower than that of those in a single-party or two-party system. It is possible,

TABLE 7.4. Successful Coups in Modernizing Countries:
1945 or Date of Independence through 1966

| | Number of Countries | Countries with Coups | |
		Number	Per cent
One-party systems	26	6	25%
Dominant-party systems	18	6	33%
Two-party systems	16	7	44%
Multiparty systems	20	17	85%

however, to compare the forms which high levels of party institutionalization assume in modernizing countries and in modernized countries. A rough division between the former and the latter can be made in terms of literacy with the line drawn at 70 per cent adult literacy. Among the 29 countries with high literacy and old parties (a major party age index of 30 years or more in 1966), no one type of party system predominated. In highly literate societies highly institutionalized party systems can take a variety of forms. In contrast ten of the sixteen countries with low levels of literacy which had highly institutionalized party systems had one-party or dominant-party systems. Six had two-party systems, and none had multiparty systems. Again it would appear that a multiparty system is incompatible with a high level of political institutionalization and political stability in a modernizing country. In modernizing countries multiparty systems are weak party systems.

The reasons for this situation are to be found in the different patterns of adaptation of the numerical party systems and the different forms that party strength assumes in those systems. In a multiparty system strong parties are normally more coherent, more complexly organized, but less flexible and less autonomous than are strong parties in a two-party system. In a strong multiparty system a one-to-one relationship tends to exist between social forces and political parties. Labor, business, landowners, urban middle class, the church, all have their own political vehicles, and institutionalized means of compromise and adaptation have developed among them. Such a strong system can exist only with a high level of mobilization and political participation. If the latter are limited, the social forces active in politics are limited, and the social base for a strong multiparty system thus does not exist. If a multiparty system does exist in these circumstances it typically reflects differences of clique and family within a restricted elite. The

TABLE 7.5. Institutionalized Party Systems
(Major Party Age Index of 30 or more in 1966)

Level of Literacy	Type of system				
	ONE-PARTY	DOMINANT-PARTY	TWO-PARTY	MULTI-PARTY	TOTAL
70% or over	8	0	9	12	29
Below 70%	9	1	6	0	16
Total	17	1	15	12	45

poor institutionalization and narrow support for the parties in such a multiparty system makes that system extremely fragile. The step from many parties to no parties and from no parties to many parties, consequently, is an easy one. In their institutional weakness the no-party system and the multiparty system closely resemble each other.

The ability of different types of party system to adapt and to expand political participation, however, may well vary over time. The crucial question concerns the extent to which the system institutionalizes procedures for assimilating new groups into the system. On this issue the evidence suggests that two-party systems and dominant-party systems, because they have more effective party competition, are likely to produce greater long-run political stability than either one-party systems or multiparty systems.

The stability of the one-party system derives more from its origins than from its character. It is usually the product of a nationalist or revolutionary struggle which stimulates extensive mobilization and institutionalization. Once the struggle is won, however, the strong party which emerges creates a one-party system, which, in turn, removes or eliminates the conditions for its own success. The continuing stability of the system thus depends upon its inheritance from the past. The more intense and prolonged the struggle for power and the deeper its ideological commitment, the greater the political stability of the one-party system which is subsequently created. One-party systems that emerge out of revolutions, consequently, are more stable than those produced by nationalist movements, and those produced by prolonged nationalist movements are more stable than those produced by movements whose struggles were brief and easy. In general, indeed, the longer a nationalist party fought for independence, the longer it was able to enjoy the power that came with independence. The Congress Party was 62 years old when independence came to India; the Neo-Destour 22 years old at the birth of Tunisia; Mapai 18 years old when Israel fought its way into the world. TANU and its predecessor had a 32-year history when Tanganyika became independent. All these parties were able to maintain a fairly vital existence in the years after independence.

In contrast, many of the nationalist parties which came into being only a few years before independence and which won independence easily had a less secure grasp on power after independence. Many African nations got independence so easily, as Emerson pointed out, that they were "cheated of their revolution." [21] Denied their revolution, they may also be denied the fruits of revolution. The prospects for political stability in Guinea appeared higher than in most of the other former French colonies in large part because the leaders of the PDG had to mobilize their followers for the struggle with France before independence and to endure the hostility of France after independence. Hostility by a colonial government toward a new government may well be a major benefit to the new government. It is also a factor whose absence cannot be fully compensated for by ritualistic incantations about neocolonialism.

In a one-party system, clearly, a new group can enter the system only by entering the party. A one-party system is, in this sense, less complex than a pluralistic party system, and consequently fewer avenues exist for the assimilation of new social forces. The political leaders of the system can hence exercise a high degree of control over the mobilization of new groups into the system. They are under no competitive impetus to broaden their appeal and to bring new groups into politics in order to stay in power. Their capacity to restrict or to control political mobilization enhances their ability to provide for the "horizontal" integration of ethnic, religious, or regional groups. In a competitive party system, in

21. Rupert Emerson, "Nation-Building in Africa," in Deutsch and Foltz, pp. 110–11.

contrast, strong incentives exist for each party to appeal to a particular group, ethnic and religious animosities are fanned by the mobilization of the masses, and the competition of the parties deepens and reinforces preexisting social cleavages.

Sustained modernization, however, poses problems for the stability of one-party systems. The strength of the party derives from its struggle for power. Once in power, what incentives does it have to maintain a high level of mobilization and organization? It can coast for a while on its inheritance from the past; to the extent that it has institutionalized high levels of participation and organization, it may be able to do this for some time. By its very nature, however, it lacks the stimulus to struggle which provides a continuing basis for political stability. For a while this impetus may come from the gap between the party and society. The ideology of the party leaders usually commits them to a thoroughgoing reconstruction of society. So long as traditional structures stand or islands of resistance remain, a stimulus exists to develop the strength and organization of the party. The party may, like the Communist Party of the Soviet Union in the 1920s and 1930s, devote itself to undermining the traditional sources of power, wealth, and status, and replacing them with structures clearly of its own making and clearly under its own control. If it thus reorders society, however, it deprives itself of social enemies to justify its existence. If, as more often happens, its ideological drive falters and it comes to terms with the society it governs, then it is likewise deprived of a raison d'être.

In the long run the struggle between the party and the groups which exist outside the political system or in a different political system (an imperial power, a traditional oligarchy) has to be institutionalized within the political system. The rationale for a one-party system, however, is often grounded on the desire to deny the existence of differences and to reassert the necessity for eliminating the struggle. The continued vitality of a one-party system thus depends upon the existence of a phenomenon which is anathema to the leaders of the system. In the absence of competition among parties, the closest functional substitute which the one-party system provides is the competition between the party hierarchy and the state bureaucratic hierarchy. The preconditions for such competition, however, are (a) that the two hierarchies remain distinct, and (b) that some rough balance of power exist between them. The struggle between the two, moreover, is a struggle between two institutions which are functionally different rather than functionally identical. Consequently, the patterns and results of the struggle resemble more those of the rivalry between executive and legislature in a presidential system of government than the rivalry between two political parties.

In the 1920s single-party systems came into being in both Turkey and Mexico. The Mexican system, as the product of a social revolution, originally mobilized a much broader segment of the rural population than was mobilized through the Turkish system which was the product of a more restricted nationalist movement. After 1946, however, Turkey shifted to a two-party system, and, as a result, the scope of popular participation, particularly rural participation, in the system broadened tremendously. In the two decades before 1946 the Mexican system was much more responsive to the needs of the rural majority than was the Turkish single-party system. In the two decades after 1946, however, the situation was reversed, and the Turkish two-party system was more responsive to the demands of the rural majority than the Mexican one-party system. Revolutionary élan waned in Mexico at the same time that the competition for peasant votes intensified in Turkey.

In addition to making the leaders of a one-party system less sensitive to the needs to expand and organize participation in the system, modernization also multiplies and diversifies the groups seeking to participate in the system. If the party leaders attempt to absorb the new groups within the framework of the single party, they achieve comprehensiveness at the price of weakening the unity, the discipline, and the élan of the party. If they exclude new groups from the party, they maintain party coherence at the price of endangering the party's monopoly of political participation and encouraging anomic and violent political behavior directed at the overthrow of the system itself. Those one-party systems which are most successful in assimilating additional social forces often tend to develop a formal or informal pattern of sectoral organization, such as exists in the Mexican PRI. If they are unable to assimilate additional social forces within the party, either the one-party system ceases to exist (as in Turkey after 1946) or the system is maintained at the price of increasing coercion and increasing instability.

The strength of a single-party system stems from its struggle against an imperial power, a traditional regime, a conservative society. Its weakness stems from the absence of institutionalized competition within the political system. Presumably a multiparty system provides this in good measure, and consequently multiparty systems should be strong party systems. Yet we have seen that this is true only in highly modernized societies where a large number of social forces have been mobilized into politics. In modernizing societies multiparty systems are weak party systems, yet party competition is supposed to produce party strength. How can this apparent contradiction be explained? The answer, of course, lies in the fact that party competitiveness and party number are not directly related. Party competition is obviously impossible in a single-party system, but it is also likely to be less in a multiparty system than in a dominant-party or two-party system. In the latter systems the leaders of parties actively compete with each other in mobilizing the voters. In a two-party system one party wins and the other party loses, and hence each party has the strongest incentive to outdo the other in mobilizing and organizing voters. In a dominant-party system, the leaders of the dominant party also have the incentive to minimize their losses to the minor parties.

In a multiparty system, on the other hand, party competition tends to be less prevalent. In a weak multiparty system in which parties are just emerging from factions, the large number of groupings precludes any effective mobilizing appeal. In multiparty systems where the parties are more solidly rooted in social forces, each party normally has its own constituency and makes intensive efforts to mobilize that constituency but party competition for the support of the same groups is less than in the two-party or dominant-party system. Each party tends to have a fixed block of voters who support it regularly, are firmly identified with the party, and are generally impervious to the appeals of other parties. Assimilation of a new social force into the multiparty system hence normally requires the creation of a new party. The system as a whole is adaptable, but its components are not. Consequently, parties rise and fall over time with changes in the social structure and composition of the politically active population. When it first appears each new party seems like a harbinger of progress and reform because it embodies the interests of a newly emerging social force. Once it has achieved a position within the political system, however, it changes as its constituency changes, and it eventually becomes the spokesman for vested interests. The party system mirrors society only too well and its component parties possess little autonomy from the social forces with which they are affiliated. Thus in Peru, the Apristas were the reform party of the 1930s, but a strangely conservative party in the 1960s. Peruvian society had changed, but they had not changed with it and they were still representing the same interests they had thirty years earlier. As a result, the way was opened for the rise of a new reform party appealing to the progressive middle class.

Party competition is usually justified in terms of democracy, responsible government, and majority rule. It can also, however, be justified in terms of the value of political stability. Electoral competition between parties tends to expand political participation and at the same time to strengthen party organization. Party competition of this sort enhances the likelihood that new social forces which develop political aspirations and political consciousness will be mobilized into the system rather than against the system.

In a dominant-party system the assimilation of new social forces typically goes through two phases. The new group first expresses its claims on the political system through a minor party which is primarily or exclusively devoted to those interests. In due course, the growth in the votes of the minor party causes the dominant party to adjust its policies and practices and to attempt to absorb the leaders and supporters of the minor party into its own framework. In a dominant party system, the leaders of the minor parties cannot hope to win control of the government, but they can hope to deny it effectively or comfortably to the dominant party. Consequently, the political appeals and activity of the dominant party are directed primarily toward countering the appeals of its strongest opponent of the moment. If the movement of opinion is to the left, the dominant party shifts in that direction to minimize the gains by the left-wing minority parties. If opinion shifts in another direction, the dominant party responds in a similar manner. The minor parties have their own specialized appeals and hence do not normally compete with each other. Each instead competes in its own way with the dominant party.

In India the grievances of particular regions have often been initially expressed through minor parties or through nonparty movements, but the Congress Party has then often absorbed the active protagonists of these grievances into its own structure. In Israel elections typically pivot about the struggle between Mapai and its most important opponent of the moment, with Mapai adapting its strategy and appeals to minimize the strength of that opposition. In the regional elections in Nigeria a somewhat similar pattern tended to develop in the 1950s. In 1957, for instance, the NCNC won 64 out of 84 seats in the parliament of the Eastern Region despite strong Catholic opposition on the educational issue. Independent candidates, however, received almost 20 per cent of the total vote; the leadership of the NCNC responded to this challenge by appointing Catholics to five of the fourteen positions in the regional cabinet although only one Catholic was in the cabinet before the election. In a dominant-party system, new groups thus first express their demands through a party of pressure and then are absorbed into the party of consensus.[22] If they are not assimilated into the dominant party, they may still function as permanent parties of pressure on the periphery of the major party. The dominant party system thus provides safety valves for the expression of the discontent of particularistic groups and at the same time strong incentives for the assimilation of such groups into the dominant party if they appear to have a popular appeal.

The pressures for the expansion of political participation are normally more intense in a two-party system than in any other type of system. The party out of power has the obvious incentive to mobilize new voters into the political system to outflank its opponent. In Uruguay, for instance, the rivalry between Colorados and Blancos was, in part, responsible for the early and, for Latin America, unprecedented incorporation of the urban working classes into the political system in the first part of the twentieth century. By mobilizing this group Batlle insured the dominance of the Colorado Party for the next half century. The problem in the two-party system, indeed, is that participation may expand so rapidly as to introduce serious cleavages into the system. Groups may be mobilized but not assimilated. An "excess of democracy" and "increased popular participation" in government may, as David Donald argued with respect to the United States in the mid-nineteenth century, erode the power of government and its capa-

22. These terms are from Rajni Kothari, "The Congress 'System' in India," *Asian Survey, 4* (December 1964), 1161 ff. See also Abernethy, pp. 482–89.

bility "to deal with issues requiring subtle understanding and delicate handling." [23] In twentieth-century modernizing countries, the rapid entrance of new groups into politics as a result of two-party competition has at times led to military coups in an effort to restrict participation and restore unity.

The tendencies toward the rapid expansion of political participation which inhere in a two-party system at times provoke deliberate attempts to limit this expansion. In Colombia, for instance, the two parties for long consciously maintained a limited competition restricted to members of the political elite. In the 1930s this pattern was challenged by the need to respond to the popular pressures for economic improvement. In the late 1940s the system broke down with the spread of decentralized violence and the emergence of a military dictator. That dictator, Rojas Pinilla, tried to do what the democratic system had been unable to do: to promote social reform and to identify new groups with the political system. Rojas, one observer wrote, "turned the clock forward on social achievement for the masses. He gave them status and a sense of their importance, if only because his government has emphasized their welfare. . . . In this sense, paradoxically, the military dictator is making a substantial contribution toward democracy." [24] In 1958, however, Rojas was thrown out, and the party leaders came to an explicit agreement to limit competition between them. The presidency would be alternated between Liberal and Conservative parties, and membership in the cabinet and Congress would be divided equally between them. In the words of another expert, using the same figure of speech, in 1958, "The party leaders seemed, in many respects . . . to be turning the political clock back to 1930, to an Athenian type of democracy, to conditions prevailing before the left wing of the liberal party attempted to win support from groups outside the elite." [25] The result of this agreement was a marked decline in voting and the rise of new movements and political forces, including a revived Rojas party, appealing to those whom the established parties were ignoring because they were not competing.

23. David Donald, *An Excess of Democracy* (Inaugural Lecture, Oxford, Clarendon Press, 1960) , p. 17.

24. Vernon Lee Fluharty, *Dance of the Millions: Military Rule and the Social Revolution in Colombia, 1930–1956* (Pittsburgh, University of Pittsburgh Press, 1957) , pp. 316–17.

25. Edwin Lieuwen, *Arms and Politics in Latin America* (New York, Frederick Praeger, 1960) , p. 89.

"The natural movement of societies," says Duverger in one of his most quoted and most criticized dicta, "tends toward the two-party system." [26] In fact, however, whatever "naturalness" a two-party system may have stems not from the nature or movement of societies, but from the nature of the political system. Opinion may well crystallize "round two opposed poles," but it may also be highly fragmented, and the large number and diverse character of social forces in modernizing and modern societies would appear to make a multiparty system far more natural than a two-party system. The crucial bipolarity among groups and social forces which develops in a highly institutionalized political system is between those who are in or close to power and those who are removed from power. The "natural" distinction is furnished by the division of the political system into government and opposition. If the political system is weak, lacking authority, and not highly institutionalized, this difference is not very great, and hence the impetus toward a two-party system is weak. Where government is strong and authoritative, however, those political leaders who, for one reason or another, are alienated from those other leaders in power, have strong incentives to work together to get back in power. The natural tendency is for those who wish to get into power to win the support of all disaffected or potentially disaffected social forces. The natural bipolarity is not the social one between the left and the right but the political one between the ins and the outs.

The two-party system thus most effectively institutionalizes and moderates the polarization which gives rise to the development of party politics in the first place. In a one-party system, the political leadership tends to dominate social forces. In a multiparty system, the social forces dominate the political parties. A two-party system maintains a more equitable balance between social forces and political parties. The parties compete for the support of the social forces, but each party draws its support from many forces and hence it is the creature of no single one. Unlike the multiparty system, the appearance of a new social force in politics does not necessarily require the creation of a new party. Unlike the single-party system, the assimilation of the social force does not necessarily take place through only one political organization. There is thus a certain logic to a two-party system, but it is a political logic rather than a social one, and it is grounded as much in the need

26. Duverger, pp. 215–16.

for political stability as in the attraction of popular choice and democratic liberties.

THE GREEN UPRISING: PARTY SYSTEMS AND RURAL MOBILIZATION

Parties and the Rural-Urban Gap

In most modernizing countries, a majority of the population—often a substantial majority—lives in rural areas and works in agriculture. In most modernizing countries, also, the urban population grows much faster than the rural population, in large part because of the movement of people from farms to cities. The combination of these two conditions—rural majority and urban growth—gives rise to a distinctive pattern of politics in modernizing countries. A gap develops between the political attitudes and behavior of the cities and those of the countryside. The city becomes the continuing center of opposition to the political system. The stability of a government depends upon the support which it can mobilize in the countryside.

A crucial function of political parties and the party system in a modernizing country is to furnish the institutional framework for this mobilization. Political parties are modern organizations; they are the creation of new men in urban environments. The party leaders are usually drawn from the Western-educated intelligentsia with upper- or middle-class backgrounds. For most modernizing countries, as for India in the 1950s, the recruitment of party workers "appears to occur largely in the cities and is conducted, for the most part, among office employees, shopkeepers, members of professions, and others in the middle classes." [27] If the party is to become first a mass organization and then a stable basis for government, however, it must extend its organization into the rural areas.

The party and the party system are the institutional means of bridging the rural-urban gap. The ideal party would be the one of which it could be said, in the words of Seydou Kouyate, that

the political organization has been the melting pot where the peasant and the city-dweller have met. It has pulled the former out of his isolation, cured the latter of his disdain for

27. Myron Weiner, *Party Politics in India* (Princeton, Princeton University Press, 1957), pp. 230–31.

the bush, and achieved the national unity from which it was
drawing its strength. Thus, the gap which existed between
the city and the countryside has been filled up and the various strata of the population have been unified into one single
stream oriented toward the political objectives.[28]

The obstacles to the realization of this ideal are immense. The
party is a modern organization. But to be successful it must organize a traditional countryside. Urban party leaders are often unable, psychologically or politically, to reach out for rural support.
If they are to do so successfully, they may have to modify drastically or to suppress their own modern values or goals and to
adopt the more traditional stance which appeals to the countryside. As political consciousness grows among the more traditional
groups, the party leaders are forced to choose between the values
of modernity and the values of politics. The source of political
modernity is the city; the source of political stability is the countryside. The task of the party is to combine the two. One major
test of the institutionalization of a party and the adaptability of its
leadership is the willingness of the latter to make the concessions
necessary to win the support of the countryside. The strong parties
and the stable party systems are those which meet this test. In a
modernizing society, the successful party is born in the city but
matures in the countryside.

Different types of party systems provide different bridges between city and countryside. In one-party states, the modernizing
elite typically attempts to impose controls upon the peasantry and
to permit them to become politically active only insofar as they
accept the modernizing values of the political elite. If the peasantry remain neither active nor modernized, the political leaders
in a one-party system can direct their attention to reform and
change in the urban sectors. This, in effect, was what Kemal did.[29]
In a different manner but with similar purpose, the leaders of the
Soviet Union followed a relatively restrained and hands-off policy
with respect to the rural areas during the 1920s. At some point,
however, even in one-party states, the needs of stability require

28. Seydou Kouyate, *Africa Report* (May 1963) , p. 16, quoted by Rupert Emerson,
"Parties and National Integration in Africa" in LaPalombara and Weiner, pp. 296–
97.

29. See Frederick W. Frey, "Political Development, Power and Communications in
Turkey," in Lucian W. Pye, ed., *Communications and Political Development,* pp.
313–14.

that the political system confront and resolve the issue of rural political participation. The Soviets attempted to make the countryside over in the image of the city, to destroy the traditional pattern of life, and to assimilate forcibly the peasantry to modern values through collectivization and the extension of the political apparatus of the Communist Party through the countryside. The political and economic costs of this effort were such that few other countries have tried to imitate it. In Turkey, on the other hand, the assimilation of the peasants involved breaking the one-party monopoly and permitting competition between groups within the modernizing elite to expand outside the modernizing elite. As a result, the assimilation of the peasants into the political system in Turkey took place on terms far more favorable to the peasants than it did in Russia. In general, competitive party systems tend to produce less rapid modernization but easier assimilation than monopolistic party systems.

In modernizing countries the city is not only the locus of instability; it is also the center of opposition to the government. If a government is to enjoy a modicum of stability, it requires substantial rural backing. If no government can win the support of the countryside, there is no possibility of stability. The result, in modernizing countries with democratic political systems, is a major difference in the voting patterns between city and countryside. The support for the governing party, if there is a governing party, comes from the countryside; the support for the opposition comes from the cities. This pattern is repeated over and over again on every continent. In India the principal sources of strength of the Congress Party are in the rural areas; the opposition parties both of the left and of the right are stronger in the cities. In Venezuela the Acción Democrática appealed to the countryside but found little support in Caracas. In 1958, it got 49 per cent of the national vote, 11 per cent of the Caracas vote. In 1962, although it dominated the executive and legislative branches of the national government, it elected only one of 22 city councillors in the national capital. In the 1963 national elections, the AD was the first-place party in the countryside, but came in fourth in Caracas.

The same pattern of urban opposition persisted in Korea throughout several regimes. During the 1950s the Liberal Party of Syngman Rhee dominated the countryside through fair means and foul. The opposition Democratic Party, however, had the blessing of the cities. In 1956 the Democratic candidate was elected vice president as a result of urban votes. In 1958 the Democratic Party elected 23 members of the national assembly from the five largest cities in the country, the Liberals only five. In Seoul, the opposition got 15 of the 16 seats, and no Liberal candidates were elected in the important cities of Taegu and Inchon. "Toward the end of the Rhee regime," Gregory Henderson observes, "an urban consensus against the government was achieved despite arrests, threats, economic favoritism, and surveillance." [30] The same pattern however, was repeated with the Pak government in the 1960s. In the presidential election of 1963, General Pak achieved his modest victory by virtue of his rural support; the city majorities were solidly against him. In Seoul the opposition won 12 of the 14 seats in the national assembly. Throughout its first four years in office the Pak regime was constantly harassed by the boisterous and at times violent opposition which it encountered in its own capital.

Elections in the Philippines after independence revealed a similar pattern of urban opposition to the government in power. Typically the rural vote was fairly evenly split between the government and the opposition, while the opposition got about 75 per cent of the urban vote. As a result of the failure of either party to develop a strong base of support in the rural areas, the urban vote gave the opposition the upper hand. The party in power lost four of six presidential elections during the two decades after World War II.[31] In somewhat similar fashion, the opposition Democratic Party in Turkey during the late 1940s was strong in the cities and weak in the countryside. In 1950, however, it won half the rural vote from the Republican People's Party and as a result ousted the Republican People's Party from office. In the succeeding elections, it developed a broad appeal in the rural areas which remained the principal source of support for it and its successor, the Justice Party, into the 1960s. In contrast, the Republican People's Party, having lost the support of the countryside, did well in the cities.

Voting in Pakistan has followed a similar pattern. In the 1951 Punjabi election, for instance, the Moslem League won just under 75 per cent of the seats in the provincial assembly, but only a bare

30. Henderson, p. 303.
31. See Martin Meadows, "Philippine Political Parties and the 1961 Election," *Pacific Affairs, 35* (Fall 1962) , 270 n.

50 per cent of the seats from Lahore. In the 1964 presidential elections, Ayub Khan got 63 per cent of the total vote and Miss Jinnah 36 per cent. Ayub got majorities in 13 of the country's 16 divisions, Miss Jinnah in three: Chittagong, Dacca, Karachi. "In effect," one commentator observed, "the vote meant that while the cities generally went with Miss Jinnah, Ayub's massive hold in rural areas was indisputable." [32] In the Moroccan elections of 1963 the opposition parties, the Istiqlal and the NUPF, carried the cities, while the government party won in the rural areas. In El Salvador in 1964 the opposition Christian Democrat Party elected the mayor of San Salvador and 14 congressmen, predominantly from the urban areas. But the government party, the National Reconciliation Party, won 32 seats in Congress, sweeping the rural areas by substantial margins. In the Dominican elections of 1966, Bosch carried Santo Domingo with a 60 per cent plurality, but Balaguer won the presidency by getting 62 per cent of the vote outside the capital.[33]

All these elections share two points in common. First, there is a marked divergence between rural and urban voting; the parties and candidates strong in the countryside are weak in the cities and vice versa. Second, the party which was strong in the countryside normally secured control of the national government and inaugurated a regime characterized by a high degree of political stability. Where no party had a clear base of support in the countryside, some form of instability was the result. In some instances, urban revolts may overturn rural-based governments, but in general governments which are strong in the countryside are able to withstand, if not to reduce or to eliminate, the continuing opposition they confront in the cities. Even in countries where there are no clear-cut party differences between city and countryside, the opposition in the city may manifest itself in other ways. In Lebanon, for instance:

> in many parts of the core area [Beirut] there is a disdain and even contempt for electoral politics. Acceptance of the legitimacy of the electoral system is probably stronger in the rural areas, where the system matches rather closely the traditional

32. Sharif al-Mujahid, "Pakistan's First Presidential Elections," *Asian Survey*, 5 (June 1965) , 292; Keith Callard, *Pakistan* (New York, Macmillan, 1957) , p. 55.

33. *New York Times*, October 25, 1965, p. 17, November 21, 1966, p. 12. I am indebted to Mr. Abraham Lowenthal for figures on the Dominican Republic.

organizations . . . It would seem that the ordinary people of the rural areas are more fully integrated into the political system than are the people of the capital, whose political potentialities are numerous, diverse, and uncertain.[34]

In other countries, where the electoral process is less meaningful, the contrast between rural support and urban opposition is no less real for not being manifested in voting patterns. In Iran this has long been the case: the opposition to the regime is centered in Teheran, the regime's continued existence dependent upon the acquiescence of the countryside. Even in South Vietnam, President Diem running for reelection in 1961 got only 48 per cent of the vote in Saigon, although he rolled up heavy majorities in the countryside. "What African president," President Ahmed Ben Bella asked in June 1965, "has a majority behind him in his capital?"[35] The events of a few weeks later showed that he was not one of them.

The rural-urban gap may be bridged by revolutionaries or by a military elite which consciously appeals to and organizes the countryside. But the assimilation of the rural masses can also be the product of the workings of parties and the party system either through the struggle of a nationalist party against colonial rule or through the competition of two or more parties for peasant support.

Rural Mobilization through Nationalist Struggle

In the nationalist pattern, the stimulus to rural mobilization is the effort of the intellectual leaders of the nationalist movement to mobilize popular support from the rural areas in their struggle against the colonial regime. Only rarely did this occur because only rarely were the nationalists able or required to mobilize rural support to win their goals. In other instances, such as China and Vietnam, communist parties capitalized on the limitations and hesitations of the nationalists and mobilized the peasants into politics under their auspices on behalf of both nationalism and revolution. The two most notable cases where extensive rural mobiliza-

34. Michael C. Hudson, *The Precarious Republic: Political Modernization in Lebanon* (New York, Random House, Forthcoming, 1968) , Chap. 6.

35. Ben Bella, quoted by Russell Warren Howe, "Would-Be Leader of the 'Third World,' " *New Republic, 152* (June 19, 1965) , 11; Bernard B. Fall, "Vietnam's Twelve Elections," *New Republic, 154* (May 14, 1966) , 14.

tion took place during the struggle for national independence were India and Tunisia.

In India the nationalist movement changed decisively in the early 1920s, broadening from a relatively small circle of English-educated, thoroughly westernized intellectual leaders drawn from the traditional higher strata into a more popular movement with extensive middle sector and small-town support. The key leader in this change was, of course, Gandhi, who redefined the nationalist appeal in traditional terms for mass consumption. "Popular nationalism," in the words of the Rudolphs, "is Gandhi's creation. He transformed the rather tame and select nationalism of the pre-1920s, broadening its class base and changing its ideological content." The pre-Gandhian nationalists were "the products of the new educational system, the trouser-wearing, English-speaking upper-middle classes. For the most part, they were drawn from the upper castes and the new professions." Their values were "essentially those of the British middle class of the period," and their "appeal was to the city and not the countryside, to the educated, not the illiterate. They ignored the village and the village ignored them." After 1920 Gandhi's leadership drastically altered this pattern. The old Western-style leaders were "supplemented by leaders from the more traditional culture, often from lesser castes or callings" and from "town or rural backgrounds." These had "little or no western education," they valued the old ways and looked "with a sceptical eye at the appeals of modernity. . . . Gandhi's appeal, his language, style, and methods infused nationalism with a new spirit, a spirit which was able to speak to those still steeped in the traditional culture." Indian nationalism was transformed into a "popular and tradition-tinged movement." [36]

A somewhat similar evolution occurred in Tunisia. There the shift from liberal to popular nationalism could not be accommodated within the framework of the first major nationalist organization. Instead, the Destour Party was supplanted in the early 1930s by the Neo-Destour which developed in Tunisia the same sort of popular appeal that Gandhi developed in India. The founders of the Neo-Destour went to the masses and organized them. As in India, new sources of leadership were mobilized. Unlike the Old Destour the Neo-Destour recruited its workers and

36. Lloyd I. and Susanne Hoeber Rudolph, "Toward Political Stability in Underdeveloped Countries: The Case of India," *Public Policy, 9* (1959), 155–57.

supporters from small towns and villages. "Although some of the sons of the Tunis *baldi* [old families] joined the Neo-Destour, the majority of its leadership was *afaqi* [outsiders] and its most reliable shock troops were the country peasants and Tunis plebs." [37]

In those numerous circumstances in which the Green Uprising is not launched under nationalist auspices before independence, the nationalist movement which comes to power at independence is typically an urban movement drawn from the middle and upper classes. A vast gulf may separate this urban, educated political elite from both the traditional leaders and the traditional masses of the hinterland which it presumes to rule. In some respects, the post-independence rulers may be almost as distant from the bulk of the population as the imperial elite they succeed. Societies are said to become independent when the foreign imperial power withdraws. In fact, however, the society does not become independent; some people in the society do. Independence has a differential impact on the various groups in the society, and the earlier independence is achieved in terms of the process of political mobilization, the greater the differential impact which independence has. Countering this, the policies of the imperial power may be consciously designed to minimize the power in the colonial situation of those groups who will inherit the imperial power when independence comes. "It is a cardinal principle of British Colonial Policy," said Lugard in one classic statement, "that the interests of a large native population shall not be subject to the will either of a small European class or of a small minority of educated and Europeanized natives who have nothing in common with them, and whose interests are often opposed to theirs." [38] When independence comes, however, it is independence for the "small minority of educated and Europeanized natives." The rhetoric of nationalism and sovereignty is scant covering for the transfer of power from an alien foreign oligarchy to an alien native one.

In such circumstances the nationalist intellectual elite is not likely to keep power for long. It occupies the positions of authority and hence has little incentive to mobilize additional popular support for new goals. It has arrived. But it is also vulnerable. The small amount of power in the political system means that it is

---

37. Clement Henry Moore, "The Era of the Neo-Destour," in Charles Micaud, ed., *Tunisia: The Politics of Modernization* (New York, Praeger, 1964) , pp. 81–82.

38. Lord Lugard, quoted in Abernethy, p. 169.

liable to overthrow either by some group which can command more ruthless and persuasive forms of power or by some group which can expand the power of the system and mobilize new groups into politics. If elections occur in the post-independence political system, the Westernized nationalist elite is likely to be overthrown by more populistic and traditional leaders. If no elections are permitted, the elite is likely to be overthrown by the military. Those nationalist leaders who do not mobilize popular support before independence do not rule for long after independence. Unless they can ally with one group against the other, they are done in either by outraged colonels or by outraged citizens.

The decay of narrow-based nationalist regimes was a common feature of African politics after independence. The significance of substantial rural mobilization before independence for subsequent political stability is perhaps best illustrated, however, by the contrast between Morocco and Tunisia and between Pakistan and India. In Morocco, unlike Tunisia, the principal nationalist party, the Istiqlal, never established the same primacy that the Neo-Destour did in Tunisia. In part this was because under the French the king in Morocco had been more powerful than the bey in Tunis and had played a major role in the independence movement. But also the Istiqlal, formed in 1943 by a group of urban intellectuals, never developed a mass base comparable to that of the Neo-Destour. In Tunisia the trade unions were closely associated with the Neo-Destour and the leadership of the two groups overlapped in large measure. In Morocco the trade unions and their leadership remained more distant from the Istiqlal and eventually aligned themselves with its left wing, which broke away in 1959 to form a separate party, the National Union of Popular Forces. More significantly, while the Neo-Destour mobilized support from rural tribesmen in its struggle for independence, the strength of the Istiqlal remained concentrated in the cities. As a result, after independence it was in a position to be challenged, first, by a new party, the Popular Movement, designed to represent the interests of the countryside and the Berber tribesmen and then by the king whose most intensive support came from the rural areas. In the 1963 elections the Istiqlal and the UNFP carried the cities but the political vehicle of the monarchy, the Front for the Defense of Constitutional Institutions, won a plurality by its appeal to the countryside.

In Pakistan, the Moslem League, like the Congress Party, was an old organization at the time of independence. It dated from 1906, but also for much of its life had been a small pressure group. In the mid-1930s it was "moribund" and in comparison with the Congress, it "was a defensive organization composed of some wealthy *zamindars* and a few discontented intellectuals who wanted greater access to government employment."[39] The mobilization of popular sentiment behind the Congress Party in the 1920s, however, had its impact on the League. Despite his own opposition to mass political participation, Jinnah, who secured control of the League in 1937–38, was compelled to develop a mass organization to rival the Congress and to support the goal adopted in 1940 of an independent Islamic state. The mobilization of mass opinion by one organization thus generated a countervailing mobilization by a competing organization. The greatest support for the Moslem League, however, came from those areas where Moslems were a minority. In 1947 many of these areas became part of India. The leaders of the Moslem League thus became the leaders of a new state which divorced them from their most active and best organized supporters.

In post-independence Pakistan the League lost both its constituency and its purposes. The League also lost its "popular character" and came to be dominated by West Pakistan landlords. In due course, "The party became a series of small cliques which had power or which wanted power, and its mass foundation withered away. . . . Whereas, in many countries parties are organized to promote ideas or interests shared by their members, in Pakistan politics have been a matter of personal rivalries, each leader being supported by a faction of adherents."[40] Pakistan, in a sense, achieved independence too easily. Having failed to produce large-scale popular mobilization among its future citizens before independence, its initial political leaders had little incentive to do so after independence. They effectively vetoed the national elections which might have compelled them to establish contact with popular sources of power. As a result, they were easily displaced first by civilian bureaucrats and then by military ones. And, ironically, the development of political structures in the countryside and

39. Callard, *Pakistan*, p. 34.

40. Callard, *Political Forces*, pp. 23–24; Mushtaq Ahmad, *Government and Politics in Pakistan* (2d ed. Karachi, Pakistan Publishing House, 1963), pp. 136, 142–43.

the mobilization of rural voters into the political arena in a competitive election then took place under the auspices of a military leader who despised party politics.

Rural Mobilization through Party Competition: The Conservatism of Democracy

Competitive party systems offer channels for the assimilation of rural groups into the political system. The nature of those channels depends upon the nature of the party system, whether it is dominant-party, two-party, or multiparty. The ability of the party system to assimilate the new groups depends upon the acquiescence of the previously dominant groups—whether conservative, nationalist, or military—in the loss of power. The assimilation of the rural groups frequently requires parties to adapt their economic programs to agrarian needs and to promise land reform and public investment in rural areas. In this sense, the parties may compete in proposing economic reforms for rural voters. The aspirations and expectations of rural groups are, however, usually fairly specific and moderate. If these expectations are reasonably satisfied, the rural populace reverts to its customary conservative role. In addition, whatever the nature of rural economic demands on the political system, the social and cultural values of the rural population typically remain highly traditional. Consequently, in most colonial or postcolonial societies the mobilization of the rural majority into politics through the party system has a highly traditionalizing or conservatizing effect on politics.

Traditionalizing tendencies gain strength in most societies after they achieve independence from foreign rule. Such tendencies seem to be stronger in democratic states than in authoritarian ones. They stem, in the first instance, from the extension of the suffrage to the bulk of the rural population. In the early modernizing countries, where the extension of political rights was a fairly prolonged historical process, the first phase in that process— the granting of the franchise to the urban middle class—had radical and modernizing consequences. The subsequent extension of the suffrage to the rural population often brought a conservative counterweight into the political balance.

In 1848 in Germany the liberals preferred a system of property qualifications for voting; the conservatives advocated universal manhood suffrage. In England Disraeli also saw and exploited the conservative benefits of broader suffrage. Similarly, in the mid-twentieth century "rural voting can be more difficult to handle for the more progressive sectors of the Latin American middle classes." [41] Where the rural masses were able to vote in Brazil, "The main social function of suffrage was that of *preserving the existing power structure*. Within the traditional patterns, suffrage added opportunities for displaying and reinforcing feudal loyalty. At the same time, it reinforced and legalized the political status of the landowner." [42] The introduction of universal suffrage in Ceylon after 1931 had similar effects. "In effect the workers transferred into their wage-earning role elements of quasi-feudal deference. In return for the use of land, or the bullocks lent or rented, or emergency aid in time of family crises, or a chit to a doctor or lawyer, the peasant gave his vote." In the 1950s in eastern Turkey, it was reported that "In these still backward regions, where there is still almost complete illiteracy and much religious fanaticism, whole communities voted for the ruling party at a mere word from the local landowner." [43] The extension of the suffrage to the rural masses in a society which otherwise remains highly traditional strengthens and legitimizes the authority of the traditional elite.

The conservative effects of rural voting often persist after the extension of modern political agitation and organization into the countryside. Competition among traditional groups often promotes the modernization of those groups: in Nigeria, for instance, Ibo and Yoruba leaders competed with each other in extending education to their people. Competition among modern urban groups, on the other hand, promotes the traditionalization of those groups as they attempt to enlist the support of the traditional rural masses. In Burma, after 1921, "The general pattern was one in which the modernizers first fell out among themselves whenever they were confronted with demanding choices of policy, and then tended to seek support from among the more traditional elements

41. José Nun, "A Latin American Phenomenon: The Middle Class Military Coup," p. 79.

42. Emilio Willems, "Brazil," in Arnold M. Rose, ed., *The Institutions of Advanced Societies* (Minneapolis, University of Minnesota Press, 1958), p. 552; italics in original.

43. W. Howard Wriggins, *Ceylon: Dilemmas of a New Nation*, pp. 107–08; *The Times* (London), December 12, 1960, quoted in George E. Kirk, "Political Problems of Selected Poly-ethnic Countries in the Middle East: Iraq, Syria, Iran, Turkey, Cyprus" (unpublished paper, Fifth World Congress, International Political Science Association, Paris, 1961), pp. 18–19.

which in time gained the ascendency." Similarly, in India, "Peasant protest is often mobilized and directed by one urban elite in an attempt to weaken or destroy the political power of another urban elite, for the urban areas are the centers of parties radiating their influence out to the villages." [44] In reaching out to the villages, the urban elites are forced to reformulate and modify the modern appeals which are effective in the cities. Both the competition among traditional groups and that among modern groups help to bridge the gap between modern elite and traditional mass. In the former, the masses come to accept at least some of the modern goals of the elite; in the latter the elites come to accept at least some of the traditional values of the masses.

Electoral competition in postcolonial countries thus seems to direct the attention of political leaders from the urban to the rural voter, to make political appeals and governmental policies less modern and more traditional, to replace highly educated cosmopolitan political leaders with less educated local and provincial leaders, and to enhance the power of local and provincial government at the expense of national government. These tendencies promote political stability but at the same time may obstruct modernizing reforms not directed to rural interests. The precondition for reform is, in general, the concentration of power in a single modernizing elite. The effect of democracy is to disperse power among a plurality of more traditional elites. By increasing the power of rural groups democracy also tends to promote policies aimed at rural and agrarian rather than urban and industrial development.

In a two-party system these tendencies frequently manifest themselves in a "ruralizing" election in which a rural-based political party ousts from power an urban-based one. In a multiparty system, the mobilization of rural voters into the political system takes place with greater difficulty. One or more political parties have to appear which compete for the support of the peasants. Typically, however, these parties have little support from other social groups; they are opposed by the parties appealing to other groups; and because of the difficulty of mobilizing peasants into political action, they are unable to become majority parties. Consequently, the assimilation of the rural masses into politics occurs,

44. Weiner, pp. 11–12; Pye, *Politics, Personality and Nation-Building*, p. 114.

if at all, in a disjointed and halting manner. In Latin America, where multiparty systems abound, the only instance before 1967 of successful rural mobilization within the framework of such a system was Venezuela. In this case, ideology, effective leadership, and a semirevolutionary struggle against the Gómez and Pérez Jiménez dictatorships provided the environment for the effective mobilization and organization of the peasants in *campesino* unions associated with the Acción Democrática. Conceivably similar developments could take place in Chile and Peru. The two difficulties of the multiparty system, however, are that it provides insufficient incentive for any established element within the political system to mobilize the peasants and that once such mobilization does take place it cumulates political and social cleavages so as to obstruct the easy assimilation of the peasant political movement into the political system.

In a dominant-party system, the dispersive and ruralizing effects of democracy also affect the distribution of power among the parties. They are, however, more likely to be seen in changes in the organizational structure and the distribution of power within the dominant party. In India, for instance, the 1950s witnessed a struggle between the "governmental" and "organizational" wings within the Congress Party. In this struggle the organizational wing, indeed, often did "act in a manner traditionally associated with opposition parties." Its members criticized the government; they publicized their dissatisfaction in the press; they attempted to get a majority of their own in the legislature; and they campaigned vigorously in the elections for party committees and party leaders.[45] In this struggle, the organizational wing eventually emerged victorious, with the top positions in the government and the party eventually coming to be occupied by a new group of leaders who had come up through the local and state Congress structures and who were peculiarly responsive to local, communal, and rural demands rather than to national ones.

Electoral competition in India tended to hasten the replacement of the nationalist, cosmopolitan, Western-educated leaders by more provincial, less well-educated, local-oriented leaders. In the 1962 election "virtually everywhere there was a concern by the voter for electing local men who could mediate between the voter

45. Marcus F. Franda, "The Organizational Development of India's Congress Party," *Pacific Affairs* 35 (Fall 1962), 251.

and the complex and often slow moving governmental machinery, rather than state-wide or national public figures who could speak on issues of public policy." [46] The general shift taking place within the Congress Party was perhaps symbolized by the change in the top leadership in 1965. Educated at Harrow and Cambridge, Nehru was as English as he was Indian. Shastri, in contrast, had never been outside his country when he became prime minister. His premature death and replacement by another Nehru at a time when indigenous political forces were gaining strength hastened the decline of the Congress Party.

The dynamics of democratic politics also brought rural leaders to the fore. About 15 per cent of the members of the 1947 provisional parliament in India came from rural areas; in 1962 about 40 per cent of the Lok Sabha were from such areas. Similar changes took place in the leadership of the Congress Party at the state levels. In Madras, for instance,

> the Chief Minister changed from C. Rajagopalachari, a Brahmin lawyer, to K. Kamraj, a peasant with little formal education. The former knew English and Sanskrit as well as the regional language, and he was the first Indian Governor-General and a national Congress leader. The latter was an astute local political leader who spoke only Tamil well. Kamraj was definitely not an intellectual, he was hailed as a "man of the people." This might be compared with John Quincy Adams' defeat by Andrew Jackson in the United States. [47]

Similarly Myron Weiner found that in the Congress Party in rural districts "recruitment has shifted from the urban centers to the smaller towns and larger villages, and there has been a general decline in the preponderance of the most educated higher castes and a corresponding increase in agriculturalists, in cadres of more varied educational level, and in the so-called middle castes." [48] Along with this shift in recruitment patterns also went a general devolution of power from the central leadership of the party to the chief ministries of the states and to the state party organizations.

46. Myron Weiner, "India's Third General Elections," *Asian Survey*, 2 (May 1962), 10.

47. George Rosen, *Democracy and Economic Change in India* (Berkeley and Los Angeles, University of California Press, 1966), pp. 72–74.

48. Myron Weiner, *Congress Party Elites* (Bloomington, Ind., Department of Government, University of Indiana, 1966), pp. 14–15.

In the 1950s in India and also in Ceylon, elections and democracy had "the effect of reinforcing rather than eroding the power of traditional leaders" and thus created "an intense conflict between the values of representative government and planned economic-social change." The lack of elections in the 1950s in Pakistan exempted it from this conflict.[49] In the 1960s in Pakistan, however, the workings of the Basic Democracies brought to the fore the same issue: "It is one of the inner contradictions of community development," one leading Pakistani bureaucrat observed, "that the people directing the programme represent the interests and classes which stand to lose their status, privilege and power if the programme succeeds. Today political and economic power is concentrated in the hands of the westernized elite and specially the government servants. Democratisation of the society is bound to reduce this power." [50]

Two-Party Competition and Ruralizing Elections

The three countries of south Asia neatly illustrate the three different relationships which may exist between nationalist movements and rural political mobilization. In India the nationalist elite developed widespread rural support before independence and was able to expand and refurbish this support after independence. As a result, it maintained itself in power for over twenty years. In Pakistan the nationalist elite did not mobilize popular rural support before independence and did not dare submit itself to the test of elections after independence. As a result, it was easily displaced by the erstwhile bureaucratic hirelings of the imperial power. In Ceylon, the nationalist elite was also narrowly based and did not mobilize mass support before independence. It exposed itself to the popular test, however, and was swept out of office in 1956 in what may well be termed the archetype of the "ruralizing election." This is the typical means through which a two-party system in a modernizing country accommodates mass rural participation.

Ceylon, 1956. Ceylon became independent in 1948 under the

49. Wayne Wilcox, "The Politics of Tradition in Southeast Asia" (unpublished notes, Columbia University Seminar on the State, November 13, 1963) , p. 1.

50. M. Zaman, *Village AID* (Lahore, Government of West Pakistan, 1960) , quoted in A. K. M. Musa, "Basic Democracies in Pakistan—an Analytical Study" (unpublished paper, Harvard University, Center for International Affairs, 1965) , p. 26.

leadership of D. S. Senanayake and his United National Party which had been created only a year earlier. The UNP attracted many members from the Ceylon National Congress which had been organized in 1919. The latter body, however, "lacked the organizational roots in the countryside and among the lower classes in urbanized areas that its Indian counterpart developed, but it was manned by the same type of Western-educated, upper middle-class, and upper-class leadership." [51] Independence for Ceylon was fundamentally a gift of the Indians and the British: by compelling the British to grant independence to India, the Indians left them little choice but to give it to Ceylon also. The bulk of the Ceylonese population had no role in the struggle for independence. "There was no mass freedom movement in Ceylon, little self-sacrifice if any (even on the part the top leaders) and virtually no heroes and martyrs." [52]

After independence the new government was dominated by a small, upper-middle and upper class, thoroughly Anglicized, urban elite whose political vehicle was the UNP. Its members were, as one observer remarked, like "the former colonial rulers in everything but the colour of their skins." [53] This group was overwhelmingly urban, although Ceylon was 70 per cent rural. It was largely Christian, although 91 per cent of the Ceylonese were not and 64 per cent were Buddhist. Its language was English, which 92 per cent of the population could neither read nor write. In short, it was drawn from and represented a minority of less than 10 per cent of the population. The temptation such a situation offered for an appeal to the large majority of rural, Buddhist, and Sinhalese votors could not be long ignored. In 1951 one leading member of the political elite, S. W. R. D. Bandaranaike, deserted the UNP and formed his own opposition party, the Sri Lanka Freedom Party, to contest the 1956 general election. Before the election it was generally assumed that the UNP would have another easy victory. The SLFP "entered the election campaign with virtually no hope of winning. The money, the organization, and most of

51. Wriggins, p. 106.
52. D. K. Rangnekar, "The Nationalist Revolution in Ceylon," *Pacific Affairs, 33* (December 1960), 363; Wriggins, p. 81.
53. Rangnekar, pp. 363–64; Marshall Singer, *The Emerging Elite* (Cambridge, MIT Press, 1964), p. 122.

the prestigious families sided with the United National Party." [54] The electoral results, however, were a smashing victory for the SLFP and its electoral allies who polled a large minority of the votes but a secure majority in parliament with 51 of 95 seats. The UNP was reduced to eight seats, eight of its ten cabinet ministers losing their seats. The composition of the House changed dramatically.

In this election the rural lower middle class and lower class Sinhalese "suddenly discovered their political strength and shattered the monopoly of political power previously held by a small, affluent, westernized elite." [55] The inauguration of the SLFP government was dominated by the symbols of the populist, traditional revival:

> the presence in force of yellow-robed *bhikkus* (members of the Buddhist clergy) ; the beating of *magul bera* (traditional ceremonial drums) in place of a fanfare of trumpets; and, at the end of the ceremony, a great surge of friendly, interested, sarong-clad people up the steps of the House, past the departing guests, and into the Chamber itself. *"Apē ānduwa,"* they said, "It's *our* Government," as they explored the House and tried out the seats of the members they had just elected.[56]

"It was a proud day for the people," one newspaperman had written of a similar event 127 years earlier when backwoods farmers had also swarmed through governmental offices. "General Jackson is *their own* president." [57] And the parallel is apt, although the Bandaranaike revolution of 1956 was if anything more fundamental than the Jacksonian revolution of 1829. Of all the elections in southern Asia until the mid-1960s, as Howard Wriggins has pointed out, "it alone resulted in a marked transfer of political power from one segment of the population to another. This shift in the locus of power was accomplished without bloodshed, mass corruption, or intimidation of the electorate by violence. It was

54. Singer, p. 144.

55. Robert N. Kearney, "The New Political Crises of Ceylon," *Asian Survey*, 2 (June 1962), 19; Wriggins, p. 327.

56. B. M., "A 'People's Government': Social and Political Trends in Ceylon," *World Today*, 12 (July 1956), 281.

57. Amos Kendall, quoted in Arthur M. Schlesinger, Jr., *The Age of Jackson* (Boston, Little Brown, 1948), p. 6; italics in original.

not the elective confirmation of a coup d'etat, but a genuine change in leadership effected by the cumulated choice of hundreds of thousands of individual votors." [58]

The victory of the SLFP was based upon its appeals to the rural interests, Buddhist beliefs, and Sinhalese prejudices of the majority of Ceylon's population. The UNP was attacked as Western and Christian. Buddhist priests went from village to village declaring that a vote for the government party was a vote against the Buddha. By advocating Sinhalese as the sole official language, the SLFP appealed both to the lower middle class and "small intellectuals" who resented the upper class its facility in English and to the Sinhalese majority which resented the extent to which the Tamil-speaking minority (about 20 per cent of the population) had preempted positions in the government. The issues of language and religion cut across other distinctions, providing the basis for an electoral alliance and "a way for urban political leaders, rural middle-class people, and peasants all to react together in common resistance to the encroachment of Western values as they came to be identified with the UNP in 1956." [59]

In the following years the SLFP government voted to make Sinhalese the official language and carried out other programs designed to cement its ties with its rural constituency. Two consequences were severe communal violence between Tamils and Sinhalese in 1958 and the assassination of Bandaranaike by a Sinhalese extremist in 1959. The March 1960 election produced a political stalemate, but a second election in July led to another victory for the SLFP. Again its support came from the rural areas, where it received two-thirds of the vote. In contrast, it won none of the 18 seats in the large cities in the first election of 1960 and only four in the second. The attitude of the party was well expressed in Parliament by a top leader who declared that the party had established a "standard . . . a very simple standard; we stand by the interests of the rural people of this country. . . . [The] common people of this country, the rural people of this country can rest assured that we shall never let them down." [60]

The policies of the SLFP government so antagonized other elite groups, however, that a military coup was attempted in January

58. Wriggins, pp. 326–27.
59. Ibid., p. 348.
60. Mr. Dias Bandaranaike, quoted in Kearney, p. 20.

1962. This, in effect, was an attempt to regain power by elements of the older, Westernized, upper-class elite. "Nearly all of the suspected conspirators were Christians, most of them Roman Catholics. Many of them came from wealthy and prominent families, had been educated in prestige schools, and generally represented the 'privileged class' against which the egalitarianism of the SLFP is directed." [61] The coup reflected the tensions which the entry of the rural masses into politics had introduced into the political system. The victory in 1965 of the UNP in cooperation with the Federal Party representing the Tamil minority also demonstrated that the political system which had been sufficiently adaptable to absorb the rural masses was also sufficiently adaptable to permit what had become the opposition party of the urban elite to return to power under the new circumstances. The UNP was able to secure power only by adapting its appeal in such a manner as to compete with the SLFP. On the one hand, the rural masses had been assimilated into the political system; on the other hand, their entry into politics also changed the style, the semantics, the policies, and the leadership dominant within that system. A competitive party system had been successful in mediating, more or less peacefully, fundamental changes in the scope of political participation and the distribution of political power.

Turkey, 1950 and after. A shift somewhat similar to that in Ceylon occurred almost simultaneously in Turkey during the 1950s. After the end of World War II a variety of pressures and circumstances led the government of Ismet Inönü to permit a group of leading politicians within the Republican Peoples Party to break off and form an opposition party. These leaders did not differ fundamentally from those who were dominant in the RPP but they did tend to be liberal and favorably disposed toward private enterprise and thus to be associated with the Turkish business class which had developed in the 1930s and during the war. At two earlier periods during the long rule of the RPP, in 1924 and 1930, opposition parties had been briefly allowed to function, and undoubtedly the RPP leaders assumed that this new opposition group of politicians would be less of a threat to them outside the RPP than inside it. In any event, they organized the Democratic Party and contested the 1946 elections, winning about

61. Ibid., p. 26.

15 per cent of the seats in the National Assembly. During the next four years, first the Democratic Party and then the RPP in response made more and more extensive efforts to mobilize and to organize the voters in both cities and countryside. In the 1950 election the RPP again expected to win a top-heavy majority. It instead lost decisively. The Democratic Party got 53 per cent of the vote and 408 seats in the assembly; the RPP 40 per cent of the vote and only 69 seats.

The Democratic victory was compounded of a substantial majority in the cities plus an even split with the RPP of the rural vote. The election marked, however, the first step in the emergence of the rural voters as the dominant voting group in Turkish politics. During the next few years the Democratic government under Adnan Menderes made every effort to identify itself with the peasantry. Economically it pushed rural roads, agricultural equipment, farm subsidies and credits. Of equal importance, in the cultural field, it modified the strict secularism which had prevailed under the RPP, introducing religious instruction into the schools and providing government funds for the construction of mosques. Menderes, as one scholar has observed, "was the country's first ruler dramatically to place rural interests above the urban, the first to respond to the peasants' material needs, the first to give them a rudimentary sense of citizenship." [62] During the 1950s, consequently, rural support for the Democratic Party increased, at the same time that its urban middle-class support weakened. In the 1954 election the Democrats upped their percentage of the vote to 56.6. "What does it matter what the intellectuals of Istanbul think," asked Menderes, "so long as the peasantry is with us?" [63]

In the 1957 election the total vote declined and with it the Democratic share of the vote. The Menderes government turned to increasingly authoritarian methods of rule; urban middle-class opinion turned more and more against it; and in May 1960 it was ousted by the military.

The political crisis resulting in and produced by this veto coup was resolved by the speedy and responsible way in which General Gursel and his associates arranged for the return to civilian rule.

62. Dankwart A. Rustow, "Turkey's Second Try at Democracy," *Yale Review,* 52 (Summer 1963), 529.

63. Adnan Menderes, quoted in Irwin Ross, "From Ataturk to Gursel," *The New Leader, 43* (December 5, 1960), 17.

In the elections of 1961, however, the old pattern of voting reappeared. Despite all the factors working in its favor, the RPP received only 37 per cent of the vote, while the newly formed Justice Party inherited the bulk of the support of the outlawed Democrats and got 35 per cent of the vote. Four years later the Justice Party swept to a commanding victory, winning 56 per cent of the popular vote and 57 per cent of the seats in the National Assembly. Its support came from a variety of sources, but preeminent among them were the votes of the peasants. The Turkish experience, in Weiker's words, neatly illustrates

> the difficulties of simultaneous rapid reform and free multiparty government . . . the often-voiced claim of Turkish leaders that the people, if only given proper leadership, will understand the situation and make sacrifices voluntarily, has never been borne out in Turkey. The fact is that when given the free ballot, the Turkish nation has not at any time in the past voted for the representatives of rapid reform, and there are convincing reasons for believing that such an eventuality is equally unlikely today.[64]

Electoral competition produced not only an appeal to rural interests but also tendencies toward the devolution of power in what had been a highly centralized political system. In 1947, in response to the Democratic challenge, the RPP decentralized its control over nominations so that 70 per cent of its candidates for deputy would be nominated by local party organizations. Subsequently, Frey observed

> within the political party, central control and discipline have been appreciably weakened. Local forces have become so strong as to impair the party's ability even to perform necessary political tasks, such as research into its own organization. . . . Recalcitrant party leaders who have lost their central posts are now commencing to cater to local interests to regain power despite central opposition.[65]

As in India and Ceylon the character of the principal participants in politics also tended to shift from a national, westernized bu-

---

64. Walter F. Weiker, *The Turkish Revolution, 1960–1961: Aspects of Military Politics* (Washington, D.C., The Brookings Institution, 1963), p. 89.

65. Frey, in Pye, *Communications and Political Development*, p. 325; Kemal H. Karpat, *Turkey's Politics: The Transition to a Multi-Party System* (Princeton, Princeton University Press, 1959), pp. 207–08; *Time, 86* (Oct. 22, 1965), 46.

reaucratic elite "oriented toward the tutelary development of the country" to a provincial elite "oriented toward more immediate local and political advantage." [66] This change occurred most dramatically during the period of transition from one-party to competitive party rule in the late 1940s. Farmers, lawyers, and merchants replaced military officers and civil servants as the dominant groups in the National Assembly. Similarly, localism gained strength: at the peak of the one-party period about one third of the deputies had been born in the constituencies they represented; after a decade of two-party competition, two thirds of the deputies fell into this category. [67] Party competition not only brought the masses into politics but also brought the political leaders closer to the masses.

Ceylon and Turkey furnish dramatic examples of the ways in which two-party competition and the ruralizing elections facilitate the assimilation of the numerically predominant rural groups into politics. Somewhat similar cases may also be briefly cited from several other countries.

Burma, 1960. After independence Burma was dominated by the Anti-Fascist Peoples Freedom League, which won overwhelming victories in the elections of 1951–52 and 1956. In the former year the opposition was very weak and very scattered; in the latter year, the opposition was stronger and grouped together in the leftist-oriented National Unity Front. In 1958 the AFPFL split into two factions, and the resulting instability and growth in strength of insurgent groups led Premier U Nu to turn the government over to General Ne Win and the army in October of that year. Much to the surprise of many, the military government remained in power for only about eighteen months and arranged for the return of power to civilians through elections in the spring of 1960. The two principal parties contesting these elections were the "Clean" AFPFL led by U Nu and the "Stable" AFPFL led by two other leading AFPFL politicians. When the party had split in 1958 the Clean faction had kept control of the All Burma Peasants Organization, the Stable faction initially taking control of the labor and women's groups.

The 1960 election clearly posed the issue of traditionalism vs. reform. The military government of Ne Win had done much to

66. Frederick W. Frey quoted in Richard D. Robinson, *The First Turkish Republic* (Cambridge, Harvard University Press, 1963), p. 144.

67. Frederick W. Frey, *The Turkish Political Elite*, Chap. 7 and pp. 396–97.

push through needed reforms, improve efficiency in the public services, and restore law and order. Its diligence and ruthlessness,
however, had antagonized many elements in Burmese society. The
army clearly preferred a victory by the Stable faction, and U Nu consequently made the most out of the identification between the military and his electoral opponents. The alignment of political forces
closely resembled that of the Turkish elections of 1961. For the Burmese, "The laxity of the old AFPFL days was considered a lesser evil,
in spite of its frequent corrupt and inefficient character, than the
Army-led reform government with its demands for sacrifices." [68]

Equally as important as his opposition to the unpleasant needs
of reform was U Nu's identification with Buddhism and traditional values. Conscientiously and conspicuously adhering to a
non-Western style of life and behavior, U Nu stood out in marked
contrast to most other Burmese political leaders. At the beginning
of the campaign he explicitly committed himself to making Buddhism the state religion of Burma. As in Ceylon in 1956 the Buddhist monks played a key role in the campaign: "the majority
rallied to the support of U Nu and became his most effective
propagandists in the towns and villages of Burma." [69] The result
was a smashing victory for U Nu and the Clean faction which won
two thirds of the vote and two thirds of the parliamentary seats at
stake. Unlike other ruralizing elections, U Nu's support came
from all sections of the population, his party doing even better in
Rangoon than it did in the countryside.

Like the Turkish army in the 1960s, the Burmese military reluctantly allowed the more conservative party to come to power. During the two years he remained in office U Nu followed policies
which were "clearly more traditionalist than revolutionary" and
gave top priority to the implementation of his pledge to make
Buddhism the state religion.[70] In 1962, however, the Burmese
military decided that the traditionalizing and disintegrative tendencies of democracy had gone far enough, intervened again to
remove the civilian government from power, and imposed upon
Burma an austere, authoritarian, dogmatic version of military so-

68. Richard Butwell and Fred von der Mehden, "The 1960 Election in Burma,"
Pacific Affairs, 33 (June 1960) , 154.

69. Donald E. Smith, *Religion and Politics in Burma* (Princeton, Princeton University Press, 1965) , p. 242.

70. Richard Butwell, *U Nu of Burma* (Stanford, Stanford University Press, 1963) ,
p. 244.

cialism. Unlike the Turkish military, the Burmese soldiers were unwilling to accept the compromise which democracy requires between traditionalism and reform.

Senegal, 1951. Competitive party systems have also provided for the shift of power from a narrow urban base to a broader rural one in countries on the verge of independence. In Senegal, political power for decades rested in the coastal cities. After World War II the dominant party in the communes was a branch of the French Socialists (SFIO). In the 1951 legislative elections, however, it was challenged by a new group, the Senegalese Democratic Bloc (BDS), organized by Leopold Senghor, which directed its appeal to the newly enfranchised and newly politically conscious rural voters. "The enlarged rural electorate had numerical control and held the key to success in the elections . . . [which] were a victorious revolt of the new citizens, urban and rural, against the old citizens of the 'four communes.' " [71] In the election Senghor made use of rural and traditional appeals, particularly religious ones. As in Ceylon in 1956 and Burma in 1960, religious leaders and workers played a key role in the campaign. "It was the imams in the mosques," Senghor subsequently declared, "who made our triumph." [72]

Jamaica, 1944. In Jamaica party competition provided the means for accommodating new groups within the political system with little violence and virtually no disruption of orderly political processes. In the usual pattern, the People's National Party, formed in 1938 to press for independence, was originally composed of a "quite small middle class following of professional persons, civil servants, and teachers." It was modernizing, socialist, and nationalist. In 1944 the first elections under universal suffrage were held. Alexander Bustamante, the leader of the Bustamante Industrial Trade Union, which despite its name was primarily an agricultural trade union, organized the Jamaica Labor Party and mobilized the rural workers to the polls. The results were a rude shock to the middle-class PNP, which gained only 24 per cent of the total vote to 41 per cent for the JLP and 30 per cent for the Inde-

71. Paul Mercier, "Political Life in the Urban Centers of Senegal: A Study of Transition," *PROD Translations, 3* (June 1960), 10.

72. Quoted in William J. Foltz, "Senegal," in James S. Coleman and Carl G. Rosberg, eds., *Political Parties and National Integration in Tropical Africa* (Berkeley and Los Angeles, University of California Press, 1964), p. 22.

pendents. The PNP leader, Norman Manley, was a prototype of the middle-class rational intellectual and the PNP program was radical and ideological. The BITU and the JLP, on the other hand, stressed "bread-and-butter issues" and concrete material benefits rather than sweeping ideological goals. Their "followers were chiefly urban and agricultural workers" and their leader, Busta-mante, was an earthy combination of union boss and populist demagogue.[73]

The effect of the JLP victory, however, was to promote similar efforts at mass organization on the part of the PNP, which developed its own trade union organization, the National Workers Union, as a competitor for the BITU. The competition also helped the moderate wing of the PNP to win out in an intraparty struggle in the early 1950s over the extreme left wing. As a result, the PNP was able to return to power in 1955 with a substantial victory over the JLP. A few years later, the JLP in turn mobilized its rural supporters and came back into office. The competition of the two leaders and the two parties in Jamaica thus served to promote both the mobilization of the Jamaican masses into politics and their effective organization through the political parties and affiliated trade unions.

Lesotho, 1965. The dominant party as Basutoland approached independence was the Basutoland Congress Party. Organized on the model of the CPP in Ghana, it drew its support from intellectuals, teachers, Protestant missionaries, and other urban groups. Its leaders had traveled abroad and identified with pan-African movements, but they had little knowledge of or contact with the rural areas of their own country. As in Jamaica, Ceylon, and Senegal, the opposition party, the Basutoland National Party (BNP) was organized only shortly before the first general election in 1965. Its strength was in the rural areas where it benefited from the active support of the lower ranks of the chiefs and the Roman Catholic clergy. In its campaign it focused primarily on bread-and-butter issues. Much to the surprise of most observers it scored a conservative upset in the election, getting 42 per cent of the vote to 40 per cent for the BCP. Again party competition produced the victory of a conservative rural party over a more radical, nationalist, urban one.[74]

73. C. Paul Bradley, "Mass Parties in Jamaica: Structure and Organization," *Social and Economic Studies,* 9 (Dec. 1960) , 375–416.

74. See *New York Times,* May 5, 1965, p. 6.

Each of these ruralizing elections is, of course, only one turning point in a long, gradual, and at times, stormy process of political mobilization and assimilation. In some countries the process may, indeed, be so gradual that it is virtually impossible to single out any particular election as heralding a significant transfer of power from urban elite to rural mass. In the Philippines after independence, for instance, the mobilization of rural voters was strung out through a series of elections in which the incumbent president was almost always defeated at the polls. In 1953 Magsaysay swept to an overwhelming victory over President Quirino. Magsaysay's appeal in the election and his activities as president were oriented to the rural voter. In addition to his land reform law and other measures designed to enhance agricultural productivity, he also set about "opening channels for continuous political communication with the masses of rural Filipinos. . . . He brought large numbers of people into contact with the government and the presidency for the first time and established that political change was possible within the legal structure of government and that violence was neither necessary nor wise. No politician after Magsaysay could afford to ignore his goals or his image." [75] His successor, García, however, was a much more conservative and upper class figure.

In 1961, the second phase of the mobilization of the rural masses occurred when the opposition candidate, Macapagal, scored a surprising victory over García. Like Magsaysay, Macapagal came from a lower-class background and directed his appeal primarily to the rural voter. During four years of campaigning he visited almost every one of the 23,000 Filipino barrios. For the first time in Filipino history a presidential candidate successfully challenged the control the landlords and the Nacionalista party machine had exercised over the rural vote.[76] In 1965 Macapagal, in turn, was defeated by Ferdinand Marcos, who seemingly was also committed to carrying on the process of rural mobilization and agrarian reform. Thus, in the Philippines, the absence of effective party organization and of very meaningful associations between parties and social forces tended to produce a situation in which the Green Uprising occurred by degrees and under a diversity of party labels.

The clearer cases of ruralizing elections shared a number of common characteristics.

75. Grossholtz, pp. 43–44.
76. See Meadows, passim, but esp. pp. 262–63, 271–73.

1. An urban-based, middle- and upper-class, modernizing elite was ousted from power.

2. The outcome was a surprise to most political observers.

3. The victorious party won primarily because it mobilized new rural voters to the polls.

4. The leader of the victorious party was typically a former member of the modernizing urban elite who, in effect, broke from the elite and espoused more popular and traditional appeals.

5. Apart from the top leader of the incoming party, its other leaders and representatives were typically drawn from non-cosmopolitan, local, rural elites.

6. The winning party appealed to the rural voters by a combination of ethnic and religious appeals and bread-and-butter issues.

7. In many cases, the winning party benefited significantly from the work of priests, *pongyis, imams,* or other religious figures in the rural areas.

8. The victory of the opposition party was viewed by both its supporters and its opponents as marking a turning point in the political evolution of the country.

9. Once in office, the new government's policies typically aimed to please and to benefit its rural supporters.

10. The new government's policies also antagonized the old elite, often in such a manner as to provoke a military coup d'etat against it, successful in Turkey and Burma, unsuccessful in Ceylon.

11. In most, but not all, cases, the party ousted from power adapted itself to the changed patterns of political participation, made its own efforts to win mass support, and, in a few cases (Ceylon, Jamaica), was subsequently voted back into power.

Through this process two-party systems assimilate rural masses into the political system, and thus produce the bridge between rural and urban areas which is the key to political stability in modernizing countries. The comparative experience of modernizing societies, both contemporary and past, suggests that two-party systems are more successful in achieving this assimilation than most other types of political systems.

THE ORGANIZATIONAL IMPERATIVE

Social and economic modernization disrupts old patterns of authority and destroys traditional political institutions. It does not necessarily create new authority patterns or new political institutions. But it does create the overriding need for them by broadening political consciousness and political participation. Willy-nilly the United States has helped to mobilize the masses into politics in Asia, Africa, and Latin America. Consciously and conscientiously other groups have done much to organize that mobilization. "The proletariat has no weapon in the struggle for power except organization," said Lenin in 1905; ". . . the proletariat can and will become an unconquerable force only as a result of this." "The great masses of Chileans have no organization," said Frei in 1966, "and without organization no power, and without power no representation in the life of the country." [77] Organization is the road to political power, but it is also the foundation of political stability and thus the precondition of political liberty. The vacuum of power and authority which exists in so many modernizing countries may be filled temporarily by charismatic leadership or by military force. But it can be filled permanently only by political organization. Either the established elites compete among themselves to organize the masses through the existing political system, or dissident elites organize them to overthrow that system. In the modernizing world he controls the future who organizes its politics.

77. Lenin, quoted in Rustow, *A World of Nations*, p. 100, from "One Step Forward, Two Steps Backward," Robert V. Daniels, ed., *A Documentary History of Communism* (New York, Vintage, 1960), *1*, 26 f.; Eduardo Frei, quoted in William P. Lineberry, "Chile's Struggle on the Left," *The New Leader, 49* (May 23, 1966), 6.

Index